Joachim Klang

TIPS FOR KIDS

RECORD-BREAKING BRICK VEHICLES

COOL PROJECTS FOR YOUR LEGO® BRICKS

HEEL

THANKS

to pioneers and revolutionaries, some of whom I know and admire personally:

2LegoOrNot2Lego
Arvo Brothers
ArzLan
Bart Willen
Brian Corredor
Bricksonwheels
Brickthing
Bricktrix
Bruceywan
captainsmog
Cole Blaq
Cuahchic
DecoJim
- Derfel Cadarn -
Digger1221
Eastpole77
Fianat
Fraslund
Fredoichi
Gabe Umland
Gambort
gearcs
Henrik Hoexbroe
Homa
Joe Meno
Jojo
Karwik
Lazer Blade
lego_nabii
Legohaulic
LEGOLAS
Legonardo Davidy
Legopard
Legotrucks
lichtblau
‚LL'
Mark of Falworth
markus19840420
marshal banana
McBricker
Mijasper
Misterzumbi
Nannan Z
NENN
Obedient Machine
Ochre Jelly
„Orion Pax"
Paul Vermeesch
Pepa Quin
RoccoB
Sir Nadroj
Sirens-Of-Titan
Spencer_R
T.Oechsner
Taz-Maniac
ted @ndes
TheBrickAvenger
Théolego
tnickolaus
Toltomeja
x_Speed
Xenomurphy

As always, I owe thanks to my coauthor Lutz Uhlmann for the digital transformations of my constructions. Uwe Kurth tried out and checked everything—a thousand thanks for doing this. Special thanks go to Ilmar Degen for advice and support.

HEEL Verlag GmbH
Gut Pottscheidt
53639 Königswinter
Germany
Tel.: +49 (0) 2223 9230-0
Fax: +49 (0) 2223 9230-13
E-Mail: info@heel-verlag.de
www.heel-verlag.de

Author: Alexander Jones und Joachim Klang
Layout and Design: Odenthal Illustration, www.odenthal-illustration.de
Cover design: Axel Mertens, HEEL Verlag GmbH
Photography: Thomas Schultze, www.thomas-schultze.de
Translated from German by: Laila Friese in association with First Edition Translations Ltd, Cambridge, UK
Edited by: Robert Anderson in association with First Edition Translations Ltd, Cambridge, UK
Project management: Ulrike Reihn-Hamburger

Printed in Hungary
ISBN 978-3-95843-551-3

CONTENTS

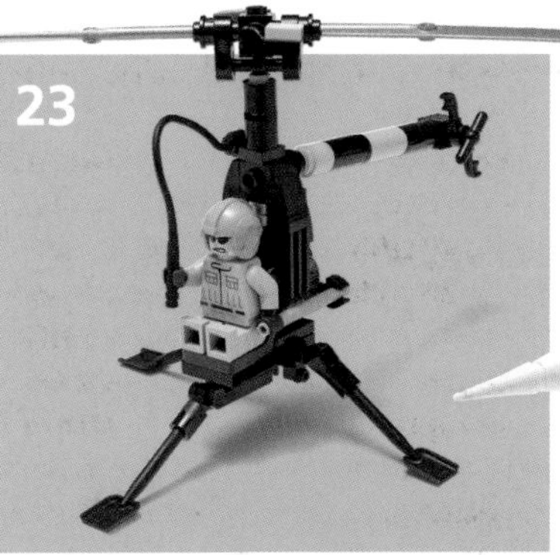

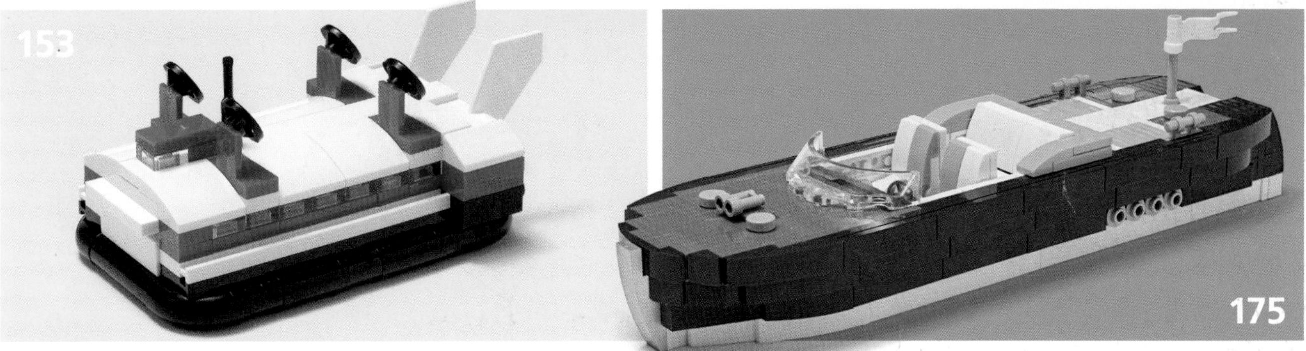

FOREWORD

You are actually holding my tenth book in your hands! A small record, I think. And that's why "record breaking" is the topic of the latest book in my LEGO® series.

In order to develop model ideas for this book, I first thought about the kinds of record we typically talk about for vehicles. As you probably did, I of course immediately thought of things like the fastest or most expensive car, boat, or plane. But, beyond that, there are also innovations, things that are the first of their kind, like the hovercraft, and then there are other interesting records, such as the type of car that has been sold the most. For air, sea, and land vehicles, there are innumerable records relating to their technical developments—from the longest journey undertaken on a single engine to the largest number of people in a car. So I put together a fairly long list of ideas for this book—but they haven't all made it into the final version and for a variety of reasons. Some ideas failed simply because they are very difficult to achieve with LEGO®—at least on a scale that can be illustrated in a "how to" guide. For example, it is really difficult to elegantly create the round shapes of a VW Beetle or a rocket car in miniature scale. Other ideas would have required such rare parts that it would be nearly impossible to construct them—or only at considerable financial cost.

I've compromised on other models by showing them on a reduced scale. For example, I really wanted to include the Concorde, but on a miniature scale its dimensions would have become huge. So I've reduced them in such a way that their implementation doesn't need too many parts.

In the end, I still had about three times as many ideas as there was space for in this book and so I had to make a choice. But, who knows, maybe one day I'll write another.

In addition to the information on the records for each vehicle that are included in the short descriptions, we decided to give you a small table with technical information.

This time we also have photos to show you some alternative ways of constructing elements of the models. Of course, I can't show you all the different ways of making each model, but the alternatives should inspire you and demonstrate that you don't always have to stick to the templates 100 percent, especially if you are missing some of the parts. Perhaps you'll find other solutions.

I also built different cars in other colors and versions, and have included photos of these here. This should also be an incentive for you to try out your own ideas and develop your own projects and not feel you have to copy my instructions to the letter.

Various versions of components have been available over the years, and we have usually used the ones available to us at the time. However, in the parts lists and overviews, as well as in the instructions, we have, as always, included all the serial numbers to help you find the parts you need.

In this context, I would like to briefly clarify the term "special bricks." The mention of "special bricks" always gives me pause for thought. Over the last few years I have heard the term mentioned again and again. But what does it really mean? In the first place, it makes me think of a

part that can be used only in a single, predetermined way. But since this word has come up in various conversations in connection with my books, this can't actually be what is meant, because I like to join up parts in different combinations. So I investigated the meaning of this term in further conversations. It turns out that for most of the people I spoke to it meant a building block that they did not think they had in their own collection. A missing part must be a "special brick" because everyone thinks his or her own collection is massive. I can't disagree with this interpretation on principle, but let's take a closer look at the LEGO® range.
According to the BrickLink database there were about 9,900 different shapes available in 2017, including plates, bricks, tiles, windows, tires, figures, etc., but excluding printed parts such as faces. Over the years, however, the availability of individual elements has been variable: Some bricks didn't appear in particular sets for many years, but new ones are constantly being added. It is also worth mentioning that about 133 different colors are available. Statistically speaking, there are 1 million different LEGO® parts in existence.

I once read that, since 1954, LEGO® has produced over 500 billion bricks. If you joined them up, you could circle the world three times over. Statistically speaking, every person in the world has 93 LEGO® bricks each.

With this range in mind, then, I have designed each model bearing in mind which bricks you are likely to have in your collection. Since I always try to create templates that will be as accurate as possible, I also often have to buy new sets or get hold of the specific bricks I need. My collection may be large, but it can never be complete. So, if I want to use a particular brick, I have to find out where I can get it—and sometimes these are actually quite ordinary bricks that I'm sure you'll have in your collection but which I have, however, already used in another model, e.g.

Let's take a look at the Lancia Stratos in this book by way of an example, and at the 1 x 1 quarter circle tiles in red from set 21306 (The Beatles Yellow Submarine). You could replace them with 1 x 1 square tiles, but in this instance it's easier to simplify the model than to refine it later. So, do decide for yourself which bricks you want to use and check your collection to see which shapes and colors you already have.

To be fair, I do have to distinguish between special parts, rare parts, and Q-parts. There are also bricks that were included in a set only once, like the quarter circle red tiles. Then there are parts that haven't been produced for many years. In this case, however, you can often make do with similar parts if they are missing from your collection. Q-parts are parts that have never been included in a set or only a long time ago. With BrickLink you can use the search terms "RARE" or "HTF" (hard to find) to find them. However, I try to avoid using such parts in my instructions. There is an ever-increasing abundance of new shapes, and over the past five years alone the diversity of parts has almost doubled.

So have a look at your collection, see what you have to choose from, and let the bricks inspire you. My conversations over the past few years have shown that people have started playing with LEGO® again in earnest, and

sometimes this has been down to my books. This makes me very happy! That's what it's all about. But please don't get annoyed if you don't manage to assemble a model from this book in one evening. As with any other hobby, you'll develop your skills further and get deeper into your hobby and you'll also gradually increase your collection. After all, someone starting out in stamp collecting won't have the Blue Mauritius straightaway, will they?

I've tried to design my models so that they can be reconstructed by following my instructions. I hope you enjoy browsing and building.

AH-64 APACHE

The AH-64 Apache was developed by the American company Hughes Aircraft and is now made by Boeing. With a climbing power of 6,400 meters, when the series first came out in the early 1980s, it maintained this record by far compared to similar helicopters. It is designed for two crewmen, with the pilot sitting in the back row on a raised seat.

SERVICE CEILING:	*6400 m (20,997 ft)*
OPERATIONAL RANGE:	*482 km (300 miles)*
WEIGHT:	*5165 kg (5.7 t)*
TOP SPEED:	*293 km/h (182 mph)*
HP:	*1696*

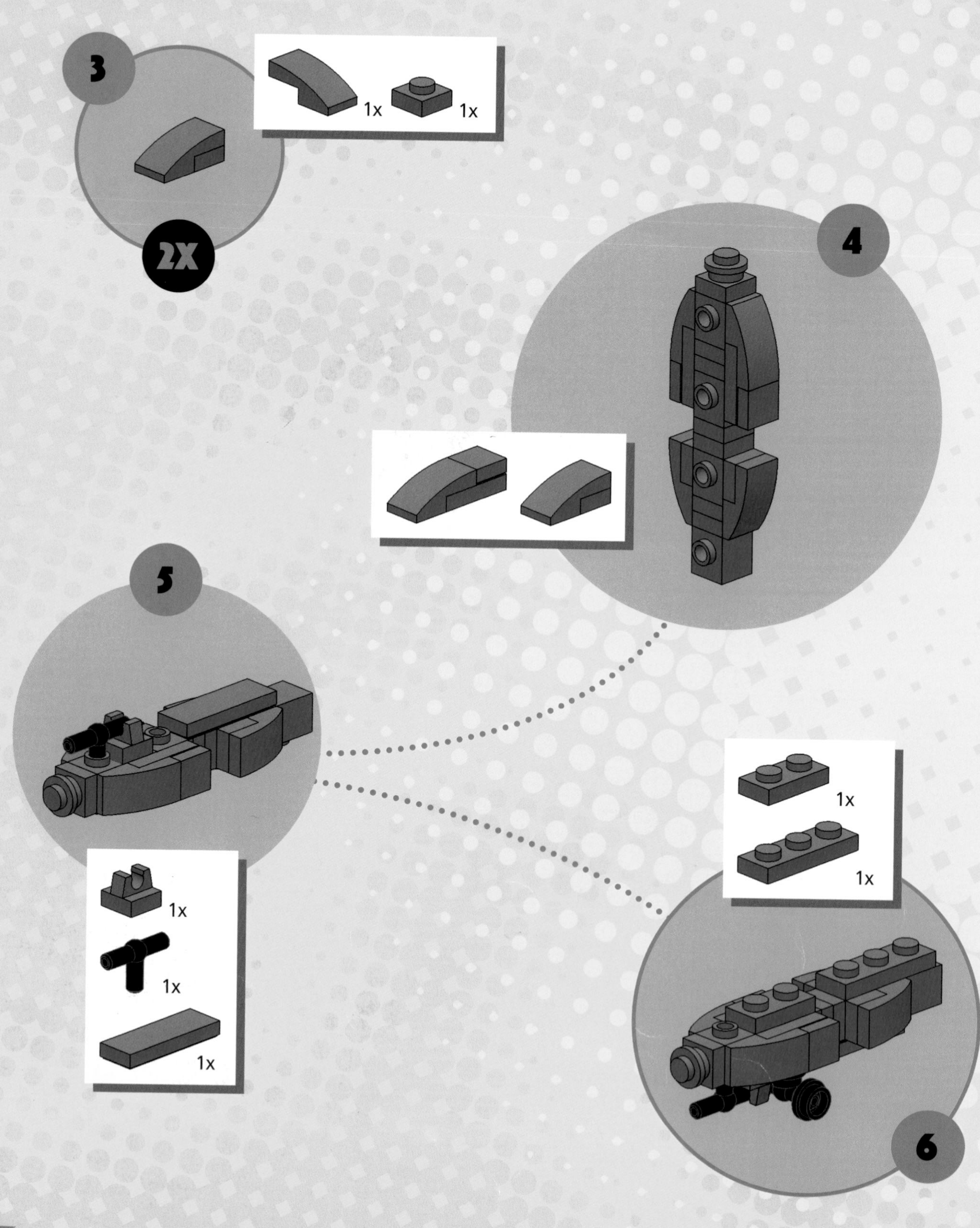
3
1x
1x
2X
4
5
1x
1x
1x
1x
1x
6

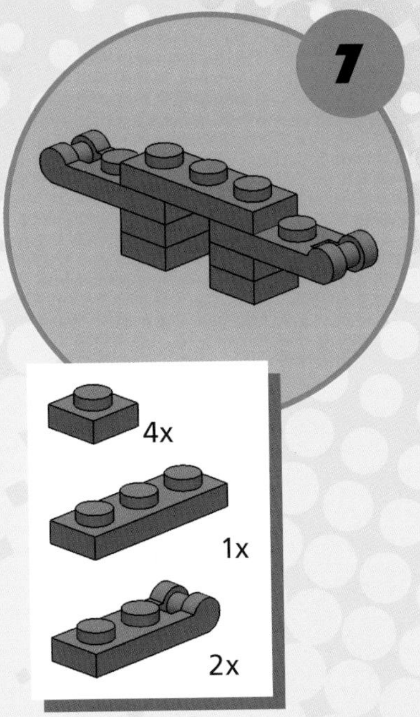

7

4x

1x

2x

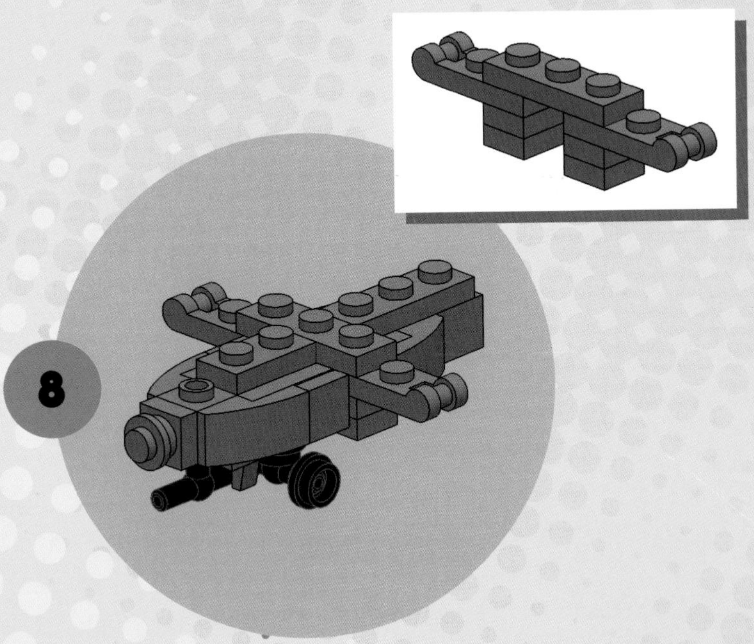

8

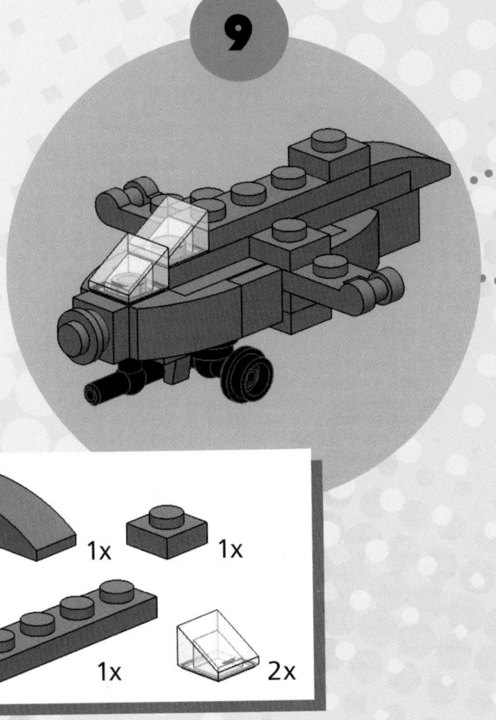

9

1x 1x

1x 2x

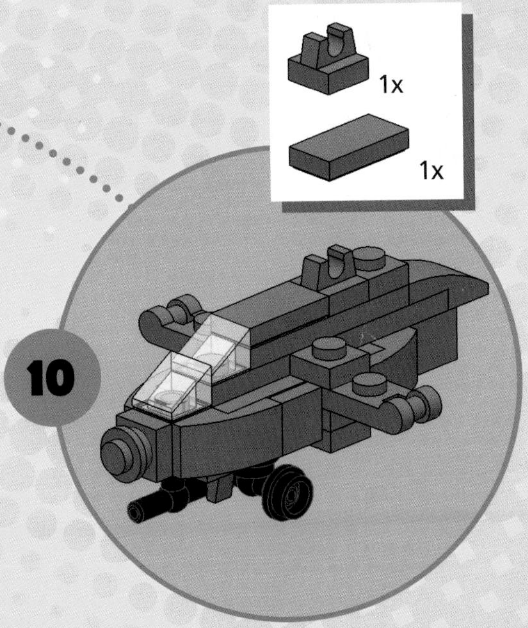

1x

1x

10

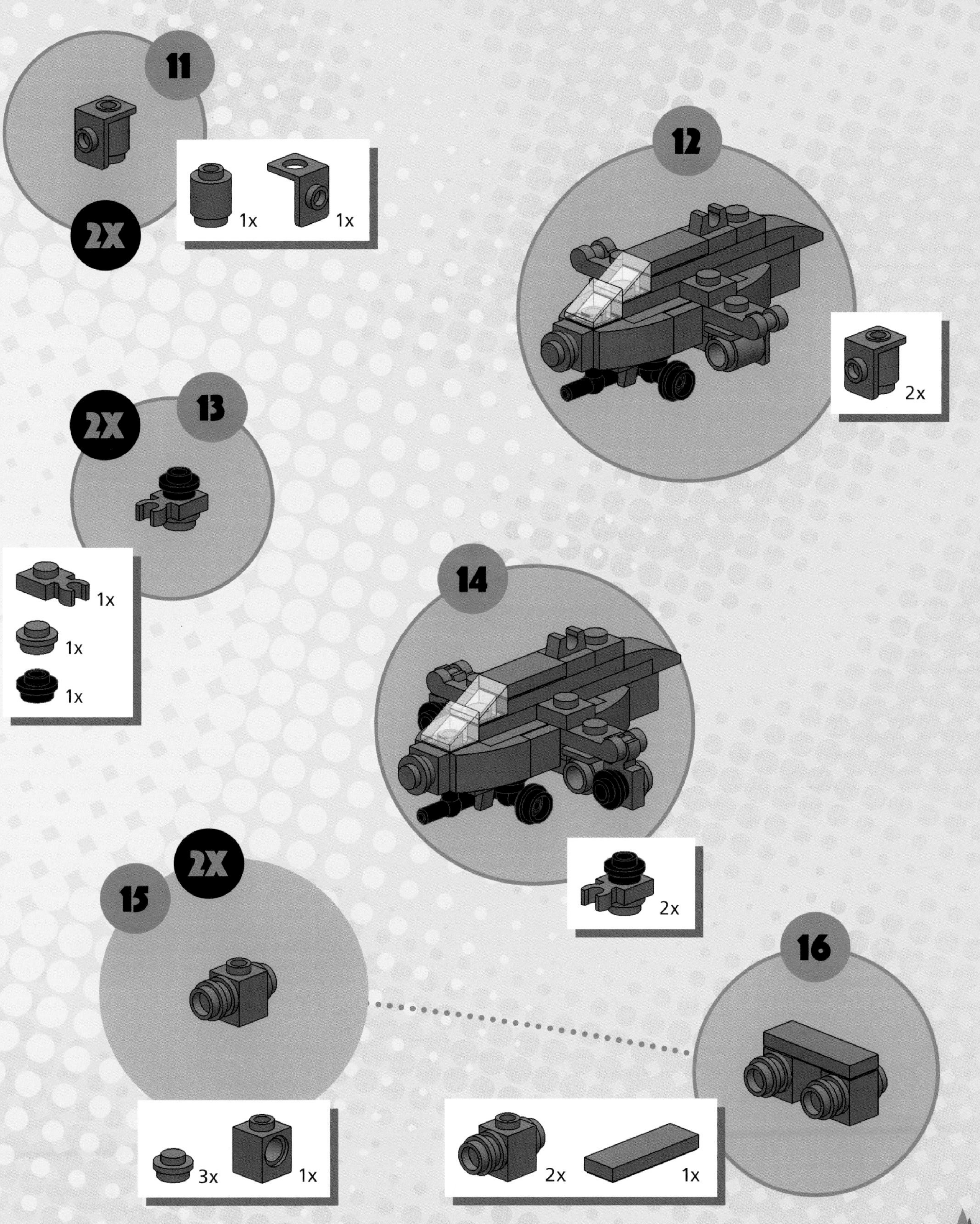
11
2X
1x
1x
12
2x
13
2X
1x
1x
1x
14
2x
15
2X
3x
1x
16
2x
1x

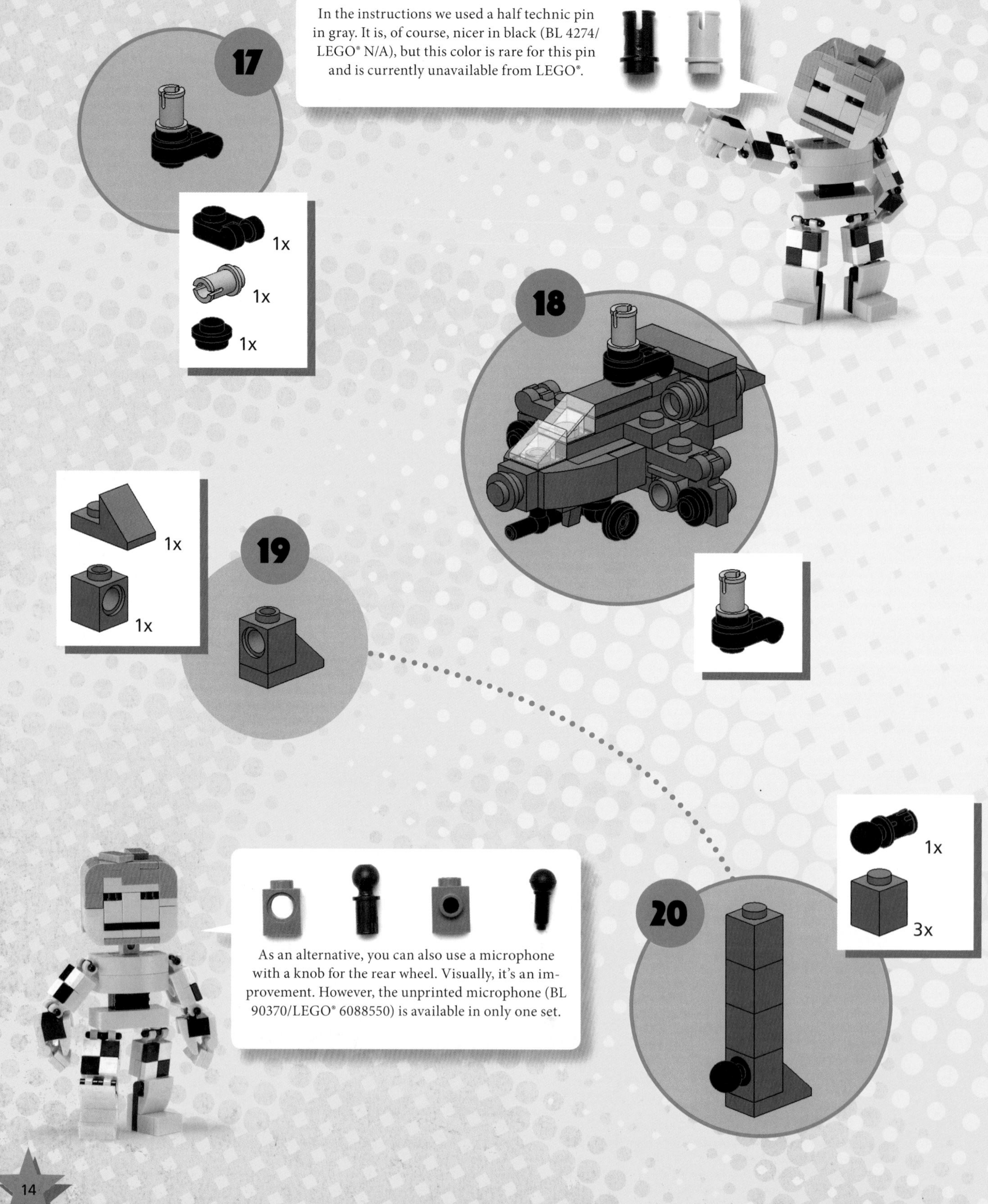
17
1x
1x
1x
In the instructions we used a half technic pin in gray. It is, of course, nicer in black (BL 4274/ LEGO® N/A), but this color is rare for this pin and is currently unavailable from LEGO®.
18
19
1x
1x
20
1x
3x
As an alternative, you can also use a microphone with a knob for the rear wheel. Visually, it's an improvement. However, the unprinted microphone (BL 90370/LEGO® 6088550) is available in only one set.

21

1x

1x

1x

22

1x

1x

23

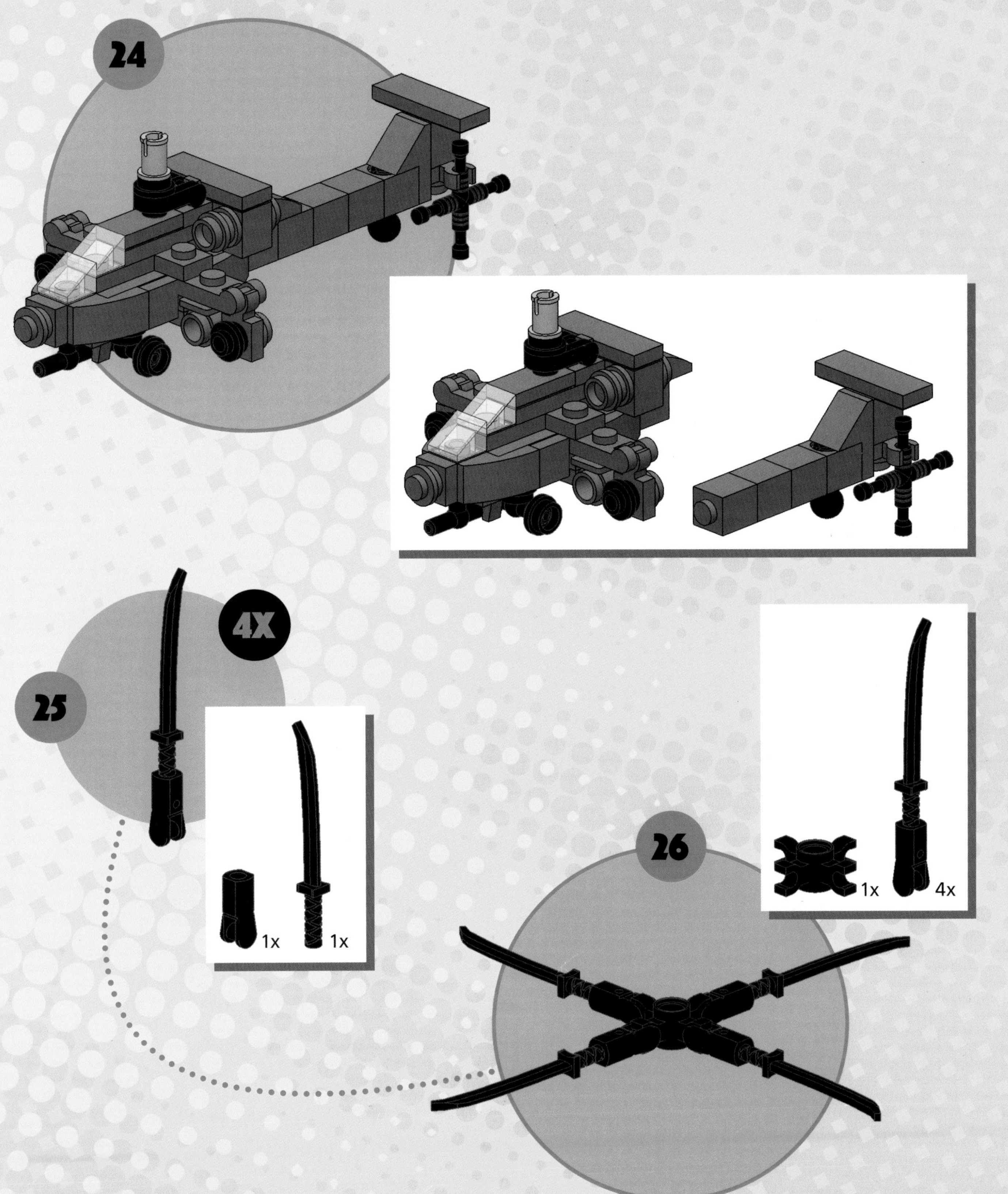
24
4X
25
1x
1x
26
1x
4x

27

PARTS LIST

Quantity	Color	Element	Element Name	LEGO® Number
4	Black	23443	Bar Tube with Handle	6143318
2	Dark Bluish Gray	42446	Bracket 1 x 1 - 1 x 1	4210469
3	Dark Bluish Gray	3005	Brick 1 x 1	4211098
2	Dark Bluish Gray	3062b	Brick 1 x 1 Round with Hollow Stud	4211090
2	Dark Bluish Gray	87087	Brick 1 x 1 with Stud on 1 Side	4558955
3	Dark Bluish Gray	4733	Brick 1 x 1 with Studs on Four Sides	4210700
4	Black	30173b	Minifig Sword Katana Type 2 (Square Guard)	4114206
1	Black	604553	Minifig Tool 4-Way Lug Wrench	6030875
14	Dark Bluish Gray	3024	Plate 1 x 1	4210719
1	Black	4073	Plate 1 x 1 Round	614126
10	Dark Bluish Gray	4073	Plate 1 x 1 Round	4210633
1	Black	26047	Plate 1 x 1 Round with Horizontal Handle on Side	6157554
2	Black	85861	Plate 1 x 1 Round with Open Stud	6100627, 6168646
3	Dark Bluish Gray	60897	Plate 1 x 1 with Clip Vertical (Thick C-Clip)	4587212
3	Dark Bluish Gray	3023	Plate 1 x 2	4211063
2	Dark Bluish Gray	60478	Plate 1 x 2 with Handle on End	4521187
2	Dark Bluish Gray	3623	Plate 1 x 3	4211133
1	Dark Bluish Gray	3710	Plate 1 x 4	4211001
2	Trans Clear	54200	Slope Brick 31 1 x 1 x 0.667	4244362
5	Dark Bluish Gray	11477	Slope Brick Curved 2 x 1	6029948
1	Dark Bluish Gray	92946	Slope Plate 45 2 x 1	4621917, 6069164
3	Dark Bluish Gray	6541	Technic Brick 1 x 1 with Hole	4210639
1	Light Bluish Gray	4274	Technic Pin 1/2	4211483, 4274194
1	Black	90202	Technic Pin Connector Round with 4 Clips	4584126, 6049760, 6052369
1	Black	6628	Technic Pin Towball with Friction	4184169, 662826
1	Black	4697b	Technic Pneumatic T-Piece - Type 2	6104209
2	Dark Bluish Gray	2555	Tile 1 x 1 with Clip	4211069, 6030710

Quantity		Color	Element	Element Name	LEGO® Number
2		Dark Bluish Gray	3070b	Tile 1 x 1 with Groove	4210848
1		Dark Bluish Gray	3069b	Tile 1 x 2 with Groove	4211052
3		Dark Bluish Gray	63864	Tile 1 x 3 with Groove	4568734

4x

2x

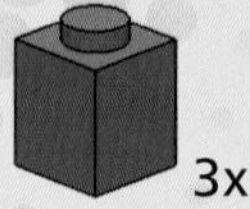
3x

2x

2x

3x

4x

1x

14x

1x

10x

1x

2x

3x

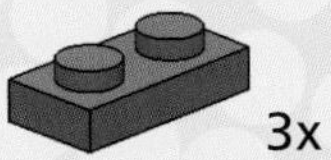
3x

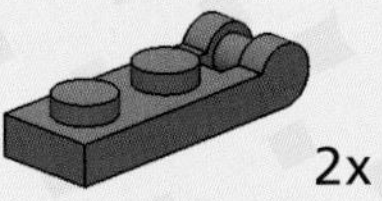
2x

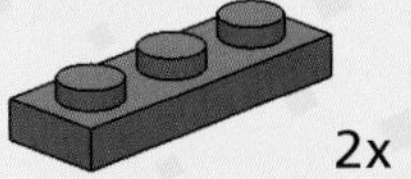
2x

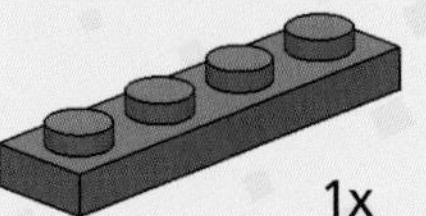
1x

2x

5x

1x

3x

1x

1x

1x

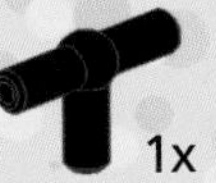
1x

2x

2x

1x

3x

ROTORCYCLE XROE-1

The Hiller ROE-1 Rotorcycle from 1958 was the smallest single-person helicopter at that time. Developed for the US Navy by Hiller and Saunders-Roe, it was, however, never used militarily. Only 12 helicopters were built, of which five are now in museums. That's why we've given the pilot a white head in our building instructions.

SERVICE CEILING:	*2804 m (9,199 ft)*
OPERATIONAL RANGE:	*267 km (166 miles)*
WEIGHT:	*140 kg (308 lb)*
TOP SPEED:	*113 km/h (70 mph)*
HP:	*40*

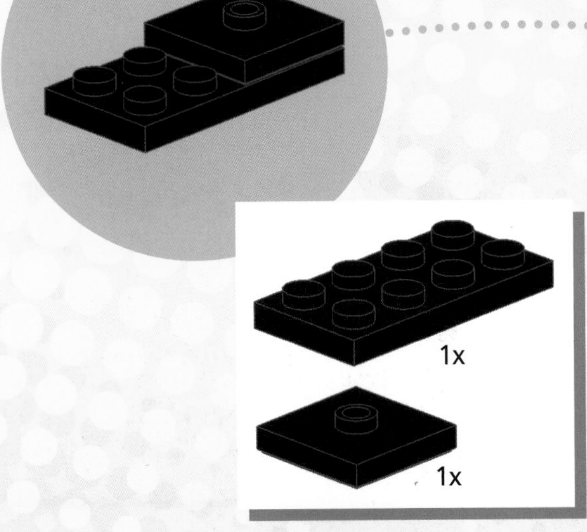

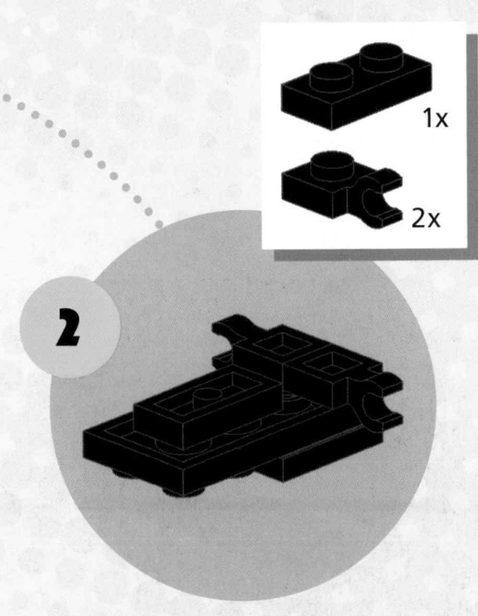

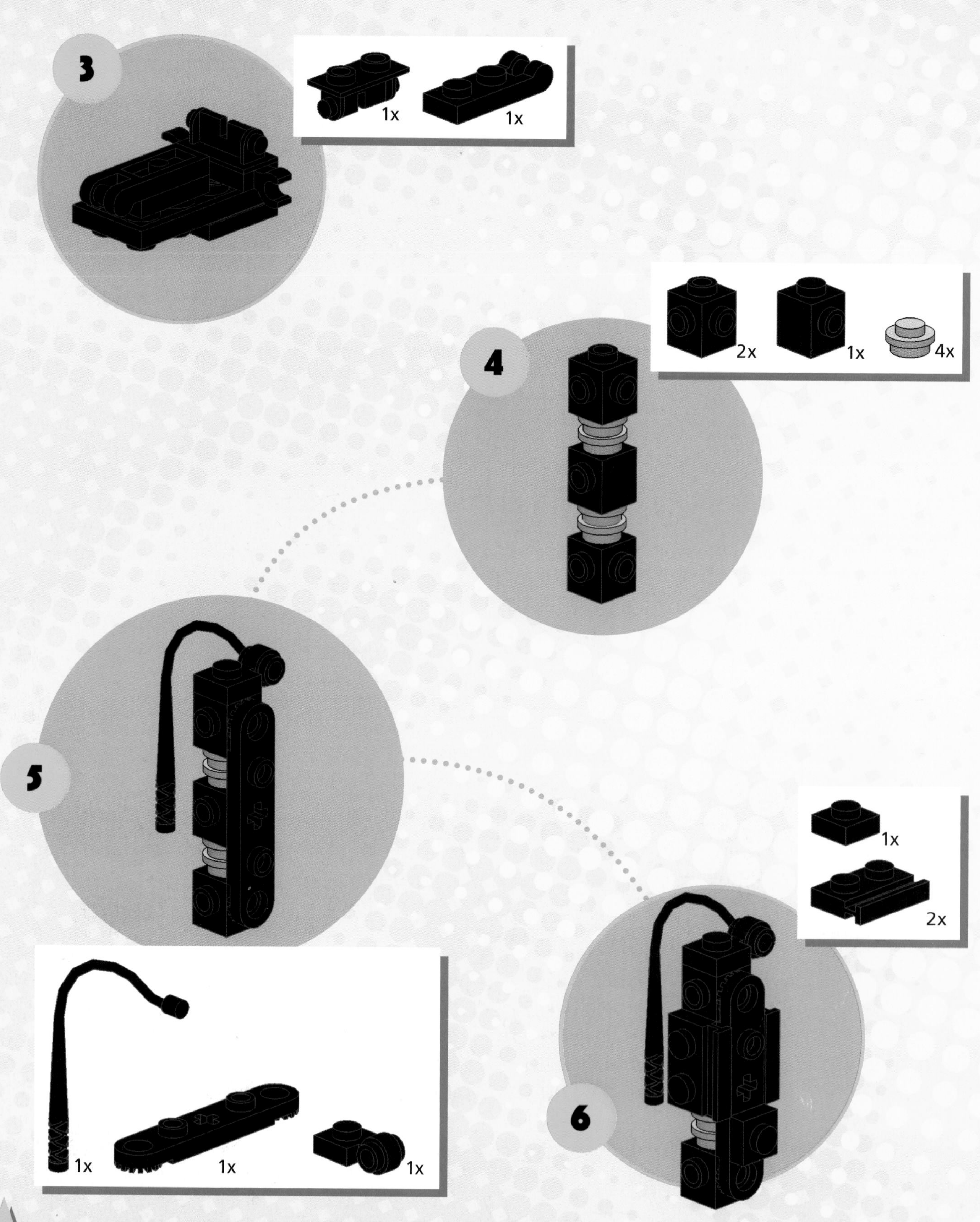

3
1x
1x
4
2x
1x
4x
5
1x
1x
1x
6
1x
2x

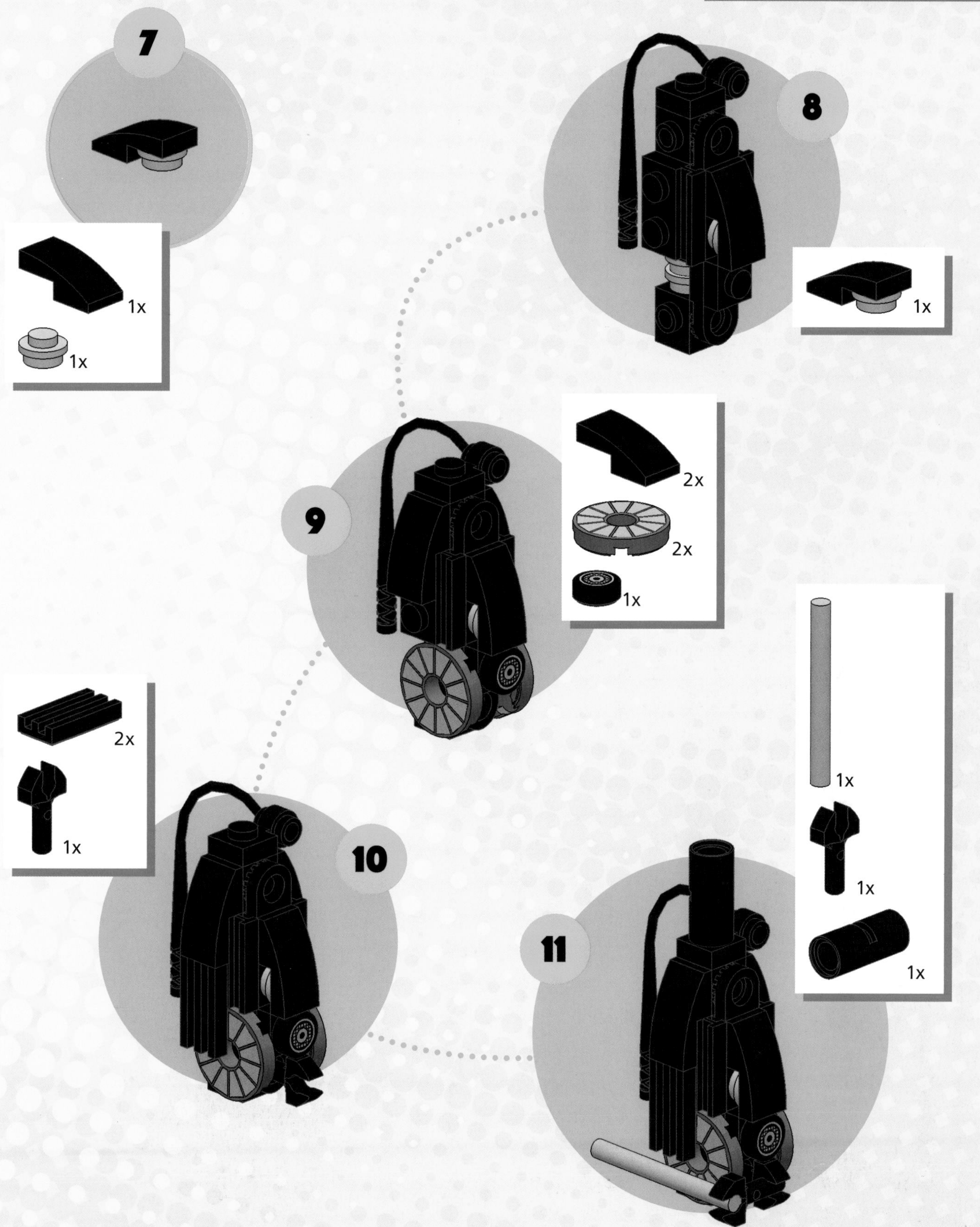
7
1x
1x
8
1x
9
2x
2x
1x
2x
1x
10
1x
1x
1x
11

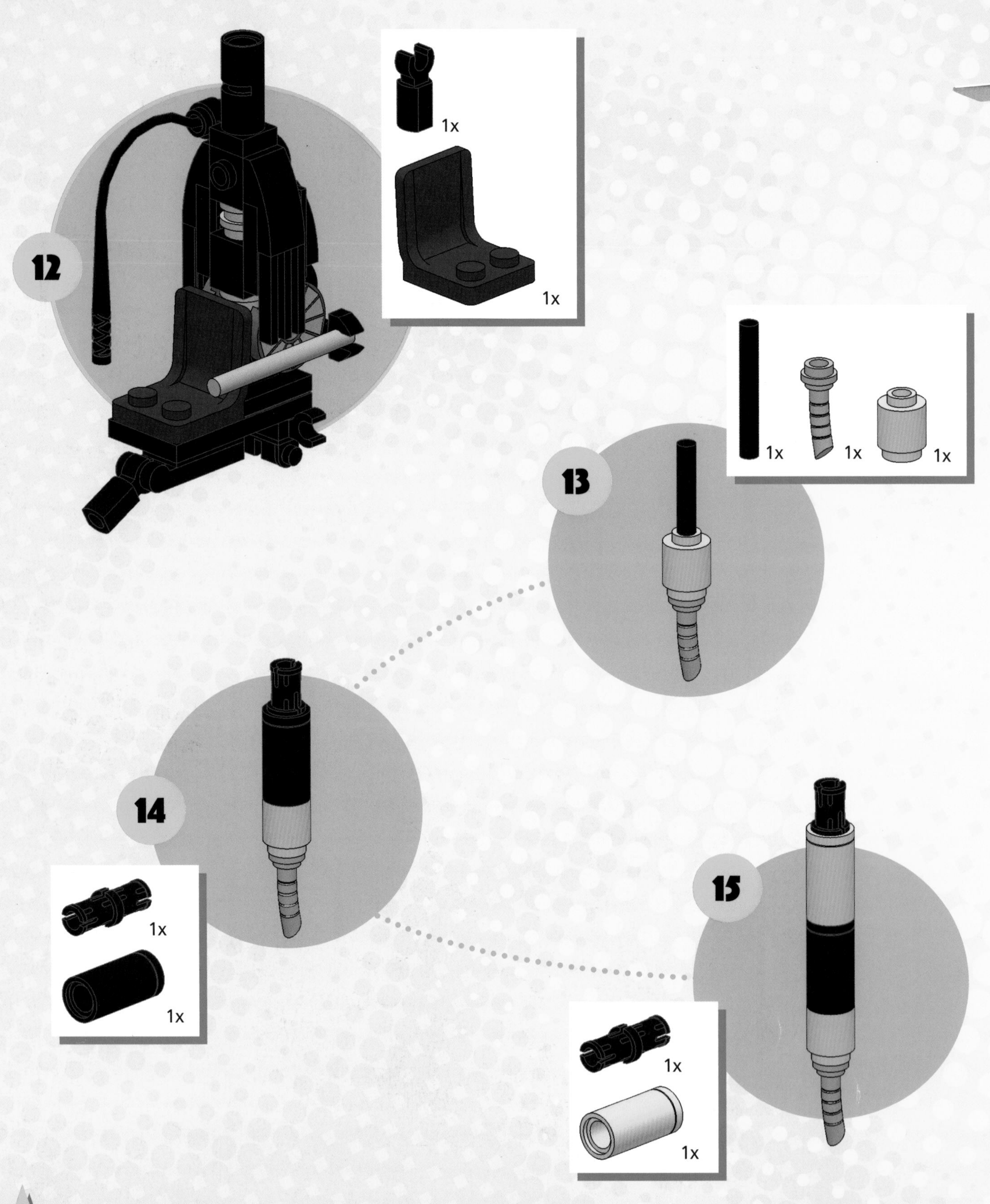
12
1x
1x
1x
1x
1x
13
14
1x
1x
15
1x
1x

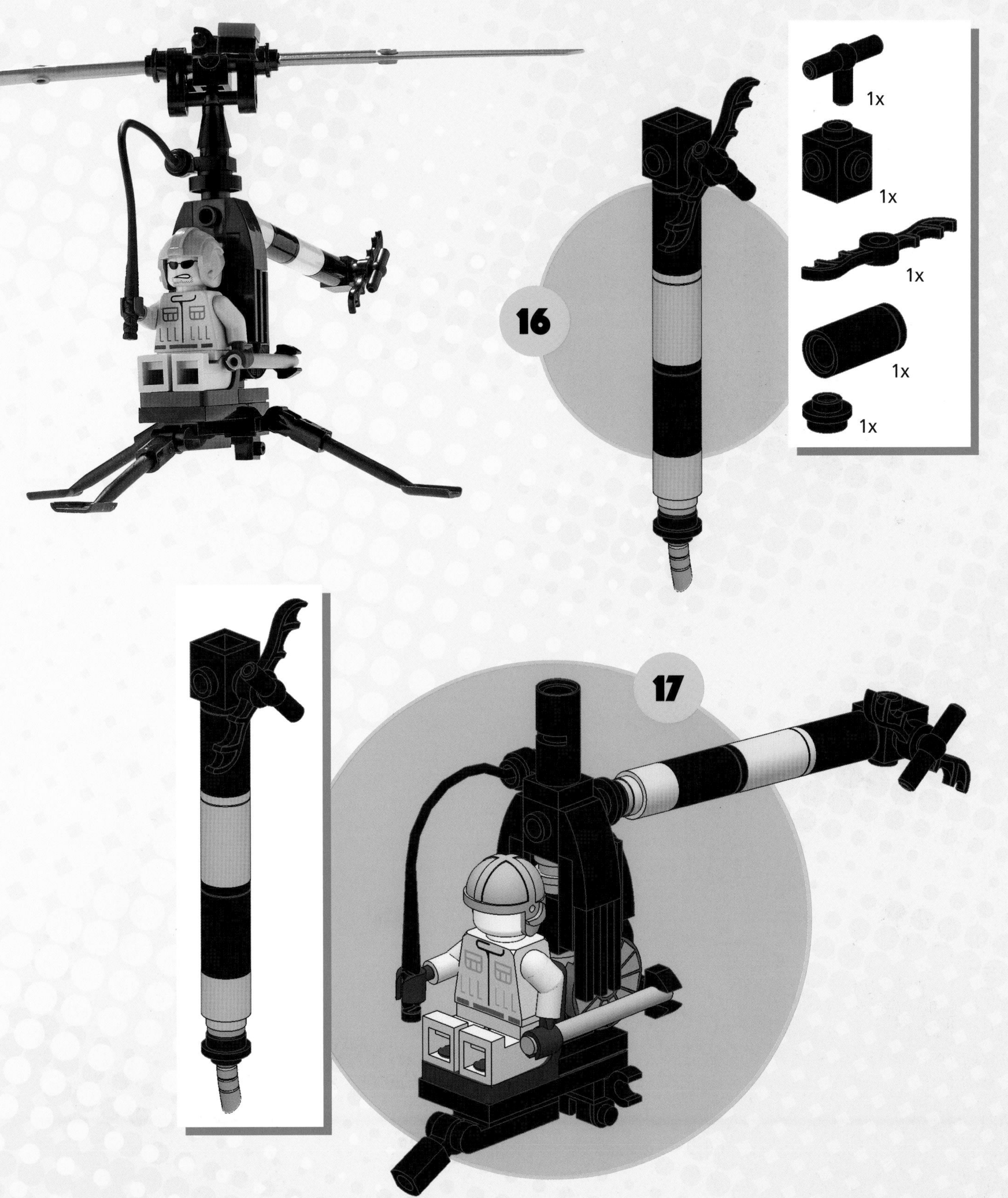

16
1x
1x
1x
1x
1x
17

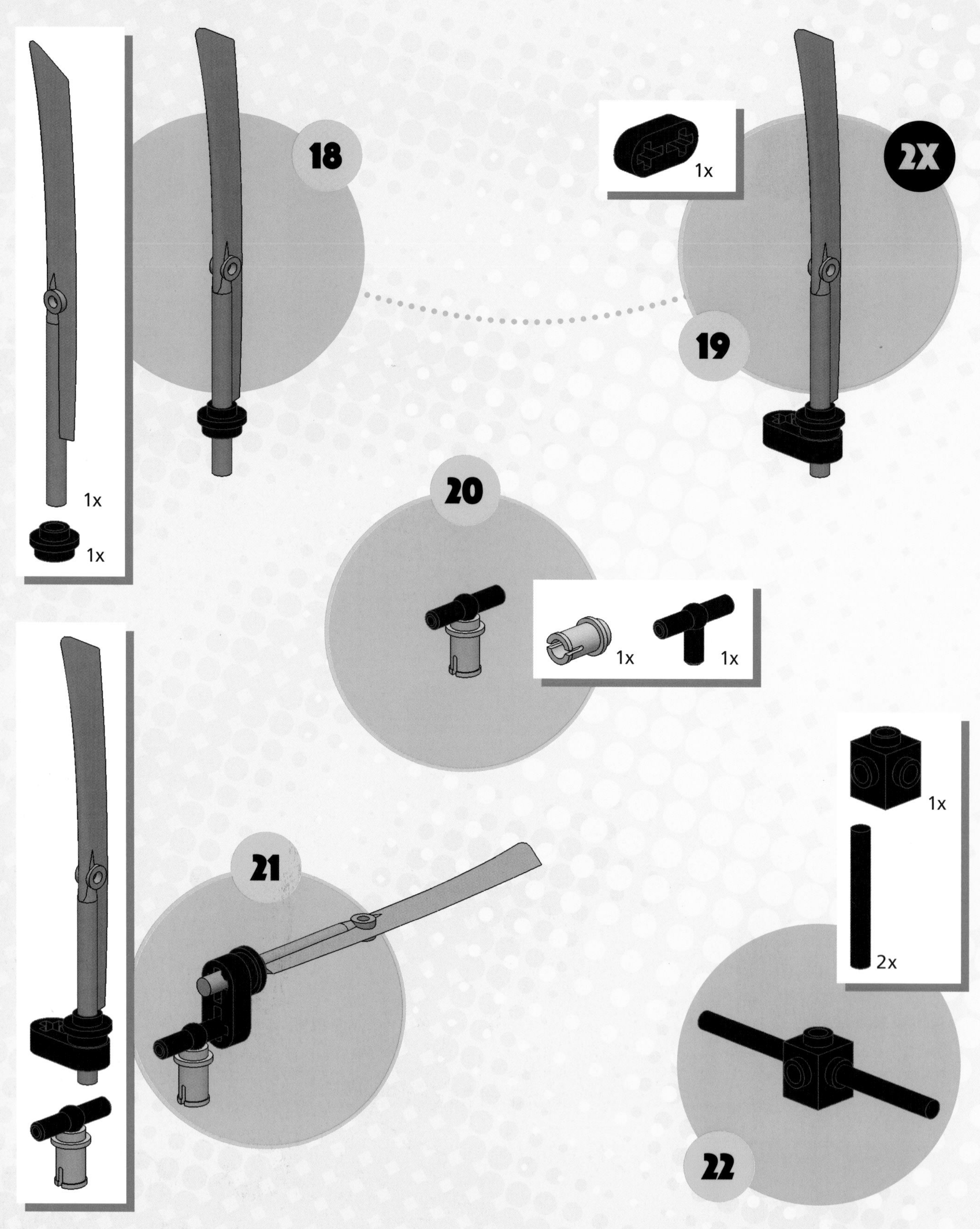

1x
1x
18
1x
2X
19
20
1x
1x
1x
2x
21
22

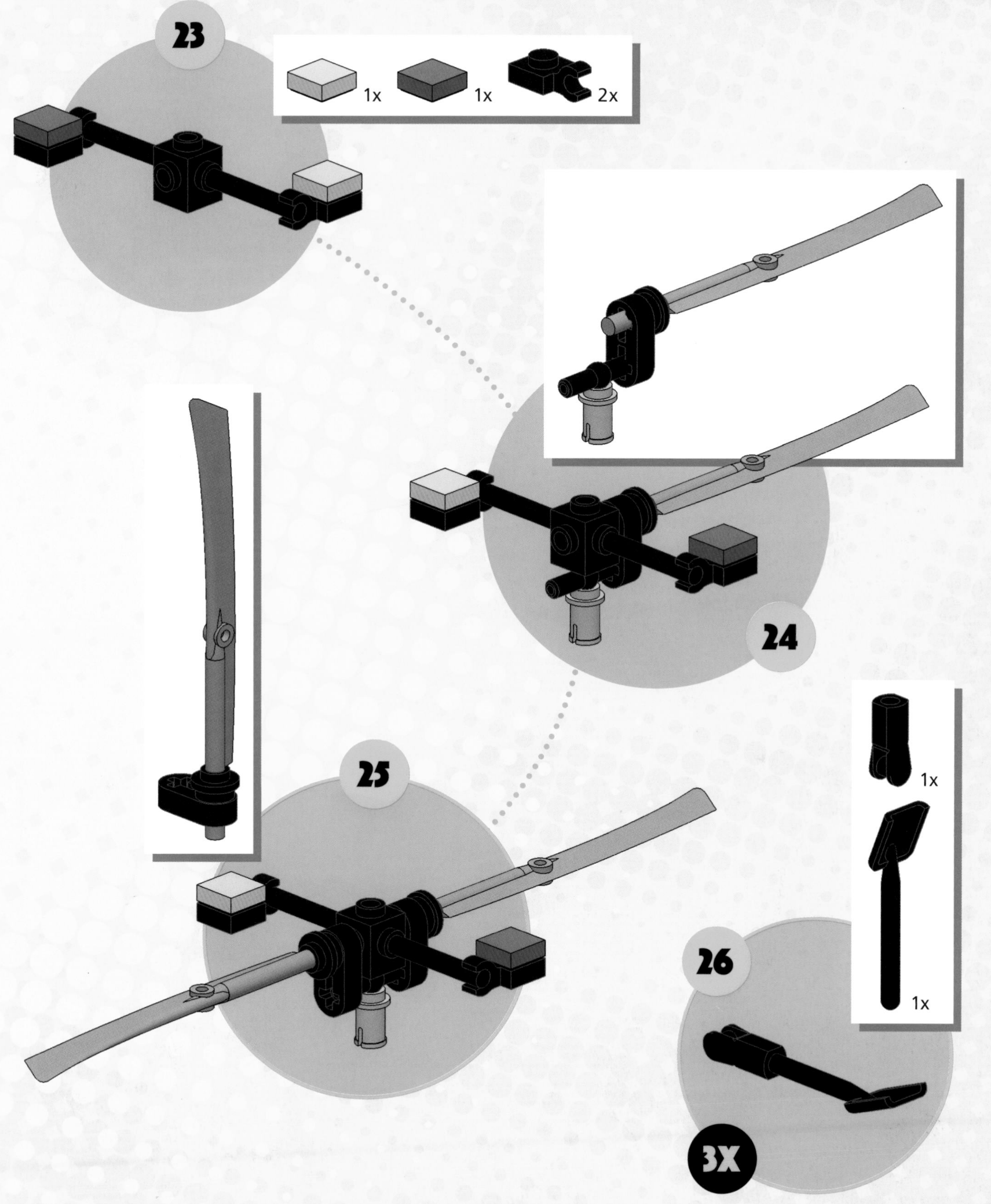
23
1x
1x
2x
24
25
26
1x
1x
3X

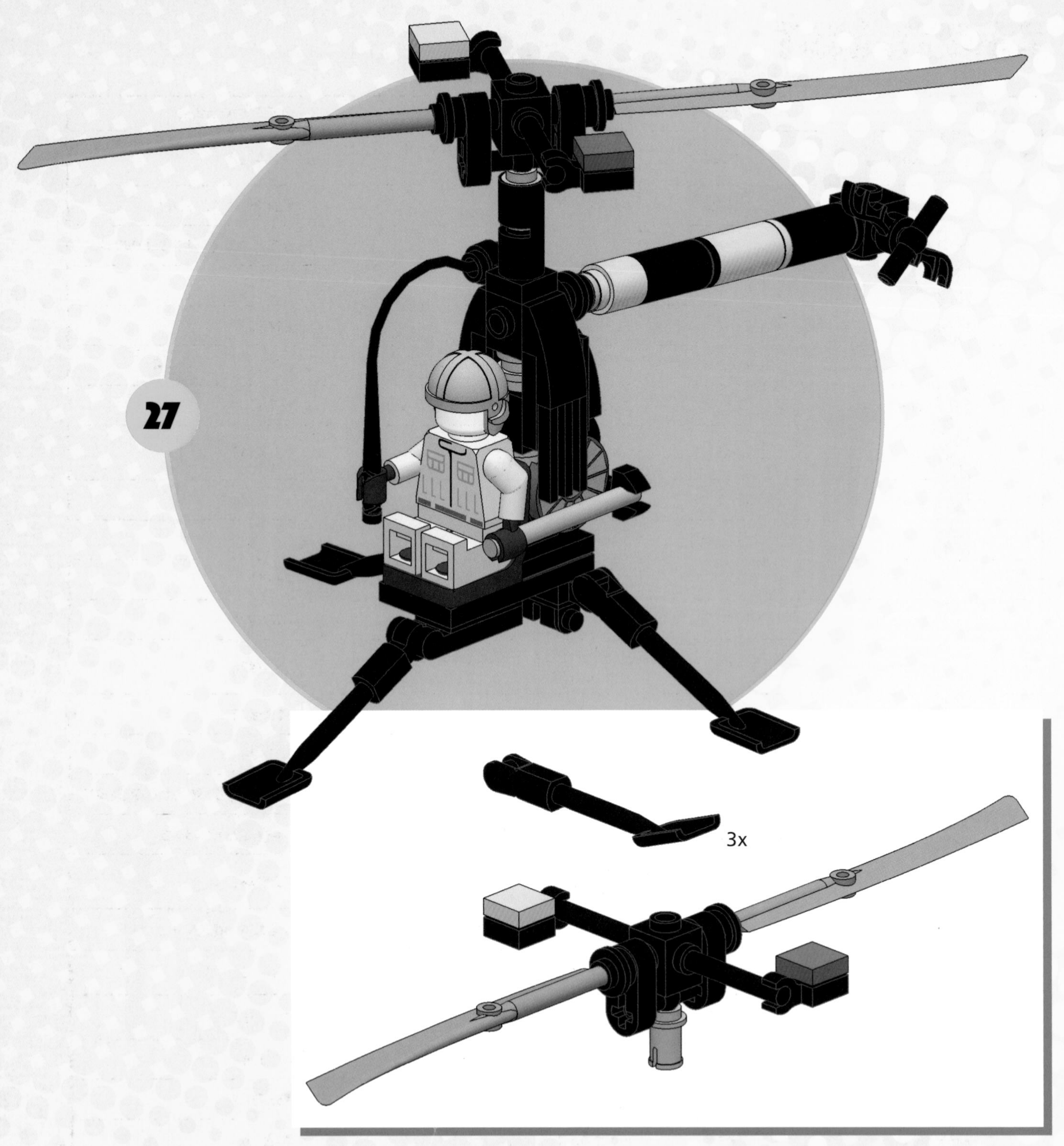
27
3x

PARTS LIST

Quantity	Color	Element	Element Name	LEGO® Number
2	Black	48729b	Bar 1.5L with Clip with Truncated Sides and Hole in Shaft	4289538
1	Light Bluish Gray	30374	Bar 4L	4211628, 6116608
3	Black	87994	Bar 3L	4566275, 4653208, 6093525
1	Black	11090	Bar Tube with Clip	6015891
3	Black	23443	Bar Tube with Handle	6143318
1	Yellow	3062b	Brick 1 x 1 Round with Hollow Stud	306224
4	Black	4733	Brick 1 x 1 with Studs on Four Sides	473326
1	Black	47905	Brick 1 x 1 with Studs on Two Opposite Sides	4214559
1	Black	3938	Hinge 1 x 2 Top	393826
1	Black	55707e	Minifig Propellor with Bat Wings	
1	Reddish Brown	4079	Minifig Seat 2 x 2	4211206
3	Black	3837	Minifig Shovel	4189009
2	Flat Silver	98137	Minifig Weapon Curved Blade 8.5L with Bar 1.5L	4654422
1	Black	88704	Minifig Whip Flexible	6092878
1	Black	3024	Plate 1 x 1	302426
5	Metallic Silver	4073	Plate 1 x 1 Round	4249039, 51809301, 6051507
3	Black	85861	Plate 1 x 1 Round with Open Stud	6100627, 6168646
4	Black	61252	Plate 1 x 1 with Clip Horizontal (Thick C-Clip)	4517925
1	Black	4081b	Plate 1 x 1 with Clip Light Type 2	408126, 4632571
1	Black	3023	Plate 1 x 2	302326
2	Black	32028	Plate 1 x 2 with Door Rail	4107761
1	Black	60478	Plate 1 x 2 with Handle on End	4515368
1	Black	87580	Plate 2 x 2 with Groove with 1 Center Stud	4565323
1	Black	3020	Plate 2 x 4	302026
3	Black	11477	Slope Brick Curved 2 x 1	6047276
2	Black	41677	Technic Beam 2 x 0.5 Liftarm	4164133, 4167726

Quantity	Color	Element	Element Name	LEGO® Number
1	Light Bluish Gray	4274	Technic Pin 1/2	4211483, 4274194
2	Black	75535	Technic Pin Joiner Round	75619
1	Yellow	75535	Technic Pin Joiner Round	75644
1	Black	62462	Technic Pin Joiner Round with Slot	4526982, 6173119
2	Black	2780	Technic Pin with Friction and Slots	278026, 4121715
2	Black	4697b	Technic Pneumatic T-Piece - Type 2	6104209
1	Black	2711	Technic Rotor 2 Blade with 2 Studs	
1	Black	98138pb064	Tile 1 x 1 Round with Speaker Pattern	6172764
1	Red	3070b	Tile 1 x 1 with Groove	307021
1	Yellow	3070b	Tile 1 x 1 with Groove	307024
2	Black	2412b	Tile 1 x 2 Grille with Groove	241226
2	Dark Bluish Gray	15535pb01	Tile 2 x 2 Round with Hole with Rotor Pattern	6117346
1	Light Bluish Gray	61199	Weapon Light Sabre Hilt Curved	4527160, 6107472

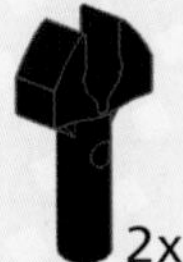
2x

3x

1x

1x

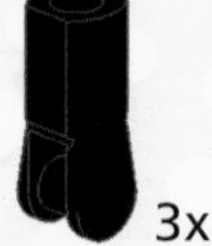
3x

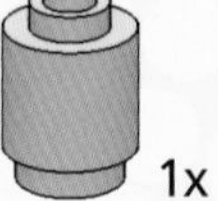
1x

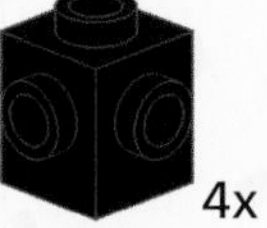
4x

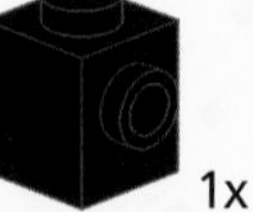
1x

1x

1x

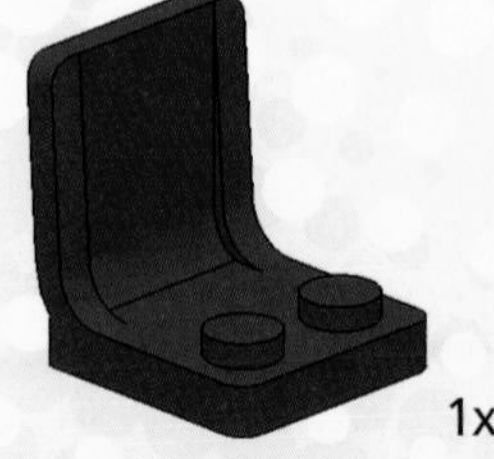
1x

3x

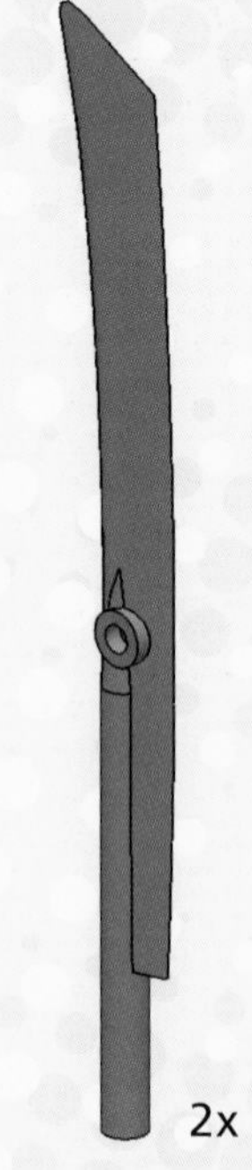
2x

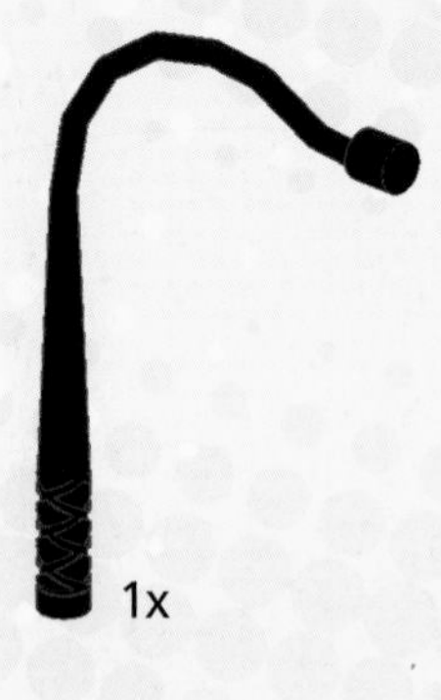
1x

1x

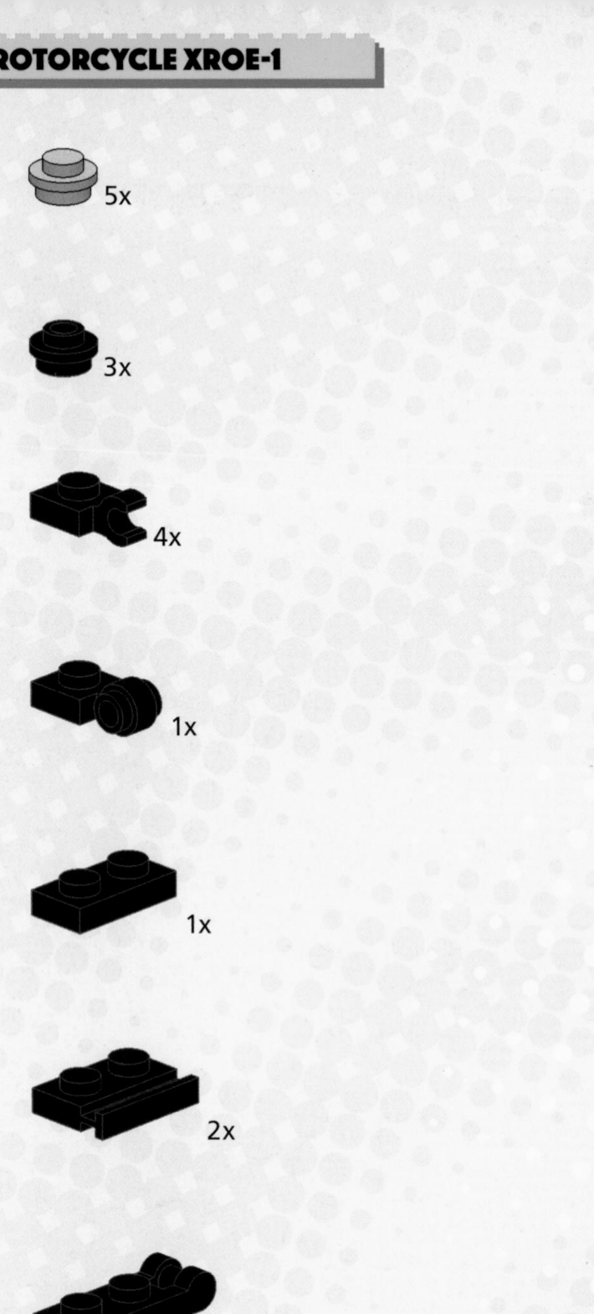
5x
3x
4x
1x
1x
2x
1x

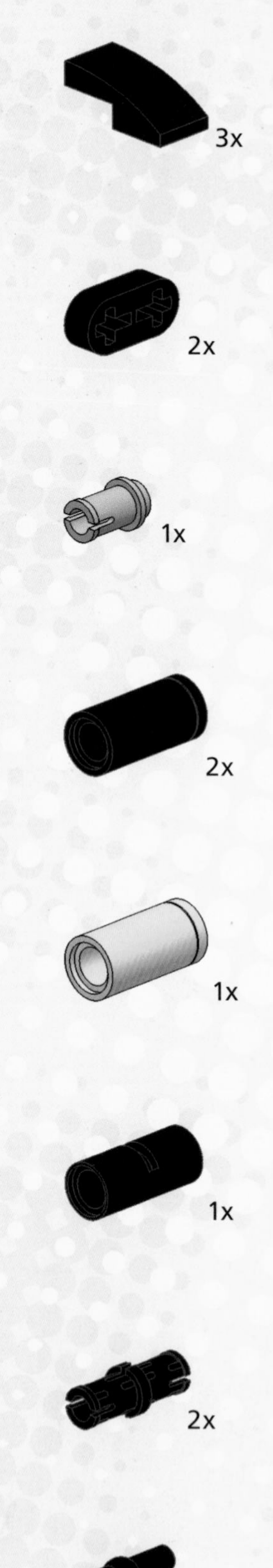
3x
2x
1x
2x
1x
1x
2x
2x

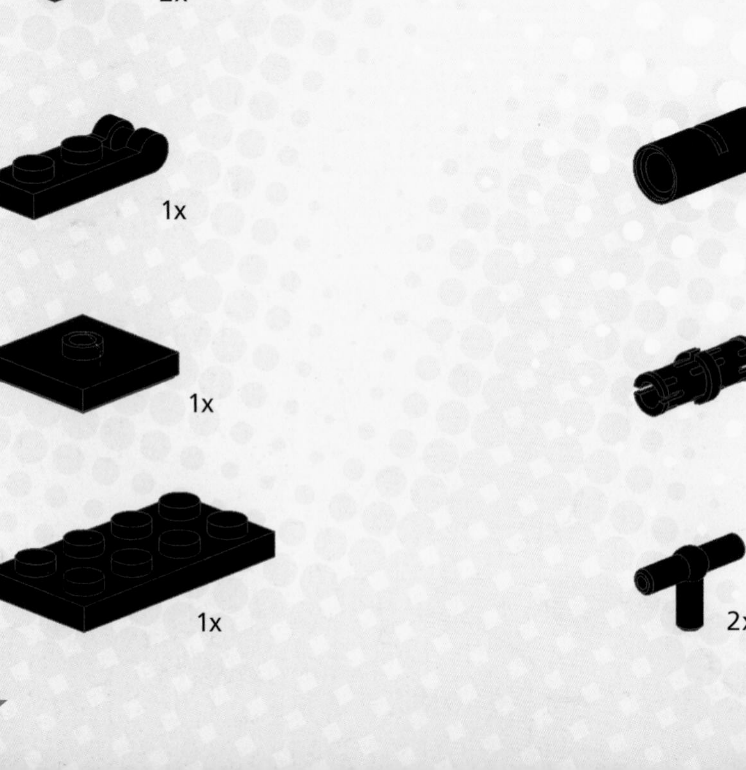
1x
1x

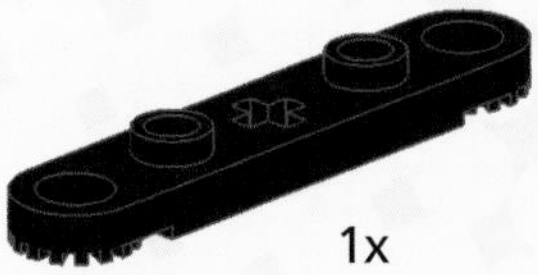

1x

1x

1x

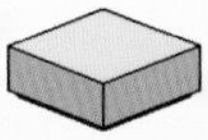

1x

2x

2x

1x

CONCORDE

The Aérospatiale/BAC Concorde 101/102 is commonly known as the "Concorde." This supersonic passenger aircraft needed only 2 hours, 52 minutes, and 59 seconds to fly from New York to London in 1996. It is an unbeaten record in civil aviation history.
Further interesting facts: On June 17, 1974, an Air France Concorde left Boston for Paris. At the same time, a Boeing 747 left Paris for Boston. Although the Concorde took 68 minutes to refuel in Paris, it still overtook the Boeing on the return flight and landed in Boston 10 minutes before the Boeing.
My replica of this delta-wing aircraft shows its flight position. The nose of the Concorde was lowered for takeoff and landing, but this is unfortunately not possible at this size in a LEGO® model.

SERVICE CEILING:	*18300 m (60,039 ft)*
OPERATIONAL RANGE:	*7250 km (4,505 miles)*
WEIGHT:	*78900 kg (87 t)*
TOP SPEED:	*2405 km/h (1,494 mph) (Mach 2,23)*
HP:	*280,000*

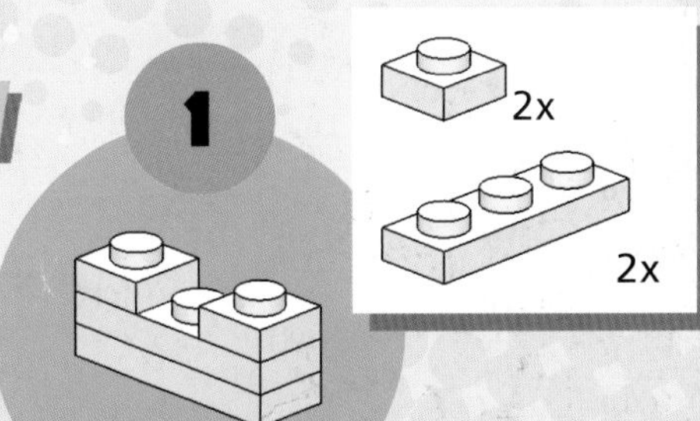

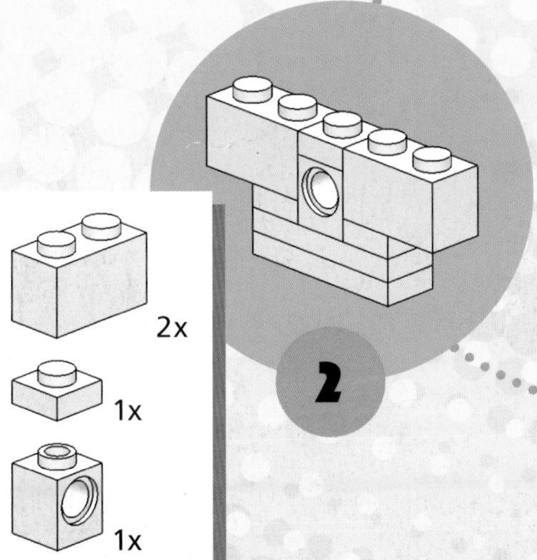

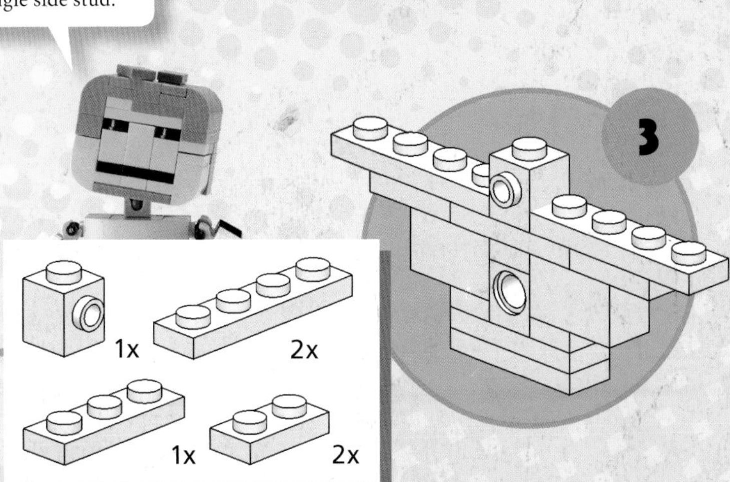

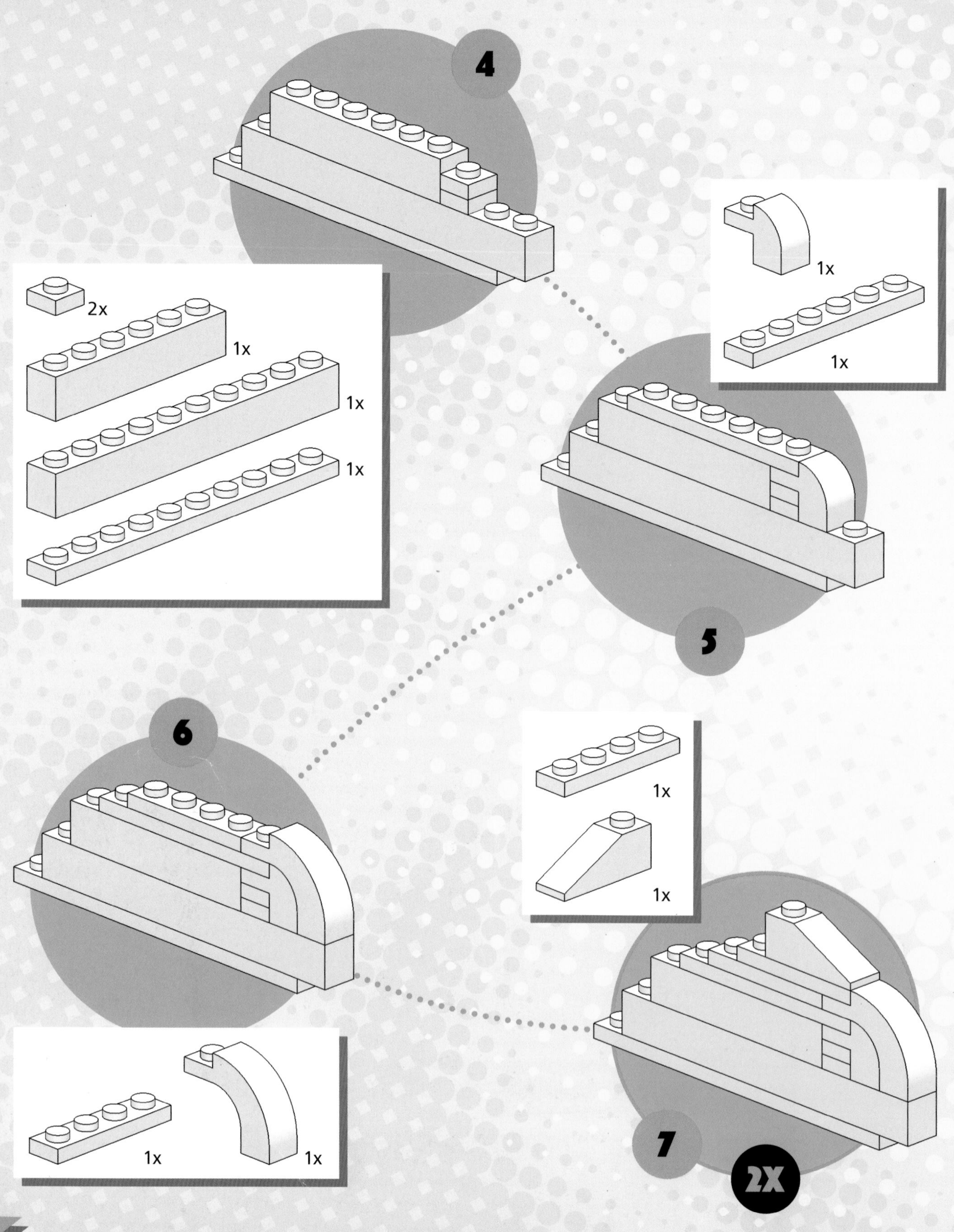
4
2x
1x
1x
1x
1x
1x
5
6
1x
1x
1x
1x
7
2X

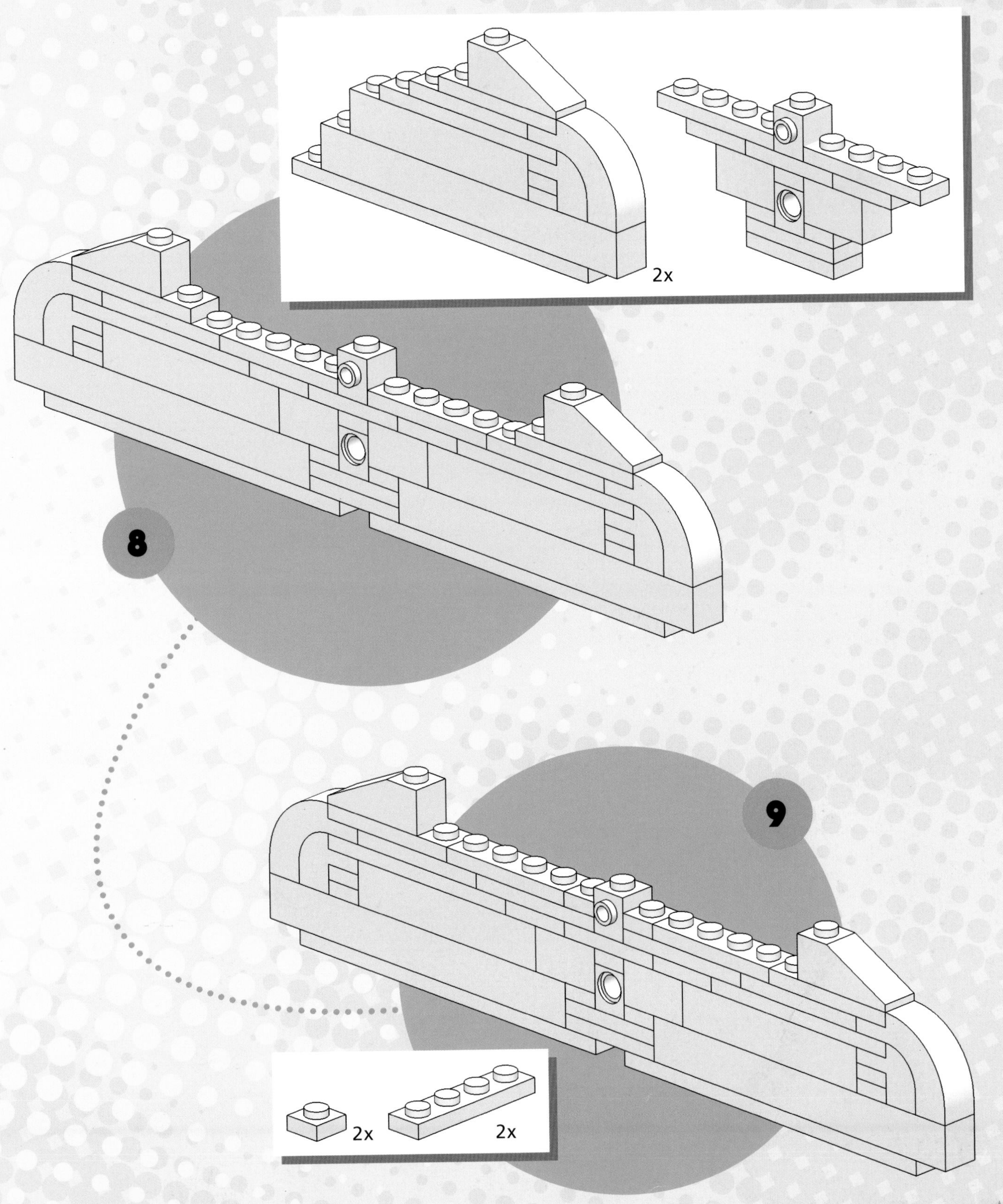
2x
8
9
2x
2x

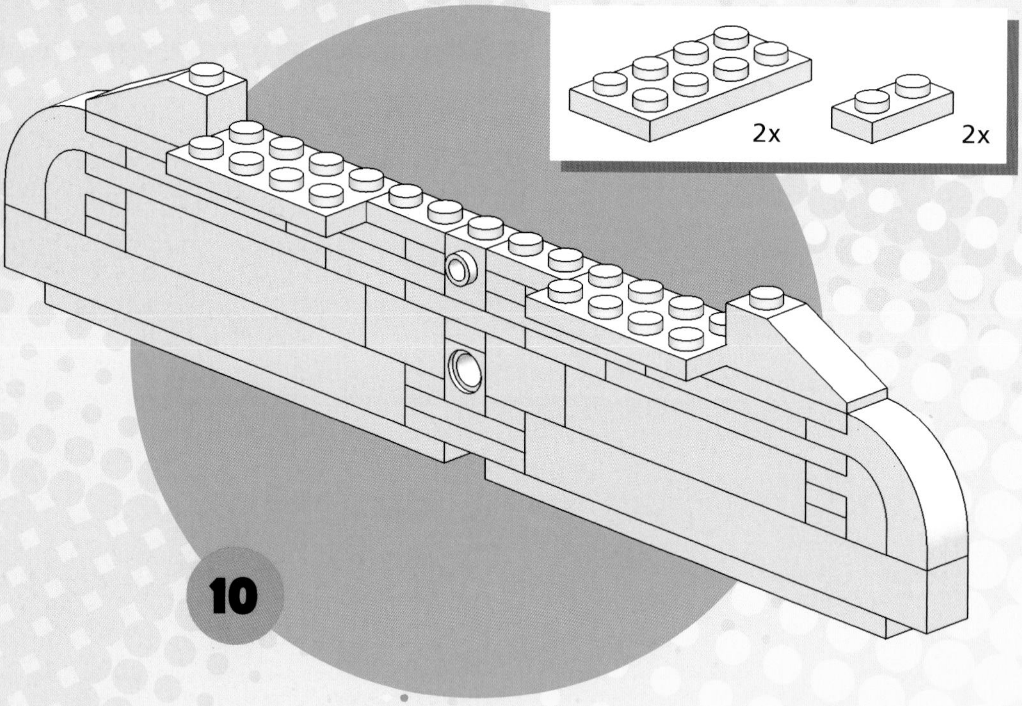

2x

2x

10

11

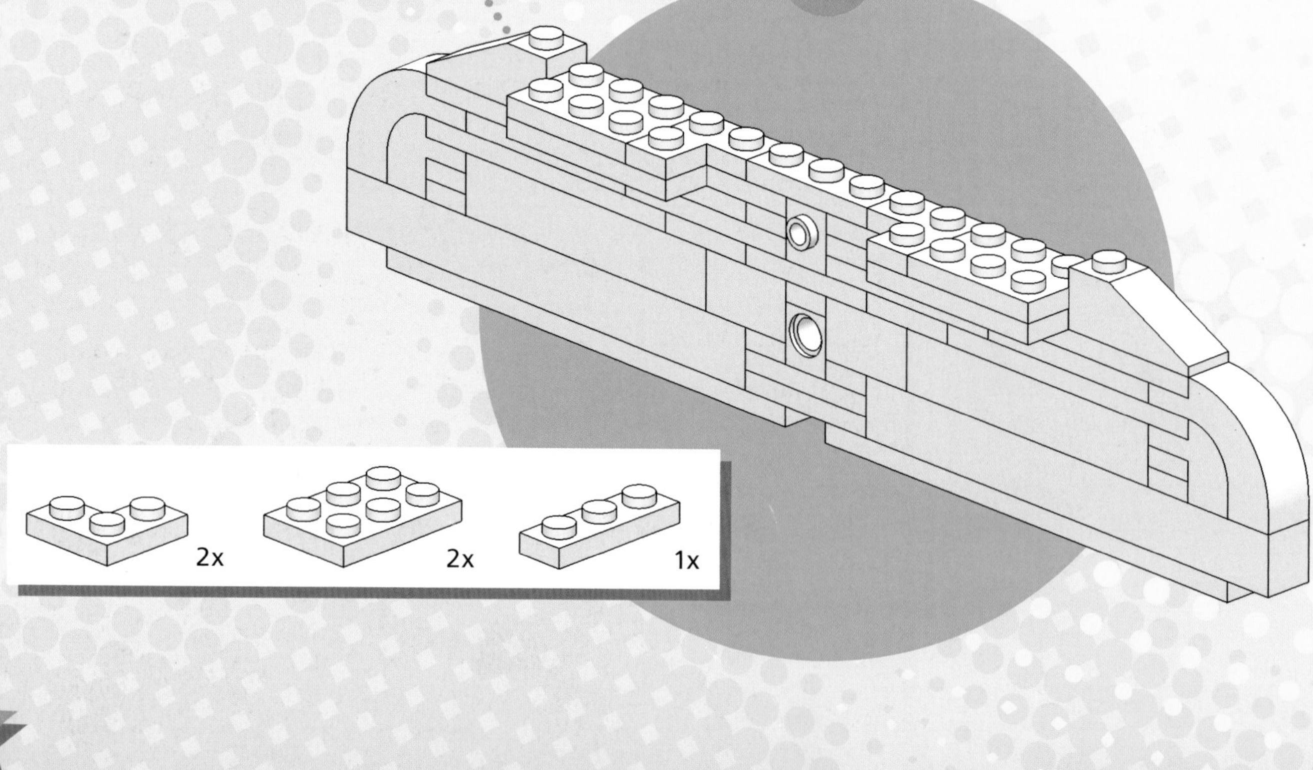

2x

2x

1x

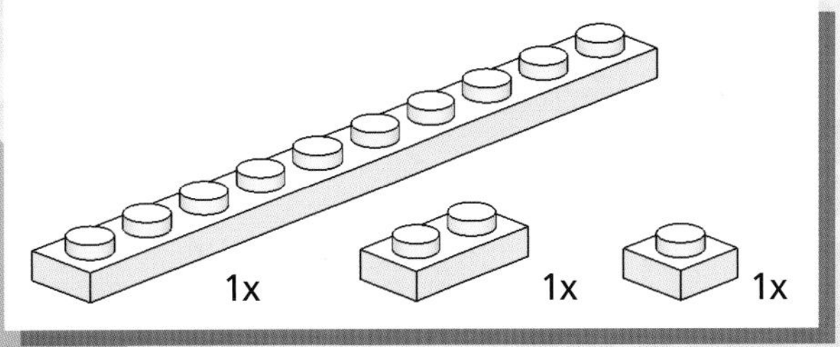

12

1x 1x 1x

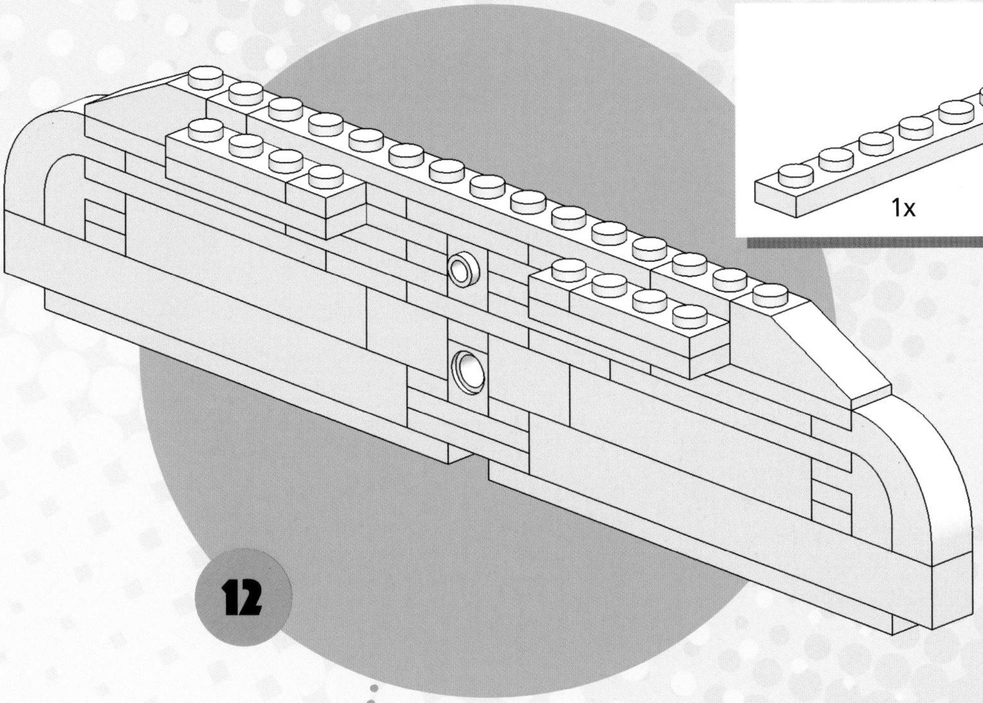

13

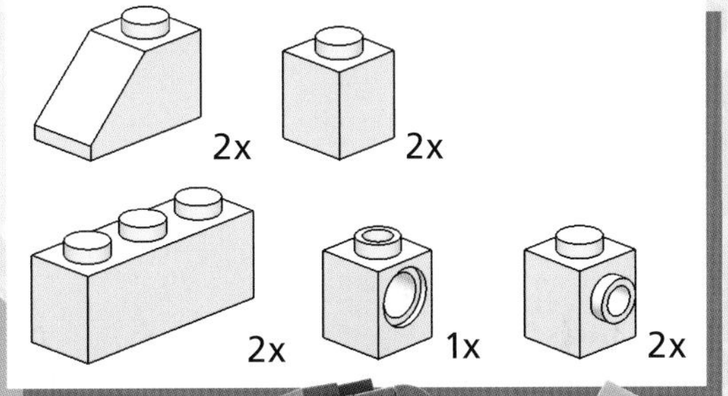

2x 2x

2x 1x 2x

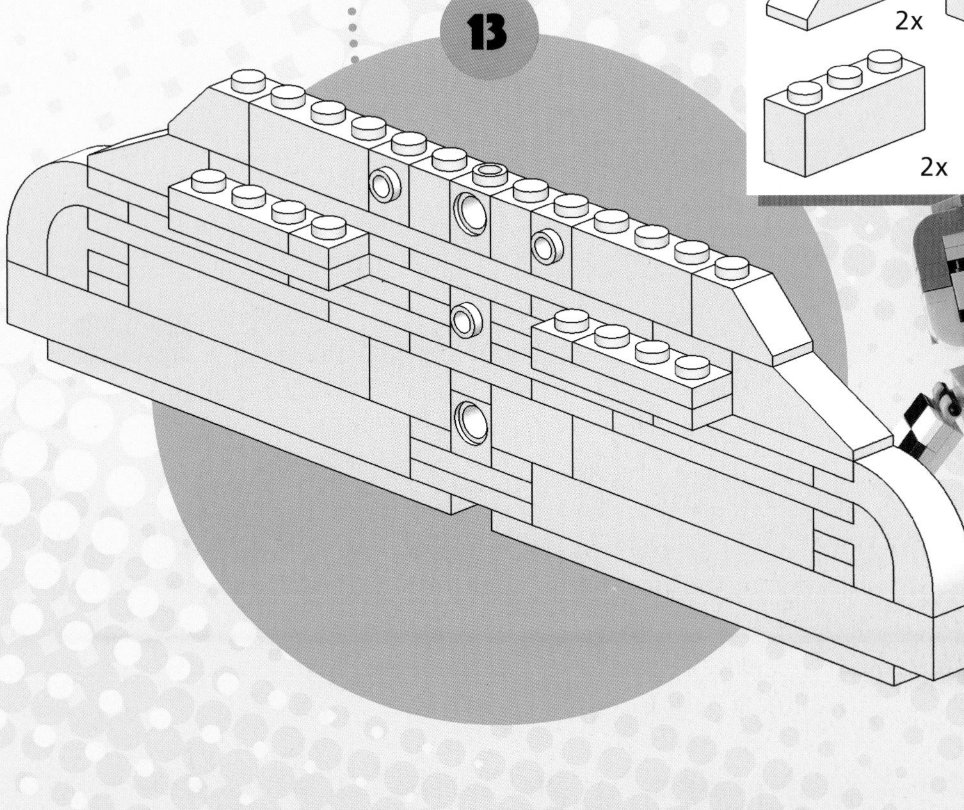

This brick only has a single side stud.

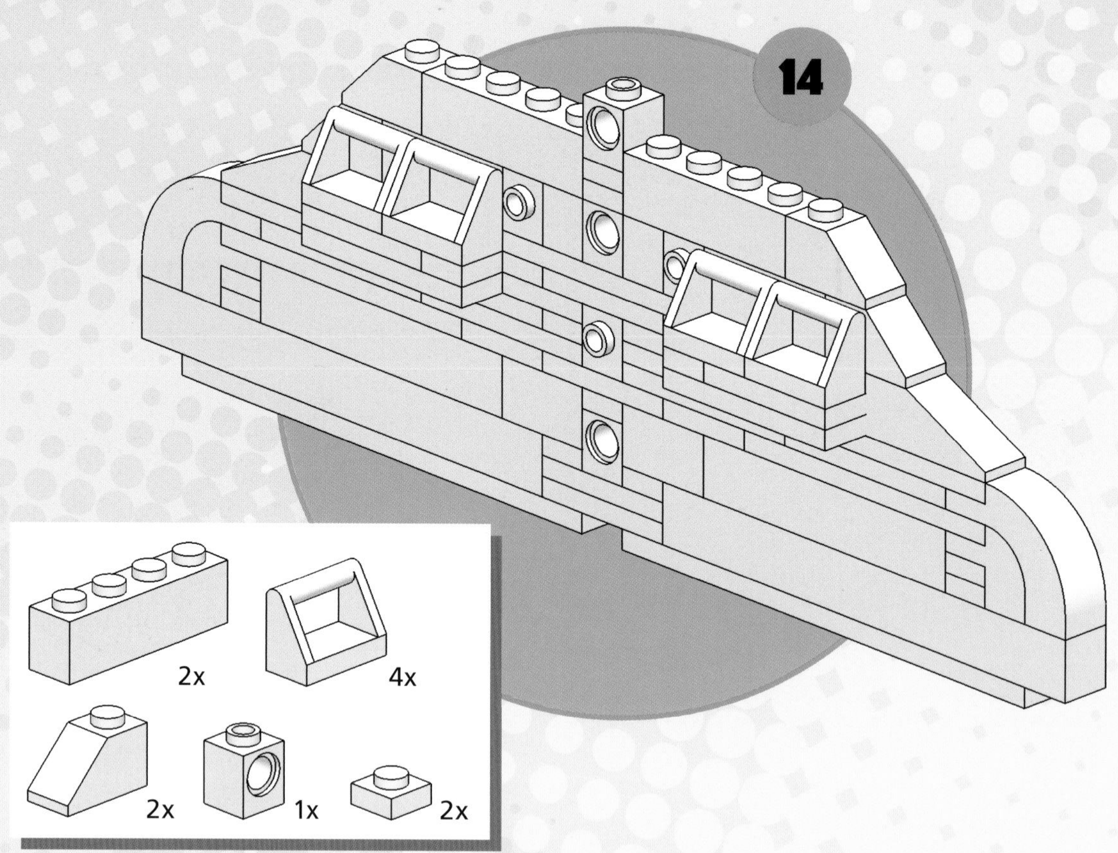
14
2x
4x
2x
1x
2x

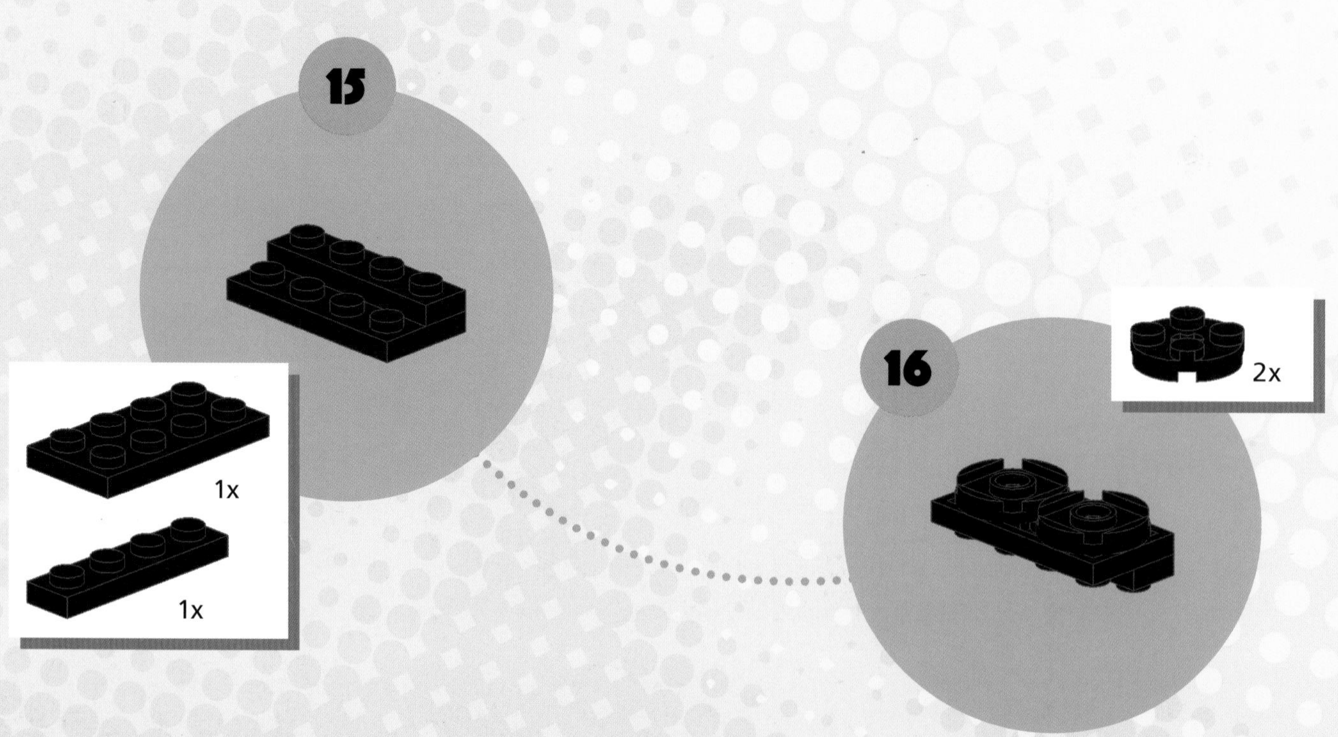
15
1x
1x
16
2x

17

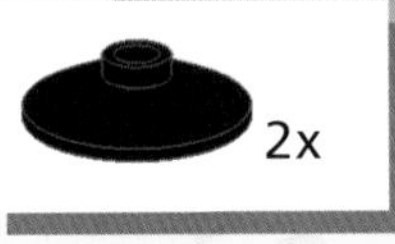

2x

18

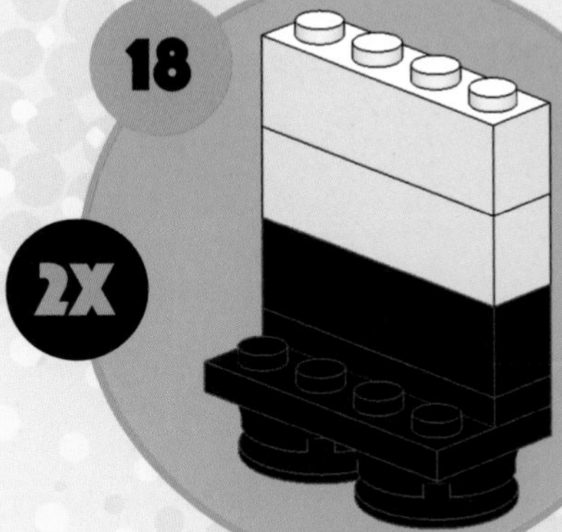

2X

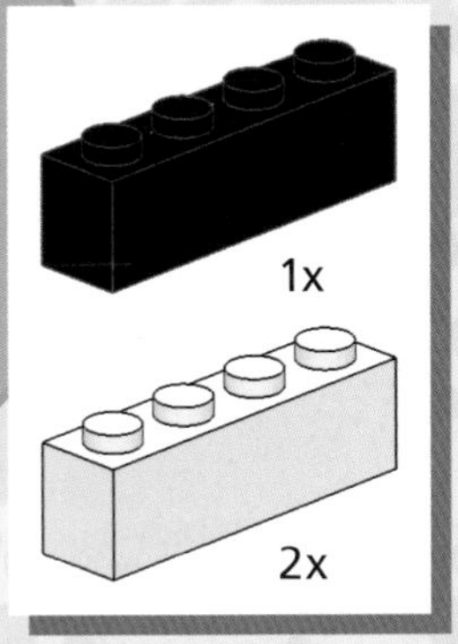

1x

2x

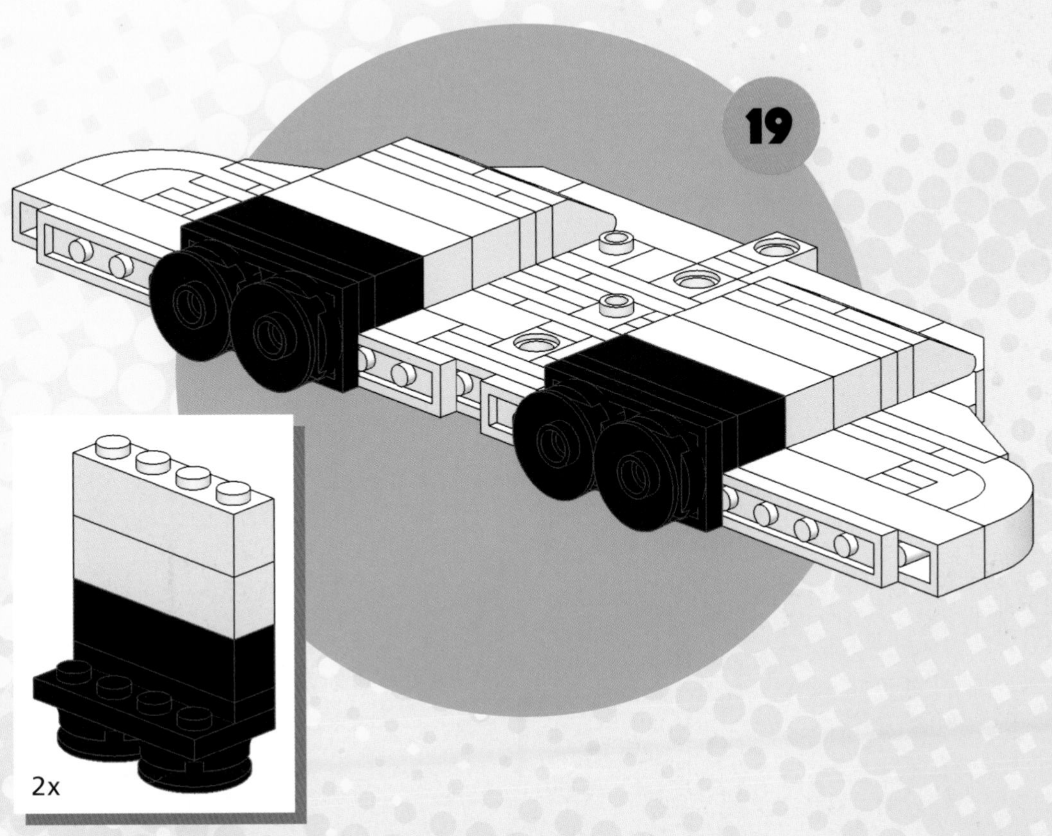

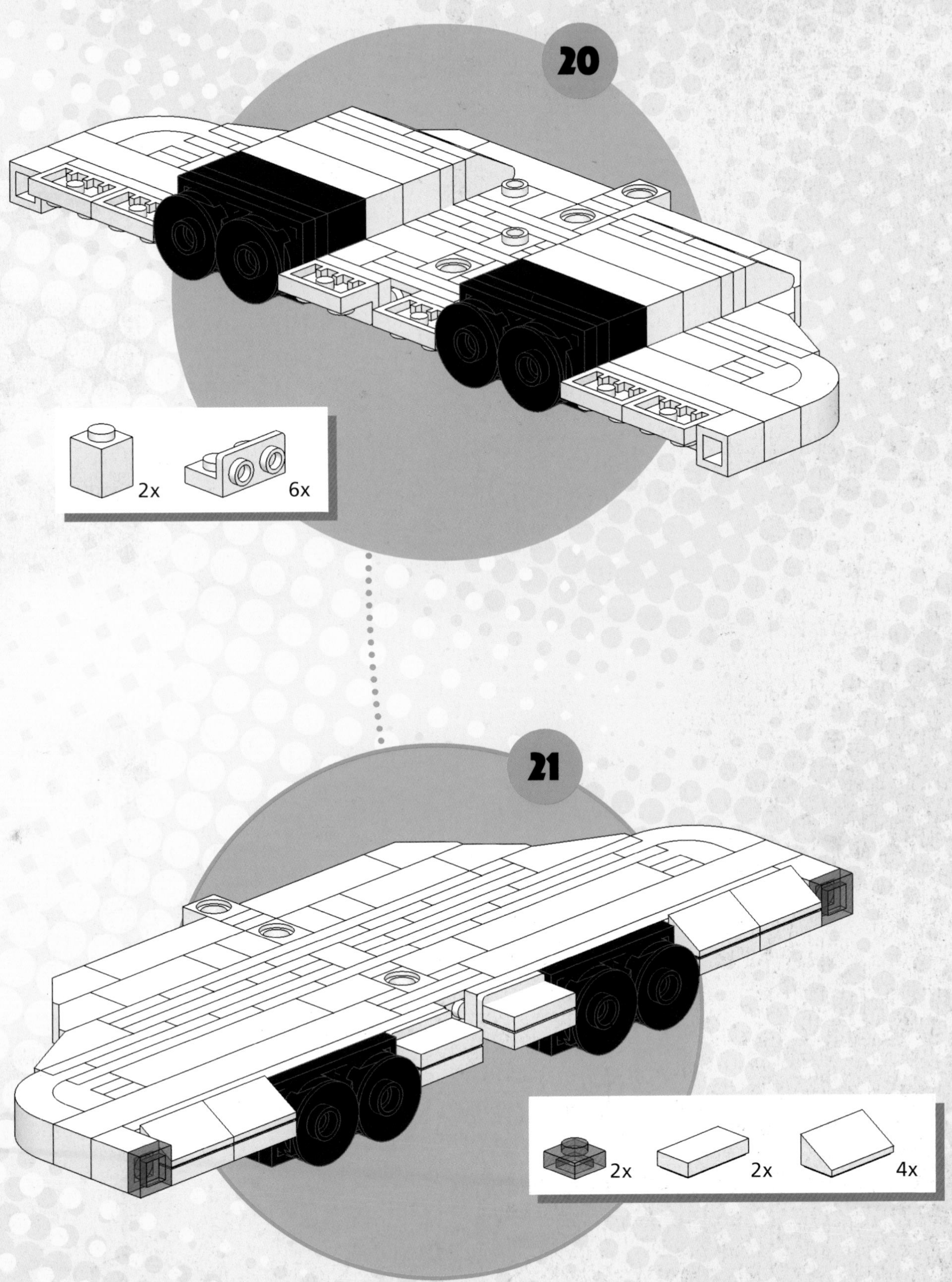
20
2x
6x
21
2x
2x
4x

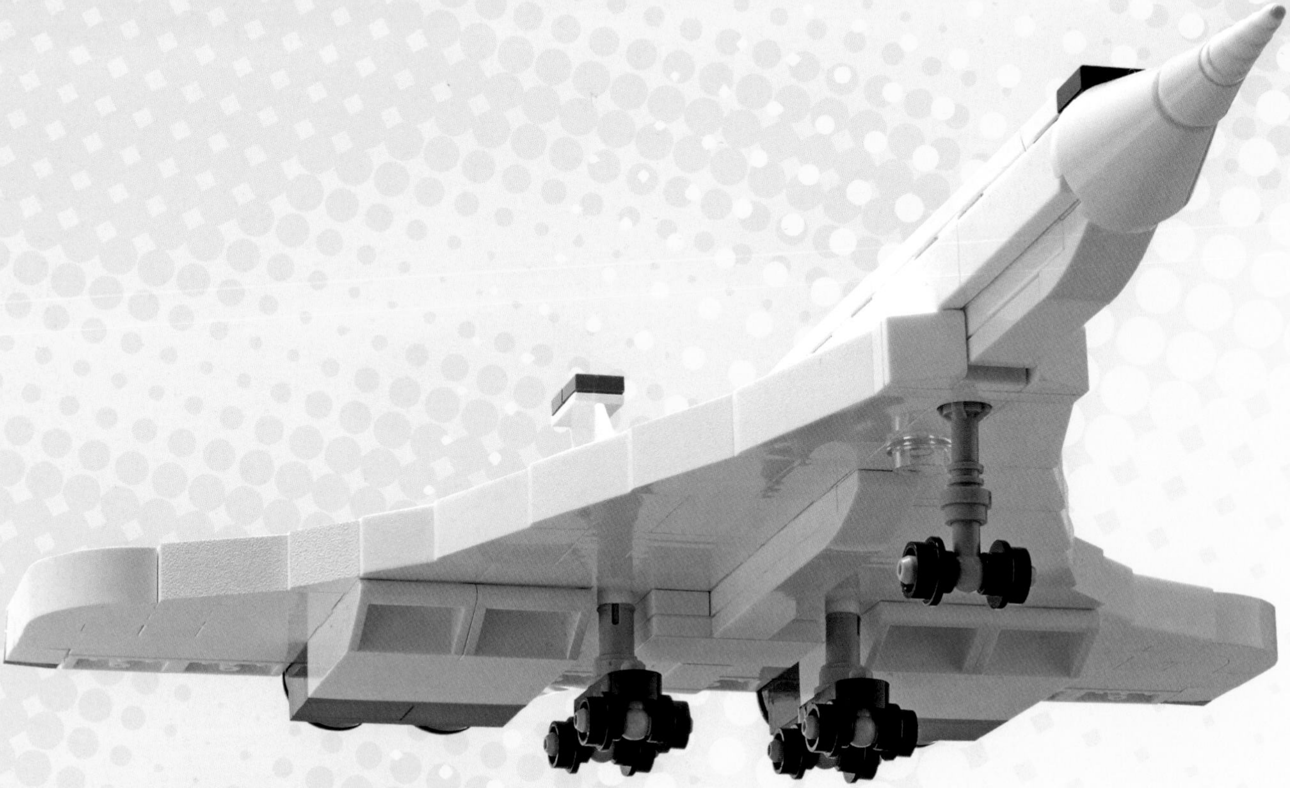

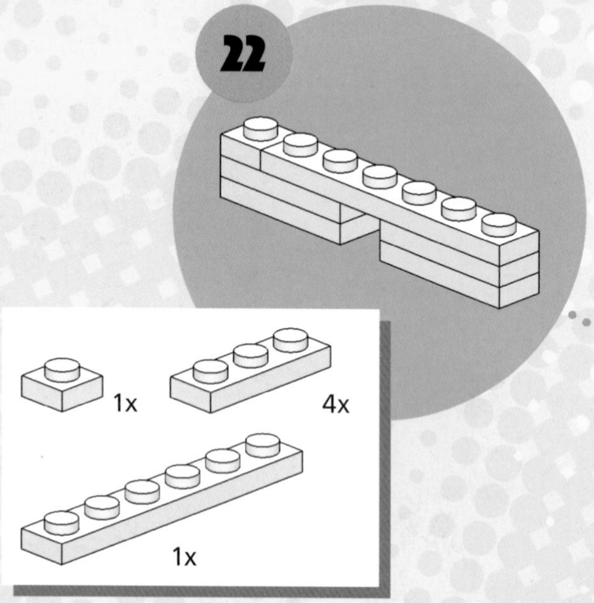

22

1x

4x

1x

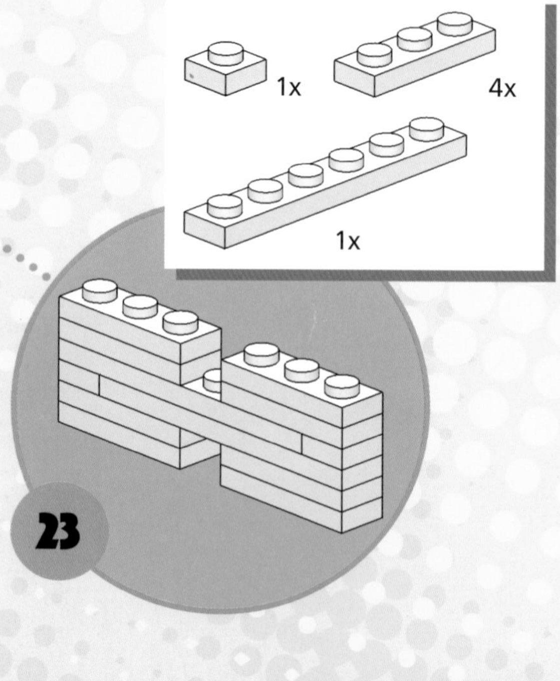

1x

4x

1x

23

24

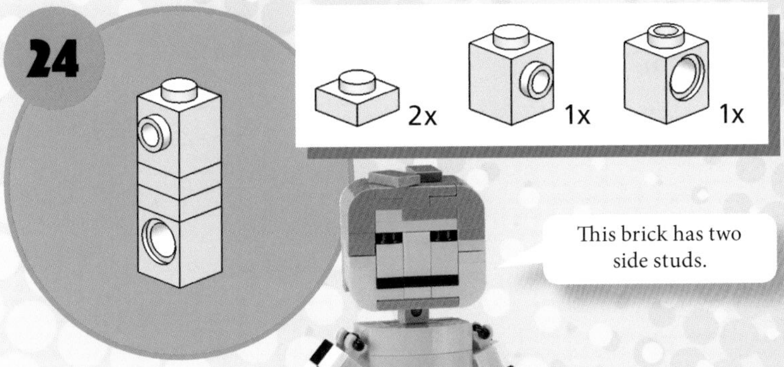

2x 1x 1x

This brick has two side studs.

2x

25

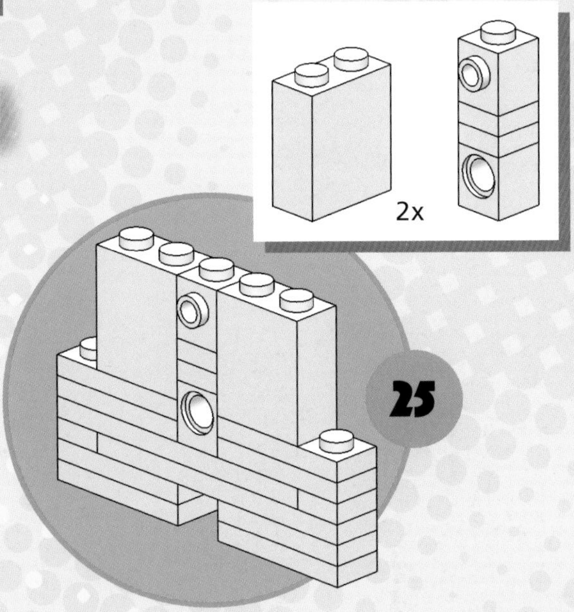

26

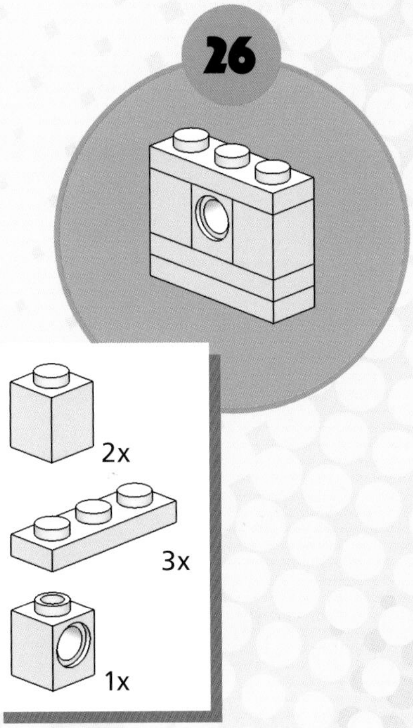

2x

3x

1x

27

6x

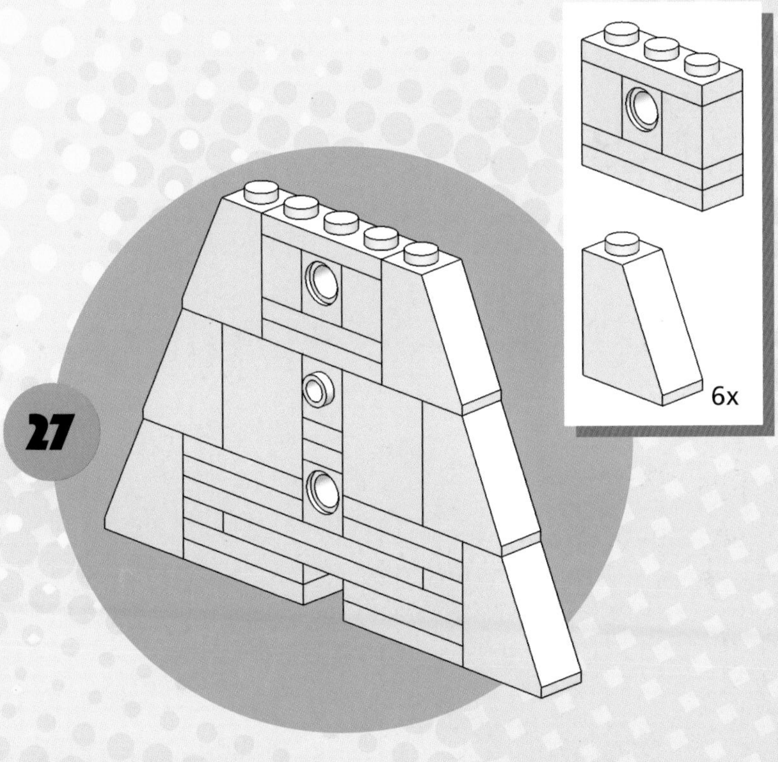

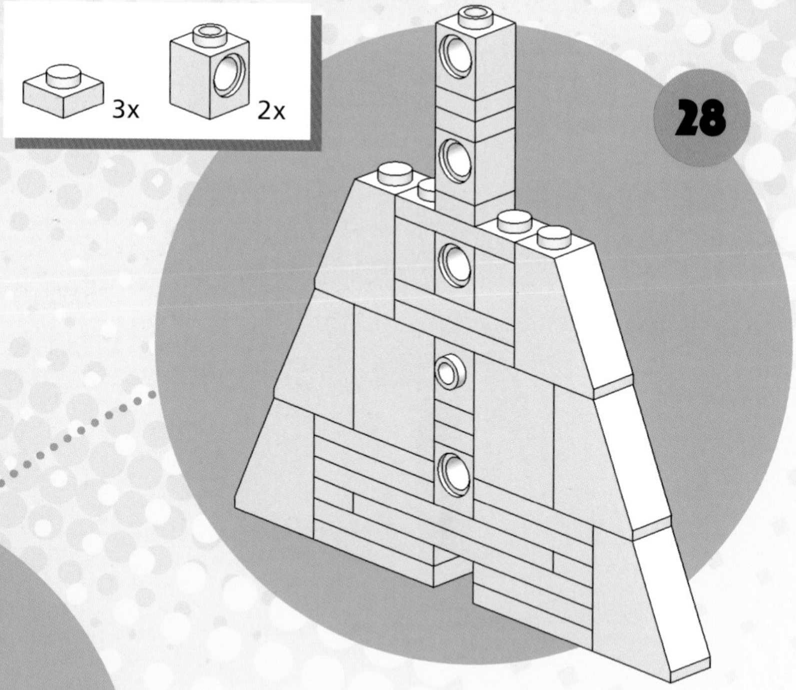

28

3x

2x

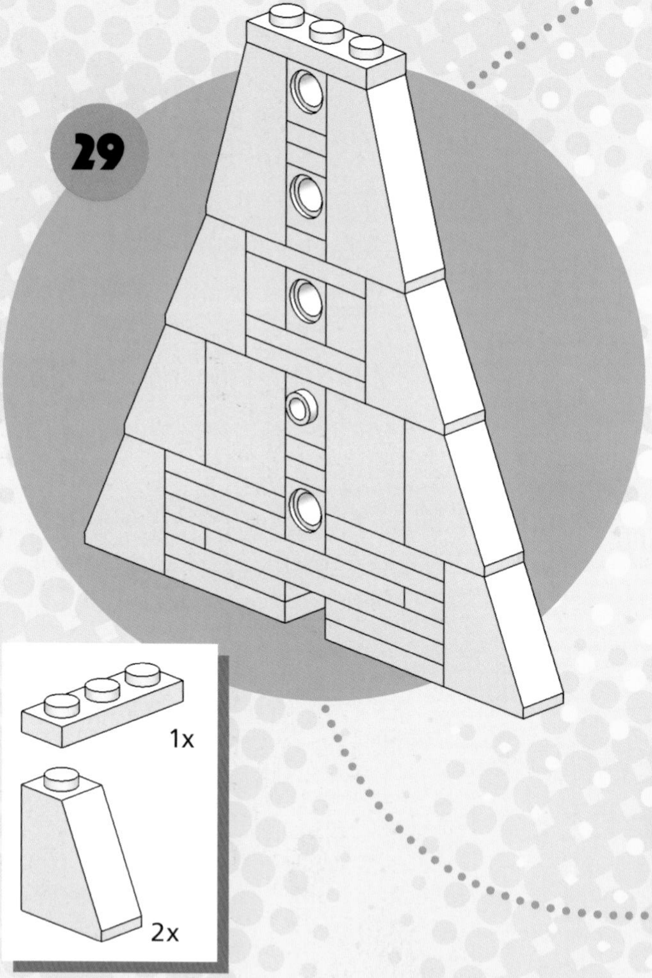

29

1x

2x

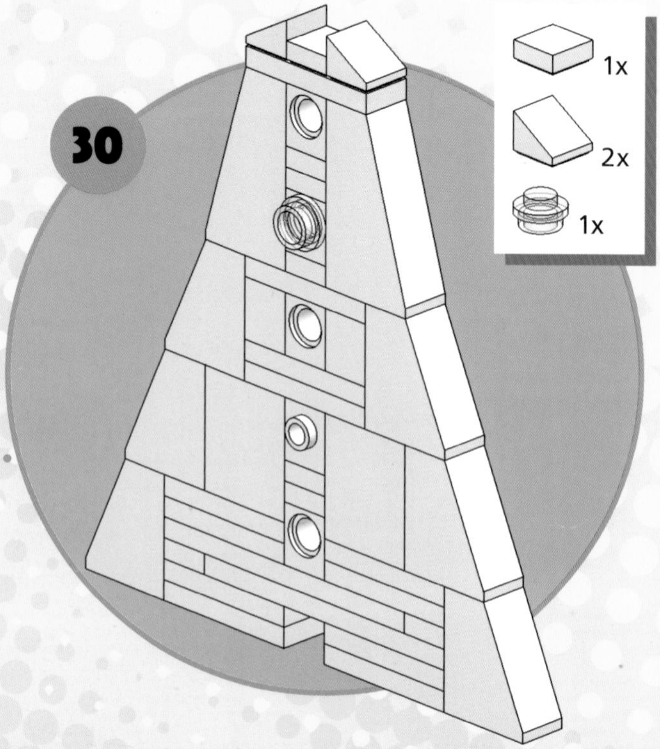

30

1x

2x

1x

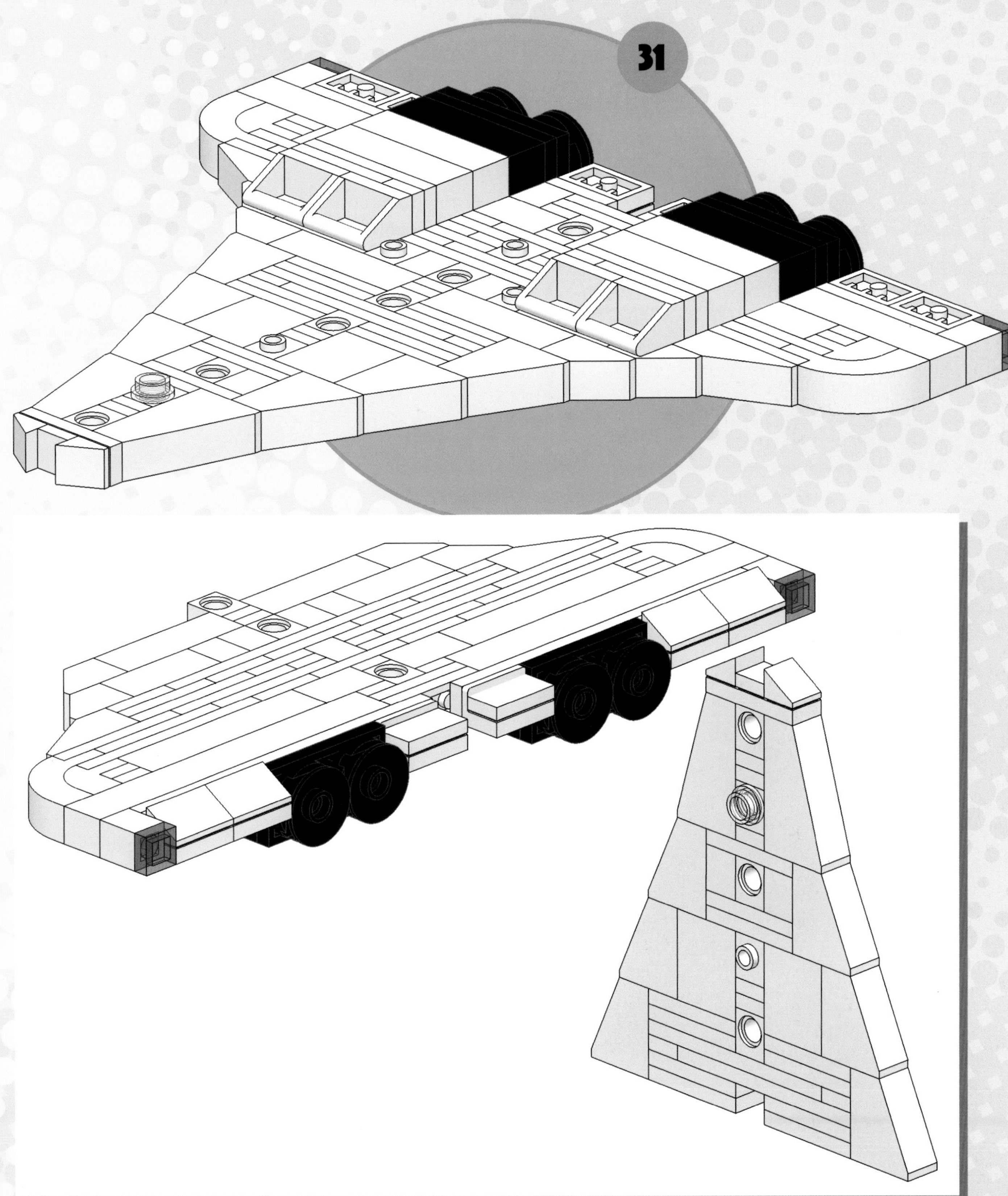
31

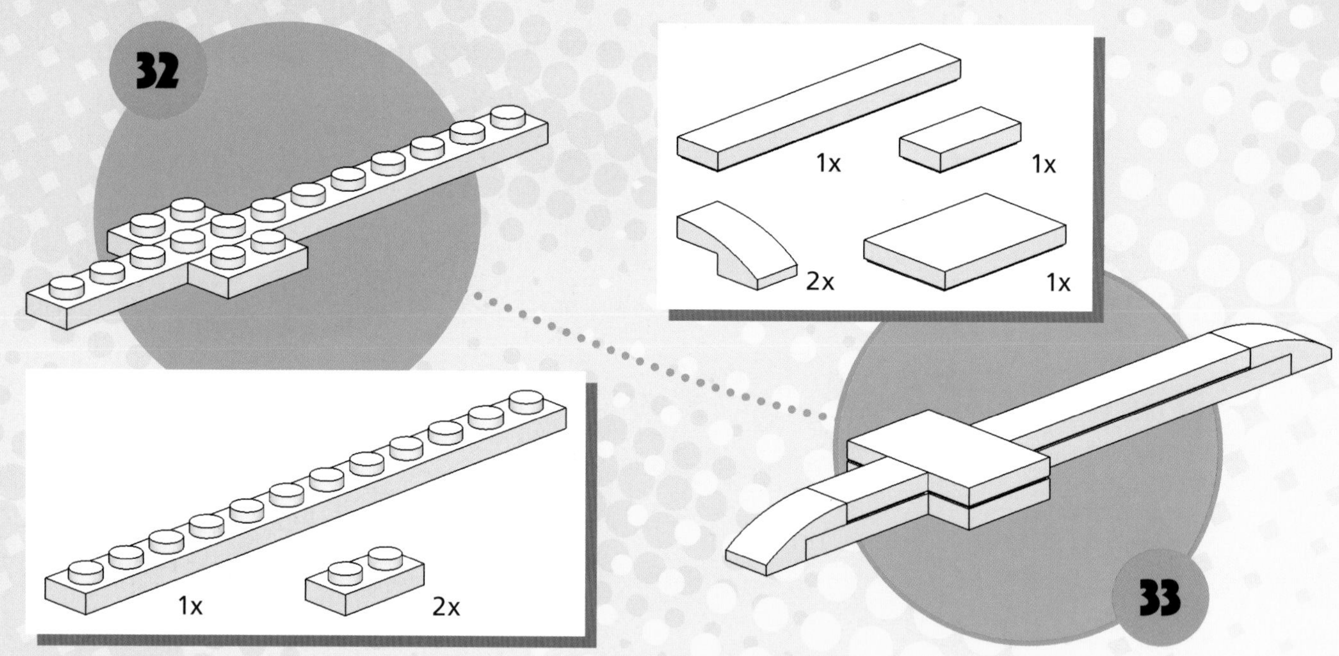

34

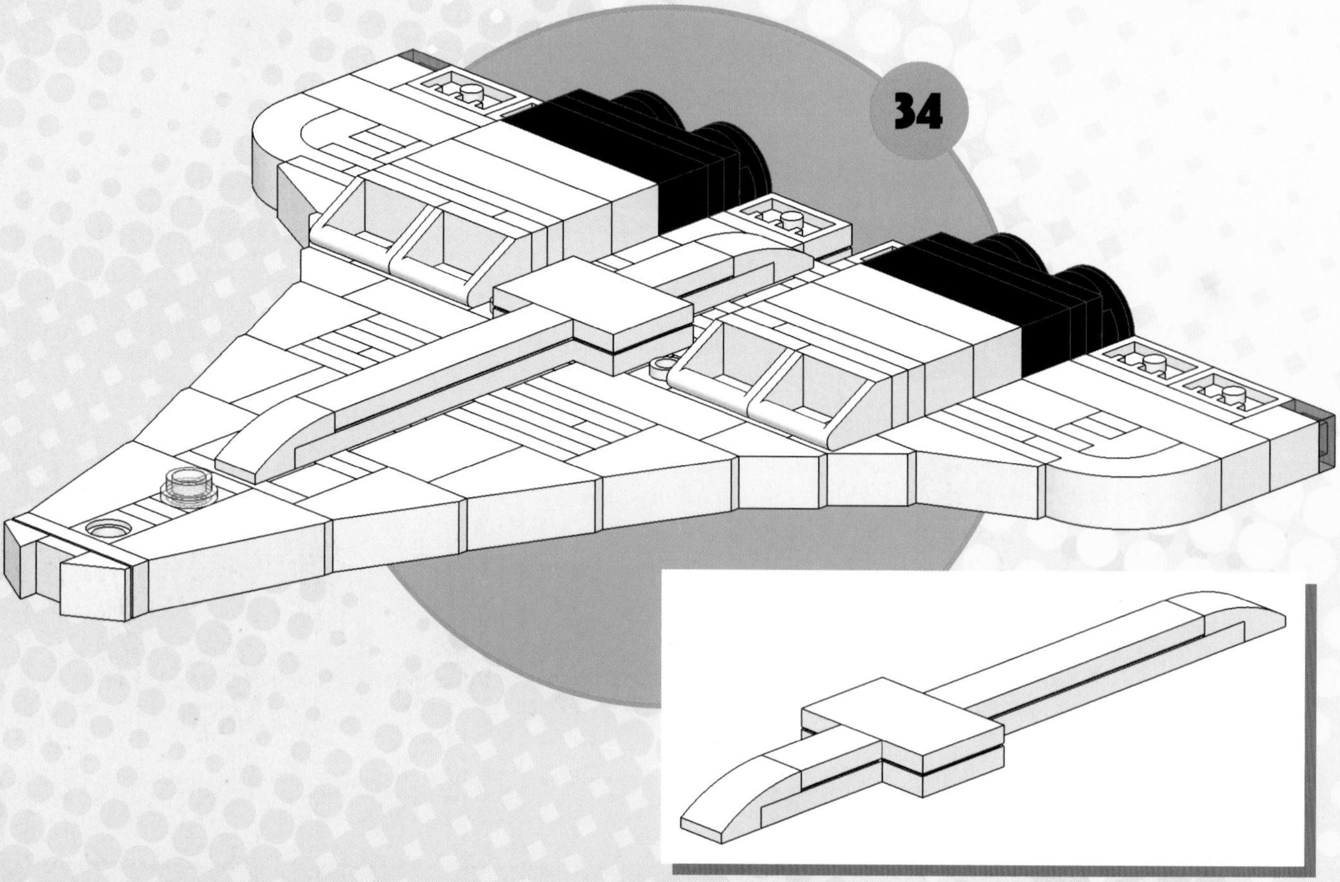

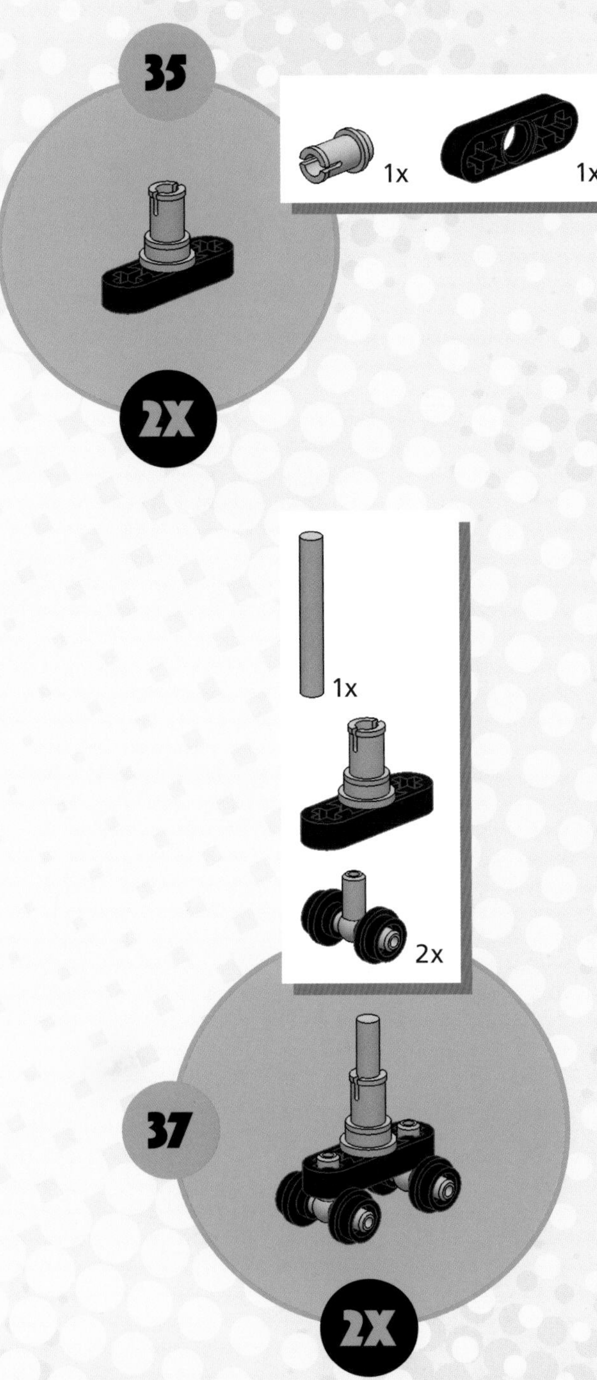
35
1x
1x
1x
2X
1x
2x
37
2X

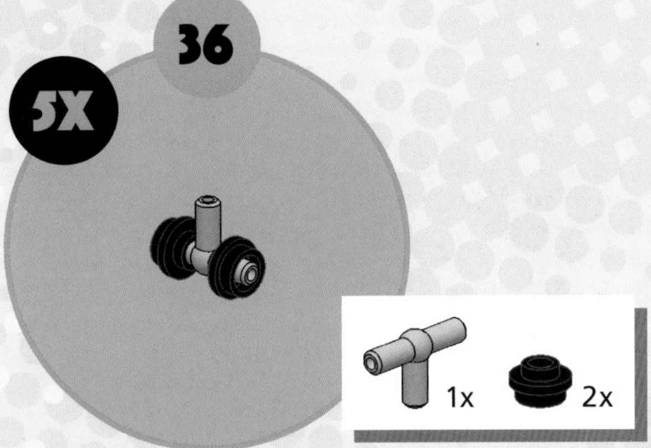
36
5X
1x
2x

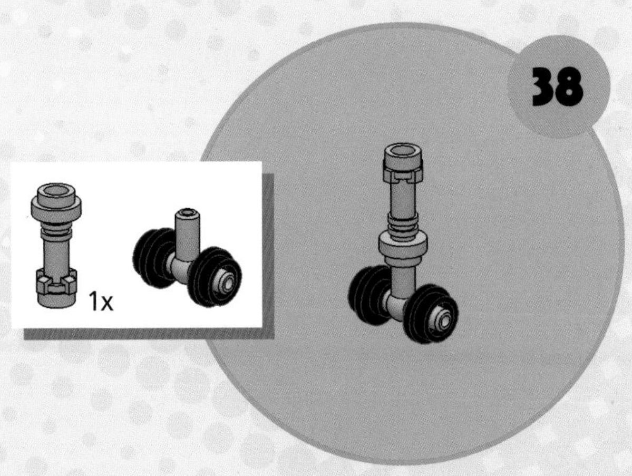
38
1x

39

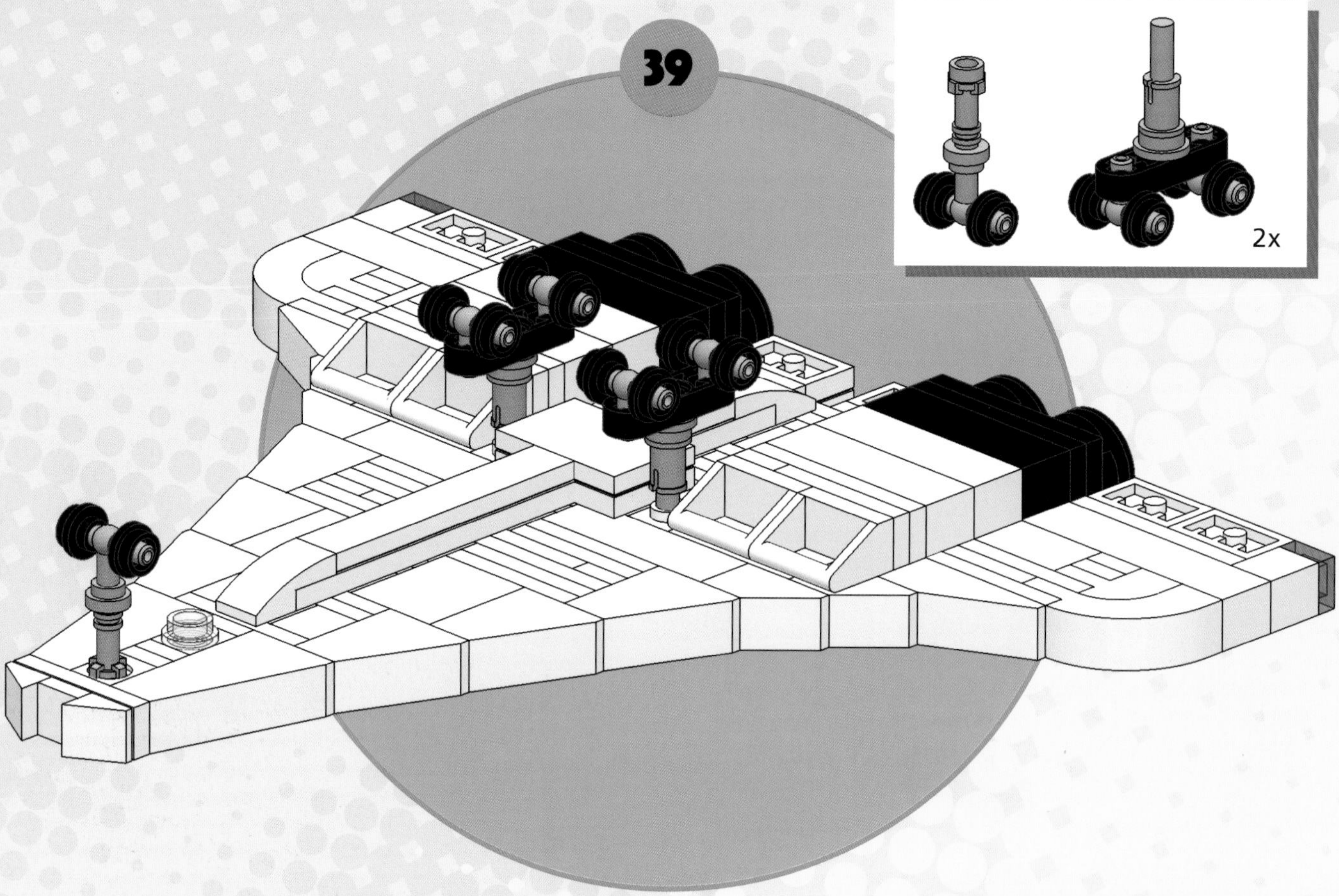

2x

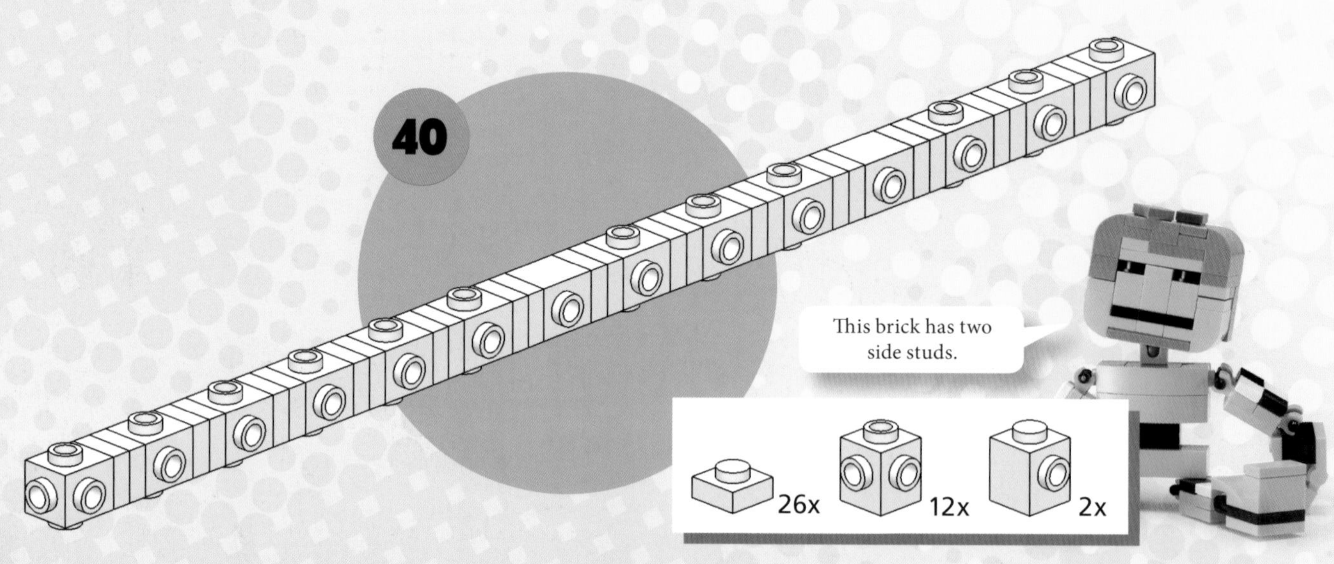

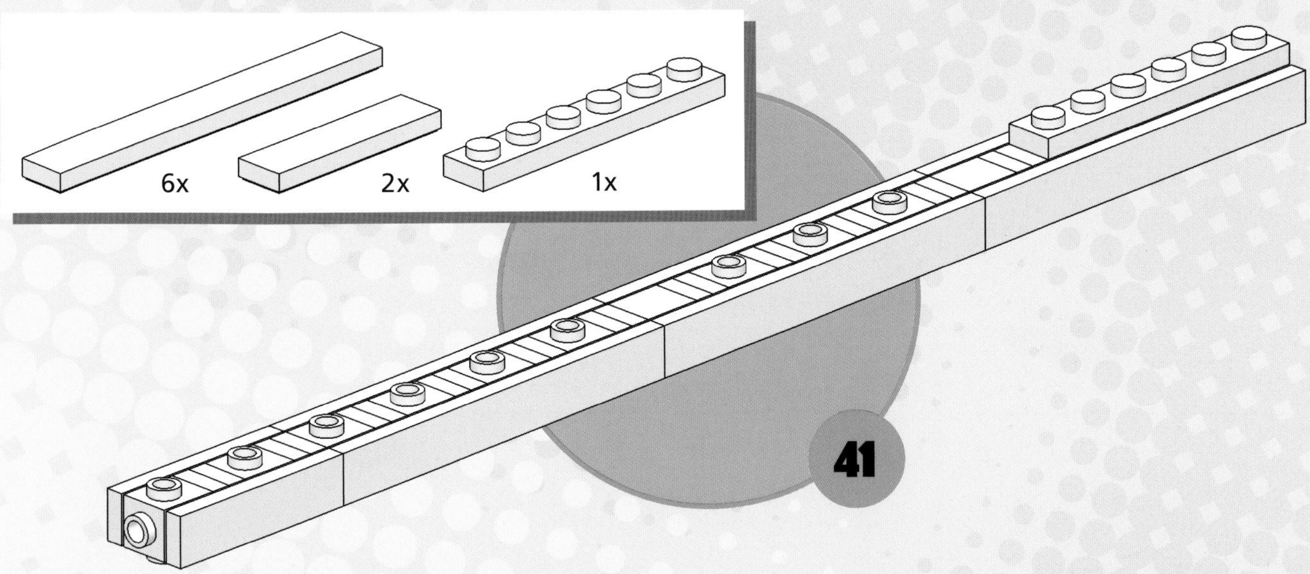

6x 2x 1x

41

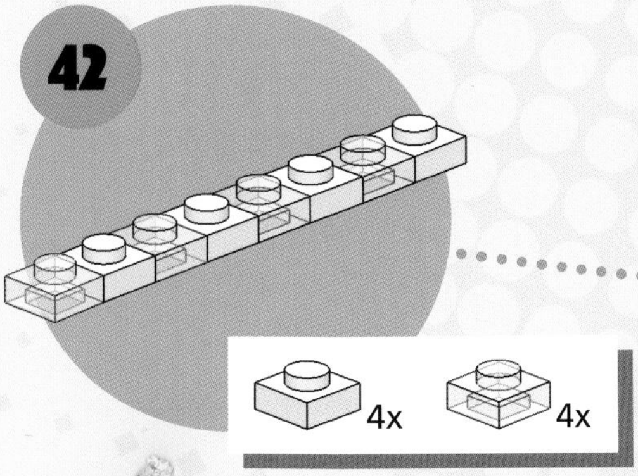

42

4x 4x

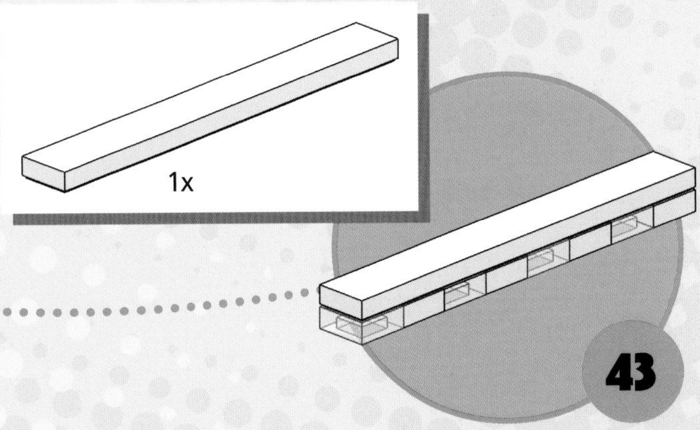

1x

43

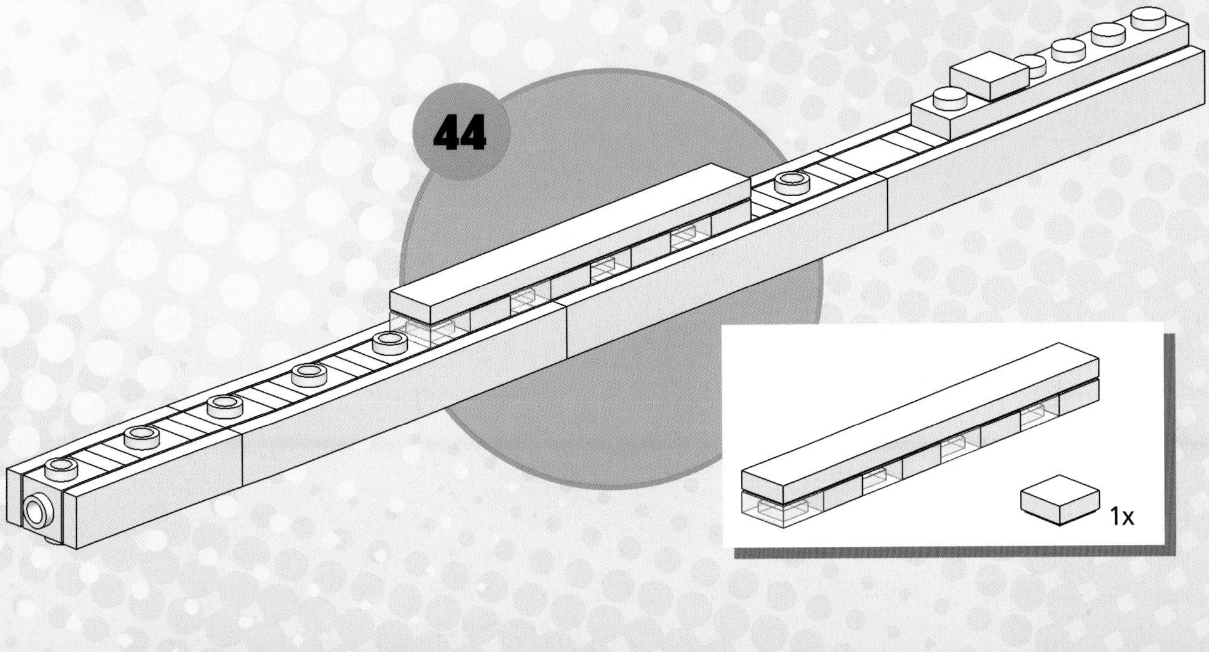

44

1x

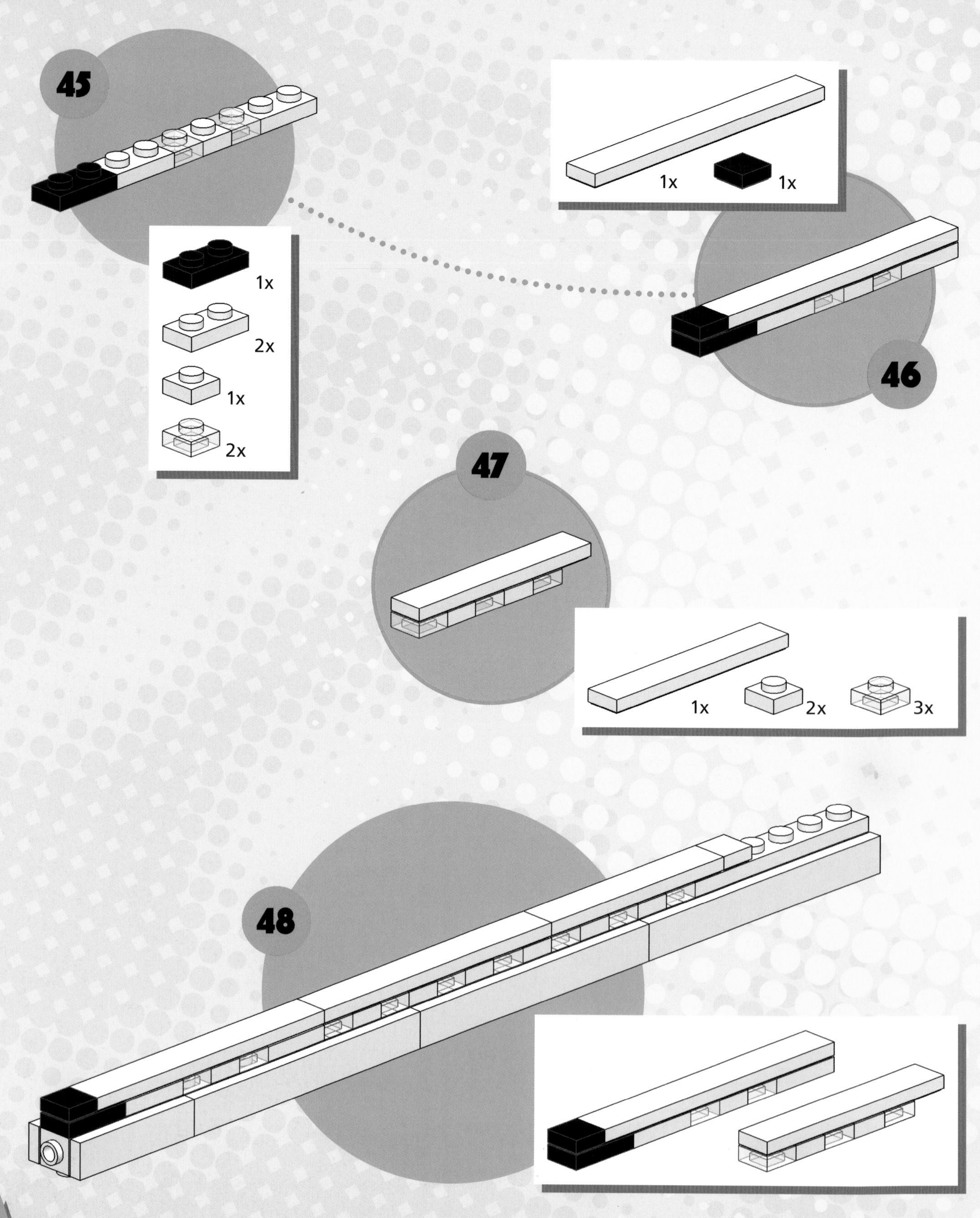
45
1x
2x
1x
2x
1x
1x
46
47
1x
2x
3x
48

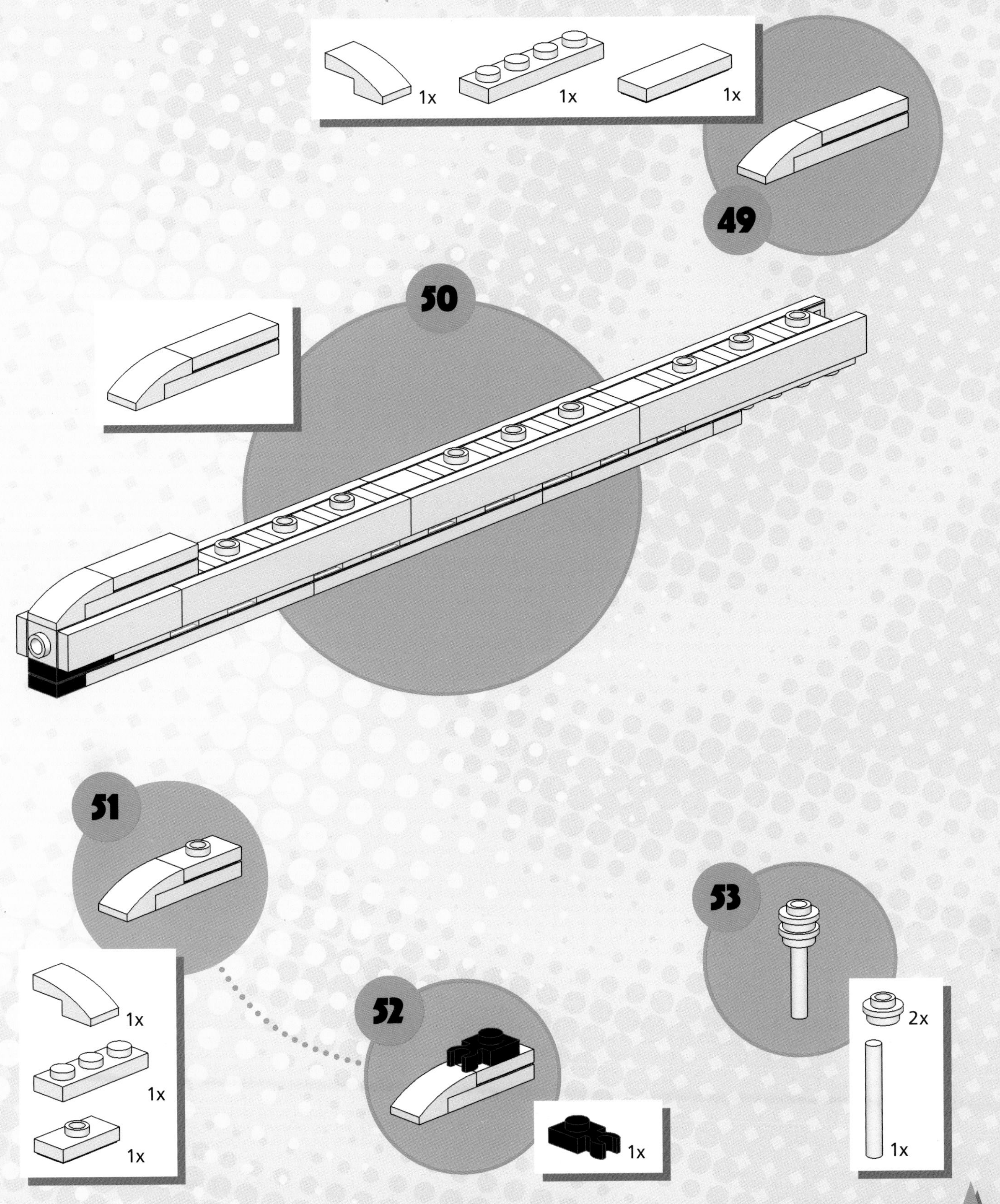
1x
1x
1x
49
50
51
1x
1x
1x
52
1x
53
2x
1x

54

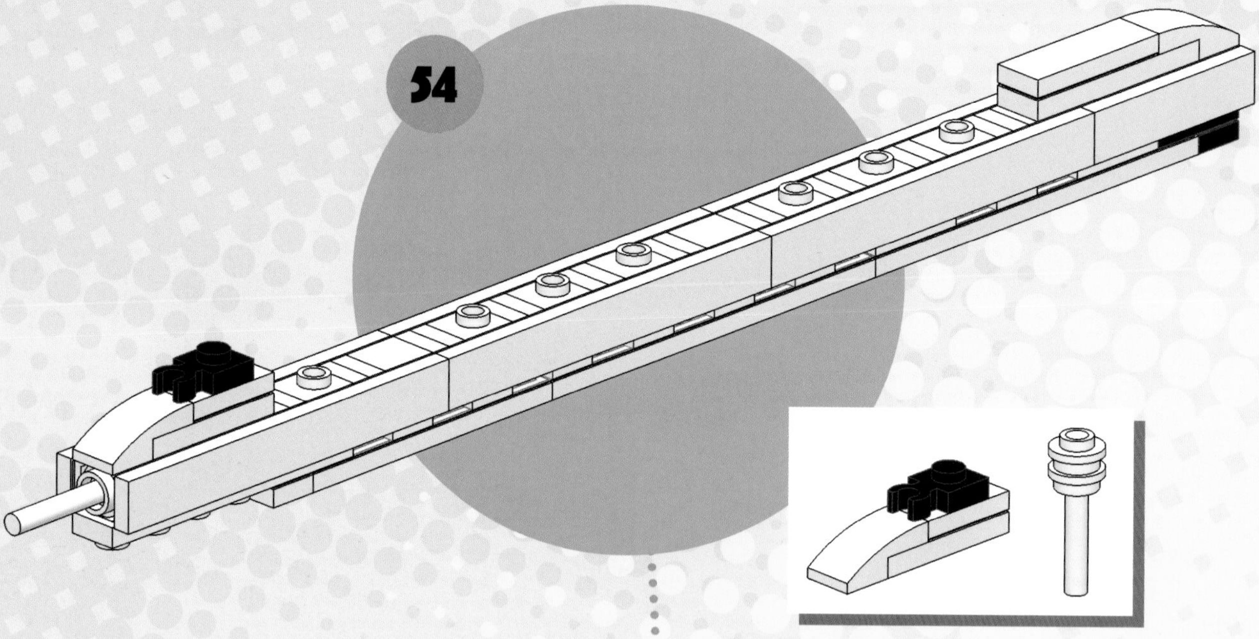

55

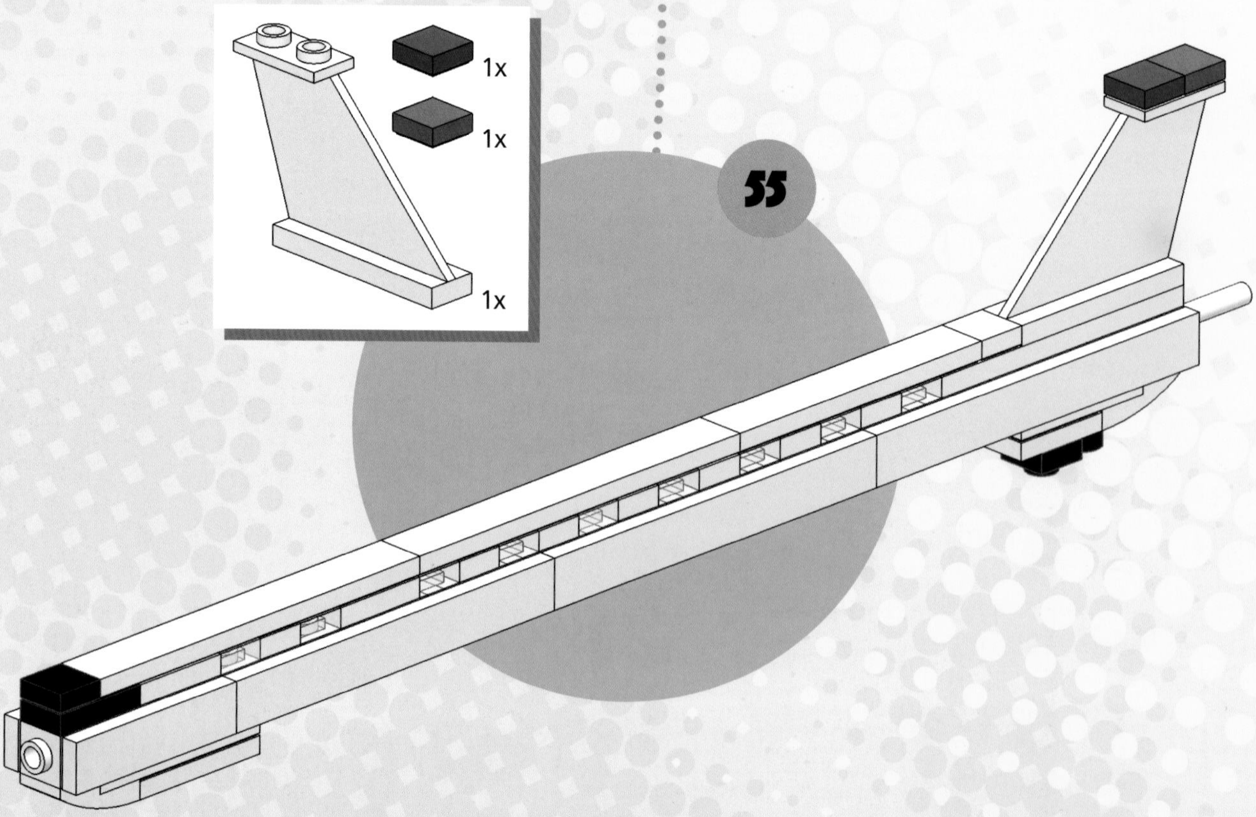

1x

1x

1x

56

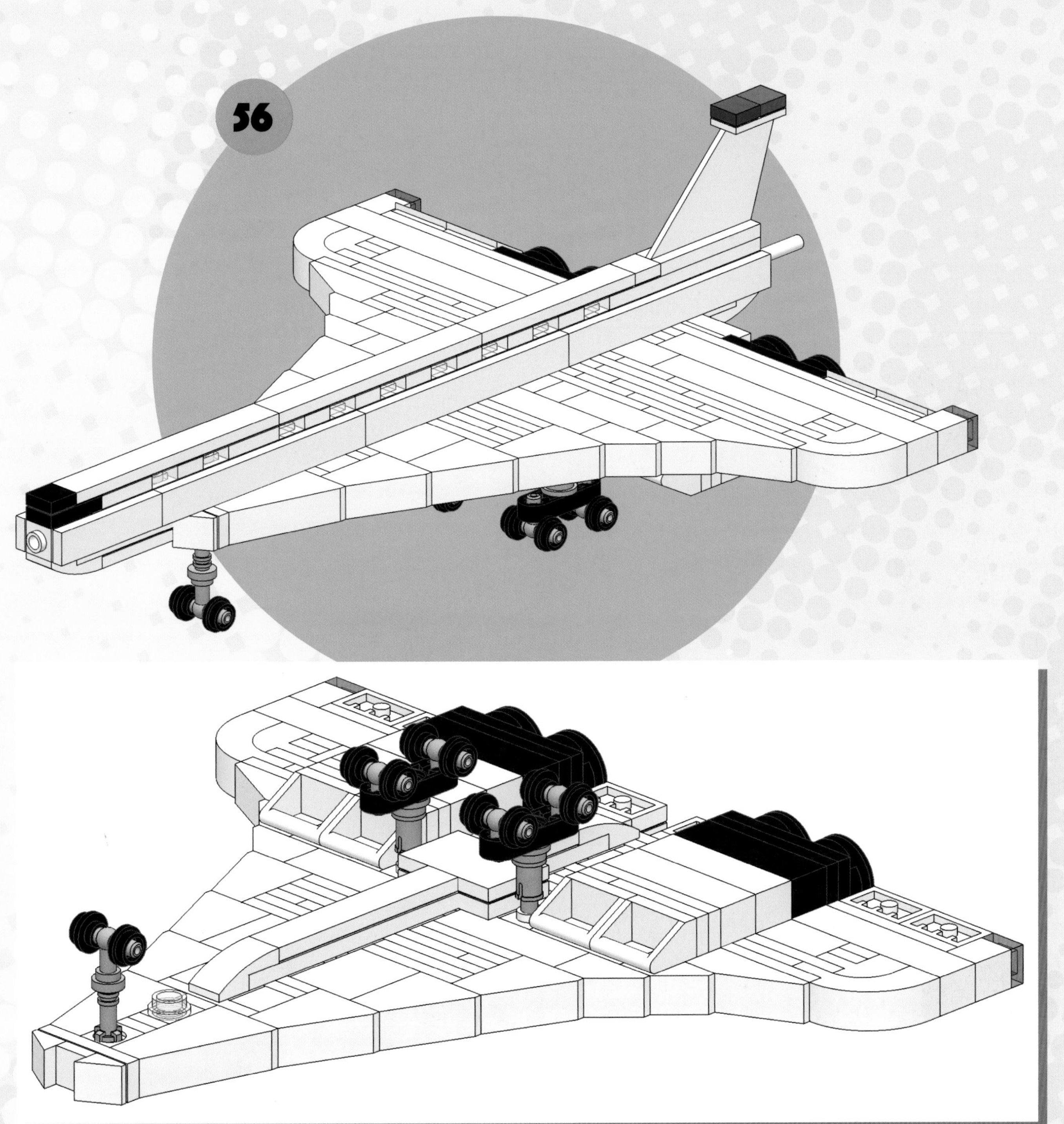

57

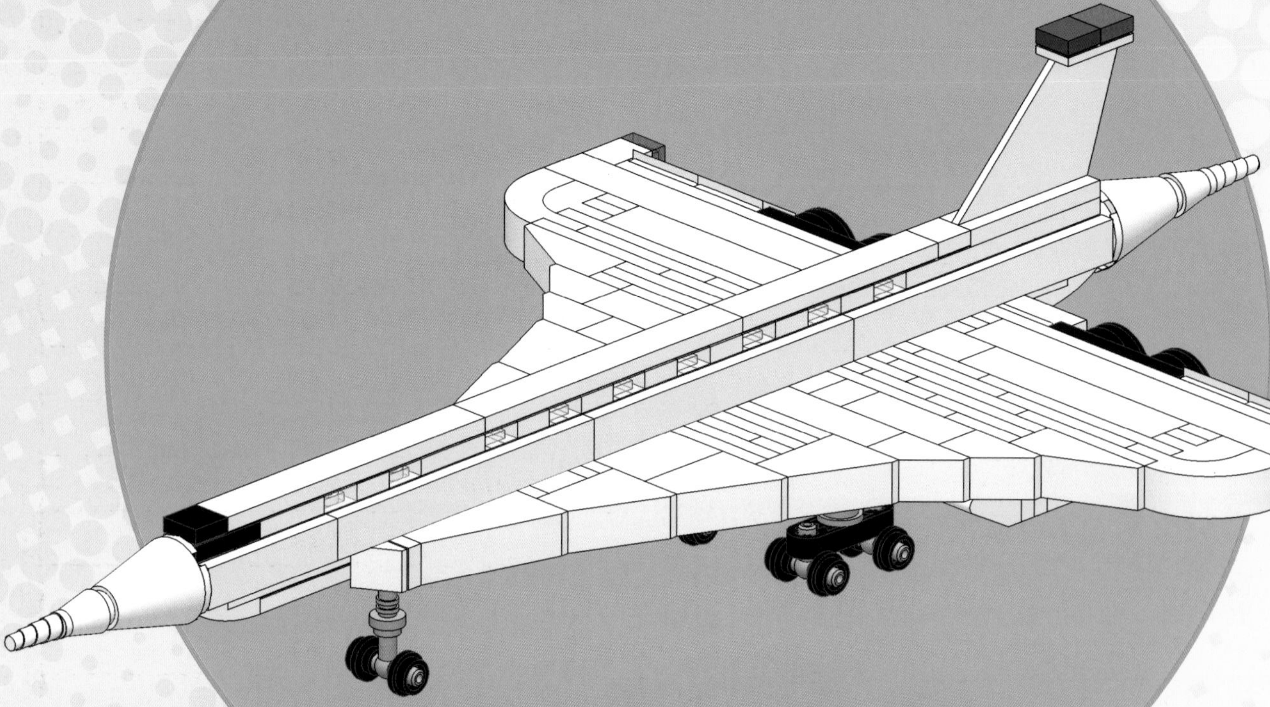

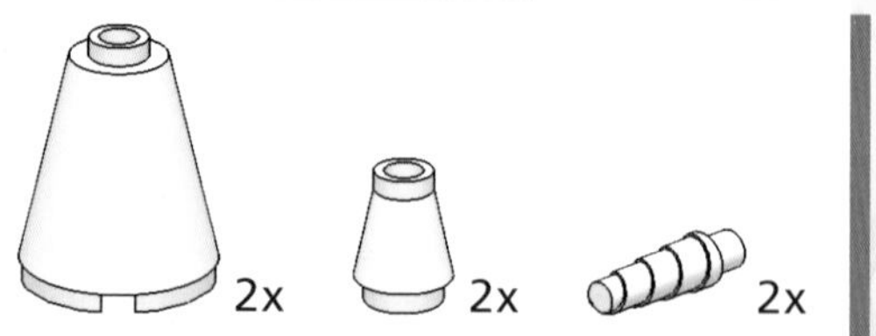

2x

2x

2x

PARTS LIST

Quantity	Color		Element	Element Name	LEGO® Number
2		White	89522	Animal Horn Spiral	6099934, 6156242
2		White	6005	Arch 1 x 3 x 2 with Curved Top	4502026, 4629913
2		Light Bluish Gray	87994	Bar 3L	6064033, 6093527
1		White	87994	Bar 3L	6019176, 6056663, 6093526
6		White	99780	Bracket 1 x 2 - 1 x 2 Up	6070698
6		White	3005	Brick 1 x 1	300501
4		White	87087	Brick 1 x 1 with Stud on 1 Side	4558952
12		White	4733	Brick 1 x 1 with Studs on Four Sides	4111971
2		White	47905	Brick 1 x 1 with Studs on Two Opposite Sides	4626882
2		White	3004	Brick 1 x 2	300401, 4613964
2		White	3245c	Brick 1 x 2 x 2 without Understud	4113261
2		White	3622	Brick 1 x 3	362201
2		Black	3010	Brick 1 x 4	301026
6		White	3010	Brick 1 x 4	301001
2		White	3009	Brick 1 x 6	300901
2		White	6111	Brick 1 x 10	611101
2		White	6091	Brick 2 x 1 x 1 & 1/3 with Curved Top	609101
2		White	4589	Cone 1 x 1	4518400, 458901
2		White	3942c	Cone 2 x 2 x 2 with Hollow Stud Open	394201, 6022158, 6044601
4		Black	4740	Dish 2 x 2 Inverted	474026
1		Light Bluish Gray	64567	Minifig Lightsaber Hilt	4212074, 4539481, 4581155
9		Trans Clear	3024	Plate 1 x 1	3000840
2		Trans Red	3024	Plate 1 x 1	3000841
52		White	3024	Plate 1 x 1	302401
1		Trans Clear	4073	Plate 1 x 1 Round	3005740
10		Black	85861	Plate 1 x 1 Round with Open Stud	6100627, 6168646
2		Light Bluish Gray	85861	Plate 1 x 1 Round with Open Stud	6124825, 6168647

Quantity		Color	Element	Element Name	LEGO® Number
2		White	85861	Plate 1 x 1 Round with Open Stud	4547649, 6168642
1		Black	60897	Plate 1 x 1 with Clip Vertical (Thick C-Clip)	4550017
1		Black	3023	Plate 1 x 2	302326
9		White	3023	Plate 1 x 2	302301
1		White	3794b	Plate 1 x 2 with Groove with 1 Centre Stud	379401
17		White	3623	Plate 1 x 3	362301
2		Black	3710	Plate 1 x 4	371026
9		White	3710	Plate 1 x 4	371001
5		White	3666	Plate 1 x 6	366601
3		White	4477	Plate 1 x 10	447701
1		White	60479	Plate 1 x 12	4514842
2		White	2420	Plate 2 x 2 Corner	242001
4		Black	4032b	Plate 2 x 2 Round with Axlehole Type 2	403226
2		White	3021	Plate 2 x 3	302101
2		Black	3020	Plate 2 x 4	302026
2		White	3020	Plate 2 x 4	302001
2		White	54200	Slope Brick 31 1 x 1 x 0.667	4244370, 4504369
4		White	85984	Slope Brick 31 1 x 2 x 0.667	4547489
2		White	4286	Slope Brick 33 3 x 1	428601
4		White	3040	Slope Brick 45 2 x 1	304001, 4121932
6		White	60481	Slope Brick 65 2 x 1 x 2	4515370
2		White	4460b	Slope Brick 75 2 x 1 x 3 with Hollow Stud	446001
4		White	11477	Slope Brick Curved 2 x 1	6034044
1		White	2340	Tail 4 x 1 x 3	234001
2		Black	6632	Technic Beam 3 x 0.5 Liftarm	4107828, 663226
7		White	6541	Technic Brick 1 x 1 with Hole	654101, 65411
2		Light Bluish Gray	4274	Technic Pin 1/2	4211483, 4274194
5		Light Bluish Gray	4697b	Technic Pneumatic T-Piece - Type 2	4211508
1		Black	3070b	Tile 1 x 1 with Groove	307026

Quantity	Color		Element	Element Name	LEGO® Number
1		Blue	3070b	Tile 1 x 1 with Groove	4206330
1		Red	3070b	Tile 1 x 1 with Groove	307021
2		White	3070b	Tile 1 x 1 with Groove	307001
3		White	3069b	Tile 1 x 2 with Groove	306901
4		White	2432	Tile 1 x 2 with Handle	243201
1		White	63864	Tile 1 x 3 with Groove	4558168
2		White	2431	Tile 1 x 4 with Groove	243101
2		White	6636	Tile 1 x 6	663601
8		White	4162	Tile 1 x 8	416201
1		White	26603	Tile 2 x 3 with Groove	6156667

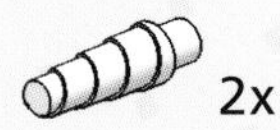
2x

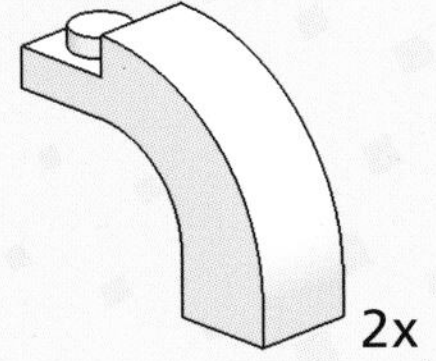
2x

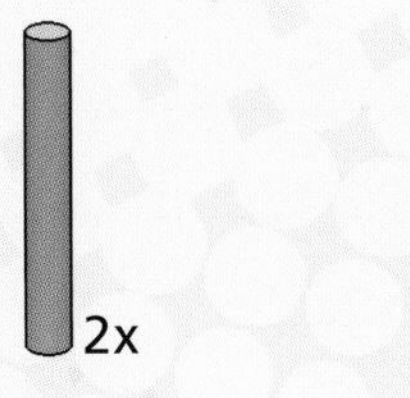
2x

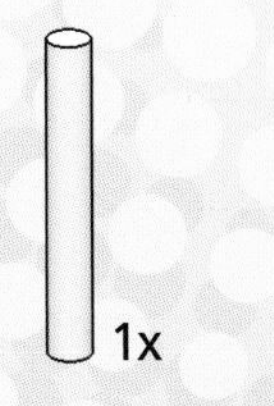
1x

6x

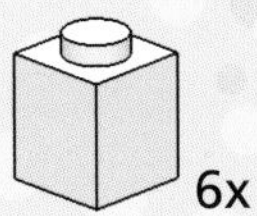
6x

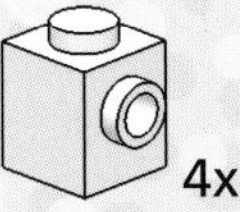
4x

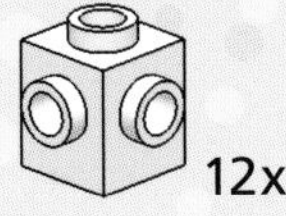
12x

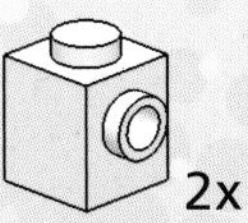
2x

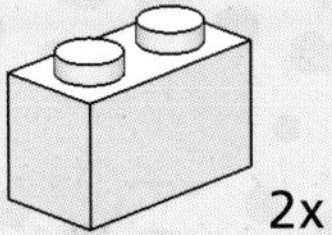
2x

2x

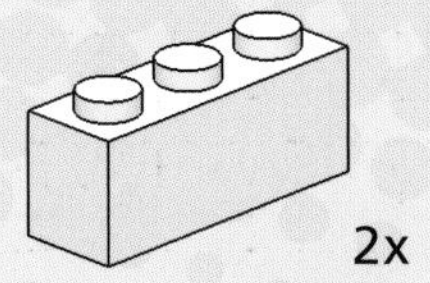
2x

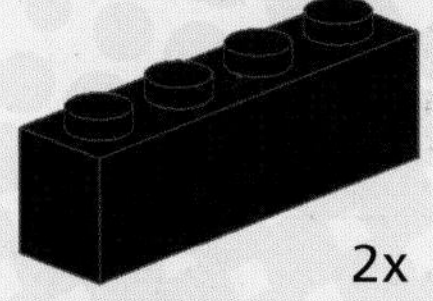
2x

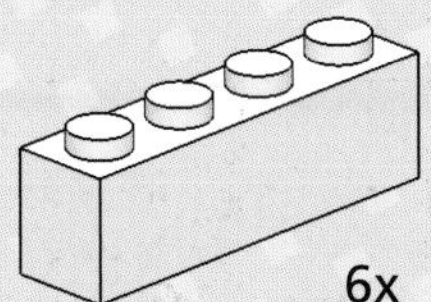
6x

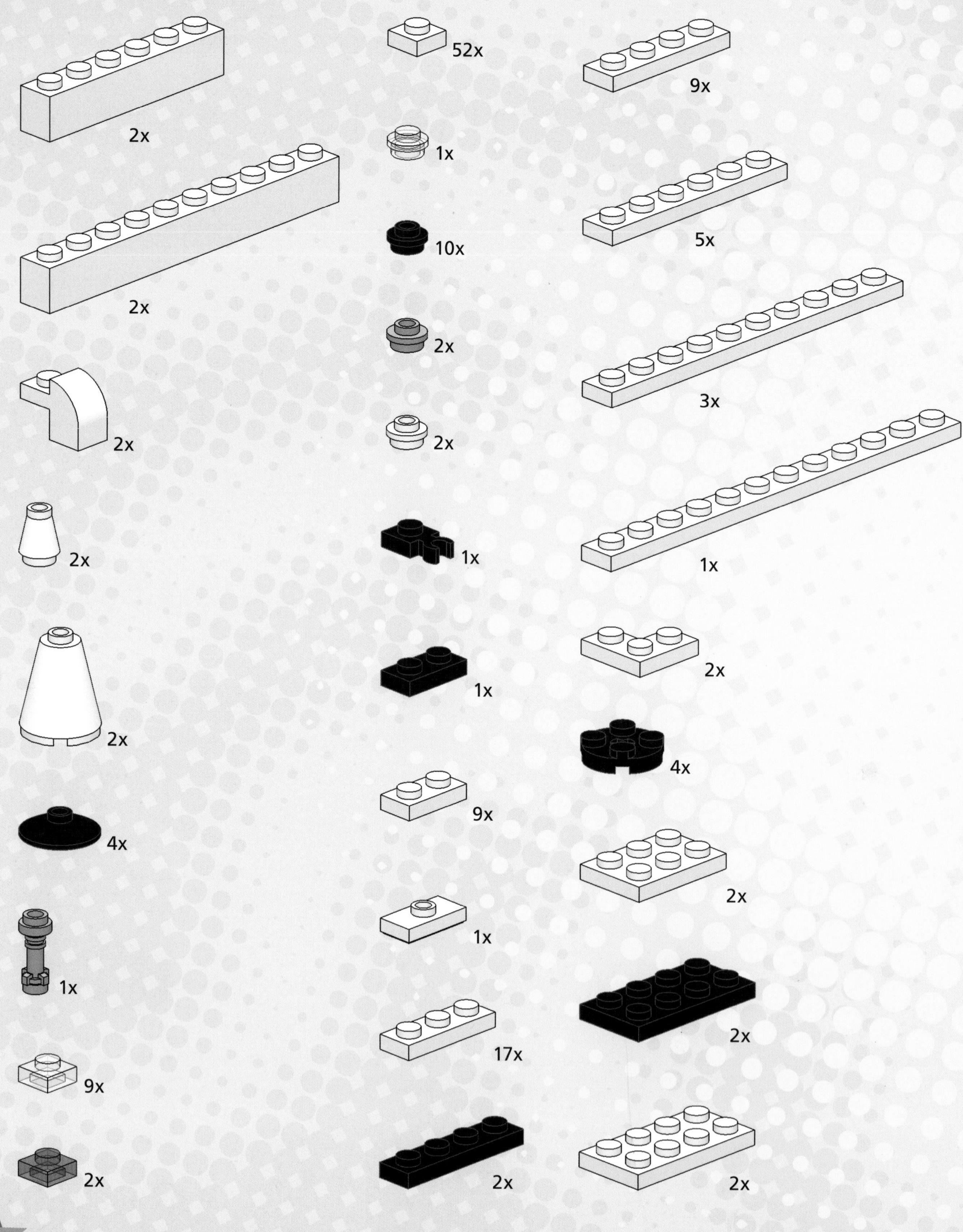
2x
2x
2x
2x
2x
4x
1x
9x
2x
52x
1x
10x
2x
2x
1x
1x
9x
1x
17x
2x
9x
5x
3x
1x
2x
4x
2x
2x
2x

2x

4x

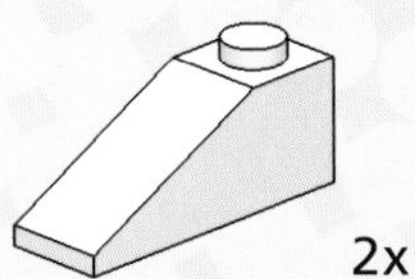
2x

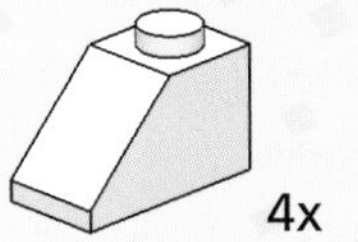
4x

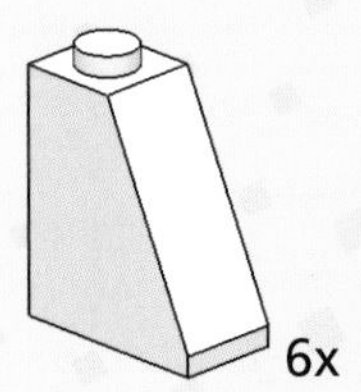
6x

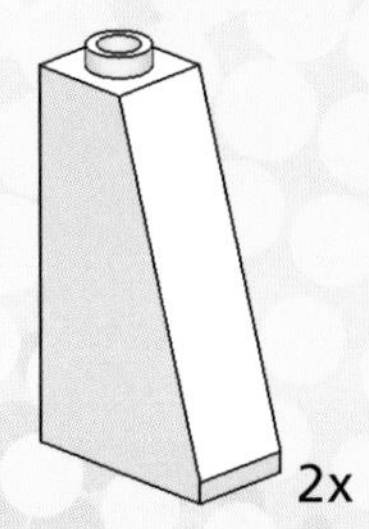
2x

4x

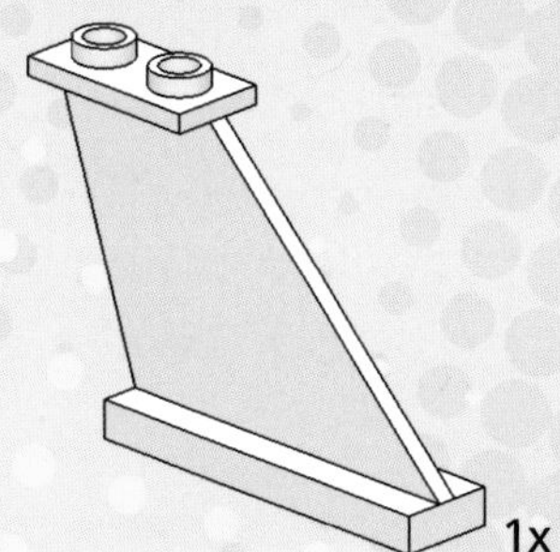
1x

2x

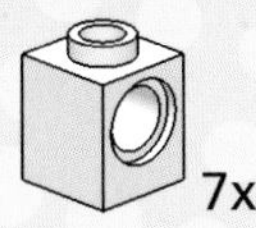
7x

2x

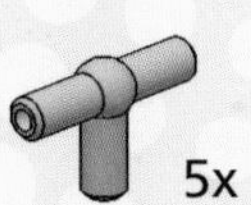
5x

1x

1x

1x

2x

3x

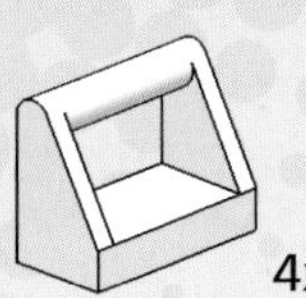
4x

1x

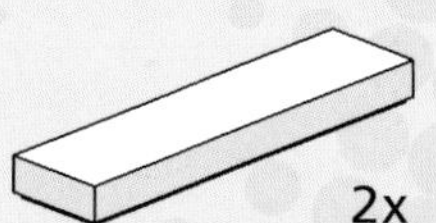
2x

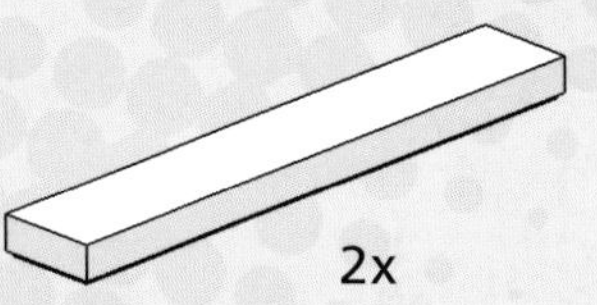
2x

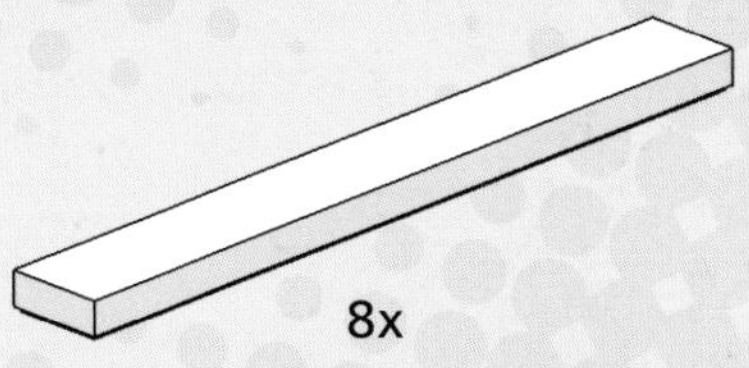
8x

1x

FIAT PANDA

Yes, even this little Panda has set a record—it's the top-selling Fiat car. My version of the model from the 1980s can be made in many typical color combinations. The windowpanes are made with three studs or one stud and these are somewhat rarer, but the cabin has to be 5 studs wide. The old tires are slightly smaller than the rim, so you need some strength to force them onto it. Warm them in your hands first and then roll them over the rims. If you've ever had to change a bike tire, you'll know all about such problems.

WEIGHT:	*700 kg (0.8 t)*
TOP SPEED:	*80 km/h (50 mph)*
HP:	*30*
TANK CAPACITY:	*40 liters (143 gal.)*

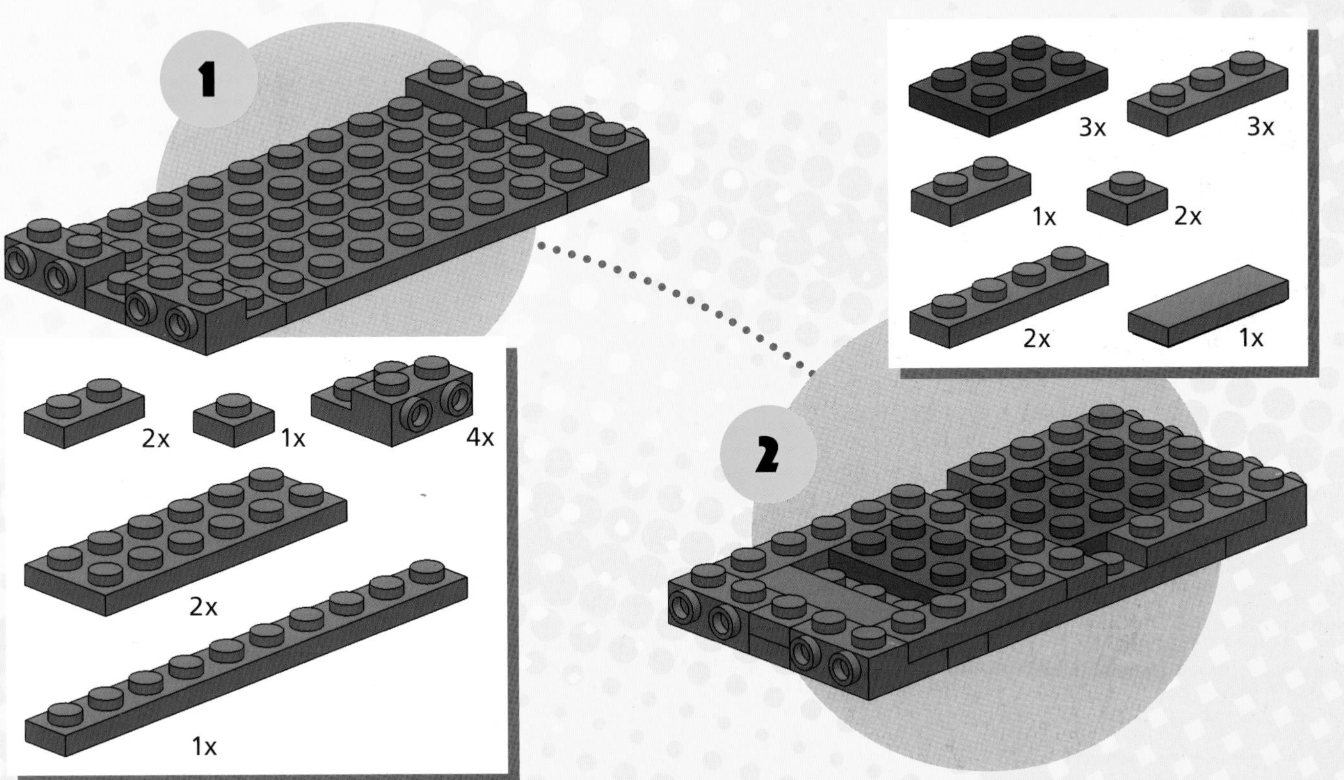

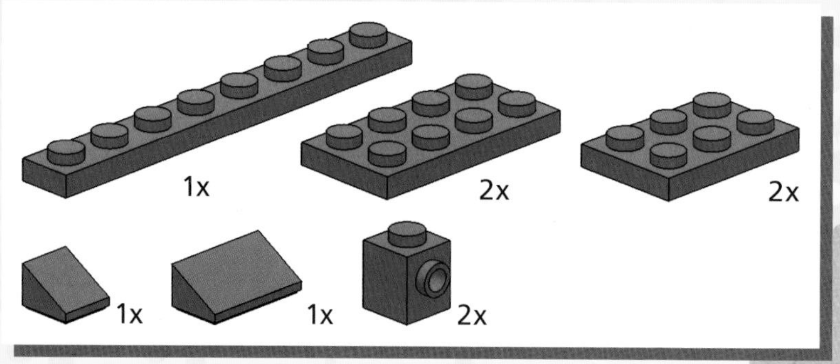

1x

2x

2x

1x

1x

2x

3

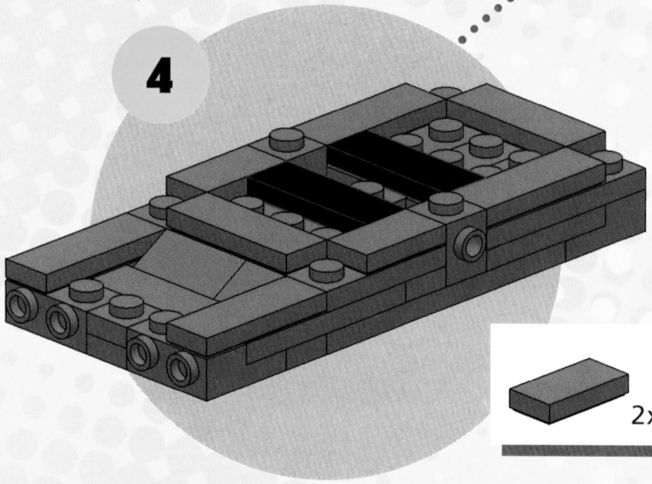

4

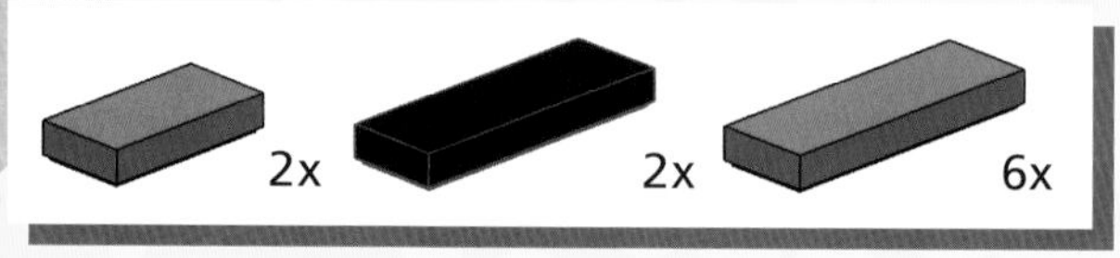

2x

2x

6x

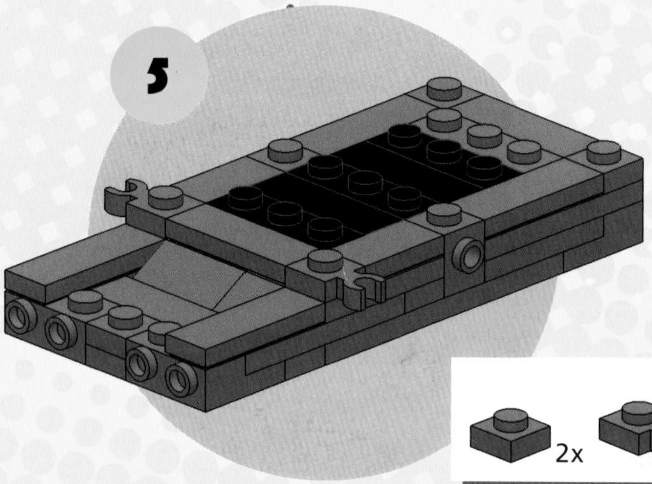

5

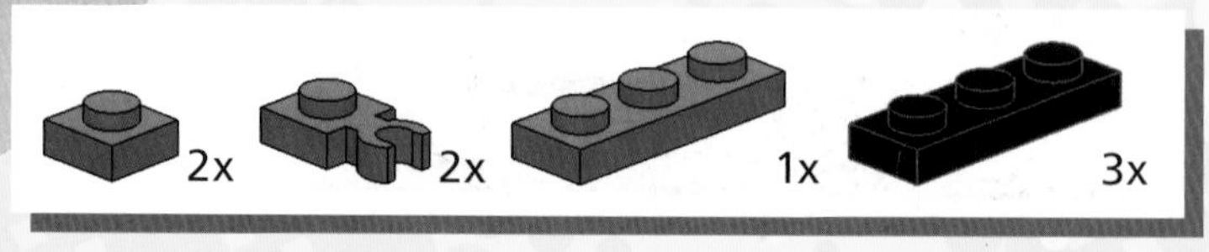

2x

2x

1x

3x

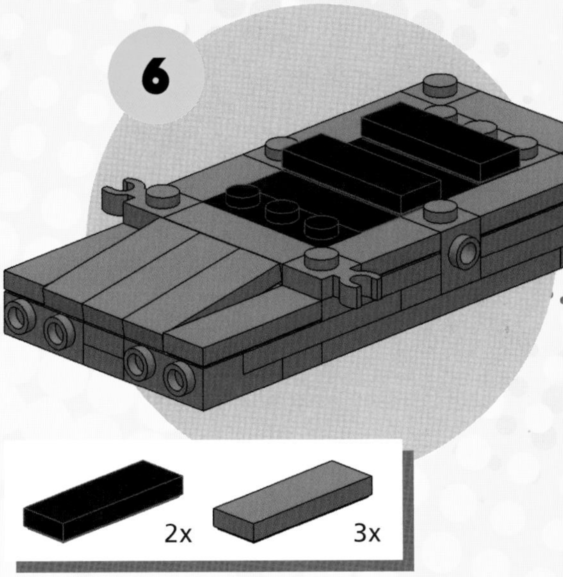

6

2x 3x

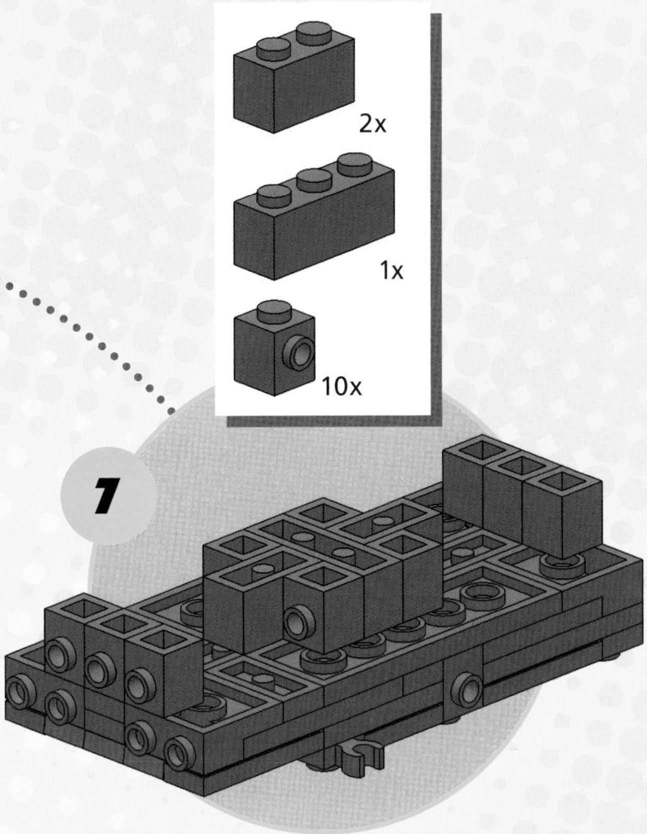

7

2x 1x 10x

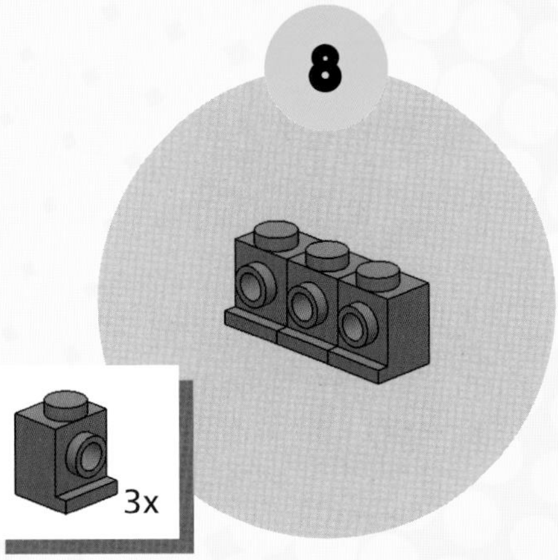

8

3x

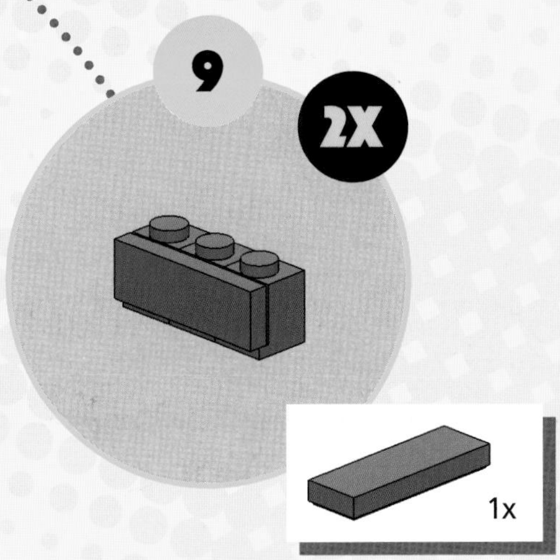

9

2X

1x

10
2x
2x

11
1x
2x
2X

1x
1x
12

2X
13
2X
1x
1x
1x

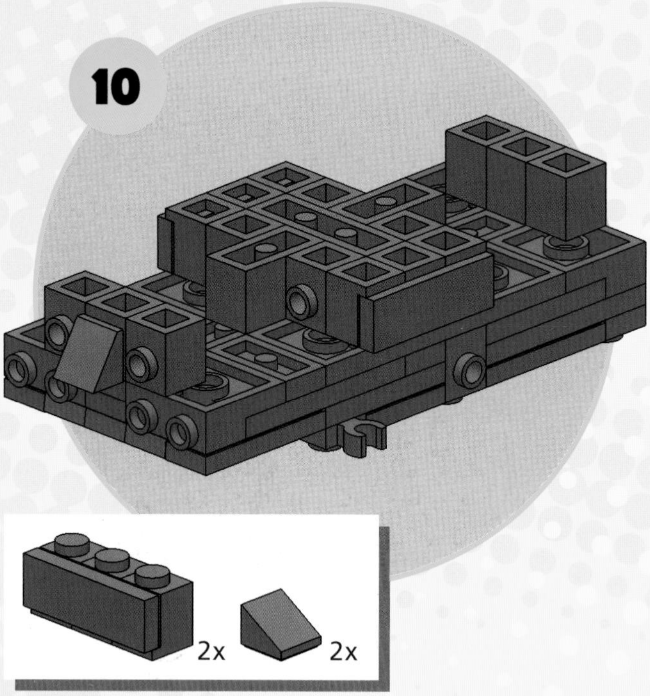

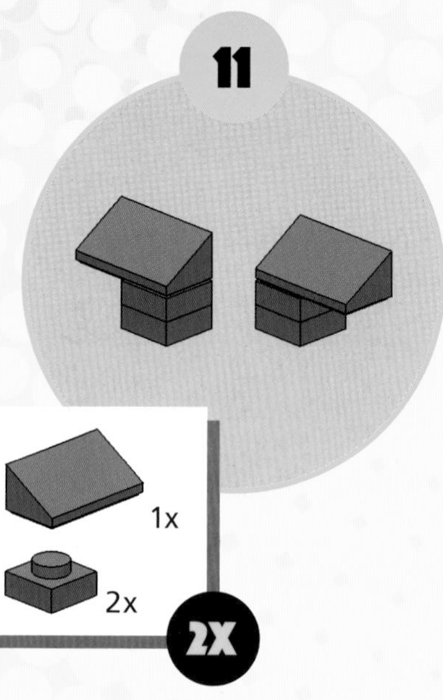

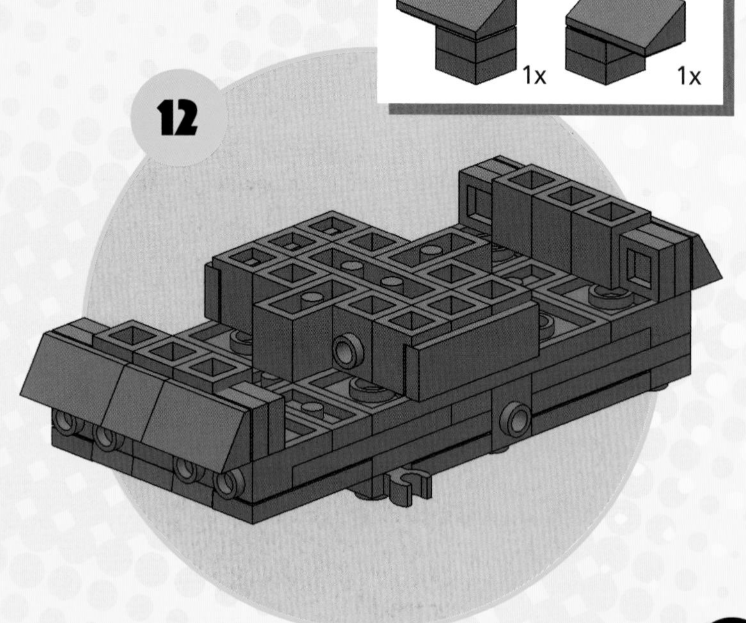

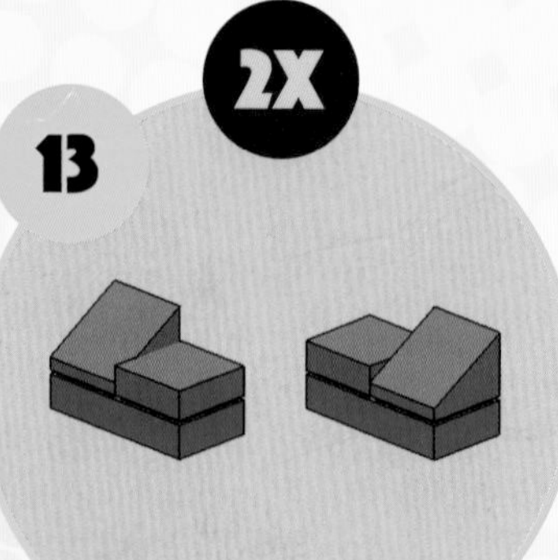

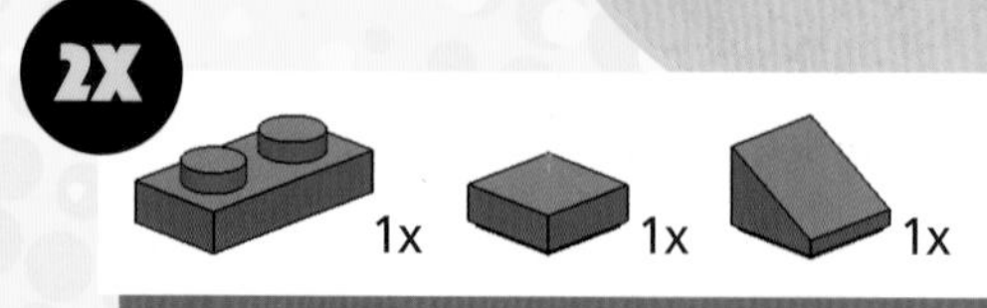

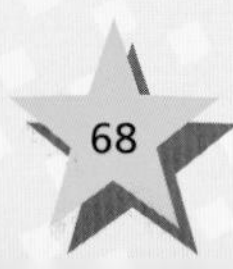

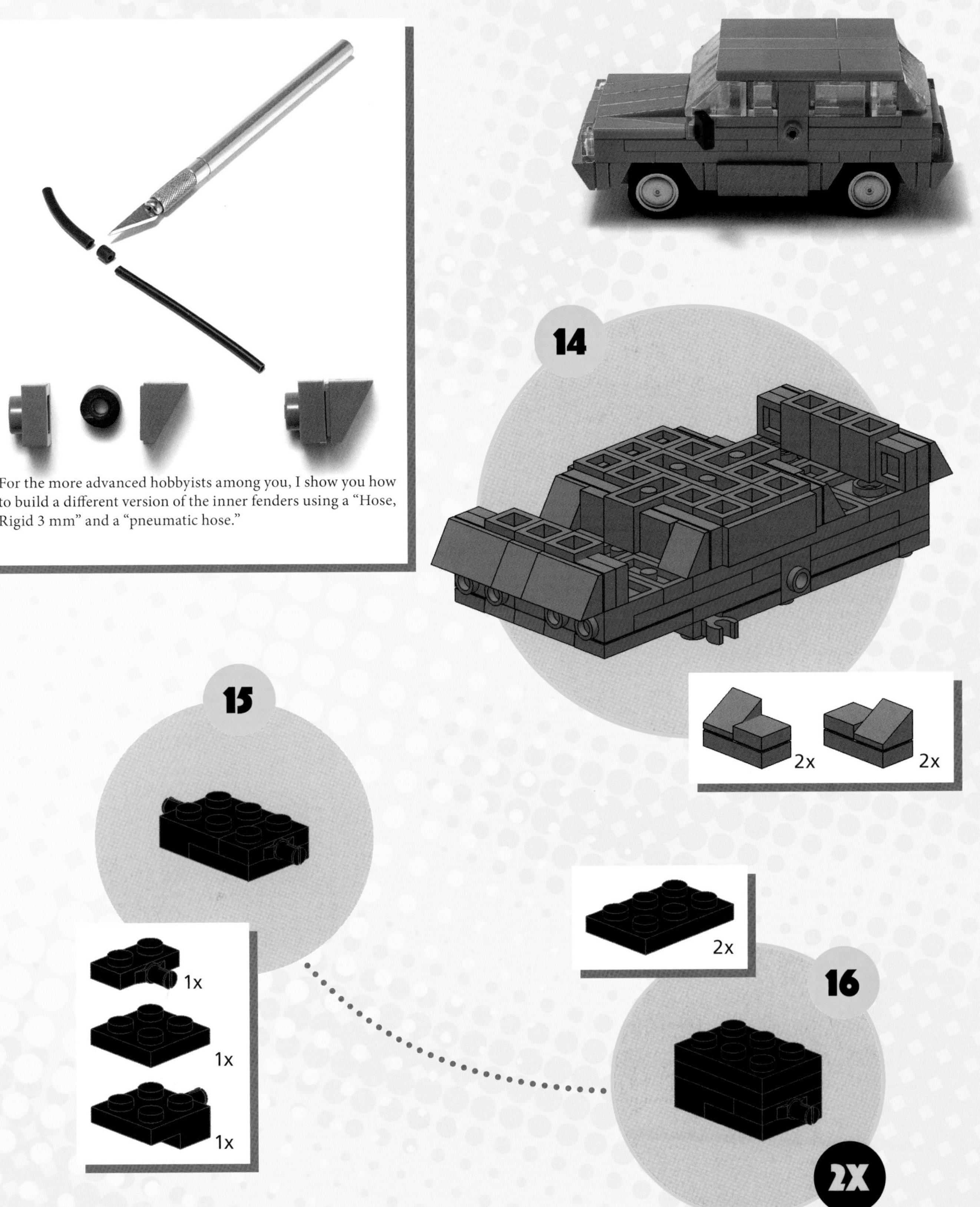

For the more advanced hobbyists among you, I show you how to build a different version of the inner fenders using a "Hose, Rigid 3 mm" and a "pneumatic hose."

17

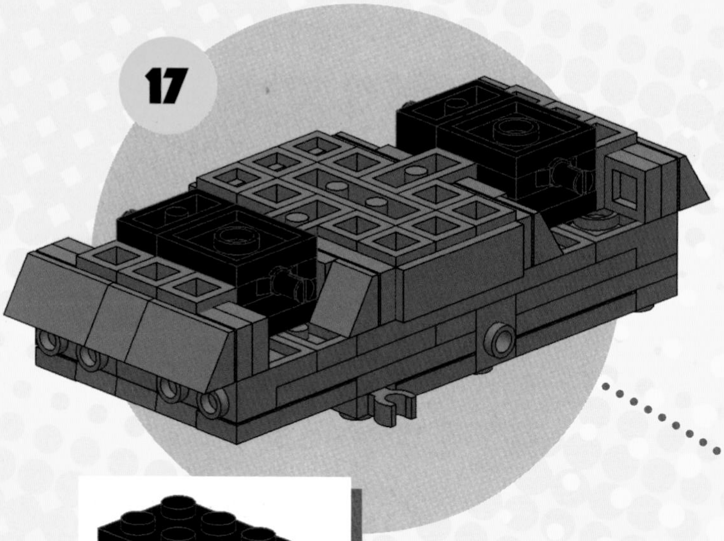

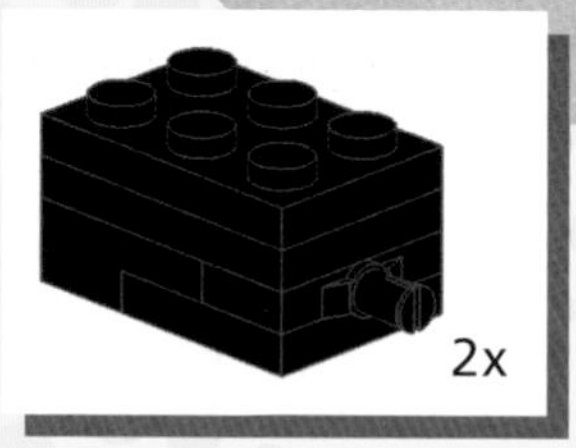

2x

18

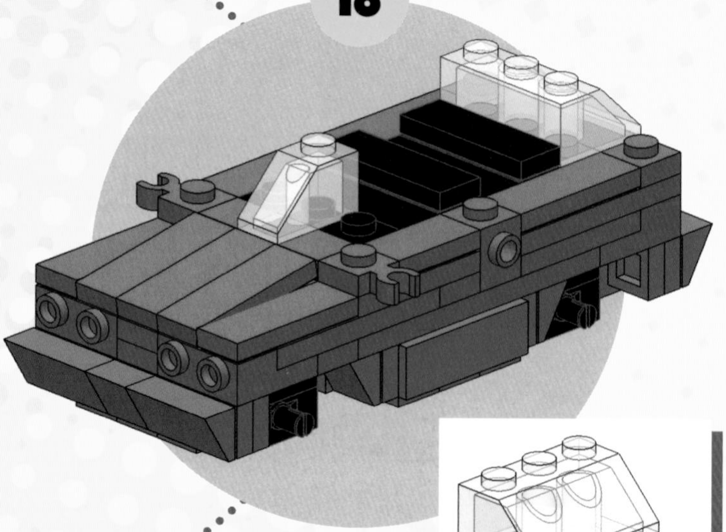

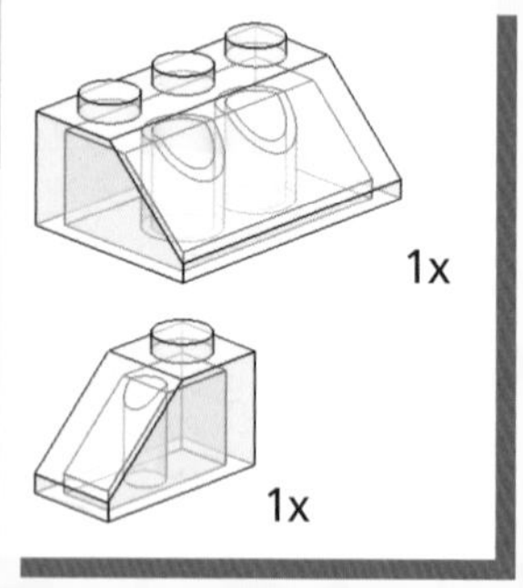

1x

1x

19

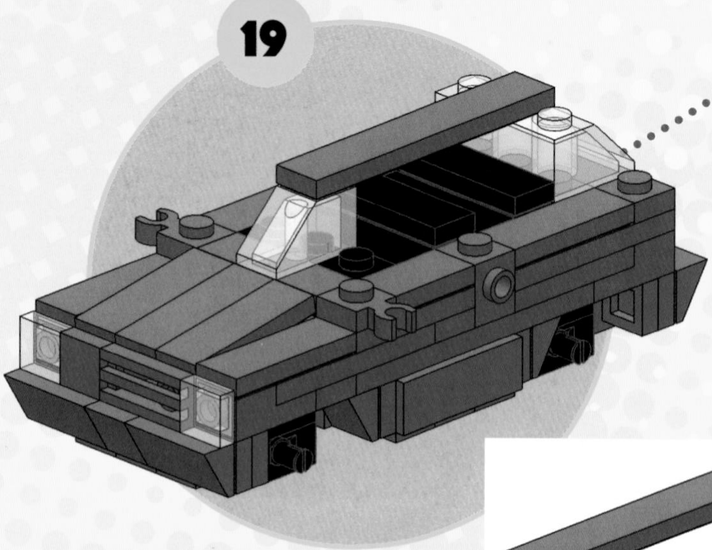

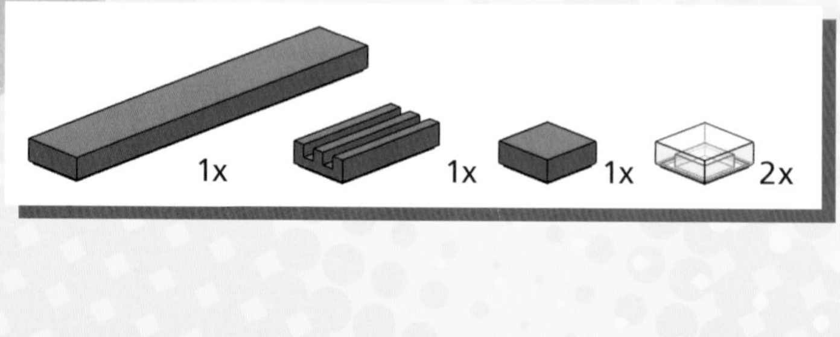

1x 1x 1x 2x

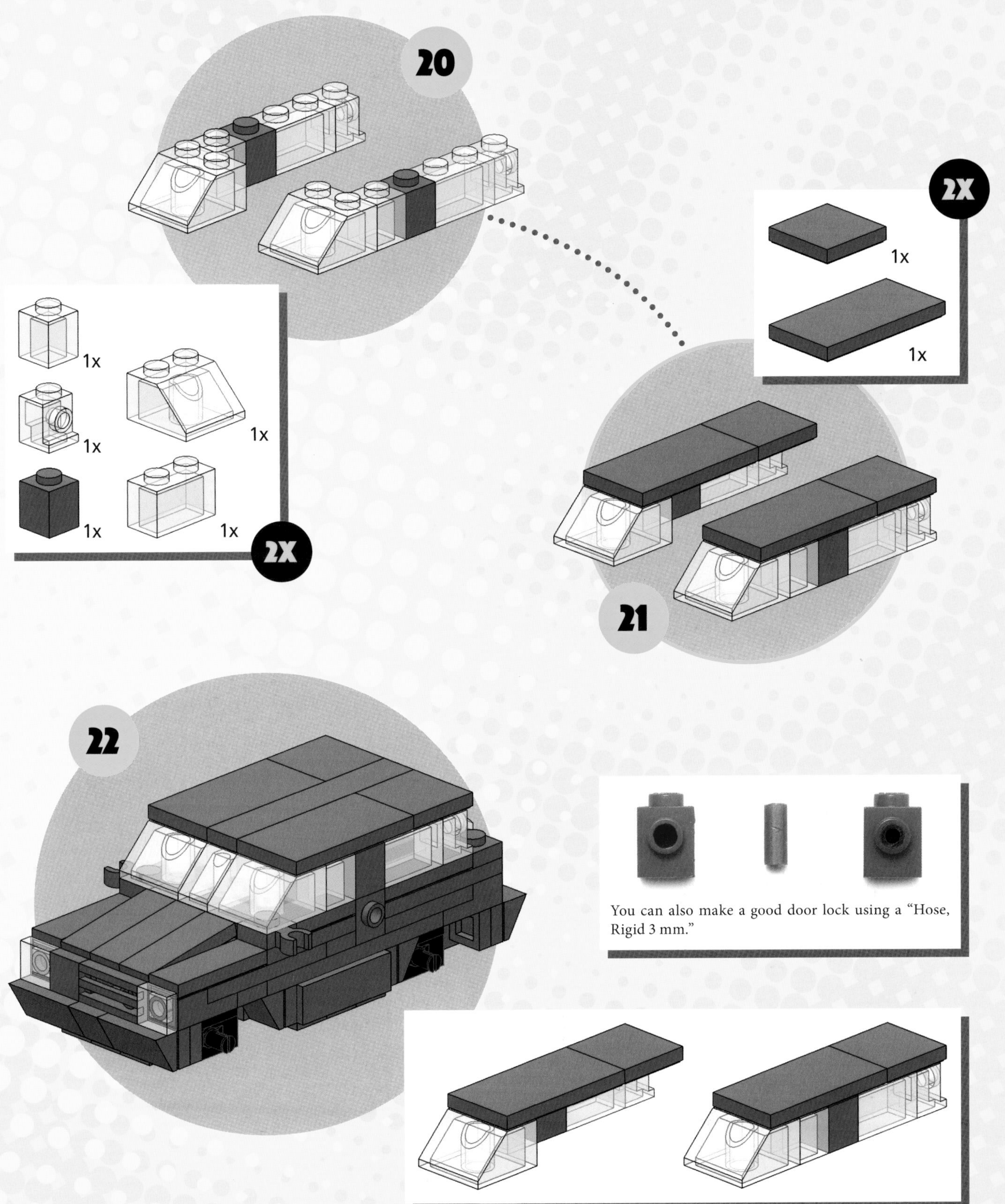

You can also make a good door lock using a “Hose, Rigid 3 mm.”

23

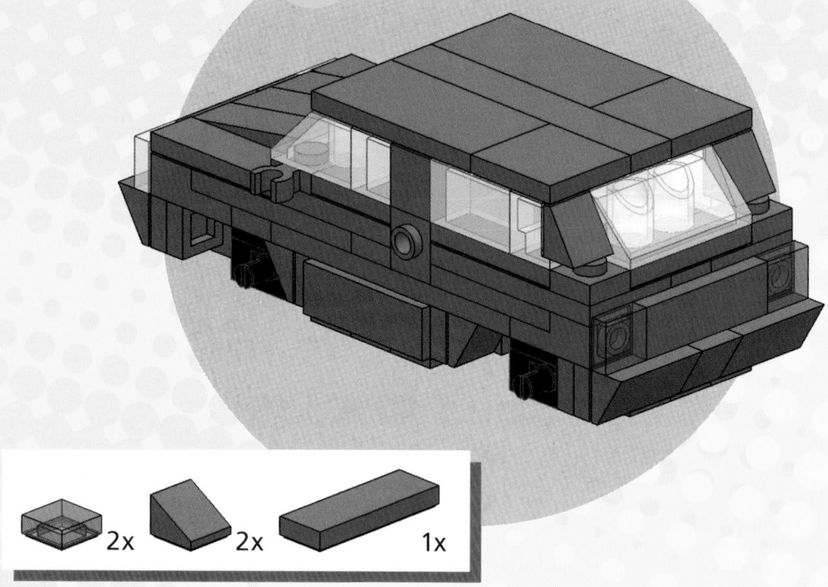

2x 2x 1x

24

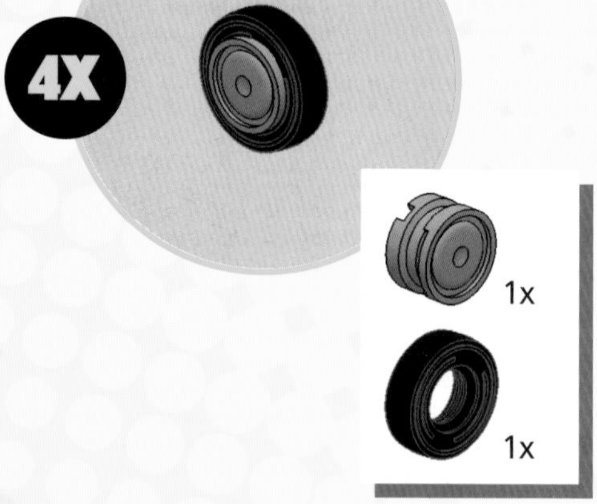

4X

1x

1x

2x 4x

25

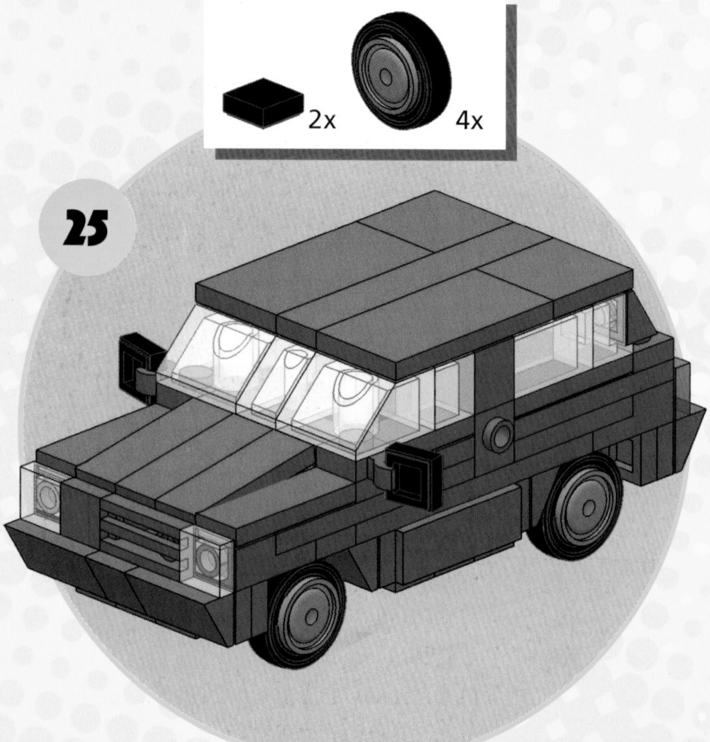

PARTS LIST

Quantity	Color	Element	Element Name	LEGO® Number
2	Red	3005	Brick 1 x 1	300521
2	Trans Clear	3005	Brick 1 x 1	4238226, 4645394
6	Dark Bluish Gray	4070	Brick 1 x 1 with Headlight	4211044
2	Trans Clear	4070	Brick 1 x 1 with Headlight	4215618
10	Dark Bluish Gray	87087	Brick 1 x 1 with Stud on 1 Side	4558955
2	Red	87087	Brick 1 x 1 with Stud on 1 Side	4558886
2	Dark Bluish Gray	3004	Brick 1 x 2	4211088
2	Trans Clear	3065	Brick 1 x 2 without Centre Stud	306540
1	Dark Bluish Gray	3622	Brick 1 x 3	4211104
8	Dark Bluish Gray	3024	Plate 1 x 1	4210719
5	Red	3024	Plate 1 x 1	302421
2	Red	60897	Plate 1 x 1 with Clip Vertical (Thick C-Clip)	
4	Dark Bluish Gray	3023	Plate 1 x 2	4211063
3	Red	3023	Plate 1 x 2	302321
2	Black	21445	Plate 1 x 2 with Wheel Holder	6122656
3	Black	3623	Plate 1 x 3	362326
4	Red	3623	Plate 1 x 3	362321
2	Red	3710	Plate 1 x 4	371021
1	Red	3460	Plate 1 x 8	346021
1	Red	4477	Plate 1 x 10	447721
2	Black	3022	Plate 2 x 2	302226
2	Black	4488	Plate 2 x 2 with Wheel Holder	448826, 6092658
4	Red	99206	Plate 2 x 2 x 0.667 with Two Studs On Side and Two Raised	6061711
4	Black	3021	Plate 2 x 3	302126
3	Blue	3021	Plate 2 x 3	302123
2	Red	3021	Plate 2 x 3	302121
2	Red	3020	Plate 2 x 4	302021

Quantity	Color	Element	Element Name	LEGO® Number
2	Red	3795	Plate 2 x 6	379521
7	Dark Bluish Gray	54200	Slope Brick 31 1 x 1 x 0.667	4244373, 4504378
2	Red	54200	Slope Brick 31 1 x 1 x 0.667	4244371, 4504379, 5074621
5	Dark Bluish Gray	85984	Slope Brick 31 1 x 2 x 0.667	4567887
1	Trans Clear	3040	Slope Brick 45 2 x 1	4130390
2	Trans Clear	3039	Slope Brick 45 2 x 2	622740
1	Trans Clear	3038	Slope Brick 45 2 x 3	
2	Black	3070b	Tile 1 x 1 with Groove	307026
4	Dark Bluish Gray	3070b	Tile 1 x 1 with Groove	4210848
1	Red	3070b	Tile 1 x 1 with Groove	307021
2	Trans Clear	3070b	Tile 1 x 1 with Groove	4162145, 6047501
2	Trans Red	3070b	Tile 1 x 1 with Groove	3003941
1	Red	2412b	Tile 1 x 2 Grille with Groove	241221
2	Red	3069b	Tile 1 x 2 with Groove	306921
4	Black	63864	Tile 1 x 3 with Groove	4558170
2	Dark Bluish Gray	63864	Tile 1 x 3 with Groove	4568734
11	Red	63864	Tile 1 x 3 with Groove	4533742
1	Red	6636	Tile 1 x 6	4113858
2	Red	3068b	Tile 2 x 2 with Groove	306821
2	Red	87079	Tile 2 x 4 with Groove	4560179
4	Black	59895	Tyre 4/ 80 x 8 Single Smooth Type 2	4516843
4	Flat Silver	93594	Wheel Rim 6.4 x 11 without Spokes	4624473

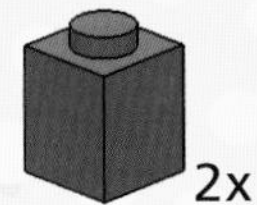
2x

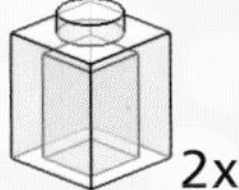
2x

6x

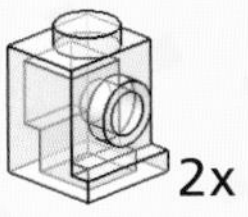
2x

10x

2x

2x

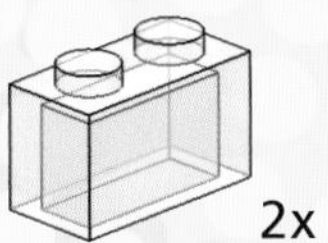
2x

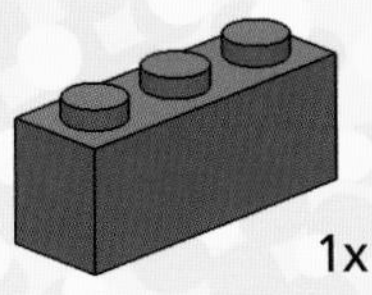
1x

8x

5x

2x

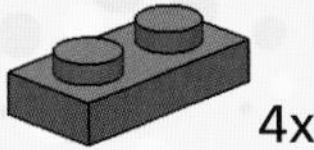
4x

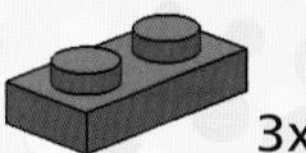
3x

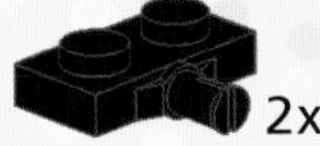
2x

3x

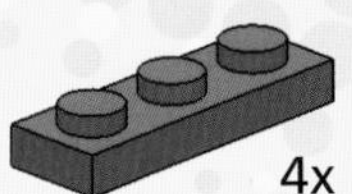
4x

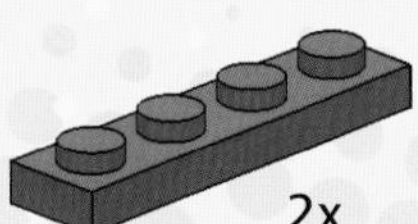
2x

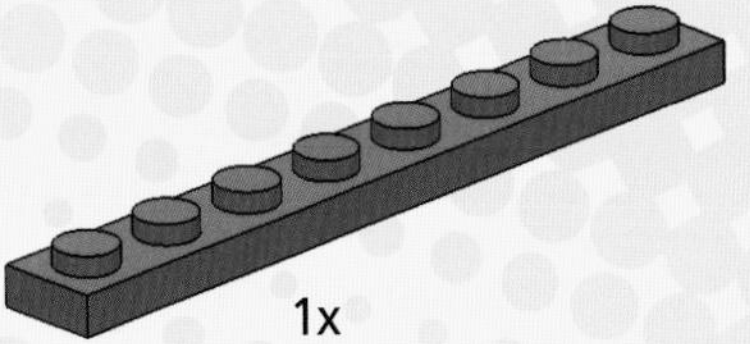
1x

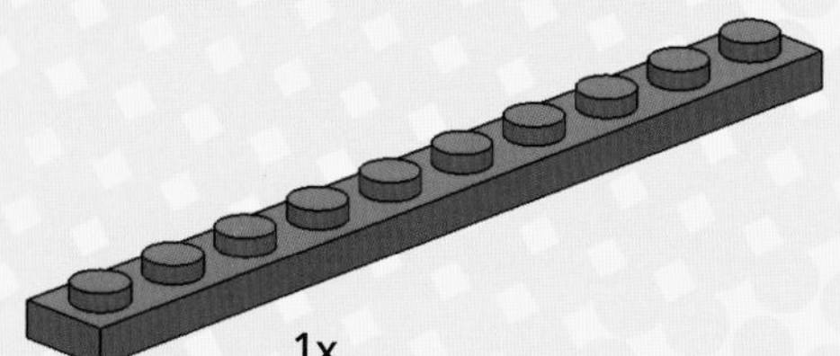
1x

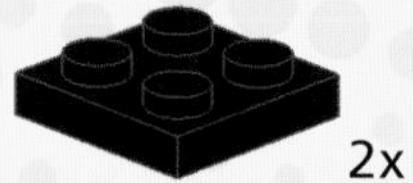
2x

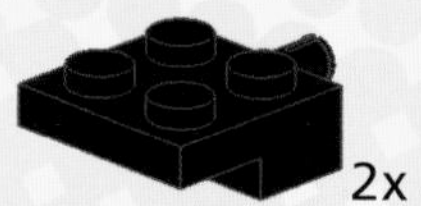
2x

4x

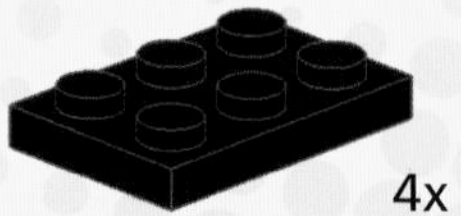
4x

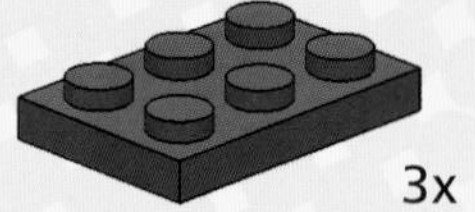
3x

2x

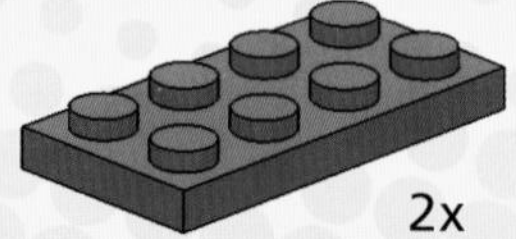
2x

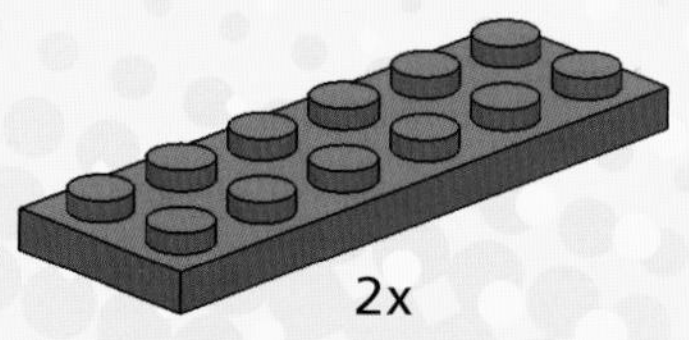
2x

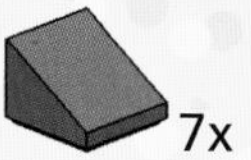
7x

2x

5x

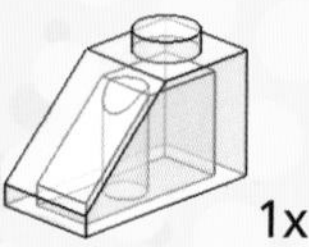
1x

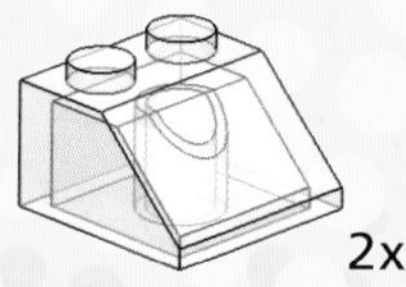
2x

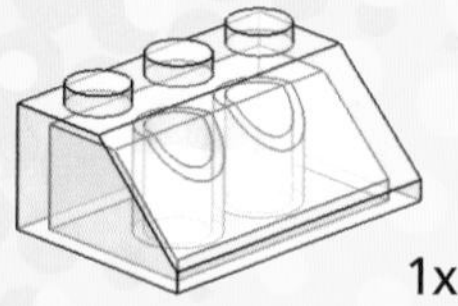
1x

2x

4x

1x

2x

2x

1x

2x

4x

2x

11x

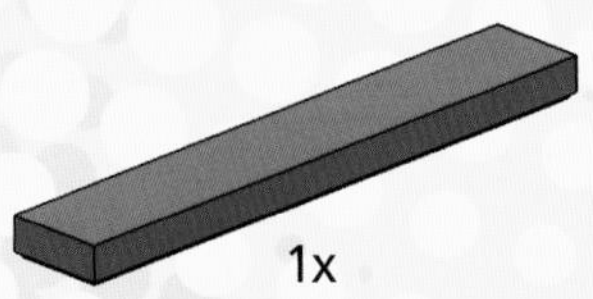
1x

2x

2x

4x

4x

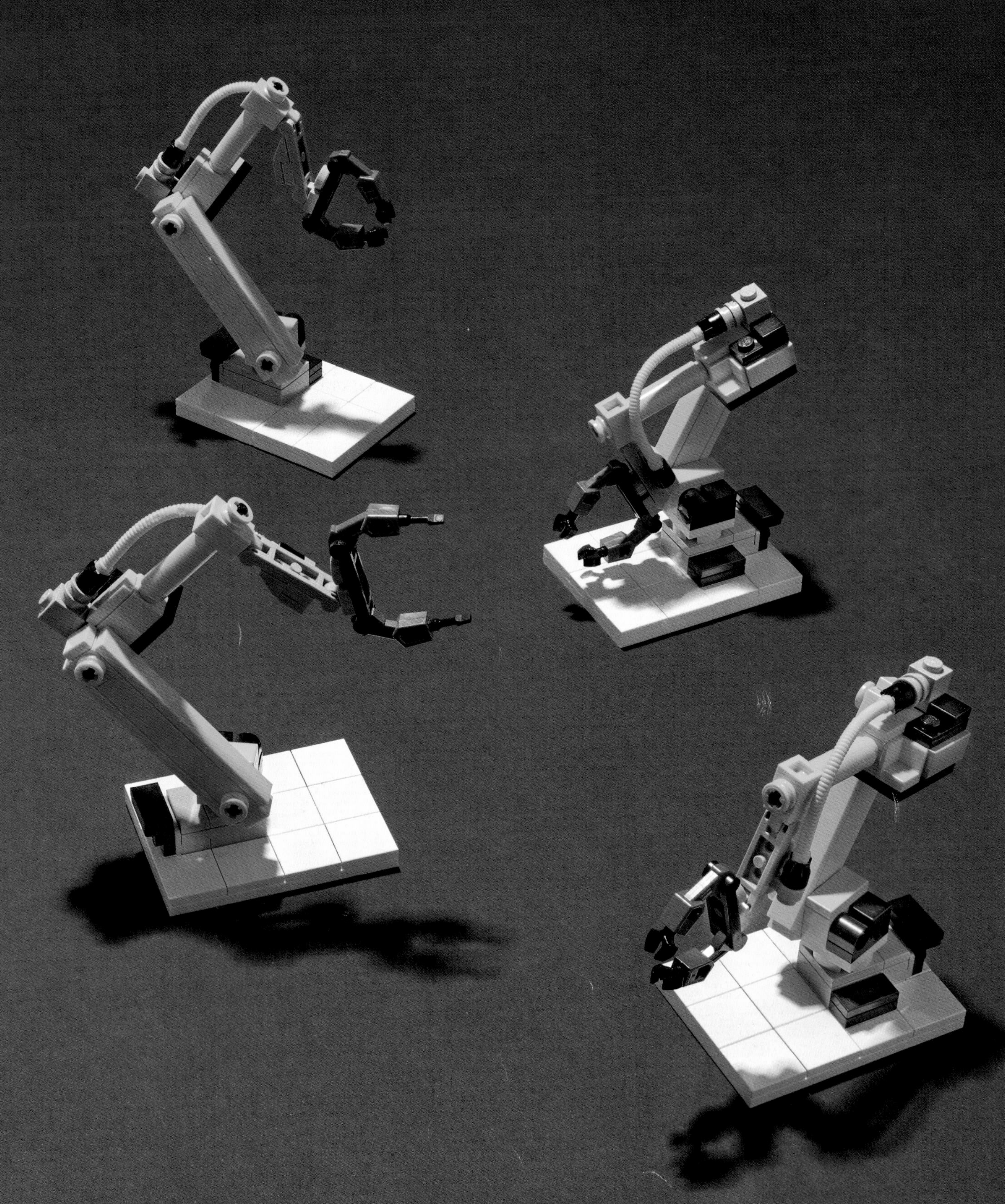

INDUSTRIAL ROBOTS

This industrial robot, inspired by me, has lured so many visitors to exhibitions I just had to include the building instructions here – even without a record. Look at the big picture, you can also attach the ends with clips instead of screwdrivers.

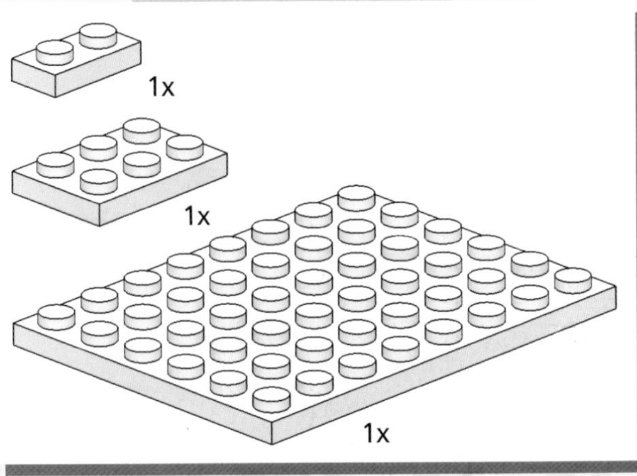

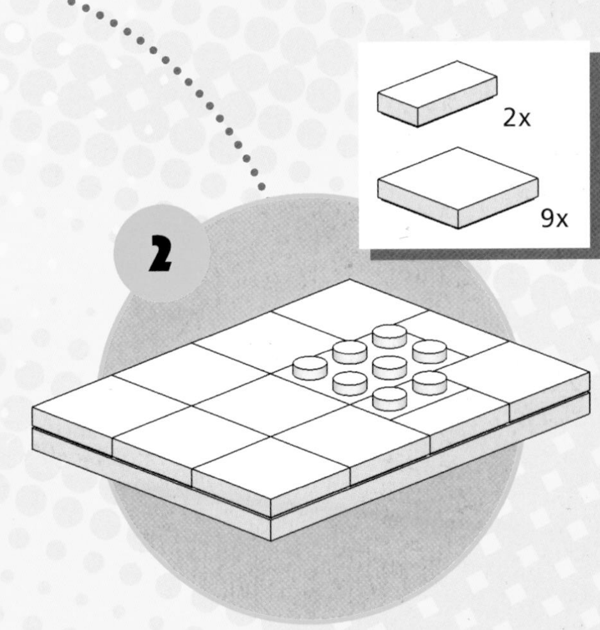

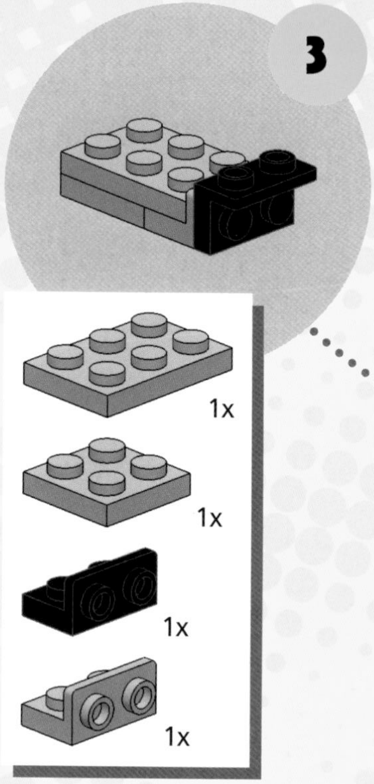

3

1x

1x

1x

1x

This plate is a rotating joint

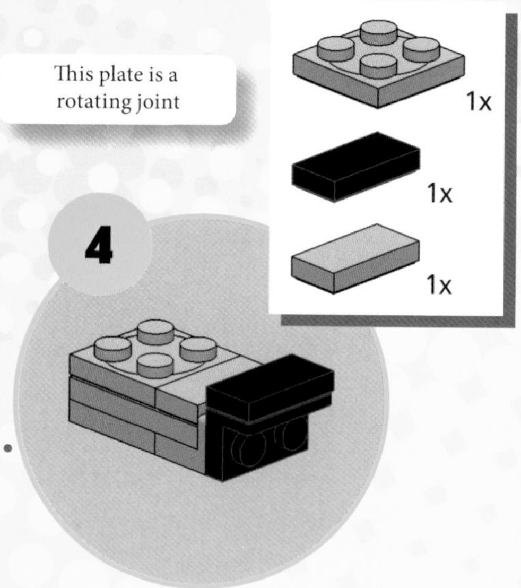

1x

1x

1x

4

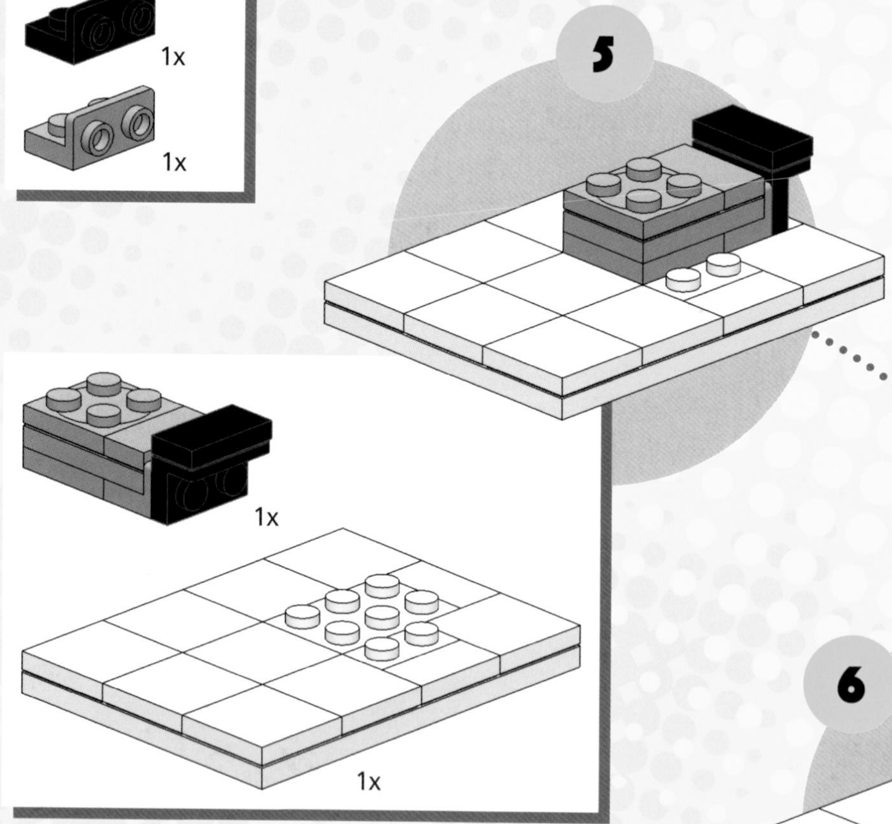

5

1x

1x

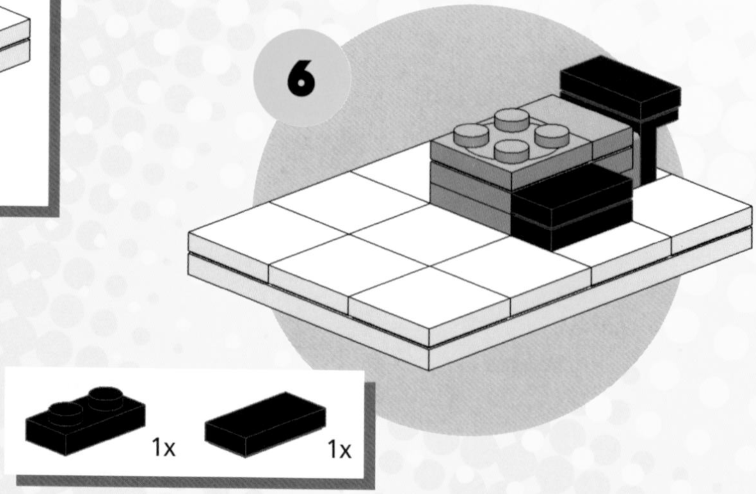

6

1x

1x

The rotating joint is best in light bluish-gray, but you can use a different color to suit your taste. Or you can create your own joint using the instructions shown here.

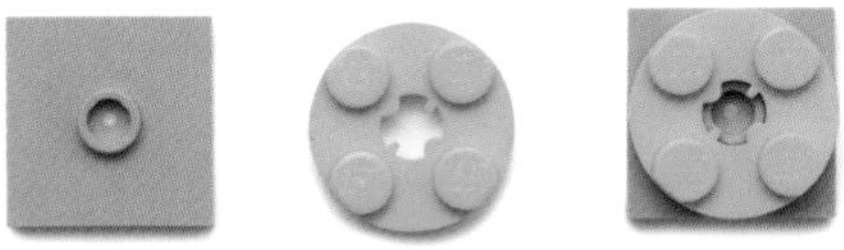

7

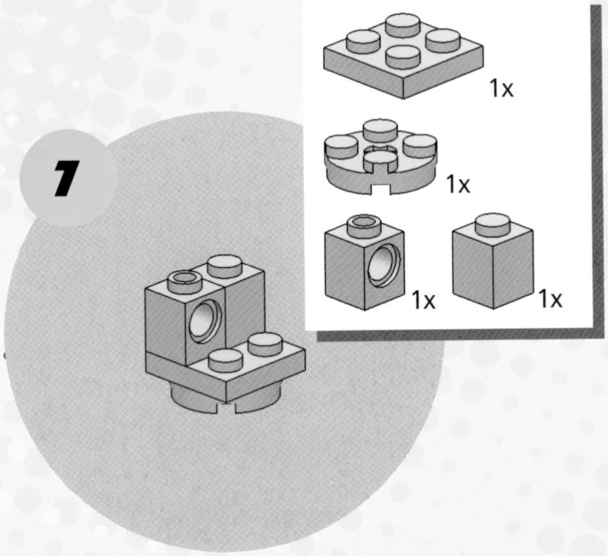

1x

1x

1x

1x

8

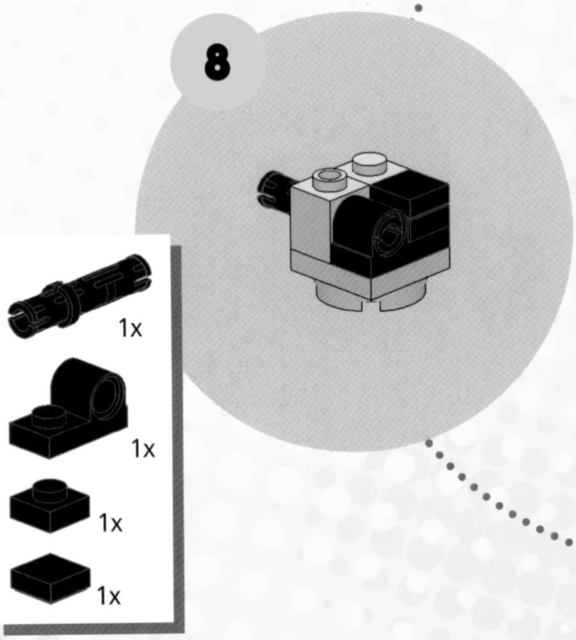

1x

1x

1x

1x

9

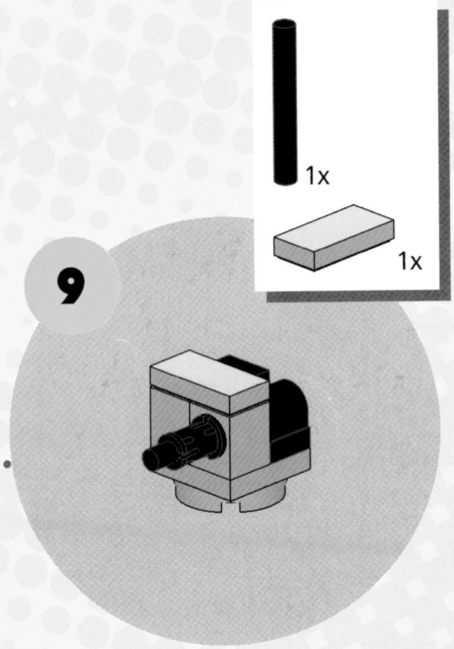

1x

1x

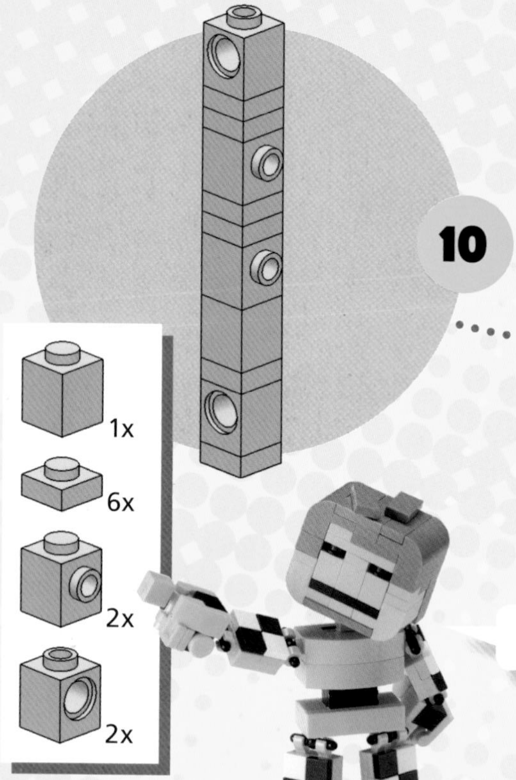

10

1x

6x

2x

2x

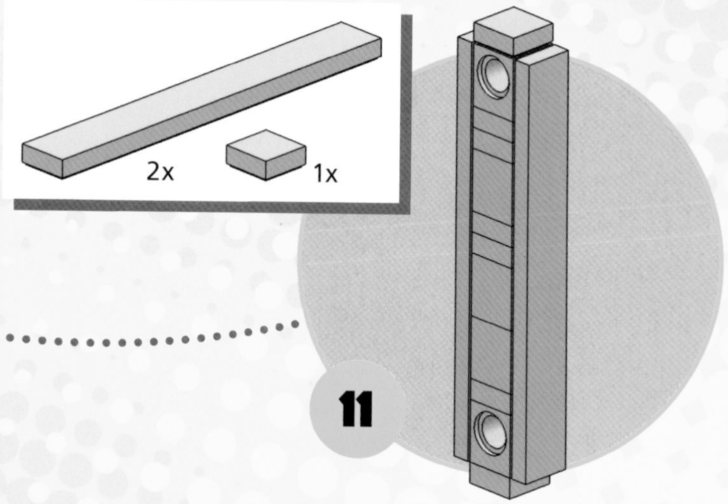

This brick has two side studs.

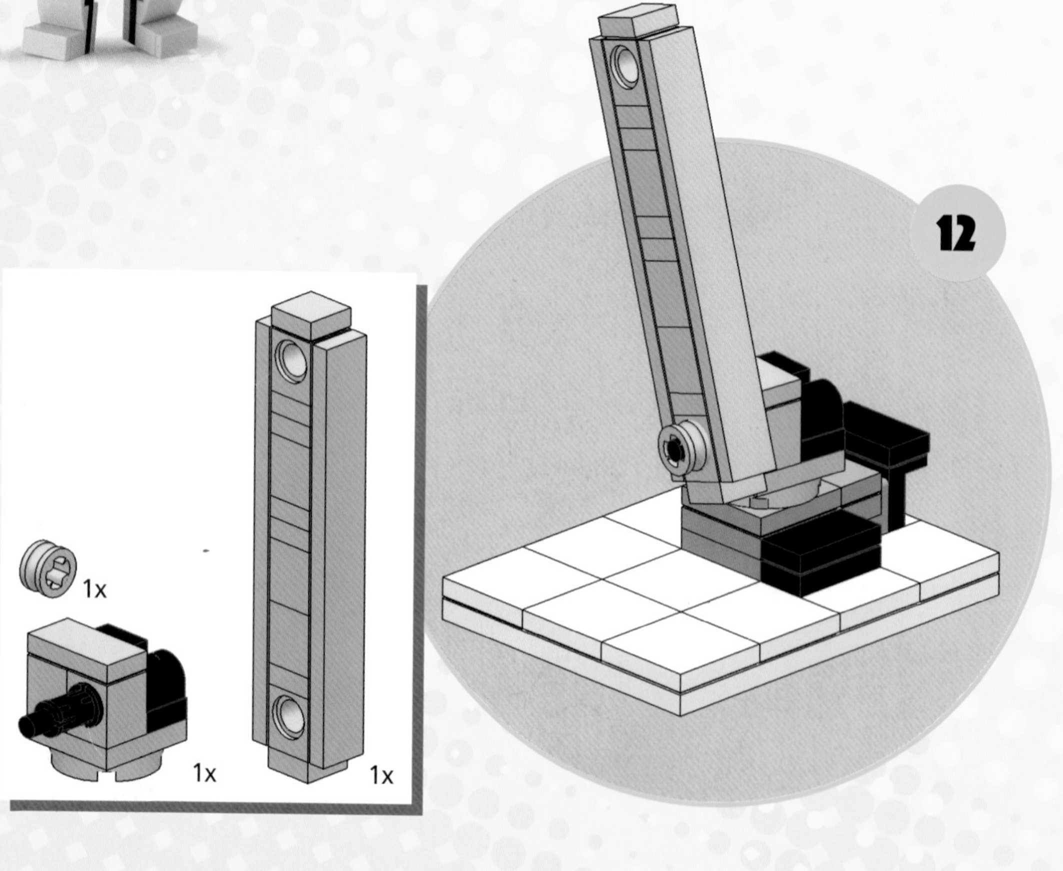

2x

1x

11

12

1x

1x

1x

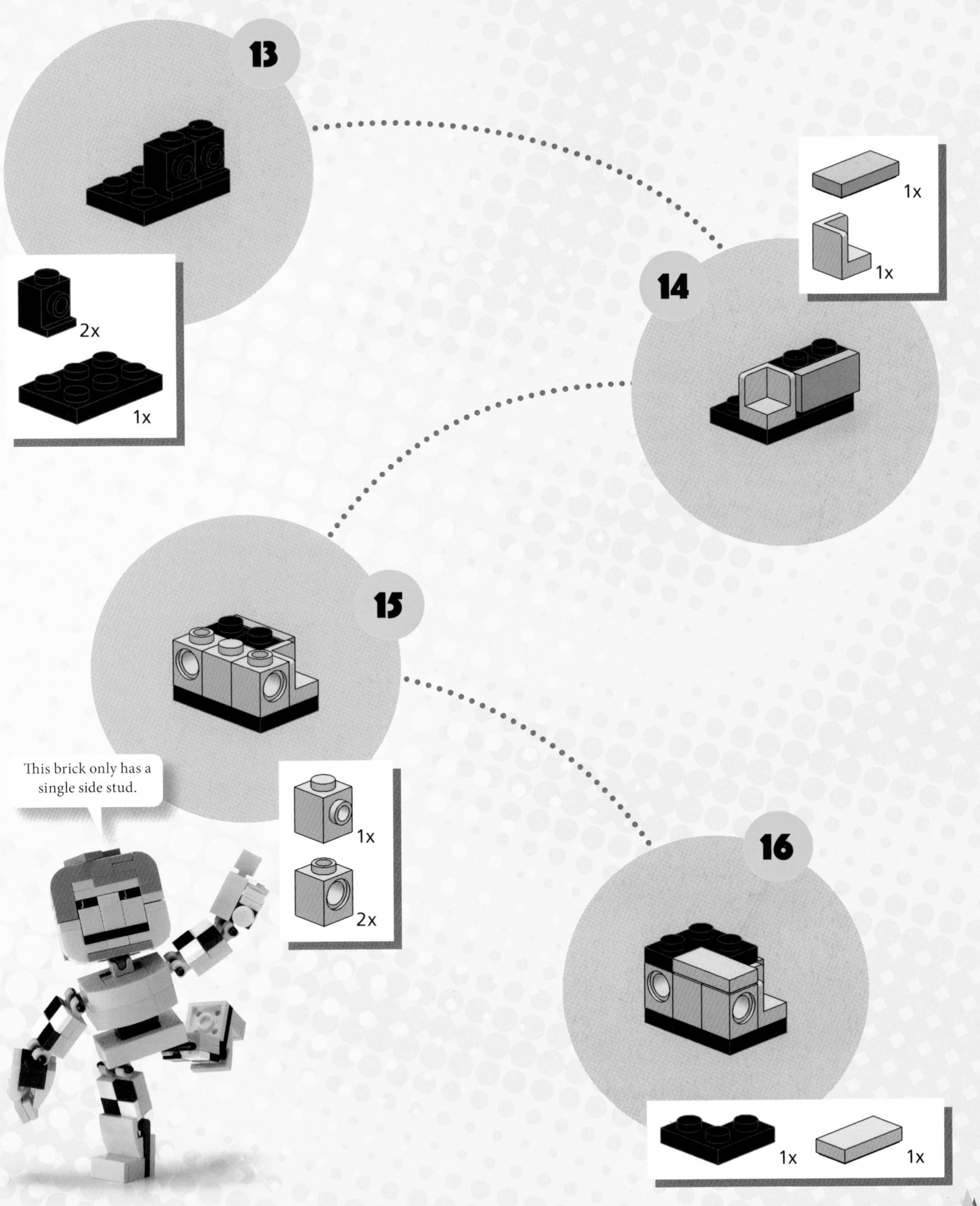
13
2x
1x
14
1x
1x
15
1x
2x
This brick only has a single side stud.
16
1x
1x

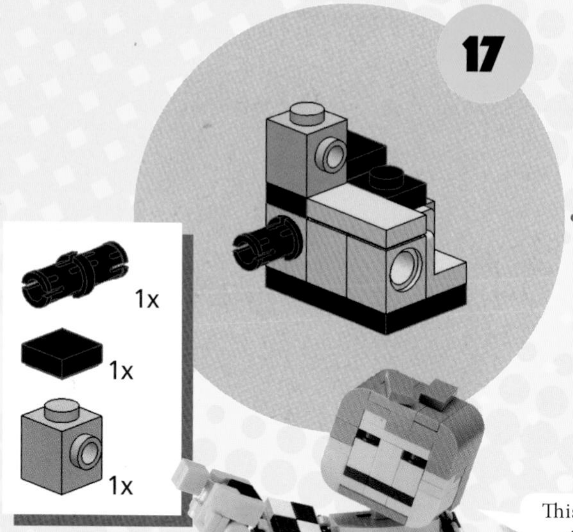

17

1x

1x

1x

This brick only has a single side stud.

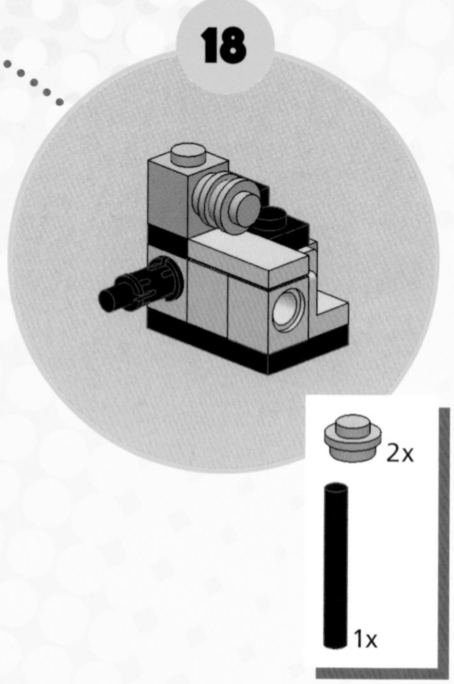

18

2x

1x

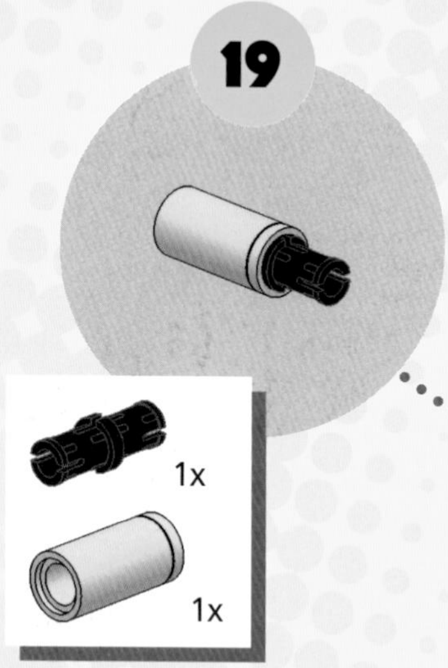

19

1x

1x

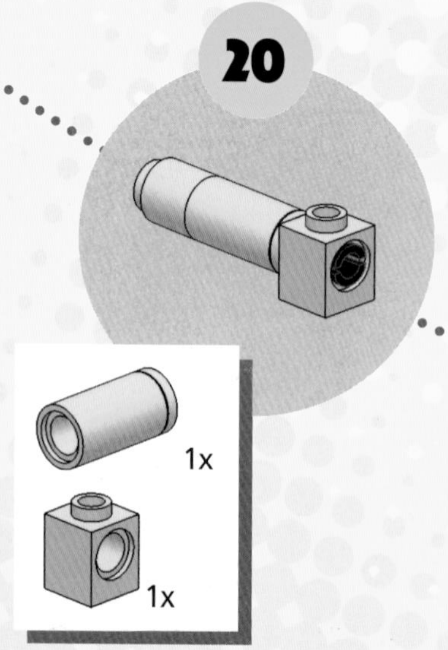

20

1x

1x

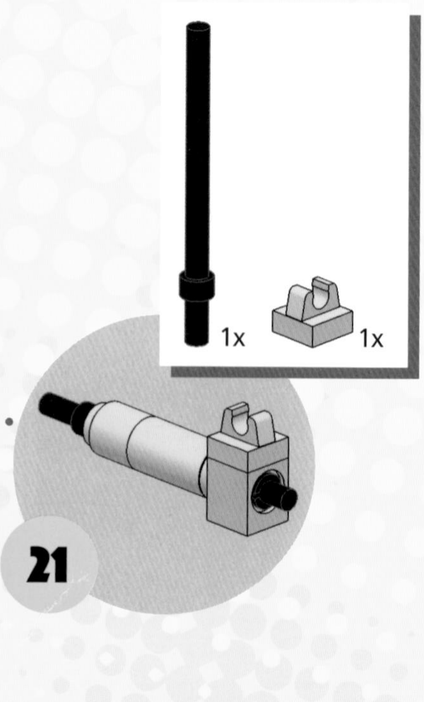

1x

1x

21

22

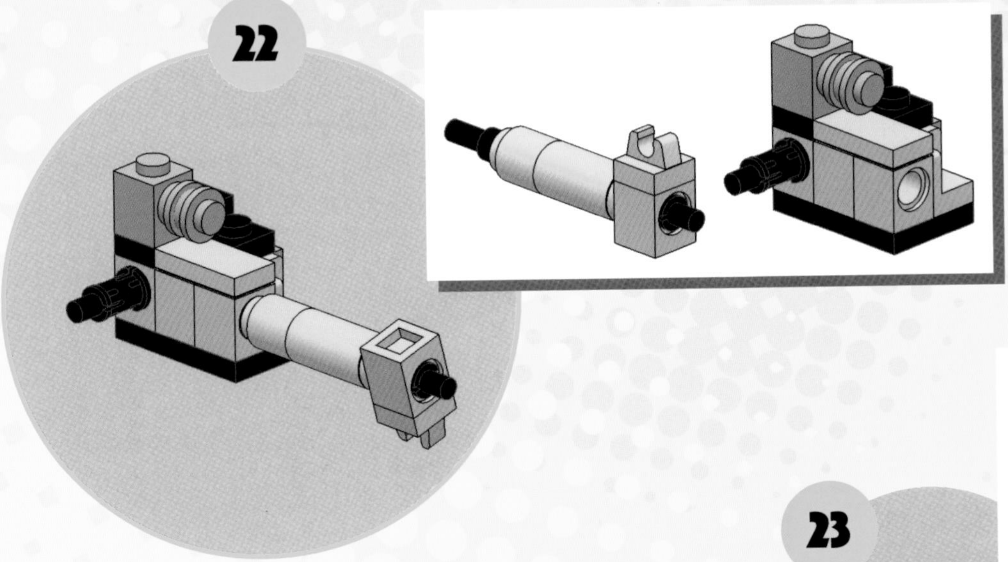

1x

1x

23

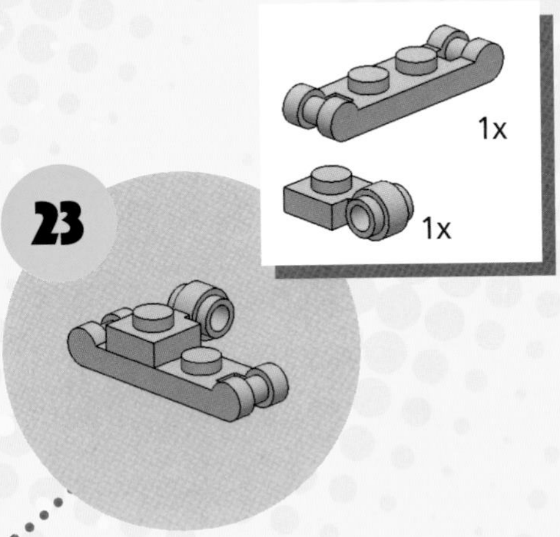

24

1x

1x

25

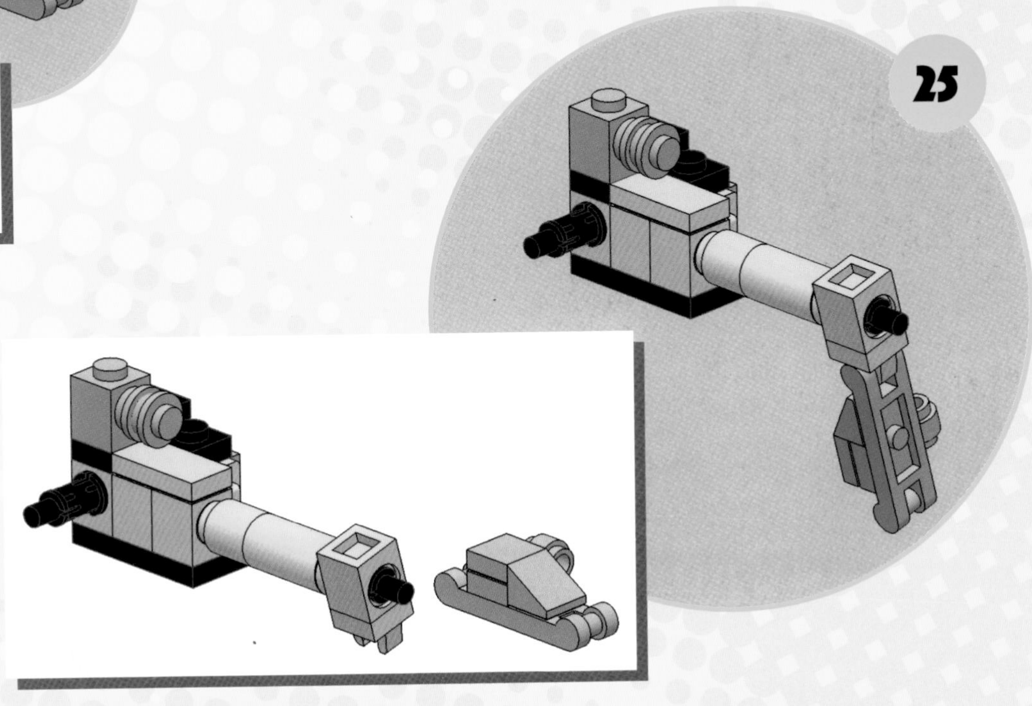

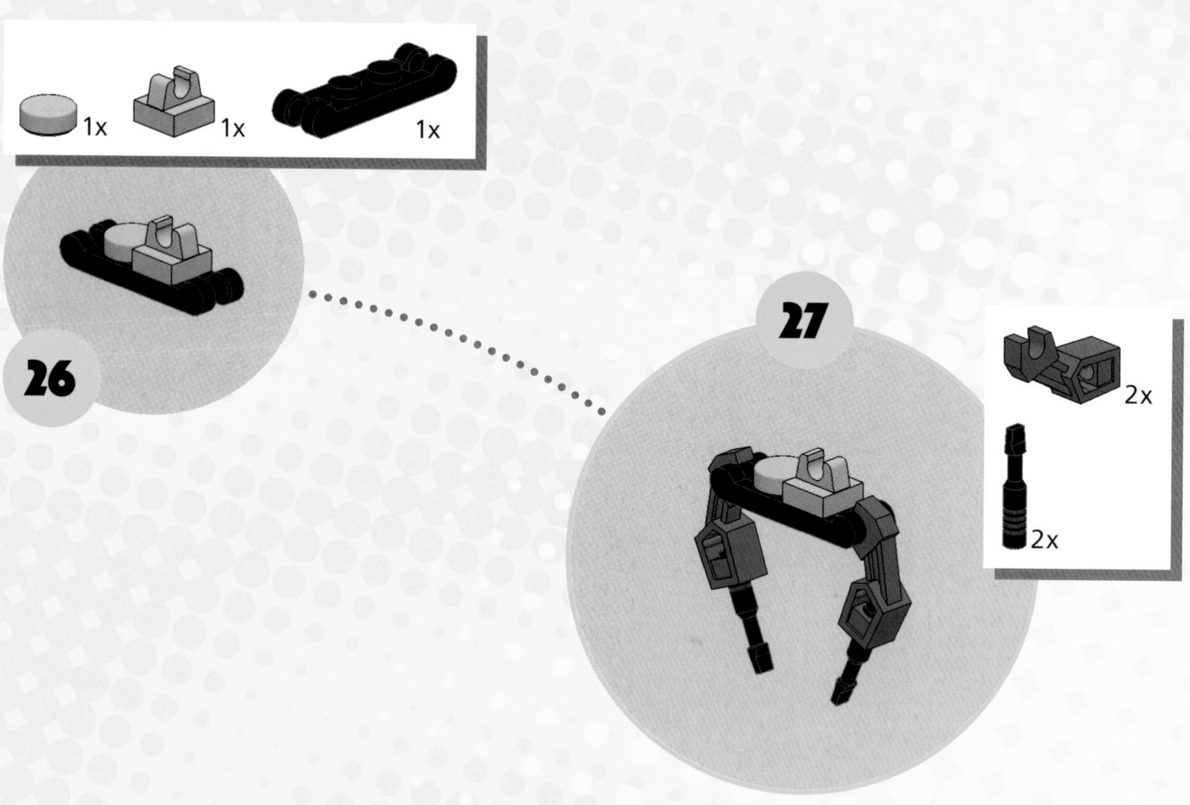
1x
1x
1x
26
27
2x
2x

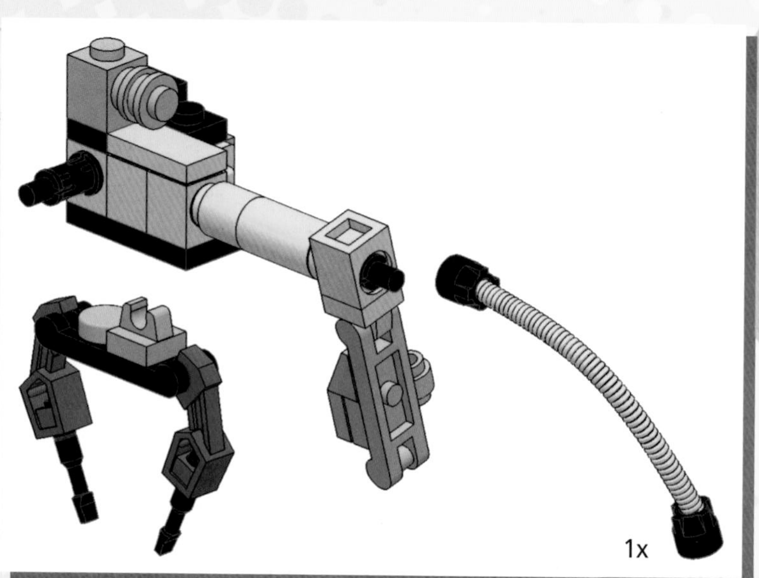
1x

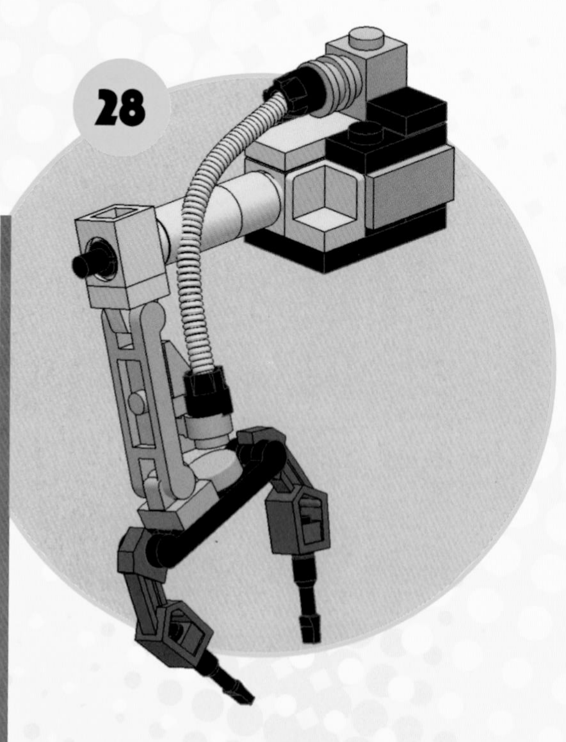
28

29

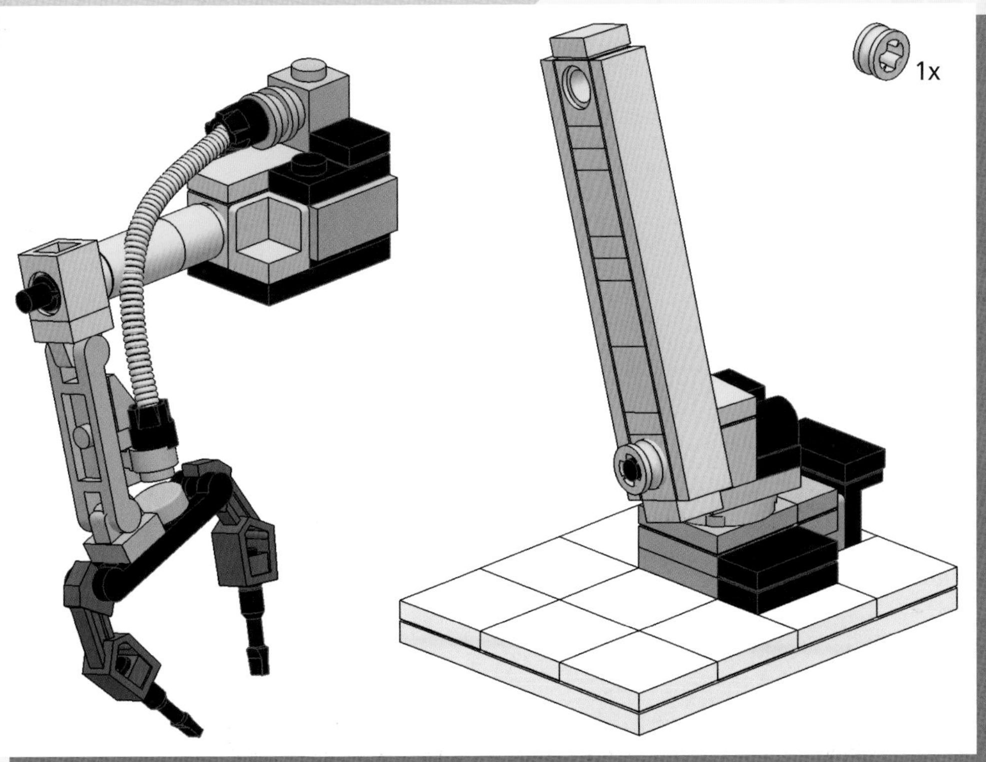

PARTS LIST

Quantity	Color	Element	Element Name	LEGO® Number
2	Black	87994	Bar 3L	4566275, 4653208, 6093525
1	Black	63965	Bar 6L with Thick Stop	4533907, 4538722, 4613957, 6061538, 6081988
1	Black	99780	Bracket 1 x 2 - 1 x 2 Up	6020193
1	Light Bluish Gray	99780	Bracket 1 x 2 - 1 x 2 Up	6004990
2	Yellow	3005	Brick 1 x 1	300524
1	Yellow	3062b	Brick 1 x 1 Round with Hollow Stud	306224
2	Black	4070	Brick 1 x 1 with Headlight	407026
1	Light Bluish Gray	87087	Brick 1 x 1 with Stud on 1 Side	4558953
1	Yellow	87087	Brick 1 x 1 with Stud on 1 Side	4624985
2	Yellow	47905	Brick 1 x 1 with Studs on Two Opposite Sides	6137920
1	Yellow	73590c02b	Hose Flexible with Black Ends with Tabs	4501980
2	Copper	53989	Minifig Mechanical Arm with Clip and Rod Hole	4291054
2	Black	11402a	Minifig Tool Screwdriver with Wide Head and 3-Rib Handle	6030875
1	Yellow	6231	Panel 1 x 1 x 1 Corner with Rounded Corners	4113238, 4201587
1	Black	3024	Plate 1 x 1	302426
6	Yellow	3024	Plate 1 x 1	302424
2	Light Bluish Gray	4073	Plate 1 x 1 Round	4211525
1	Light Bluish Gray	4081b	Plate 1 x 1 with Clip Light Type 2	4211477, 4632575
1	Black	3023	Plate 1 x 2	302326
1	White	3023	Plate 1 x 2	302301
1	Black	18649	Plate 1 x 2 with Handles on Opposite Ends	6099483
1	Light Bluish Gray	18649	Plate 1 x 2 with Handles on Opposite Ends	6093058
1	Black	11458	Plate 1 x 2 with Offset Peghole	6114987
1	Light Bluish Gray	3022	Plate 2 x 2	4211397
1	Yellow	3022	Plate 2 x 2	302224, 4613978
1	Black	2420	Plate 2 x 2 Corner	242026
1	Yellow	4032b	Plate 2 x 2 Round with Axlehole Type 2	403224
1	Black	3021	Plate 2 x 3	302126

Quantity		Color	Element	Element Name	LEGO® Number
1		Light Bluish Gray	3021	Plate 2 x 3	4211396
1		White	3021	Plate 2 x 3	302101
1		White	3036	Plate 6 x 8	303601
1		Light Bluish Gray	54200	Slope Brick 31 1 x 1 x 0.667	4521921
6		Yellow	6541	Technic Brick 1 x 1 with Hole	654124
2		Yellow	32123	Technic Bush 1/2 Smooth with Axle Hole Reduced	3212324, 4239601
1		Yellow	75535	Technic Pin Joiner Round	75644
1		Black	6558	Technic Pin Long with Friction and Slot	655826
2		Black	2780	Technic Pin with Friction and Slots	278026, 4121715
1		Light Bluish Gray	98138	Tile 1 x 1 Round with Groove	4650260
1		Light Bluish Gray	2555	Tile 1 x 1 with Clip	2555194, 4211369, 6030711
1		Yellow	2555	Tile 1 x 1 with Clip	4164060, 6030719
2		Black	3070b	Tile 1 x 1 with Groove	307026
1		Light Bluish Gray	3070b	Tile 1 x 1 with Groove	4211415
1		Yellow	3070b	Tile 1 x 1 with Groove	307024
2		Black	3069b	Tile 1 x 2 with Groove	306926
2		Light Bluish Gray	3069b	Tile 1 x 2 with Groove	4211414
2		White	3069b	Tile 1 x 2 with Groove	306901
2		Yellow	3069b	Tile 1 x 2 with Groove	306924
2		Yellow	4162	Tile 1 x 8	416224, 4189400
9		White	3068b	Tile 2 x 2 with Groove	306801
1		Light Bluish Gray	3680c02	Turntable 2 x 2 Plate with Light Bluish Grey Top	

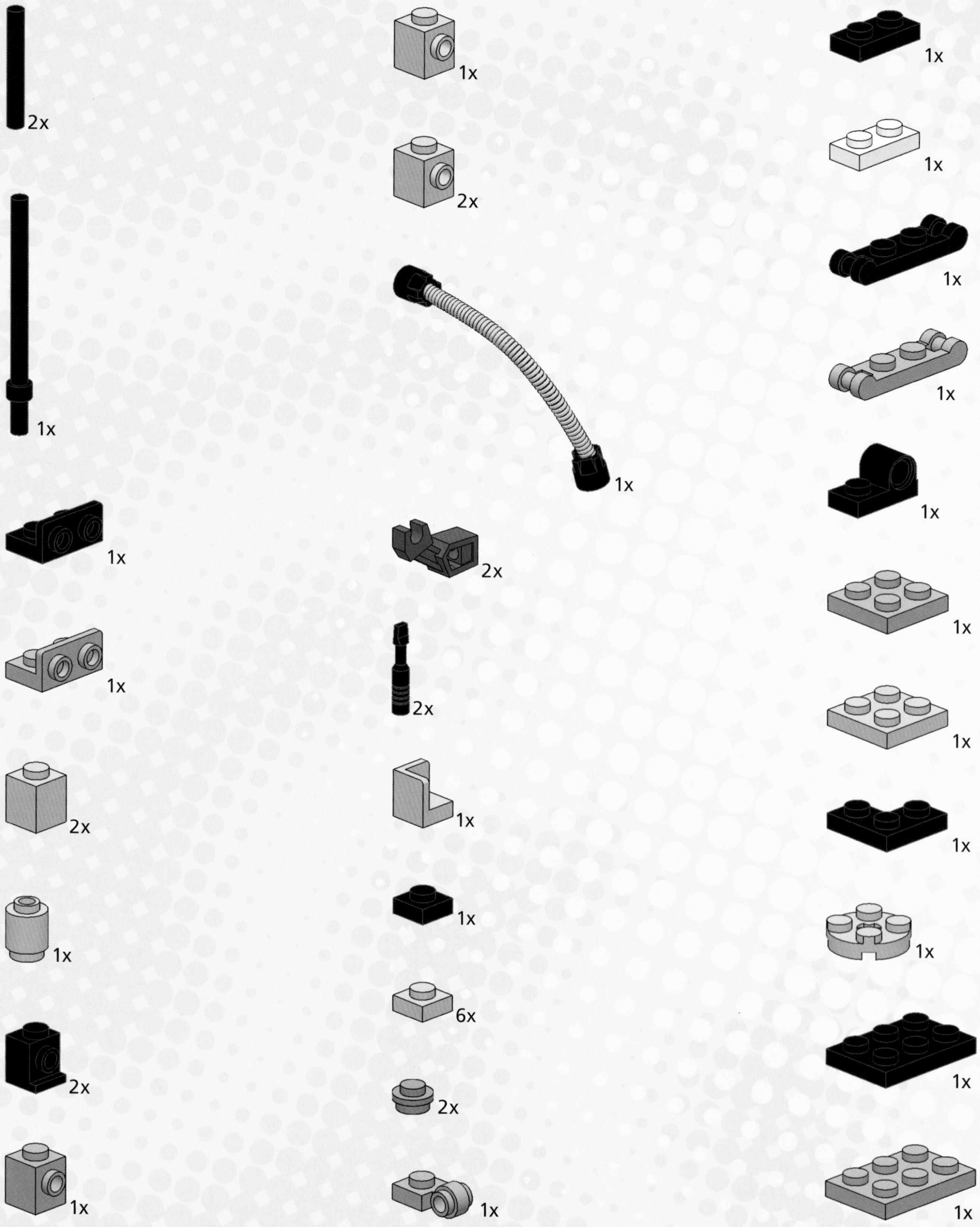

2x

1x

1x

1x

2x

1x

2x

1x

1x

2x

1x

2x

2x

1x

1x

6x

2x

1x

1x

1x

1x

1x

1x

1x

1x

1x

1x

1x

1x

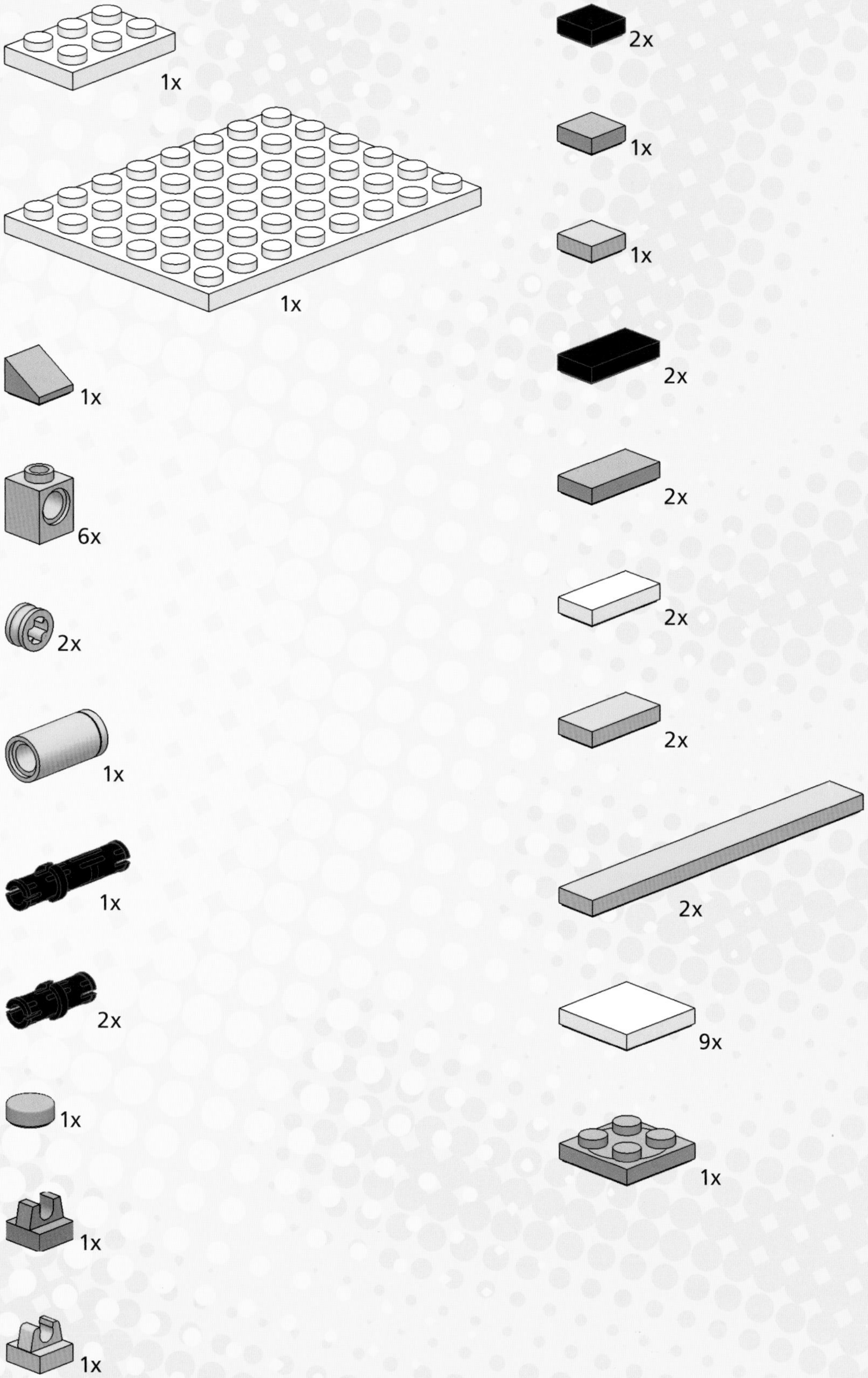

1x

1x

1x

6x

2x

1x

1x

2x

1x

1x

1x

2x

1x

1x

2x

2x

2x

2x

2x

9x

1x

CORVETTE C3 STINGRAY

In 1967 Chevrolet introduced the third generation of the Corvette. The so-called "Coke bottle design" attracted a lot of attention. I have chosen to model the 1971 Corvette C3 Stingray because at the time it held the record for the greatest engine power for a serial version. It also had a "big block" engine with 435 HP.

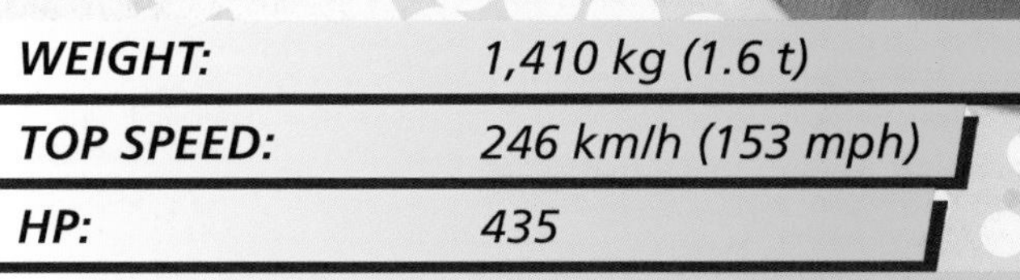

WEIGHT:	*1,410 kg (1.6 t)*
TOP SPEED:	*246 km/h (153 mph)*
HP:	*435*
TANK CAPACITY:	*90 liters (24 gal.)*

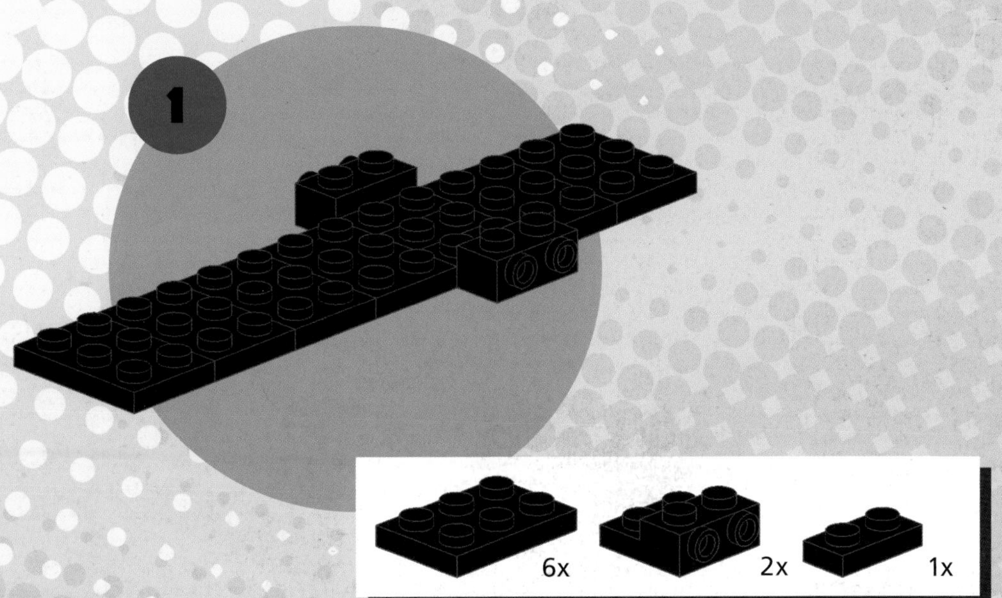

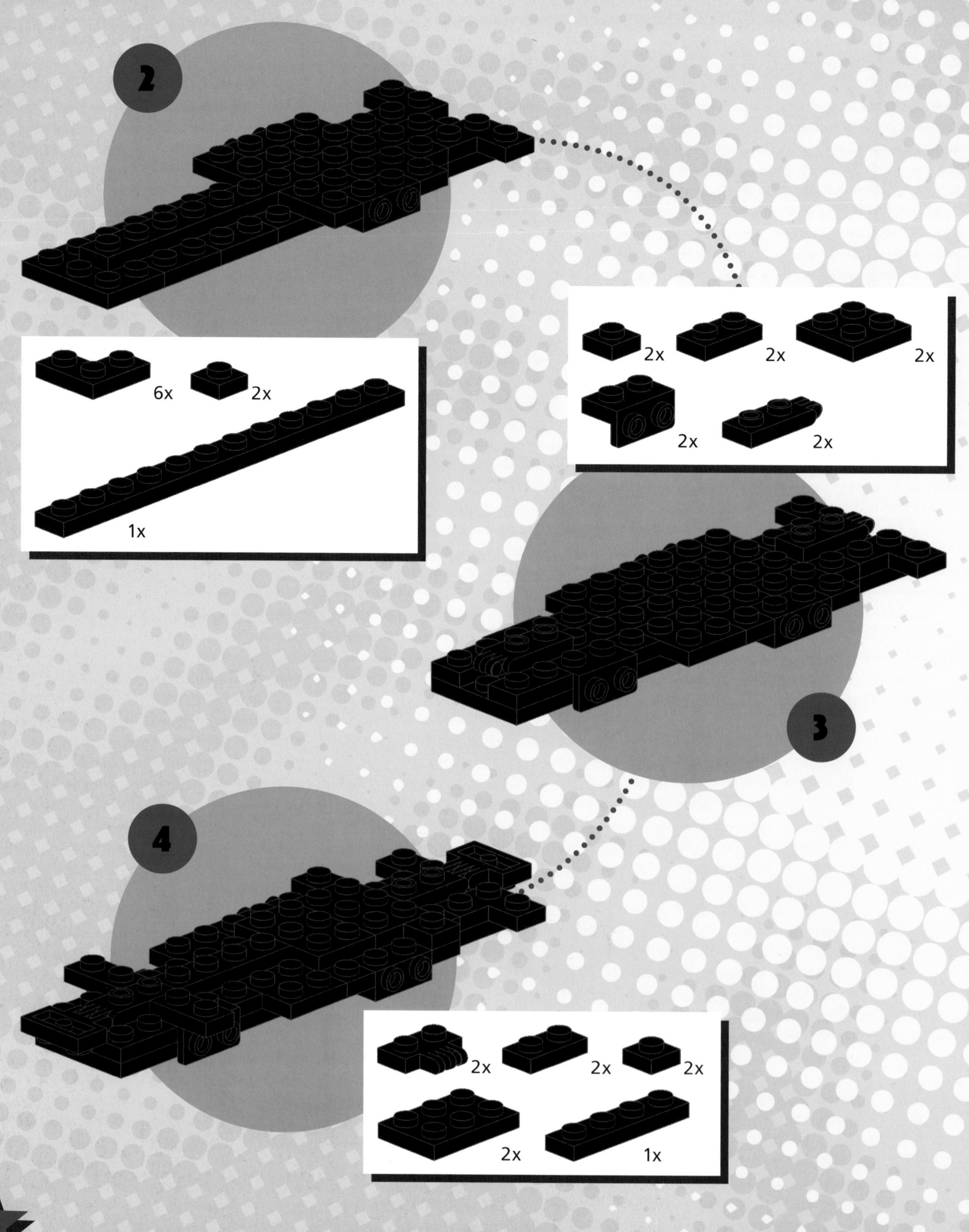
2
6x
2x
1x
2x
2x
2x
2x
2x
3
4
2x
2x
2x
2x
1x

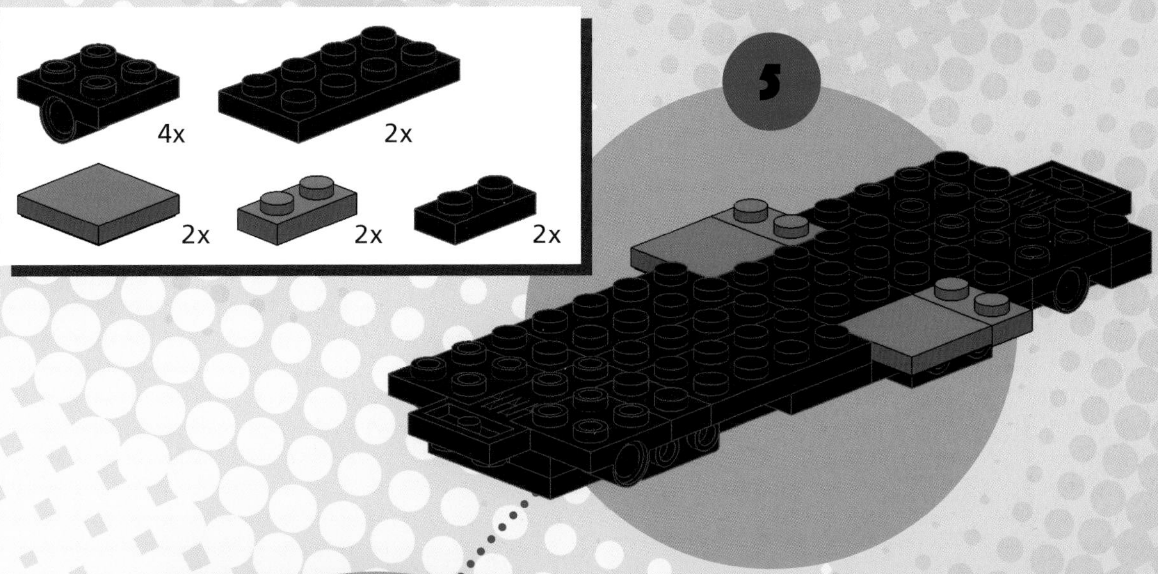

5

4x 2x
2x 2x 2x

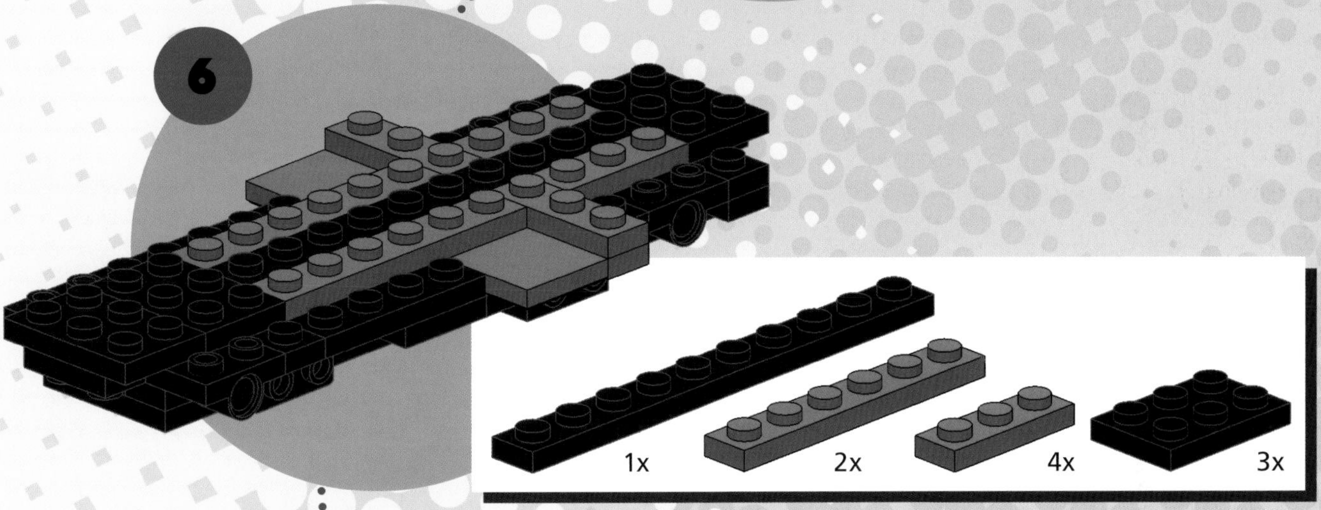

6

1x 2x 4x 3x

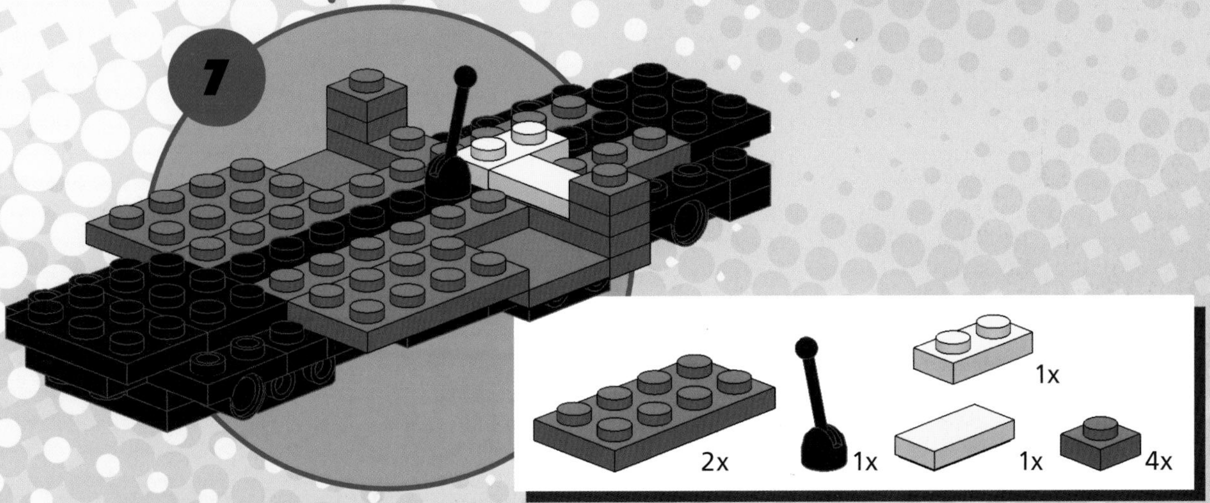

7

2x 1x 1x 1x 4x

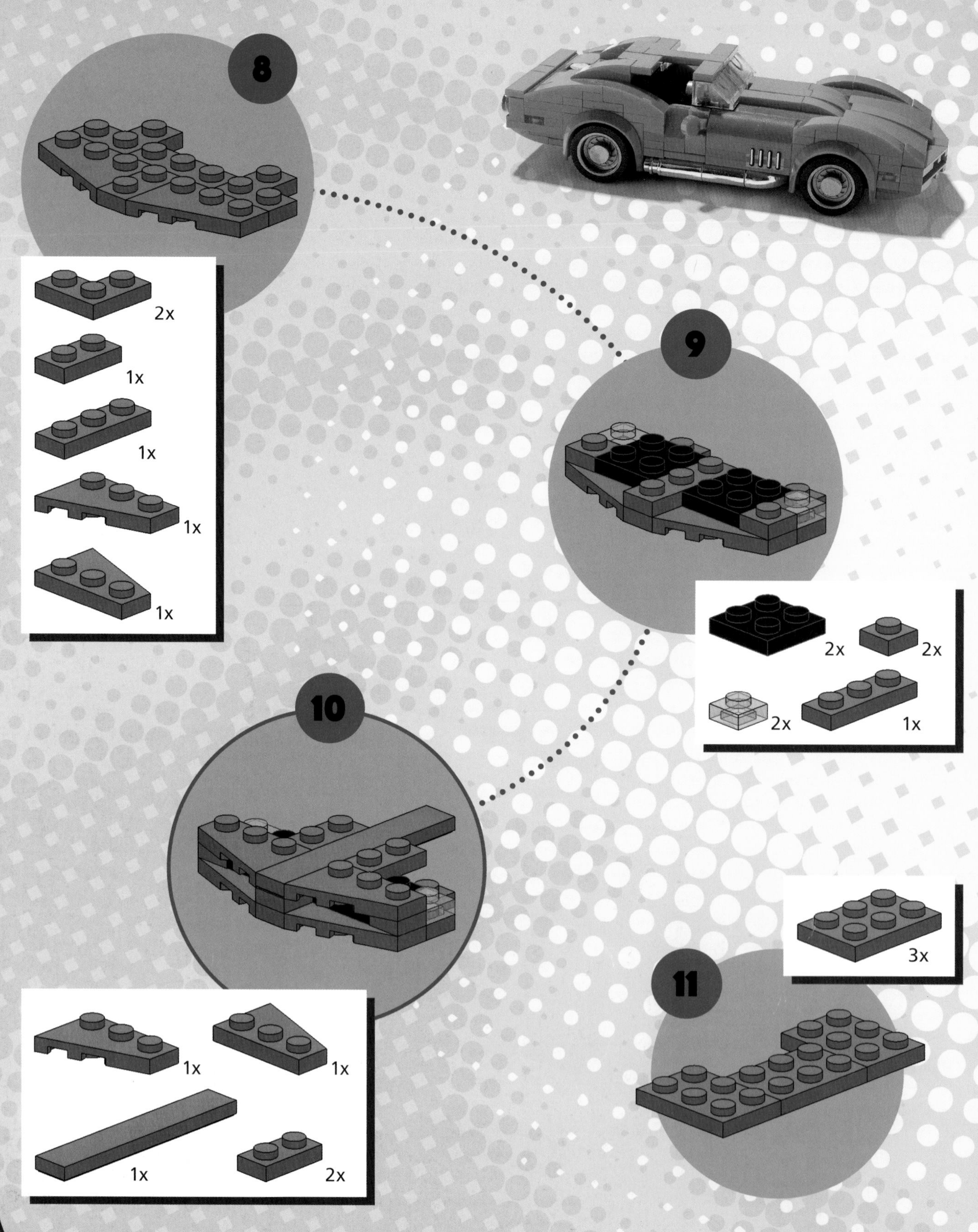
8
2x
1x
1x
1x
1x
9
2x
2x
2x
1x
10
1x
1x
1x
2x
3x
11

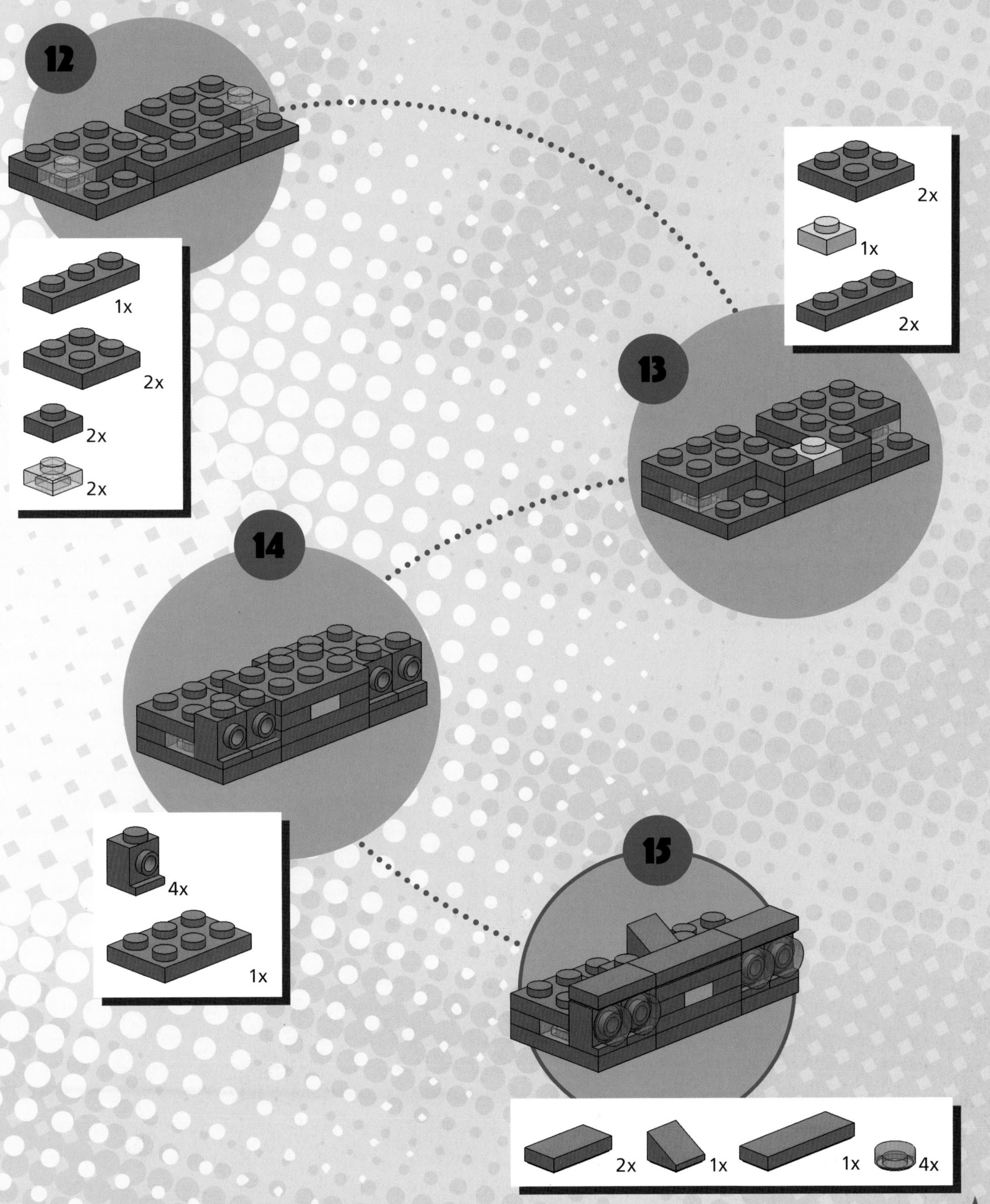
12
1x
2x
2x
2x
13
2x
1x
2x
14
4x
1x
15
2x
1x
1x
4x

16

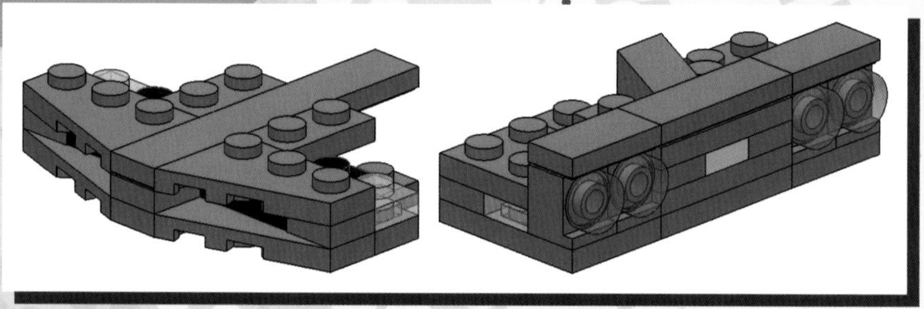

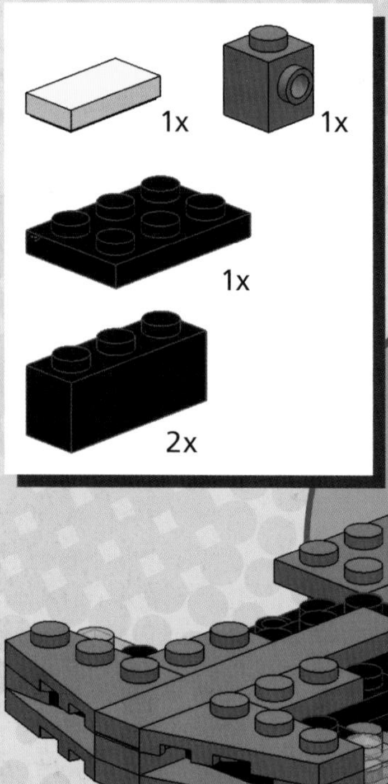

1x
1x
1x
2x

This brick only has a single side stud.

17

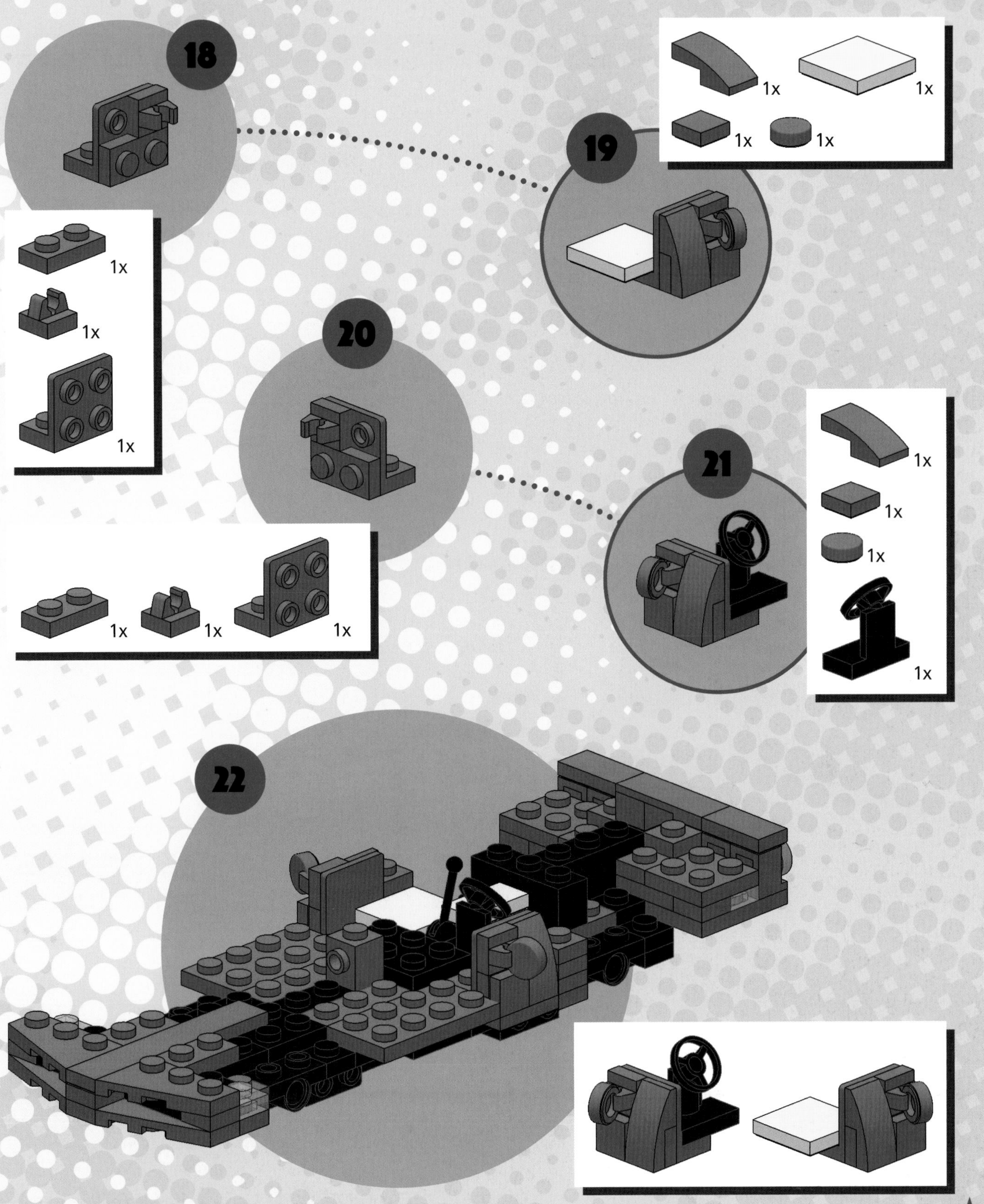
18
1x
1x
1x
19
1x
1x
1x
1x
20
1x
1x
1x
21
1x
1x
1x
1x
22

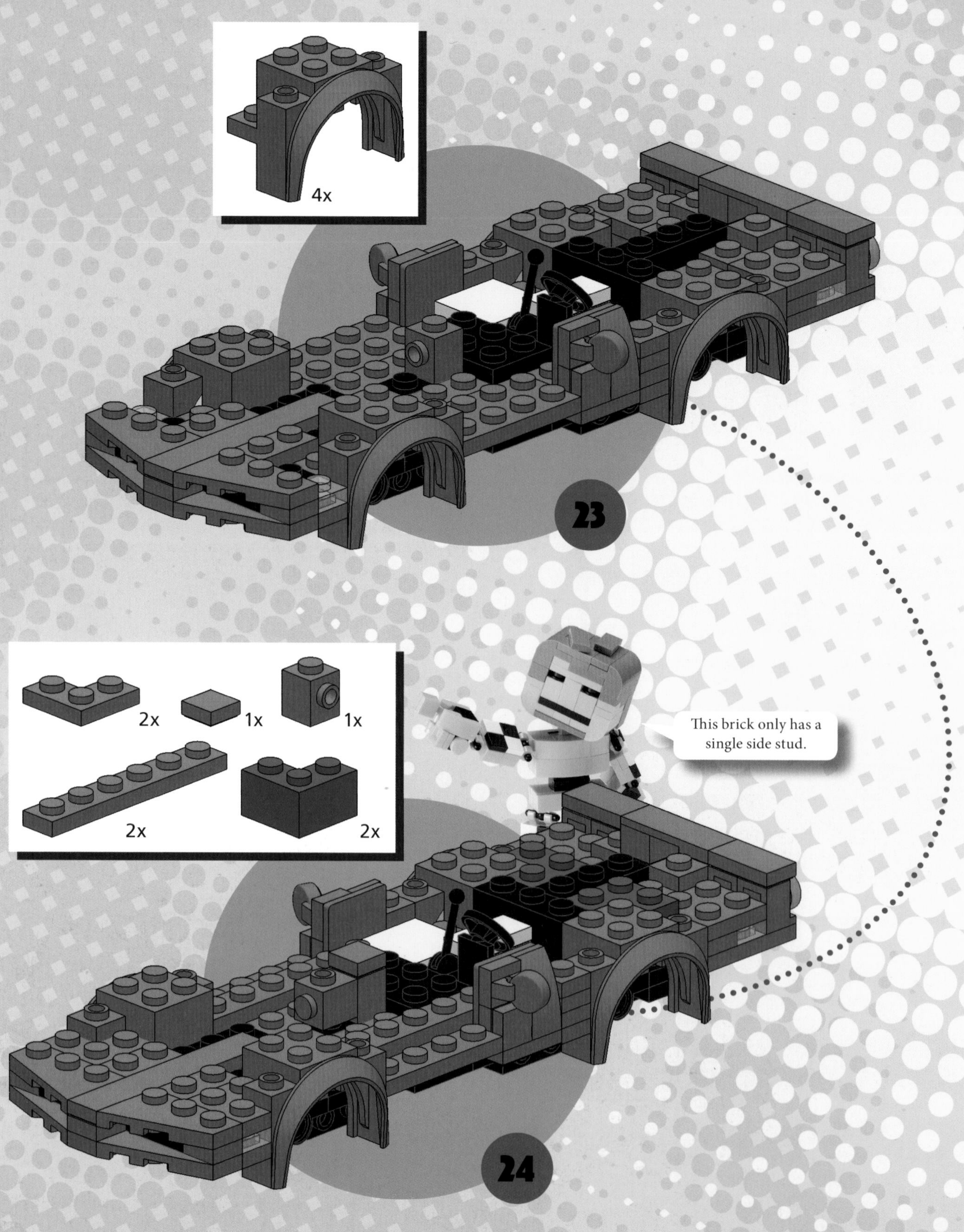
4x
23
2x
1x
1x
2x
2x
This brick only has a single side stud.
24

25

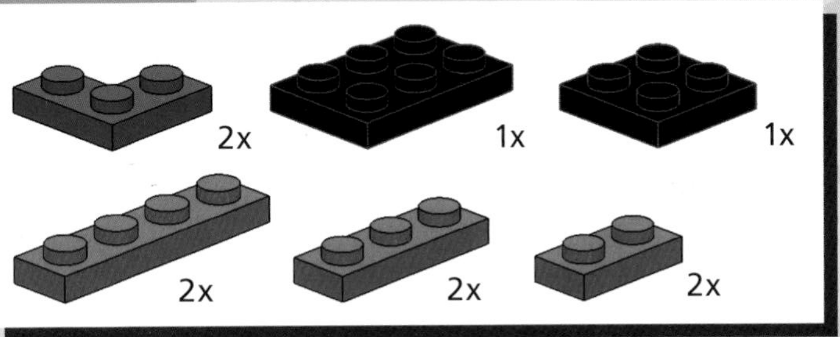

2x 1x 1x

2x 2x 2x

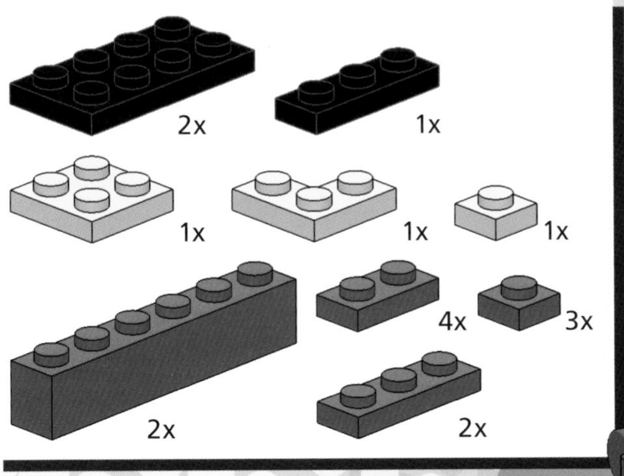

2x 1x

1x 1x 1x

4x 3x

2x 2x

26

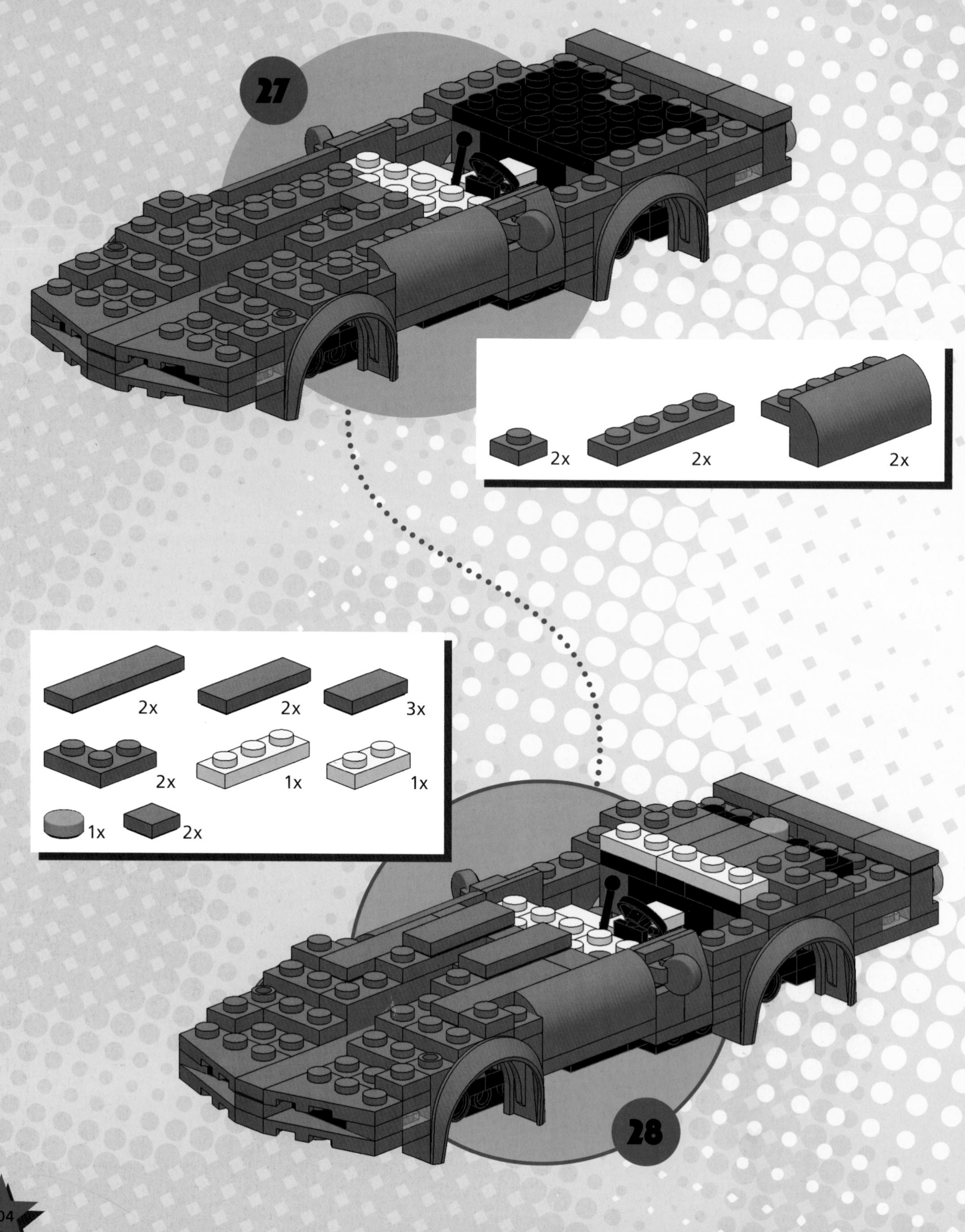
27
2x
2x
2x
2x
2x
3x
2x
1x
1x
1x
2x
28

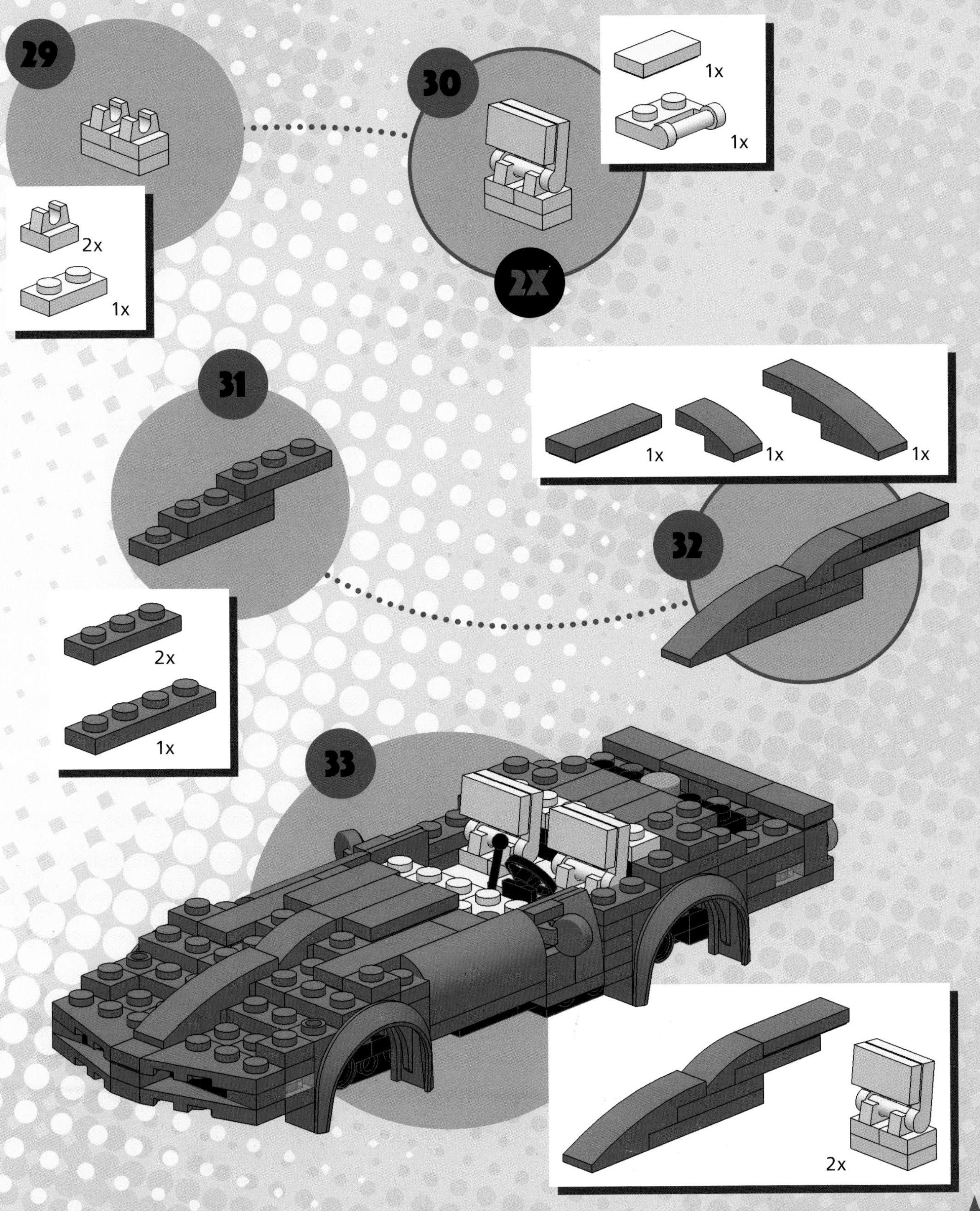
29
2x
1x
30
1x
1x
2X
31
2x
1x
32
1x
1x
1x
33
2x

34

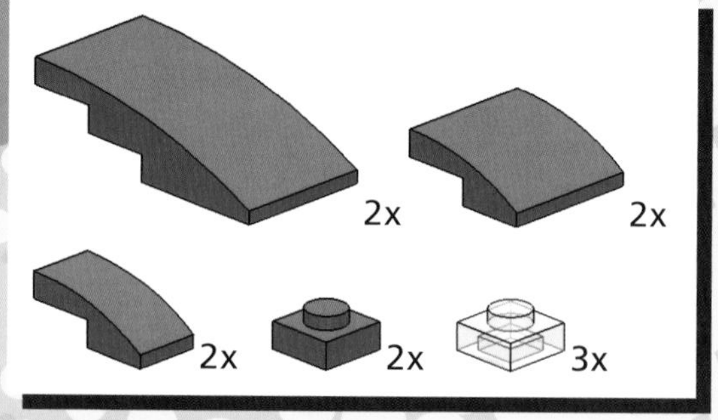

2x 2x

2x 2x 3x

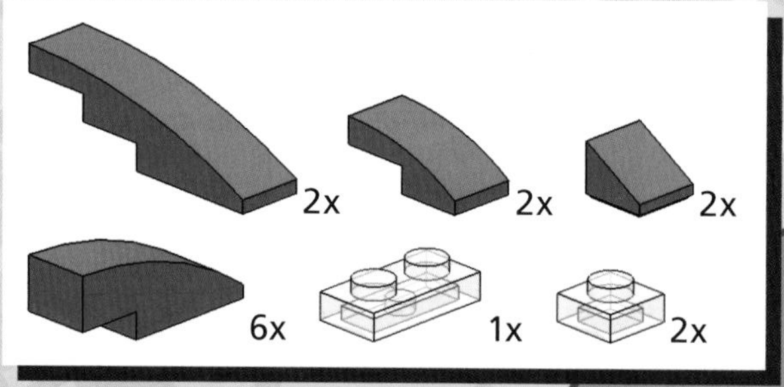

2x 2x 2x

6x 1x 2x

35

36
2x
1x
1x

37
2x
1x

38
1x
2x
2x

39
1x
2x

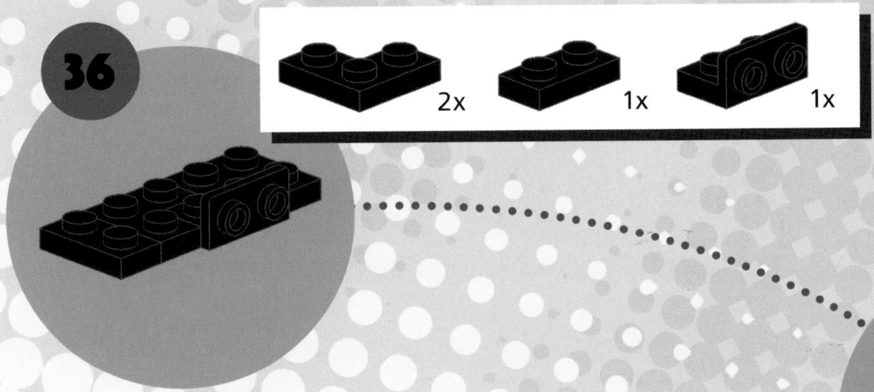

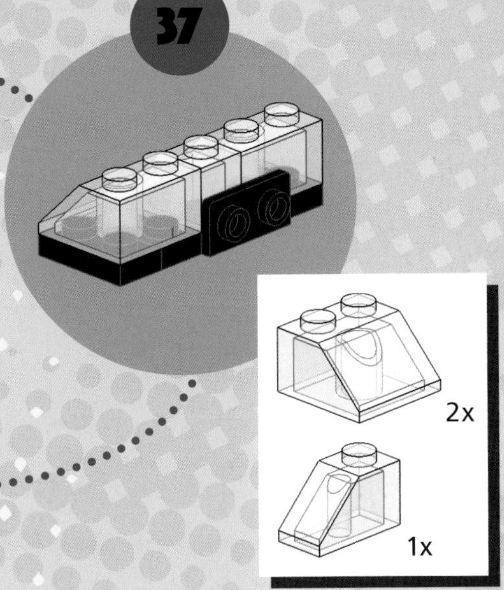

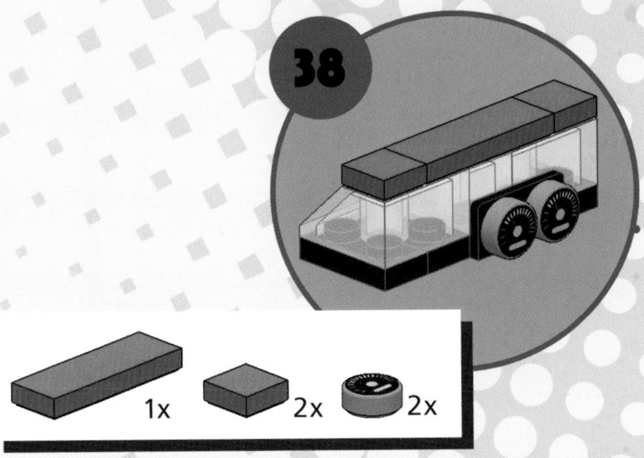

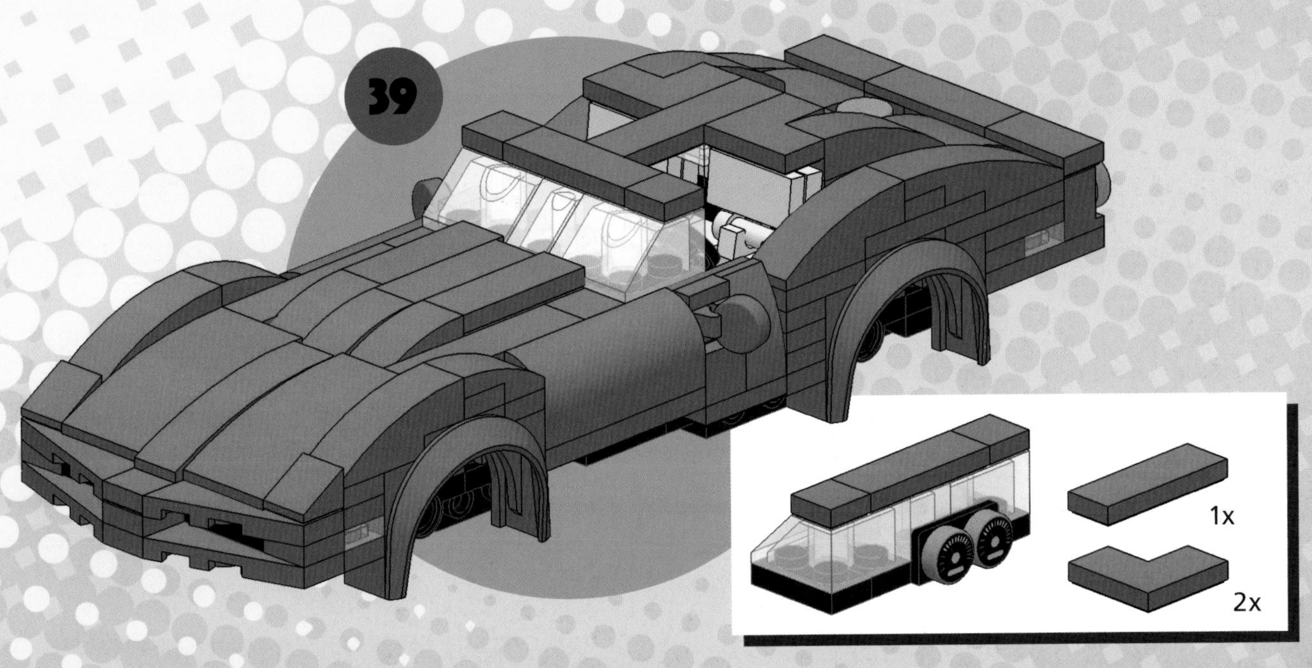

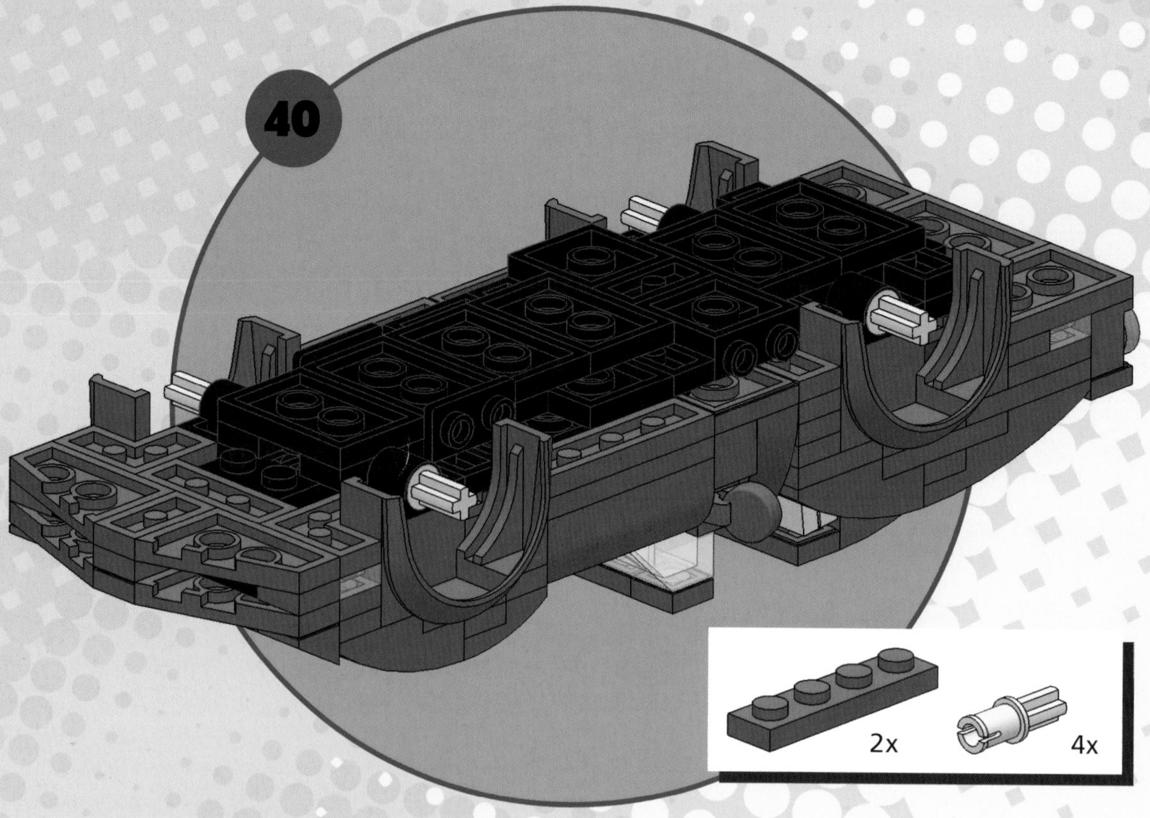

40

2x 4x

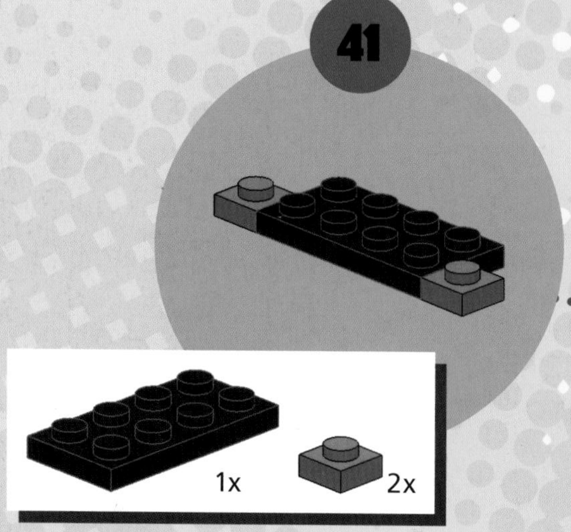

41

1x 2x

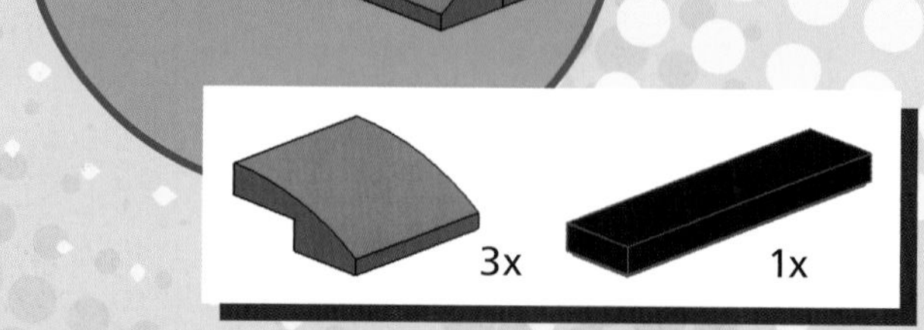

42

3x 1x

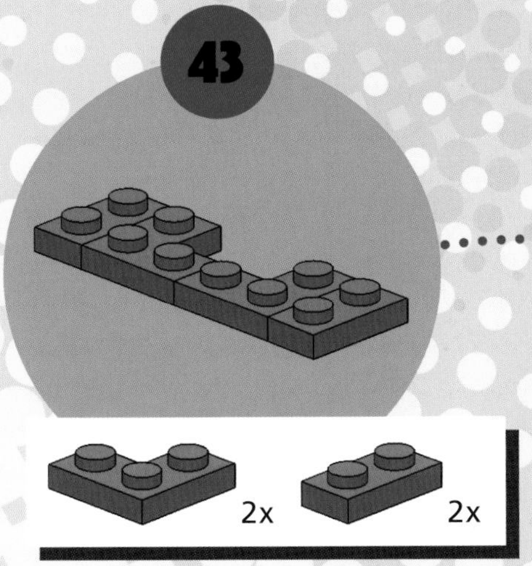

43

2x 2x

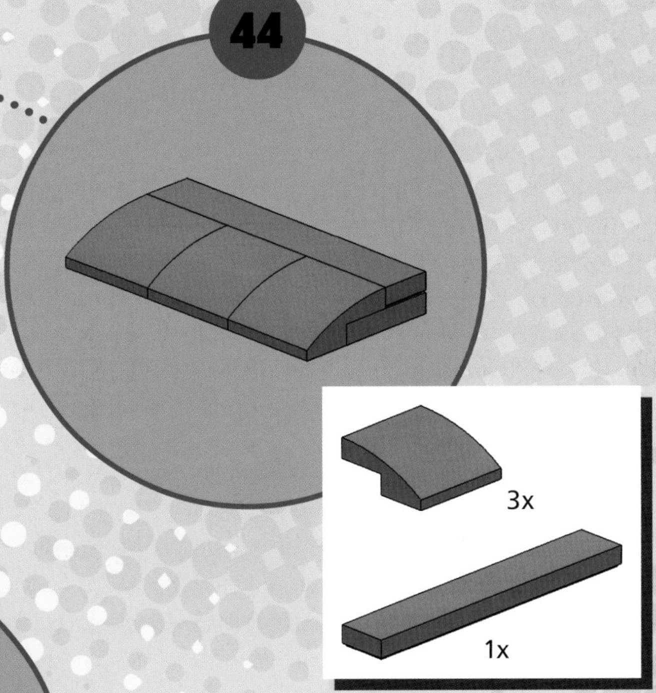

44

3x

1x

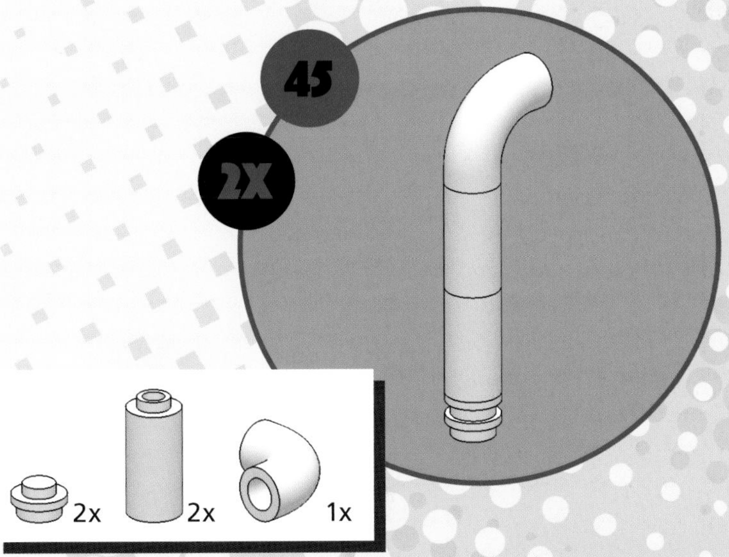

45

2X

2x 2x 1x

With small modifications you can also make a version without a side exhaust.

46

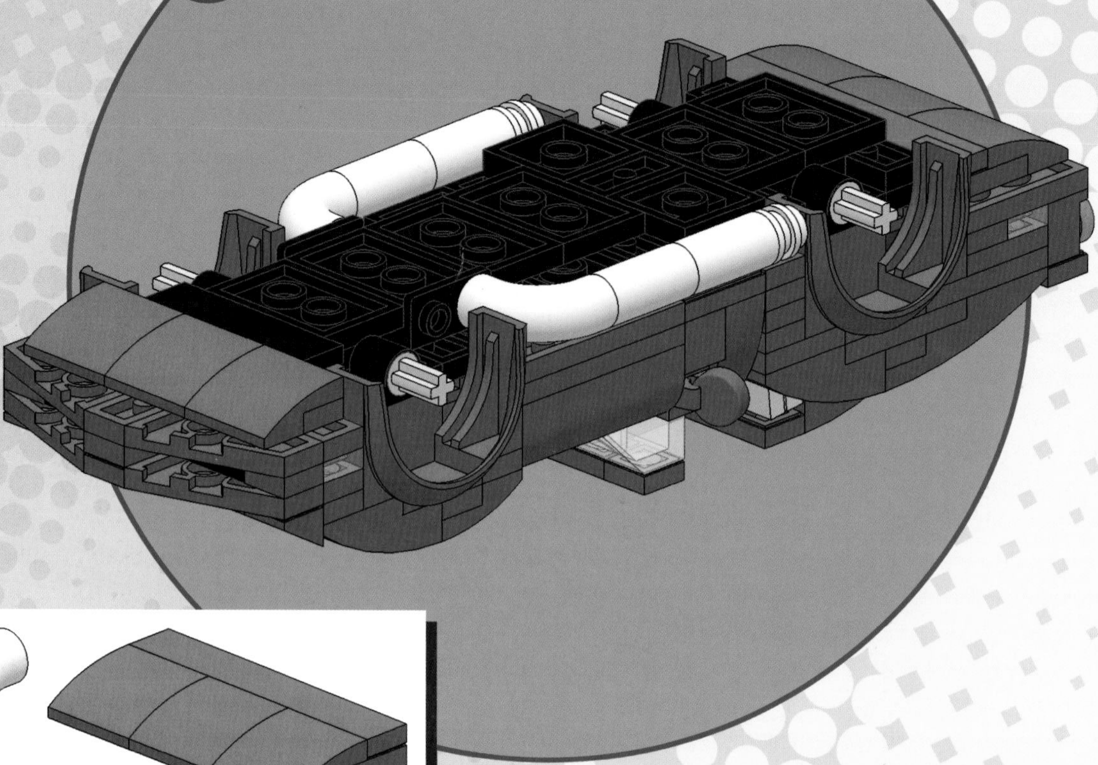

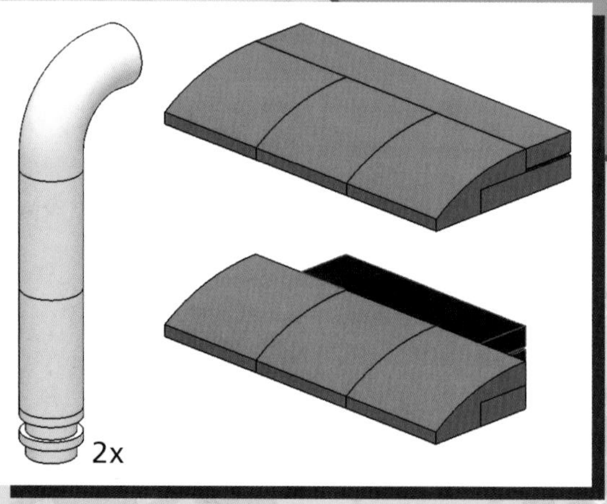

2x

47

4X

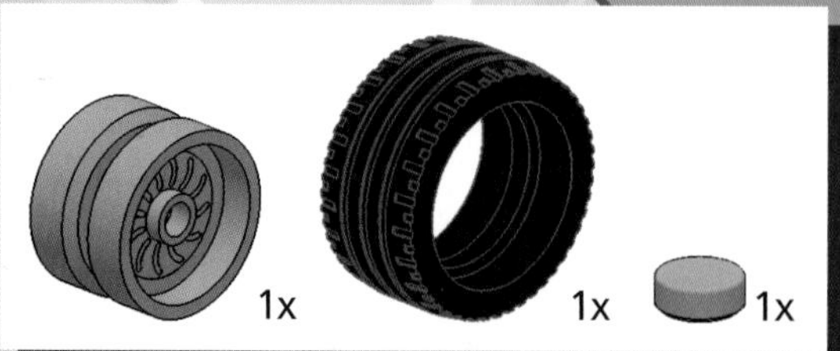

1x

1x

1x

48

4x

Look closely: A convertible can easily be turned into a model with a closed roof. You can also build the model in a different color.

PARTS LIST

Quantity	Color	Element	Element Name	LEGO® Number
2	Black	99781	Bracket 1 x 2 - 1 x 2 Down	6016172
1	Black	99780	Bracket 1 x 2 - 1 x 2 Up	6020193
2	Red	99207	Bracket 1 x 2 - 2 x 2 Up	6001806
4	Red	4070	Brick 1 x 1 with Headlight	407021
2	Red	87087	Brick 1 x 1 with Stud on 1 Side	4558886
4	Chrome Silver	71075a	Brick 1 x 1 x 1.667 Round	
2	Black	3622	Brick 1 x 3	362226
2	Red	3009	Brick 1 x 6	300921
2	Blue	2357	Brick 2 x 2 Corner	235723, 4533323, 4558606
2	Red	6081	Brick 2 x 4 x 1 & 1/3 with Curved Top	4116617
4	Red	18974	Car Mudguard 4 x 2.5 x 2.333	6102586
1	Black	3829c01	Car Steering Stand and Wheel (Complete)	73081
2	Chrome Silver	71076a	Cylinder 2 x 2 Elbow	
1	Black	4592c01	Hinge Control Stick and Base (Complete)	
2	Black	4276b	Hinge Plate 1 x 2 with 2 Fingers and Hollow Studs	
2	Black	2452	Hinge Plate 1 x 2 with 3 Fingers On Side	
6	Black	3024	Plate 1 x 1	302426
1	Metallic Silver	3024	Plate 1 x 1	4528732
17	Red	3024	Plate 1 x 1	302421
1	Tan	3024	Plate 1 x 1	4159553
5	Trans Clear	3024	Plate 1 x 1	3000840
4	Trans Orange	3024	Plate 1 x 1	4542673
4	Chrome Silver	4073	Plate 1 x 1 Round	
8	Black	3023	Plate 1 x 2	302326
15	Red	3023	Plate 1 x 2	302321
4	Tan	3023	Plate 1 x 2	4113917
1	Trans Clear	3023	Plate 1 x 2	4167842, 622540

Quantity		Color	Element	Element Name	LEGO® Number
2		Tan	48336	Plate 1 x 2 with Handle Type 2	4217562
1		Black	3623	Plate 1 x 3	362326
15		Red	3623	Plate 1 x 3	362321
1		Tan	3623	Plate 1 x 3	4121921
1		Black	3710	Plate 1 x 4	371026
7		Red	3710	Plate 1 x 4	371021
4		Red	3666	Plate 1 x 6	366621
1		Black	4477	Plate 1 x 10	447726
1		Black	60479	Plate 1 x 12	4514845
5		Black	3022	Plate 2 x 2	302226
4		Red	3022	Plate 2 x 2	302221, 4613974
1		Tan	3022	Plate 2 x 2	4114084
8		Black	2420	Plate 2 x 2 Corner	242026
2		Blue	2420	Plate 2 x 2 Corner	242023
8		Red	2420	Plate 2 x 2 Corner	242021
1		Tan	2420	Plate 2 x 2 Corner	4114077
4		Black	10247	Plate 2 x 2 with Hole and Complete Underside Rib	6061032
2		Black	99206	Plate 2 x 2 x 0.667 with Two Studs On Side and Two Raised	6052126
13		Black	3021	Plate 2 x 3	302126
4		Red	3021	Plate 2 x 3	302121
5		Black	3020	Plate 2 x 4	302026
2		Red	3020	Plate 2 x 4	302021
3		Red	54200	Slope Brick 31 1 x 1 x 0.667	4244371, 4504379, 5074621
1		Trans Clear	3040	Slope Brick 45 2 x 1	4130390
2		Trans Clear	3039	Slope Brick 45 2 x 2	622740
7		Red	11477	Slope Brick Curved 2 x 1	6029946

Quantity	Color	Element	Element Name	LEGO® Number
8	Red	15068	Slope Brick Curved 2 x 2 x 0.667	6105976
6	Red	50950	Slope Brick Curved 3 x 1	4251162
3	Red	61678	Slope Brick Curved 4 x 1	4520782, 6045937
2	Red	93606	Slope Brick Curved 4 x 2	4613174
4	Tan	3749	Technic Axle Pin	4186017, 4666579, 65625
2	Flat Silver	98138pb010f	Tile 1 x 1 Round with Gauge with red pointer Pattern	6030333
5	Flat Silver	98138	Tile 1 x 1 Round with Groove	4655241
2	Red	98138	Tile 1 x 1 Round with Groove	6063445
4	Trans Red	98138	Tile 1 x 1 Round with Groove	4646864
4	Tan	2555	Tile 1 x 1 with Clip	4206665, 4542411
2	Red	93794	Tile 1 x 1 with Clip with Centre Notch	4617081
7	Red	3070b	Tile 1 x 1 with Groove	307021
5	Red	3069b	Tile 1 x 2 with Groove	306921
4	Tan	3069b	Tile 1 x 2 with Groove	30695, 4114026
5	Red	63864	Tile 1 x 3 with Groove	4533742
1	Black	2431	Tile 1 x 4 with Groove	243126
3	Red	2431	Tile 1 x 4 with Groove	243121
2	Red	6636	Tile 1 x 6	4113858
2	Red	14719	Tile 2 x 2 Corner	6078641
2	Red	3068b	Tile 2 x 2 with Groove	306821
1	Tan	3068b	Tile 2 x 2 with Groove	4185177, 4251986
4	Black	18977	Tyre 11.2/ 28 x 17.6 Intermediate	6102596
4	Flat Silver	18976	Wheel Rim 11 x 18 with Vented Disc Brake	6102594
2	Red	43723	Wing 2 x 3 Left	4180533, 4372321
2	Red	43722	Wing 2 x 3 Right	4180504, 4372221

2x

1x

2x

4x

2x

4x

2x

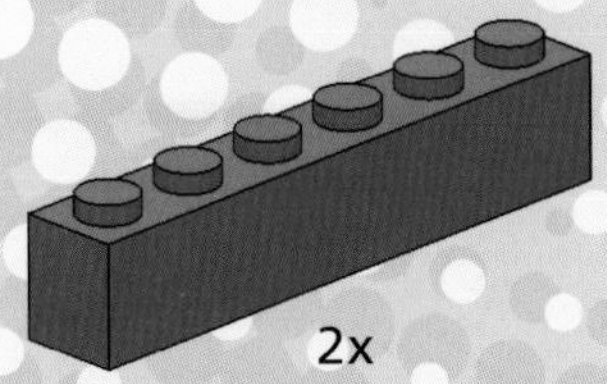
2x

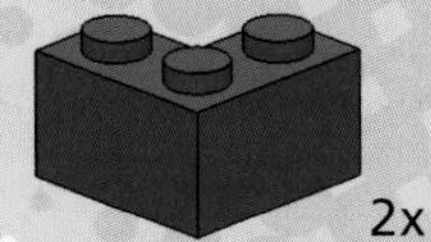
2x

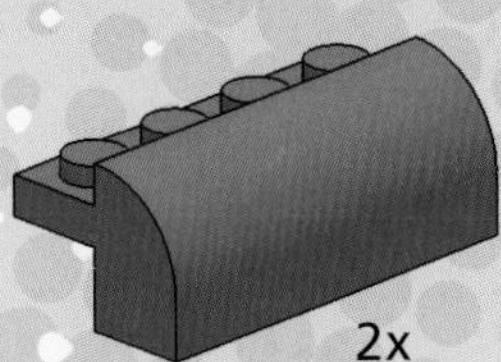
2x

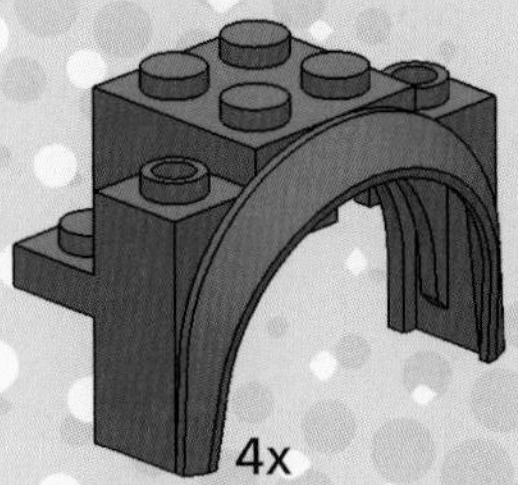
4x

1x

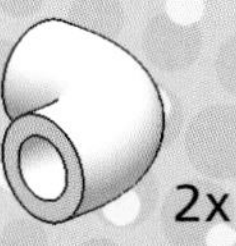
2x

1x

2x

2x

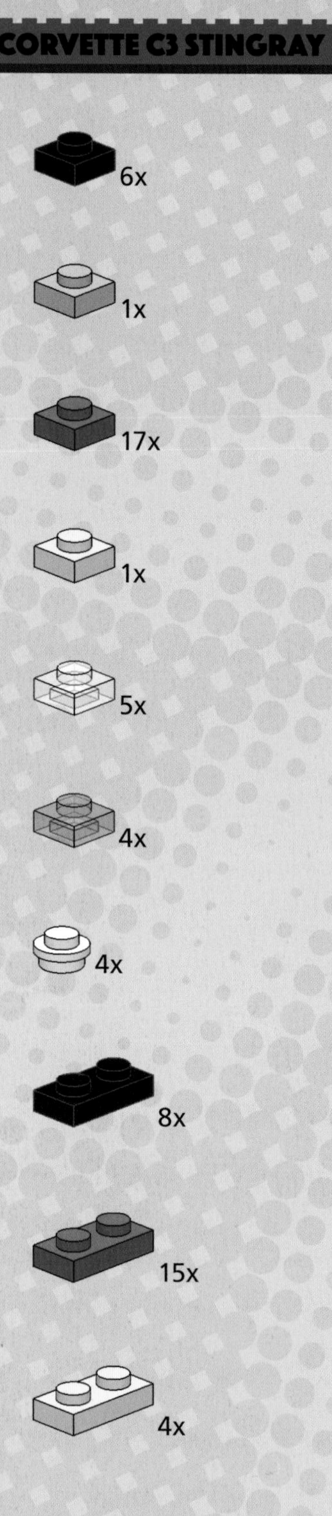
6x
1x
17x
1x
5x
4x
4x

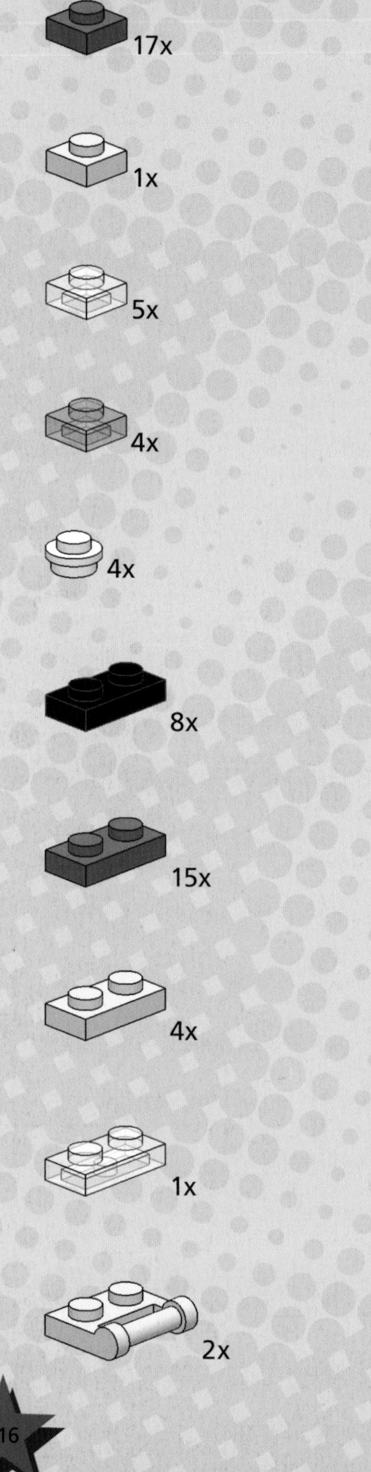
8x
15x
4x
1x

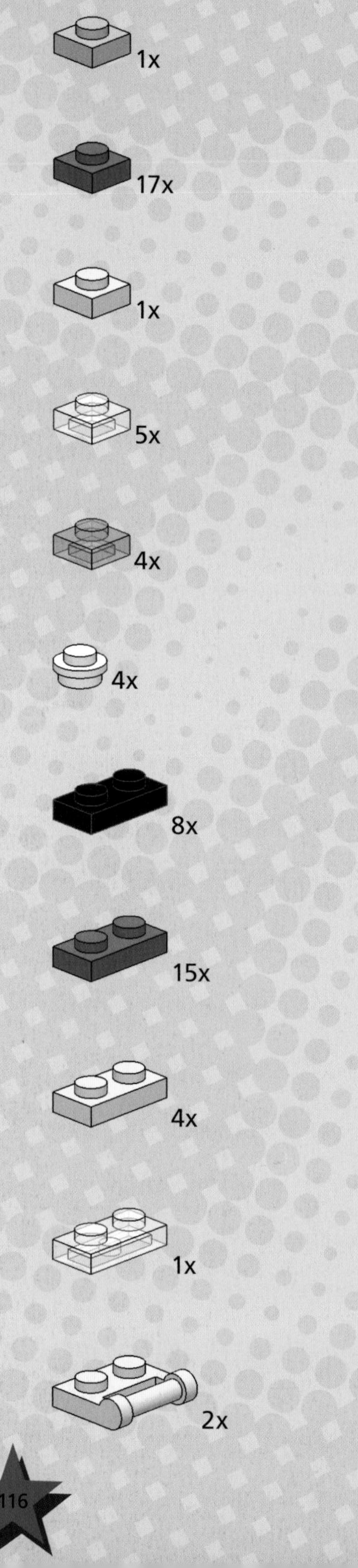
2x

1x

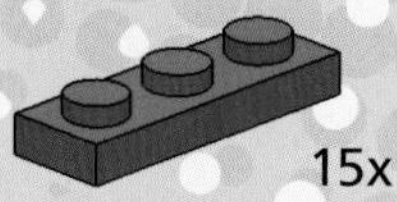
15x

1x

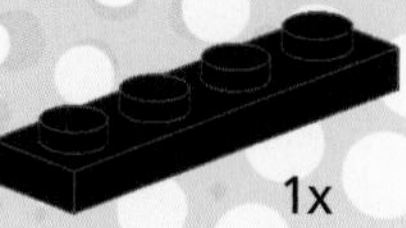
1x

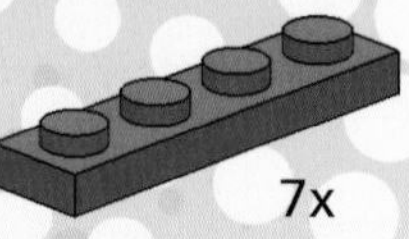
7x

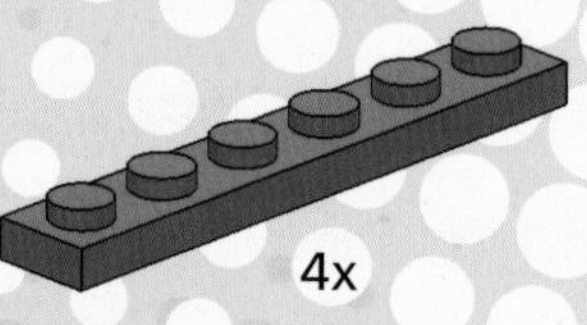
4x

1x

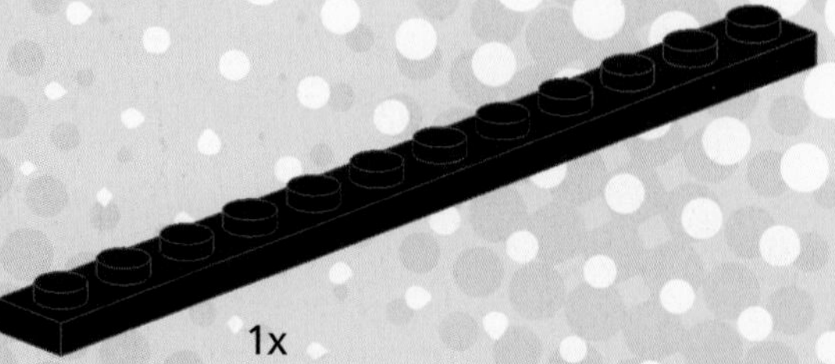
1x

5x

4x

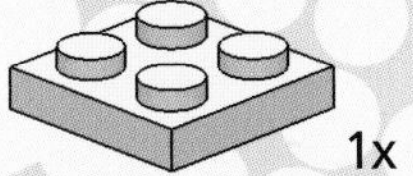
1x

8x

2x

8x

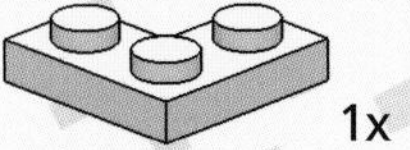
1x

4x

2x

13x

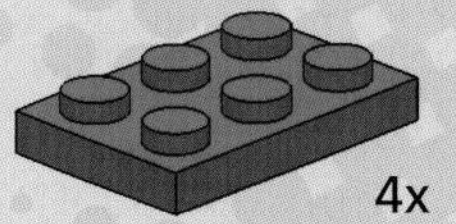
4x

5x

2x

3x

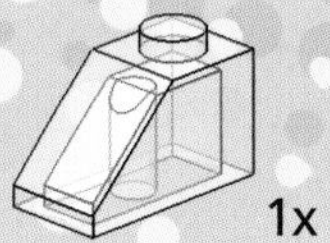
1x

2x

7x

8x

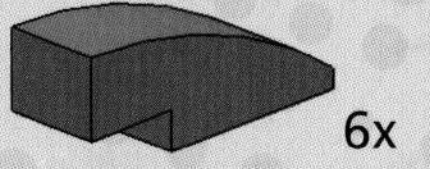
6x

3x

2x

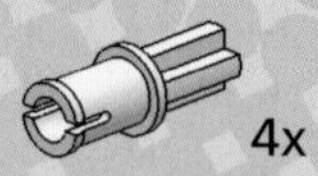
4x

2x

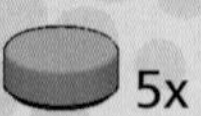
5x

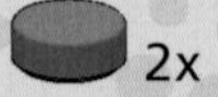
2x

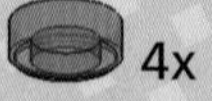
4x

4x

2x

7x

5x

4x

5x

1x

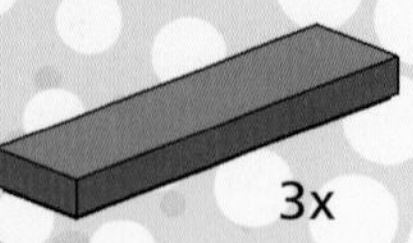
3x

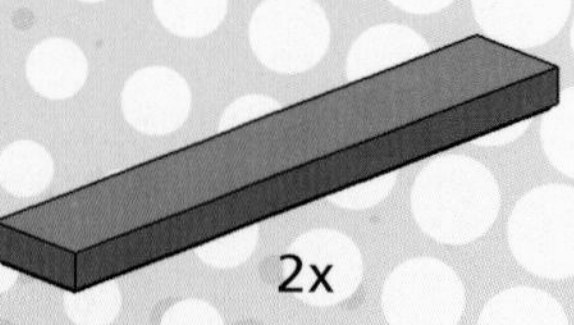
2x

2x

2x

1x

4x

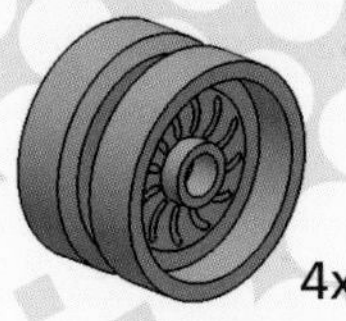
4x

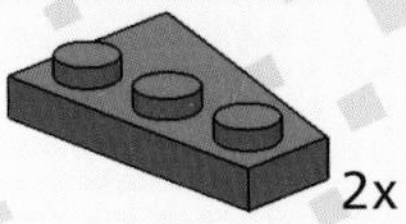
2x

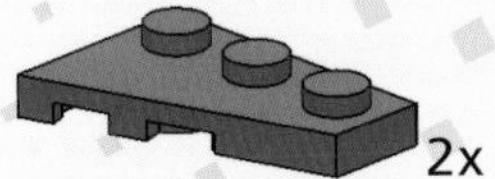
2x

Energy
WAX
1

Energy
WAX
1

LANCIA STRATOS HF

A legend! The Lancia Stratos HF was the first car in the world designed for a rally. It won the World Rally Championship three times in a row, in 1974, 1975, and 1976. A road version came out later, but only 495 of these were produced. You can see pictures of my red reconstructed version of this speedster later on.

WEIGHT:	*980 kg (1 t)*
TOP SPEED:	*80 km/h (50 mph)*
HP:	*280*
TANK CAPACITY:	*80 liters (21 gal.)*

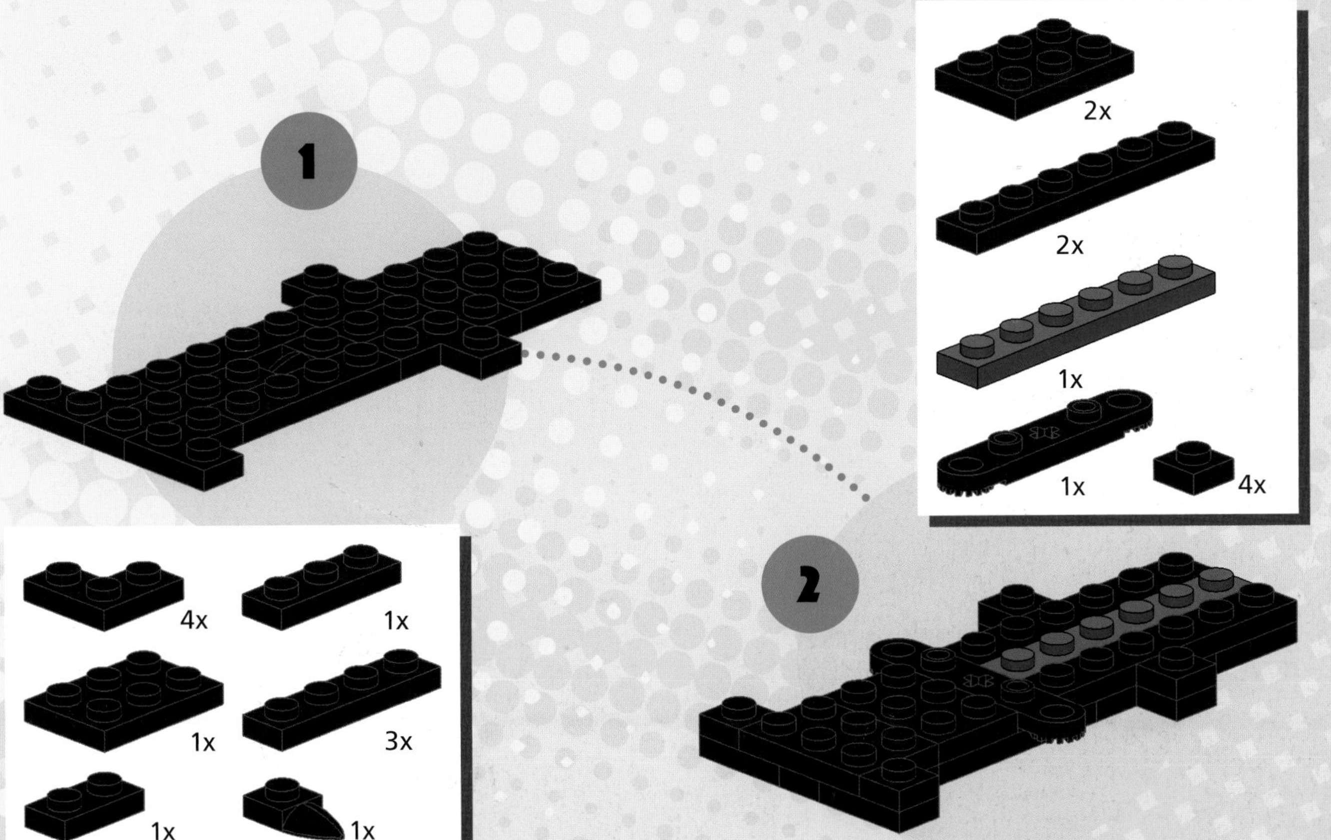

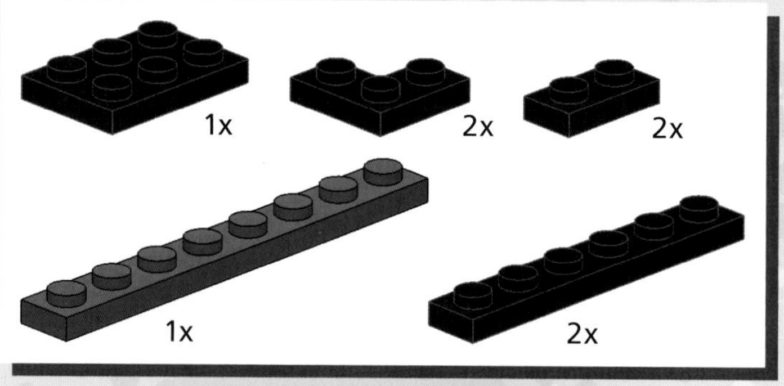

1x
2x
2x
1x
2x

3

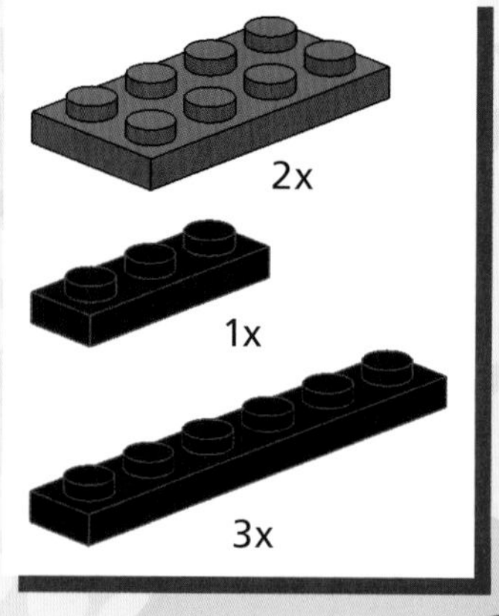

2x
1x
3x

4

5

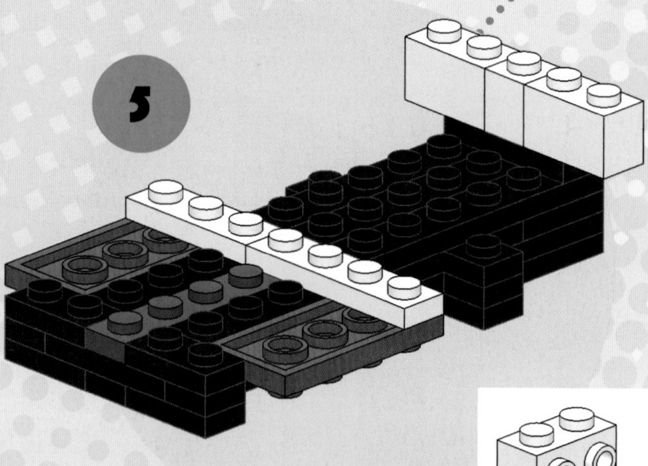

This brick only has a single side stud.

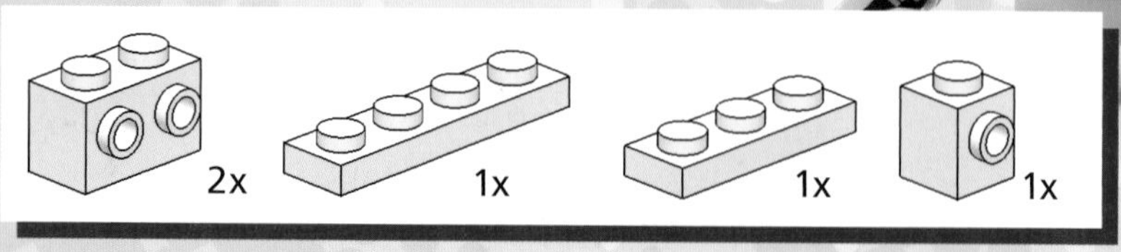

2x
1x
1x
1x

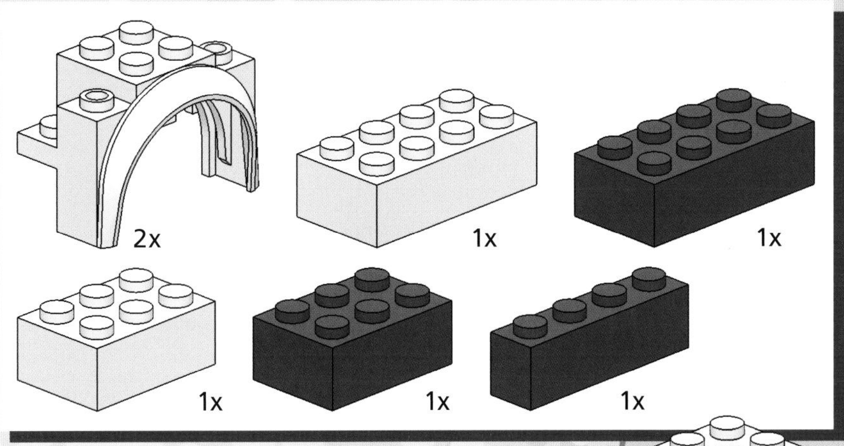

6

2x
1x
1x
1x
1x
1x

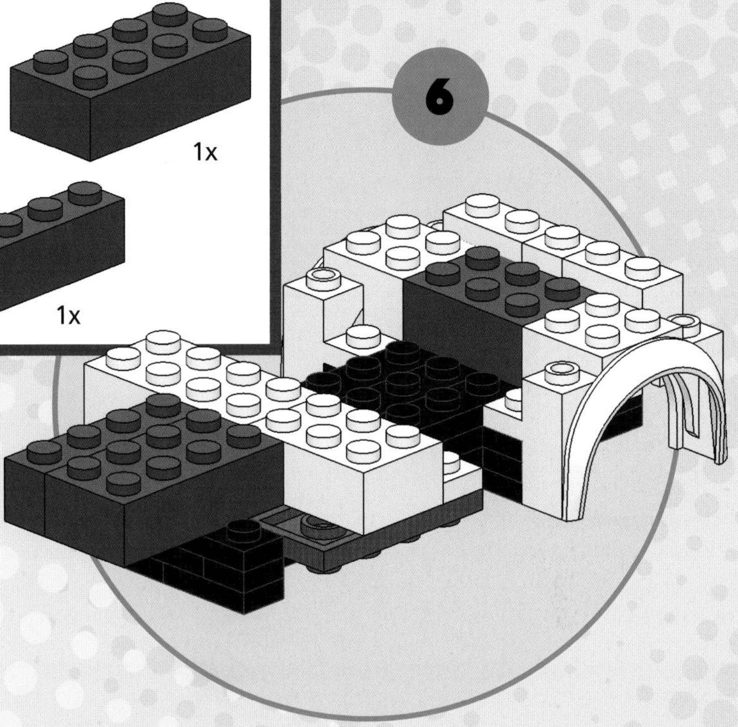

7

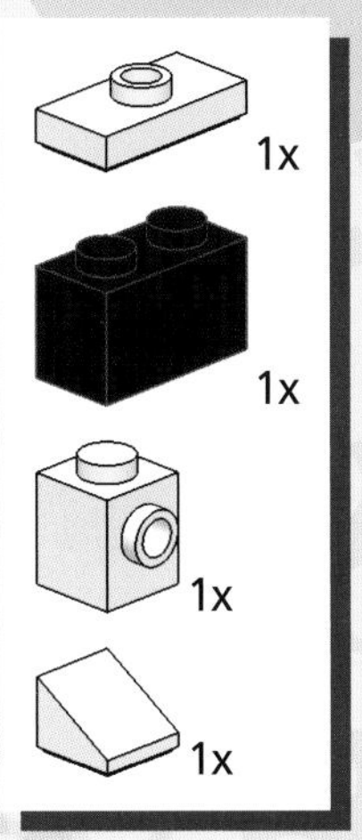

1x
1x
1x
1x

8

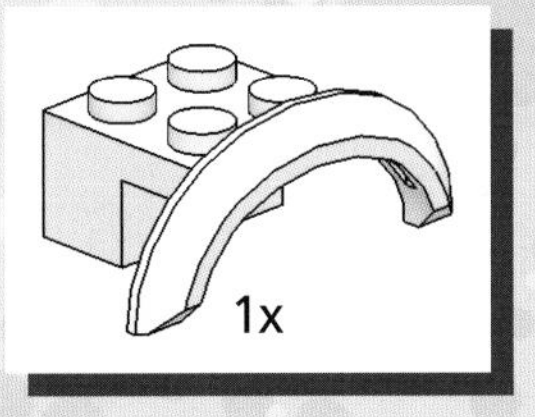

1x

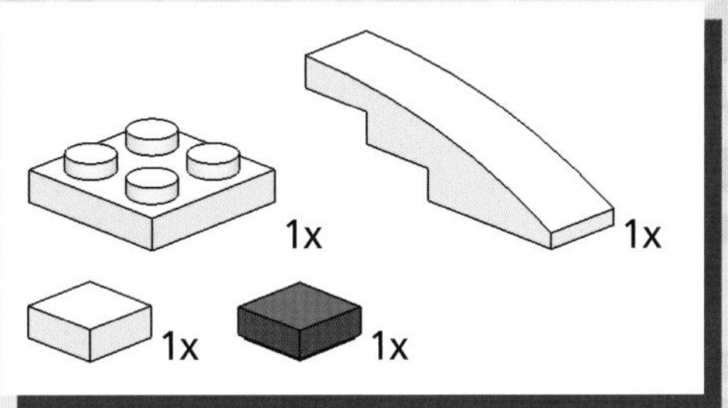

9

1x
1x
1x
1x

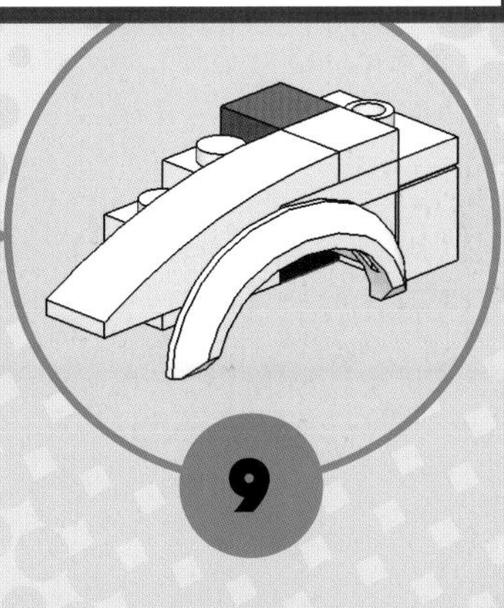

10

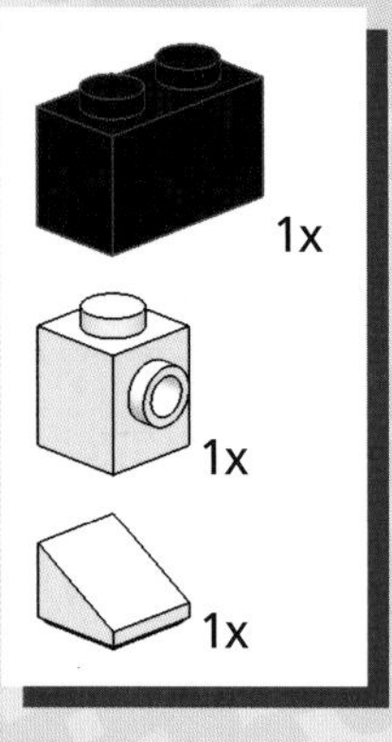

1x

1x

1x

11

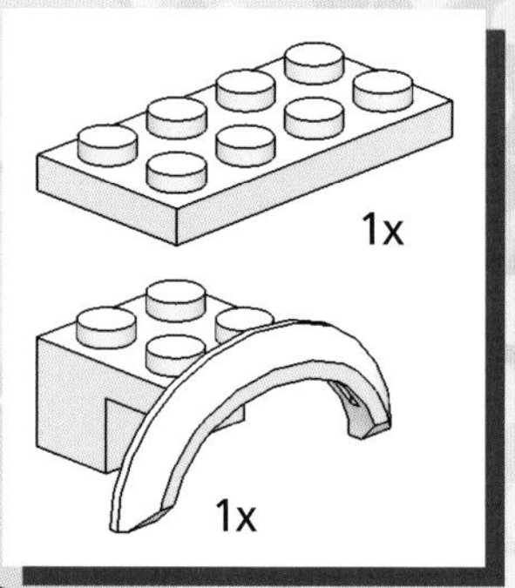

1x

1x

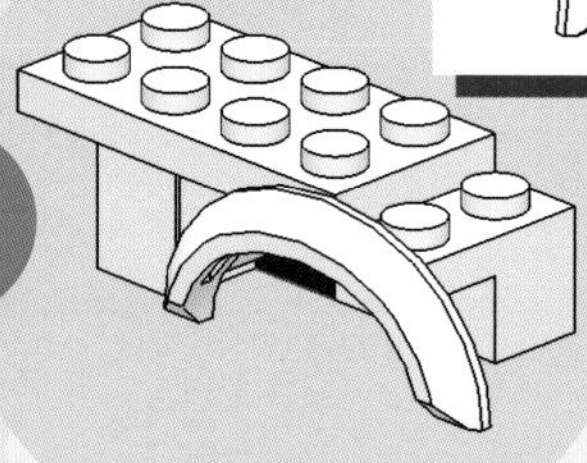

12

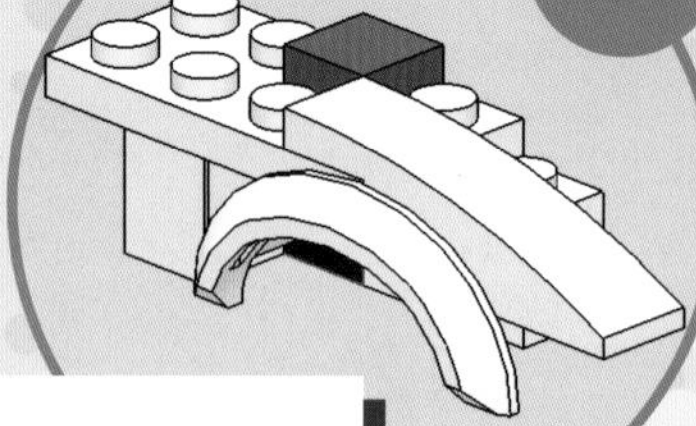

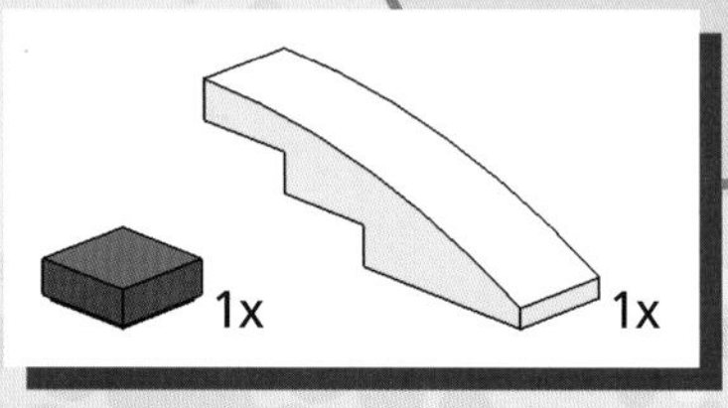

1x

1x

1x

1x

13

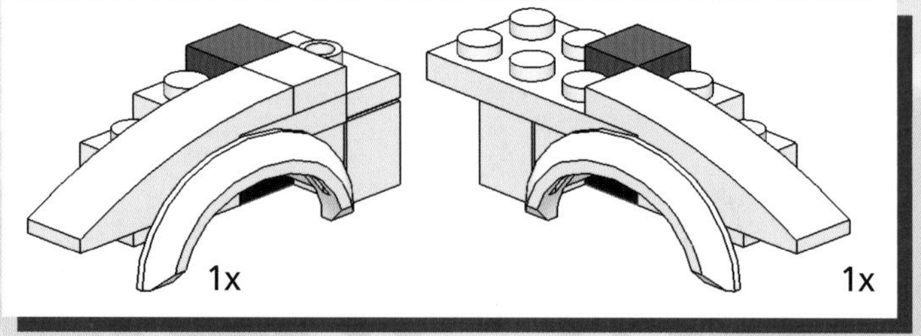

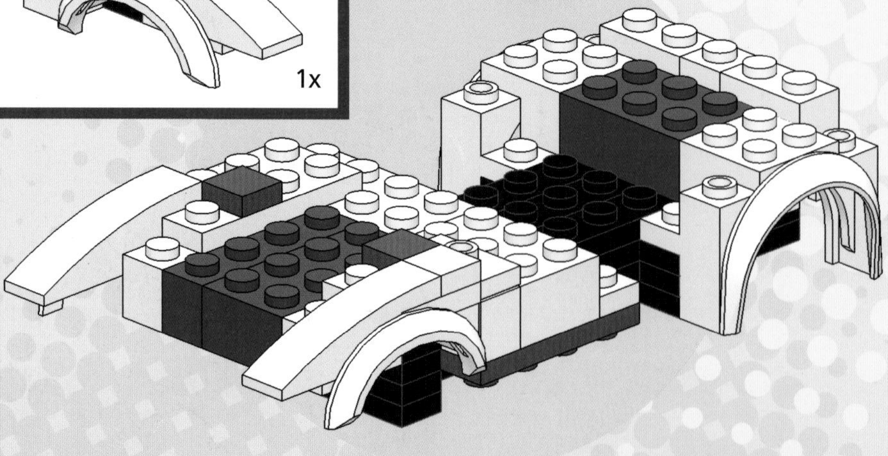

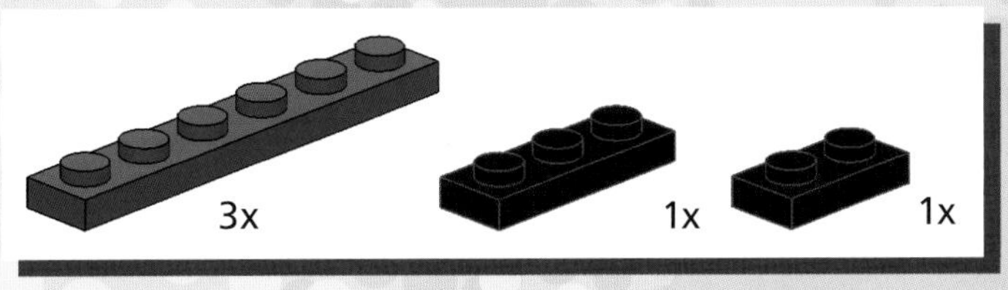

3x 1x 1x

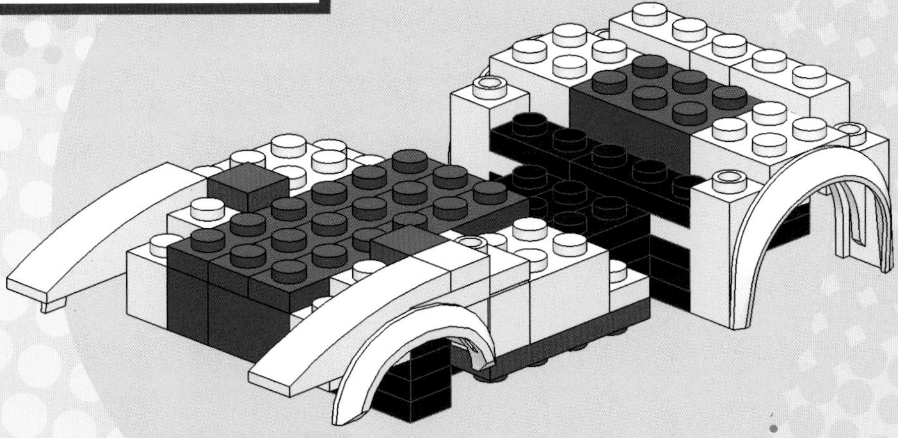

14

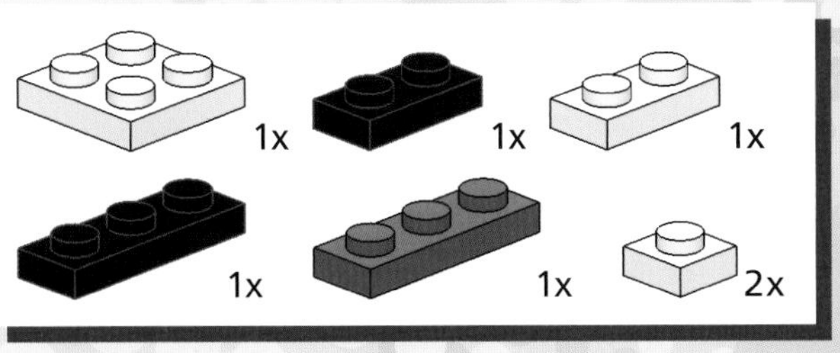

1x 1x 1x

1x 1x 2x

15

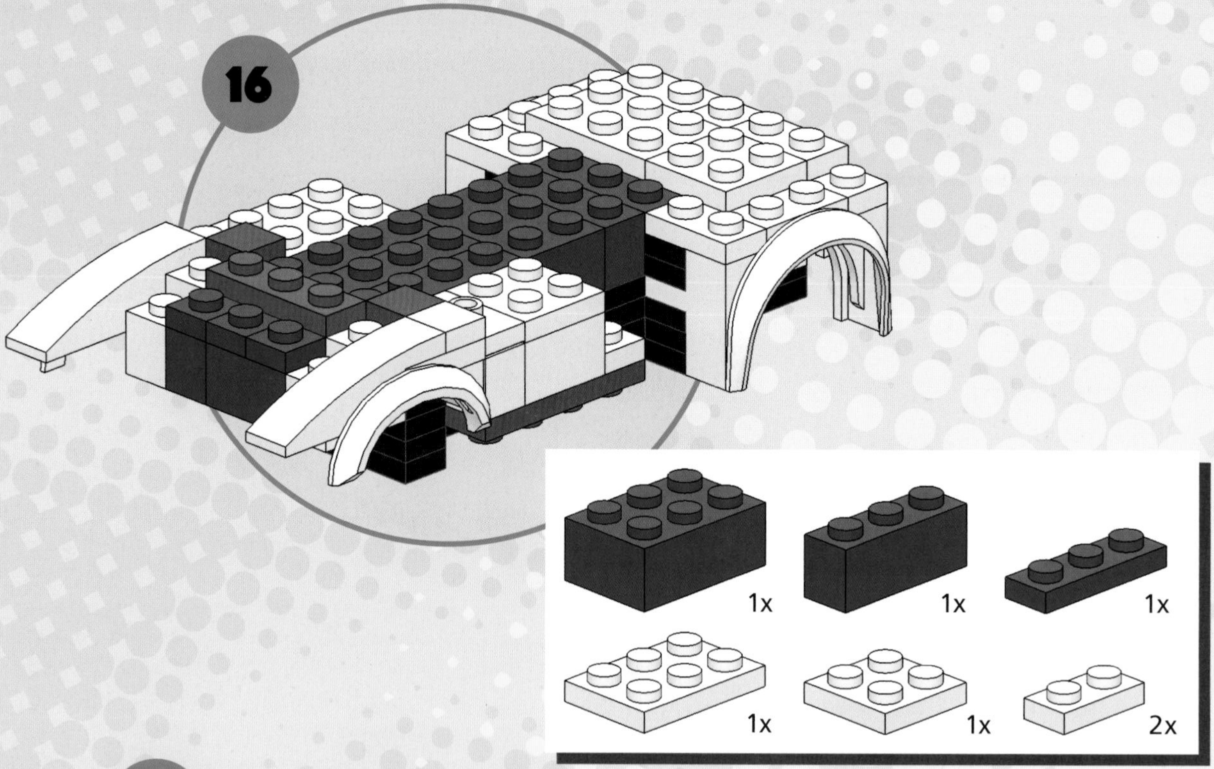

16

1x 1x 1x
1x 1x 2x

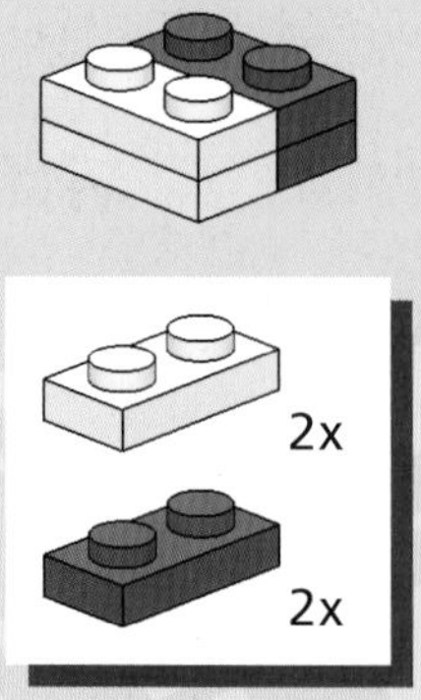

17

2x
2x

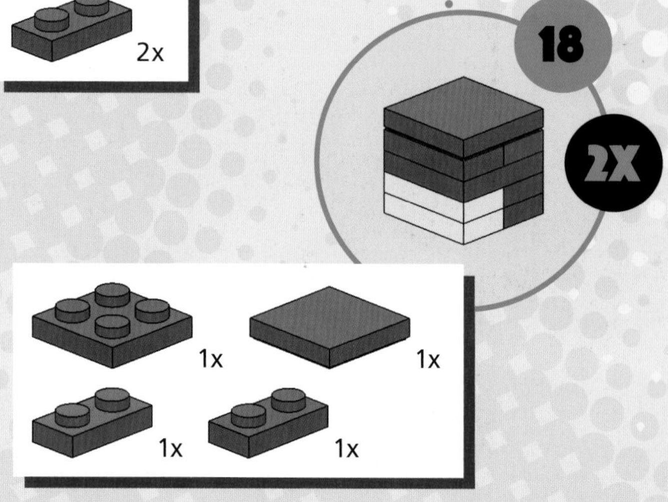

18

2X

1x 1x
1x 1x

These bricks only have a single side stud.

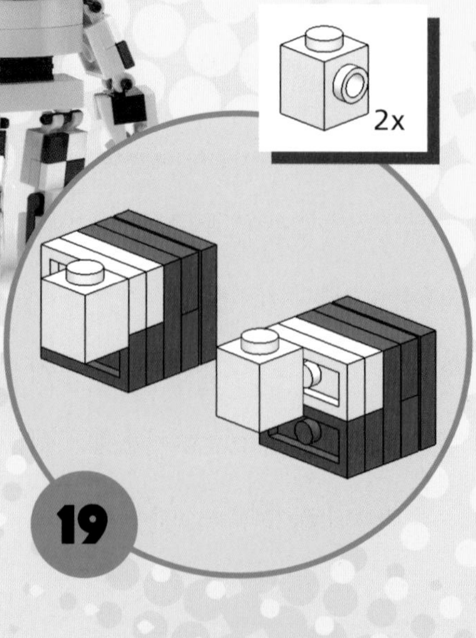

2x

19

20

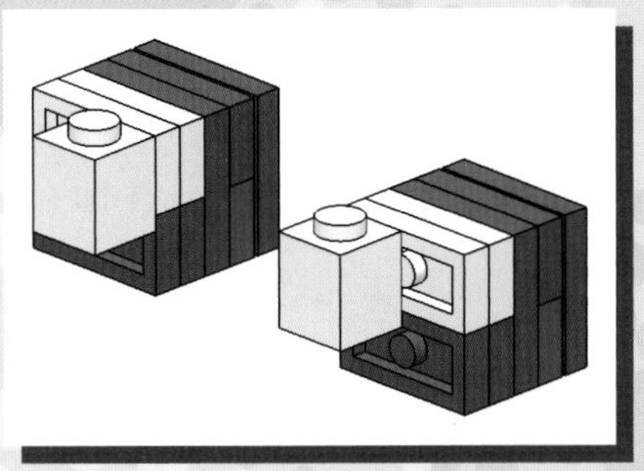

21

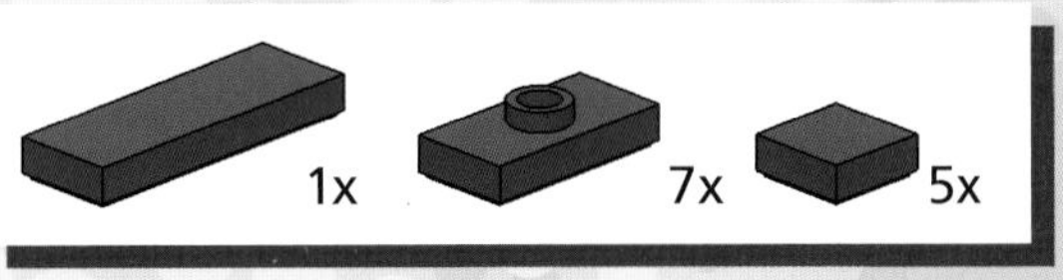

1x 7x 5x

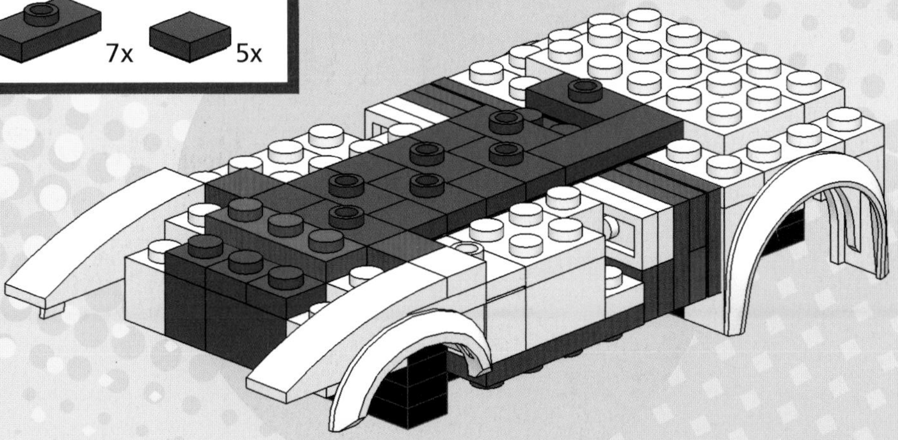

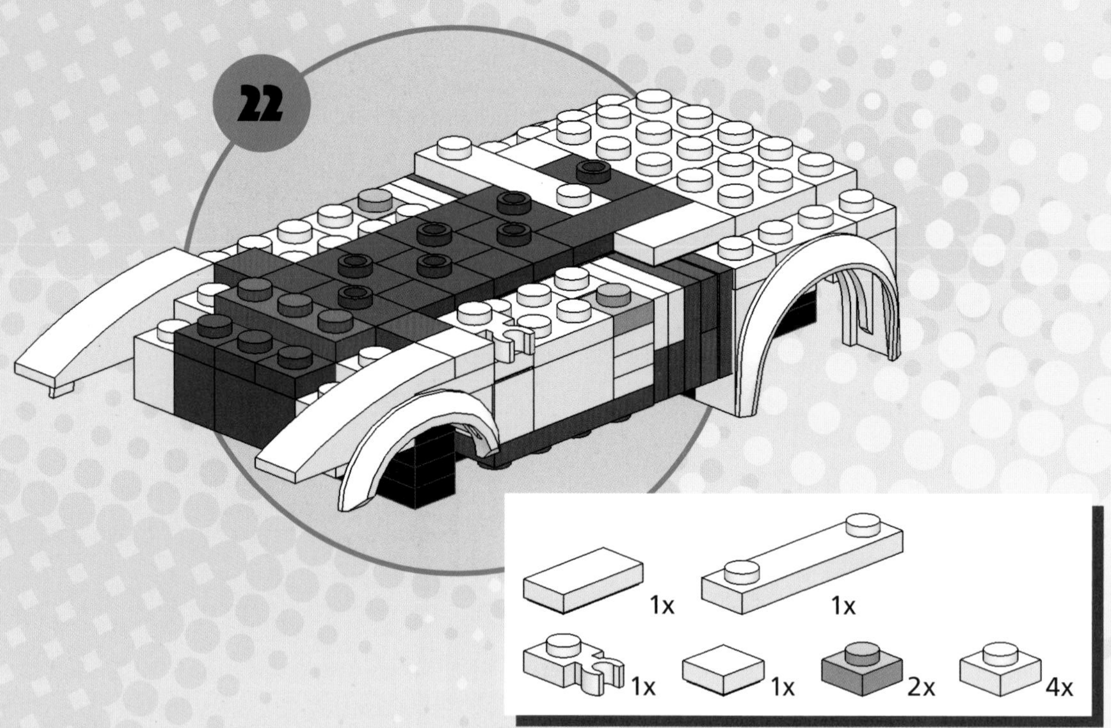
22
1x
1x
1x
1x
2x
4x

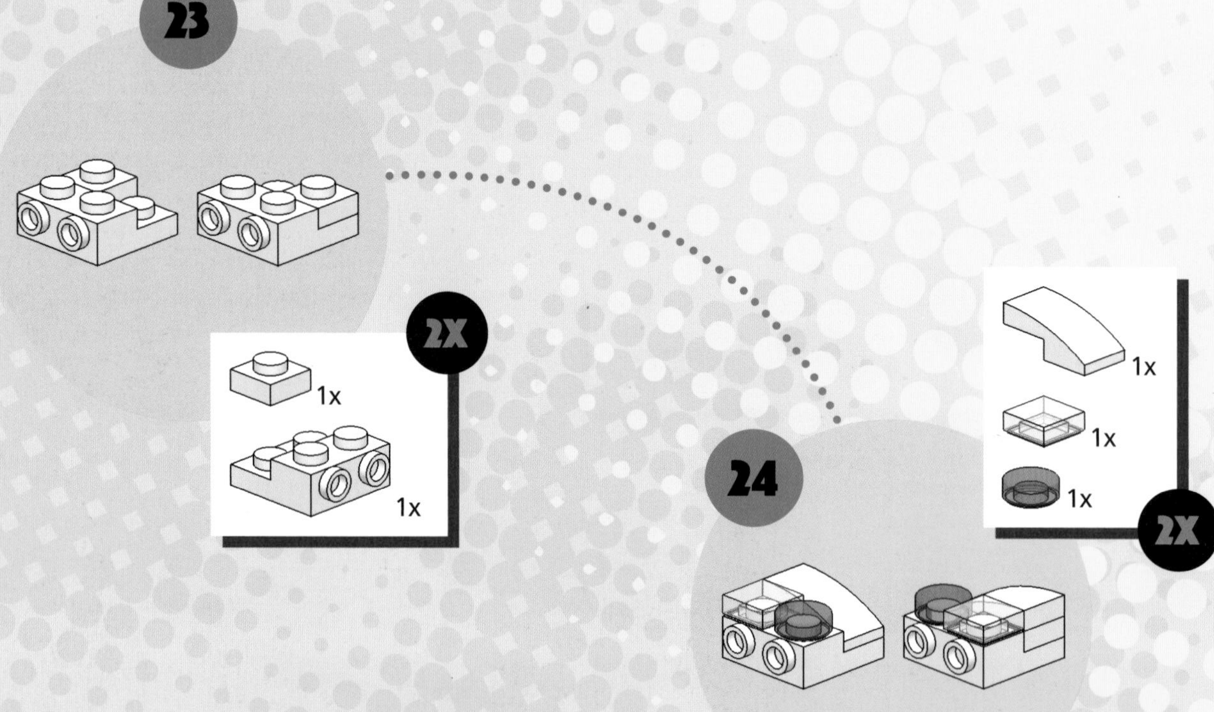
23
2X
1x
1x
24
1x
1x
1x
2X

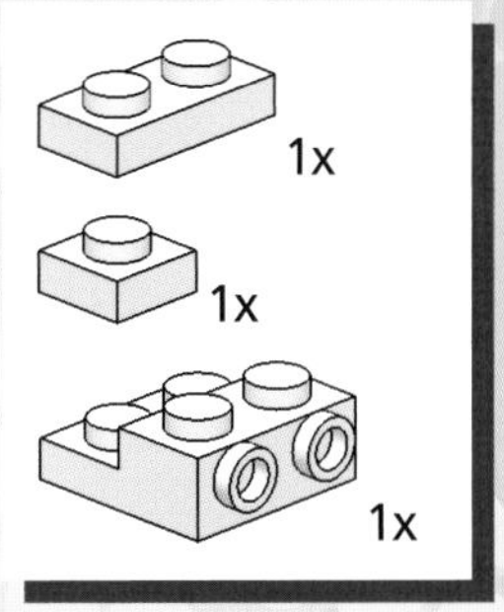

1x
1x
1x

25

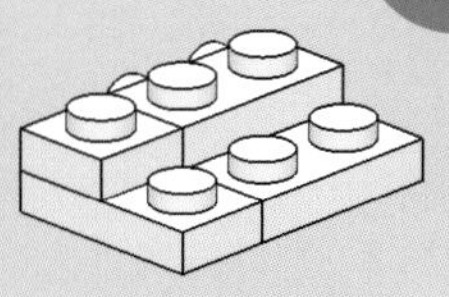

26

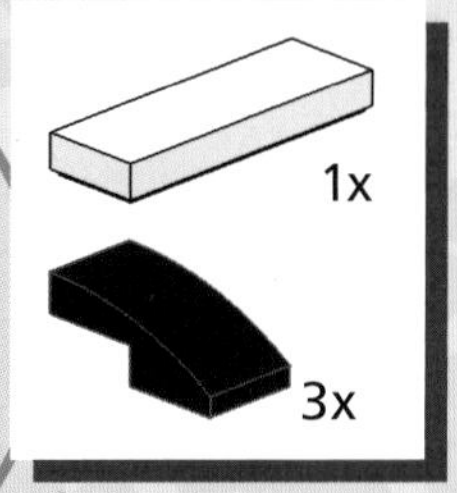

1x
3x

27

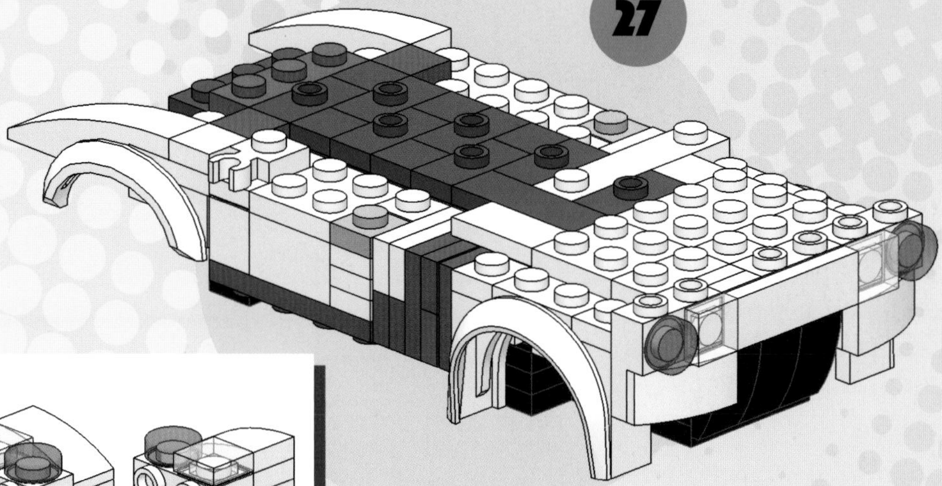

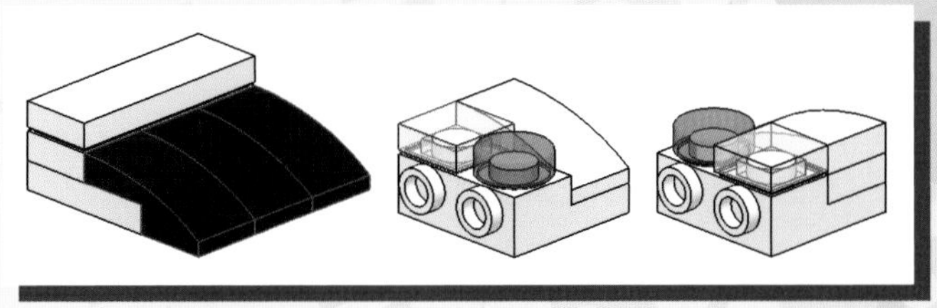

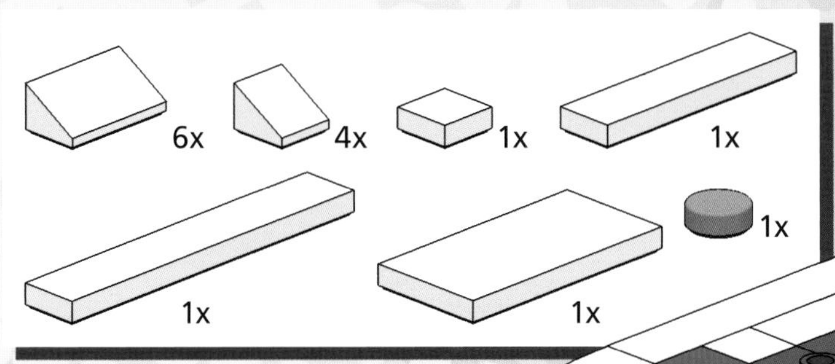

6x 4x 1x 1x
1x 1x 1x

28

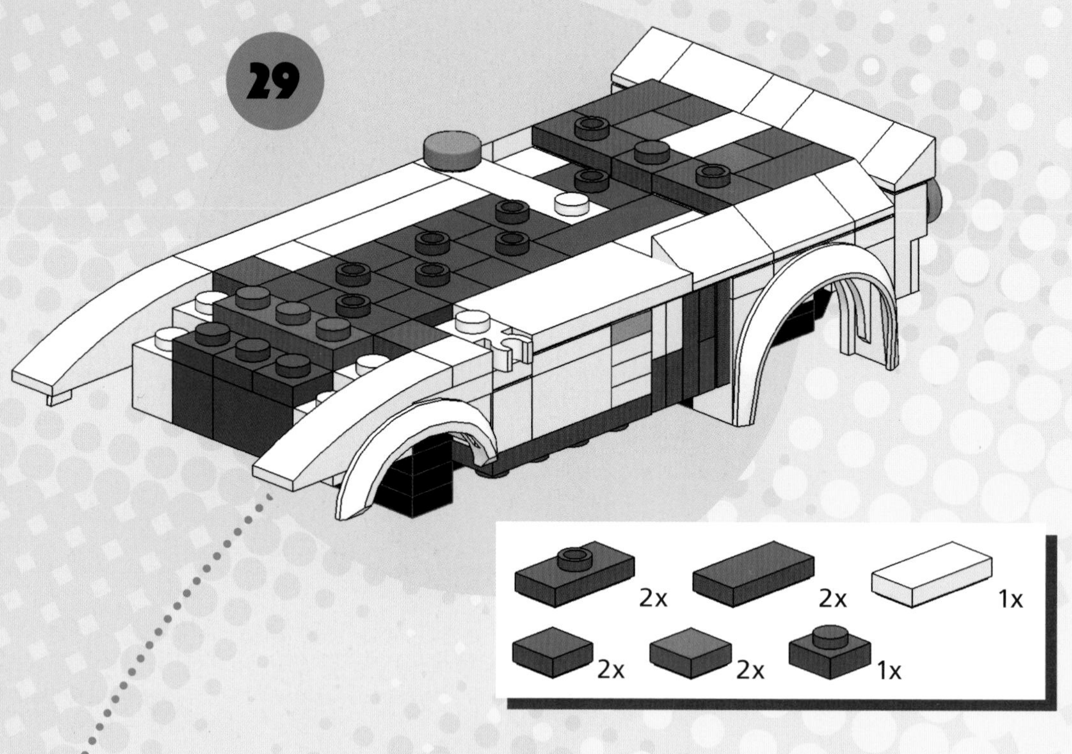
29
2x
2x
1x
2x
2x
1x

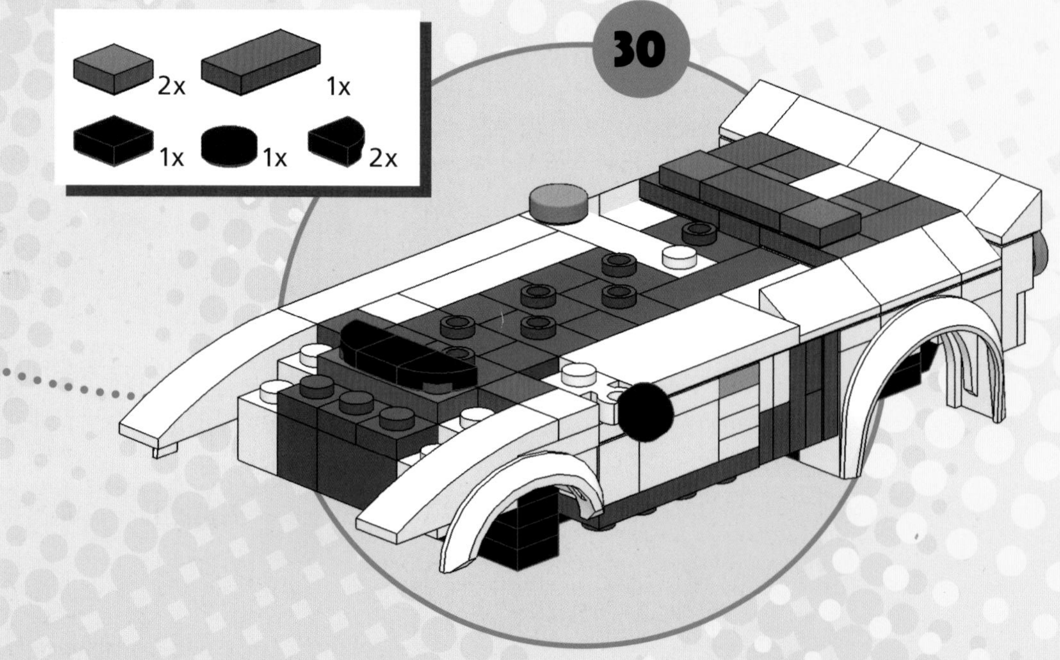
30
2x
1x
1x
1x
2x

31

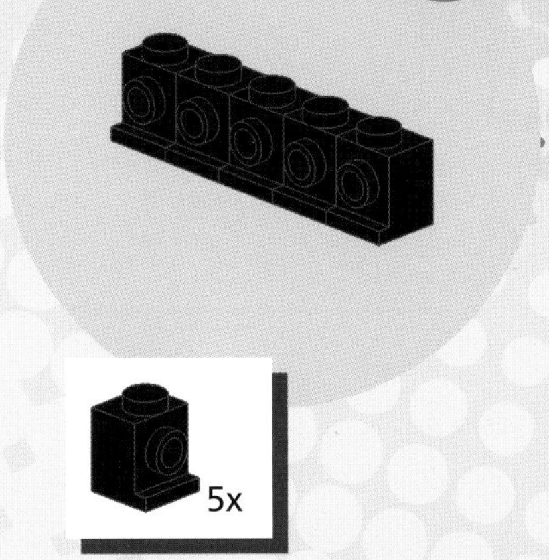

5x

32

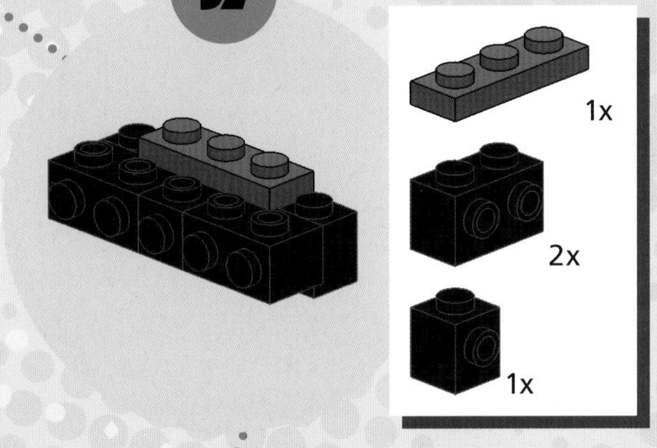

1x

2x

1x

33

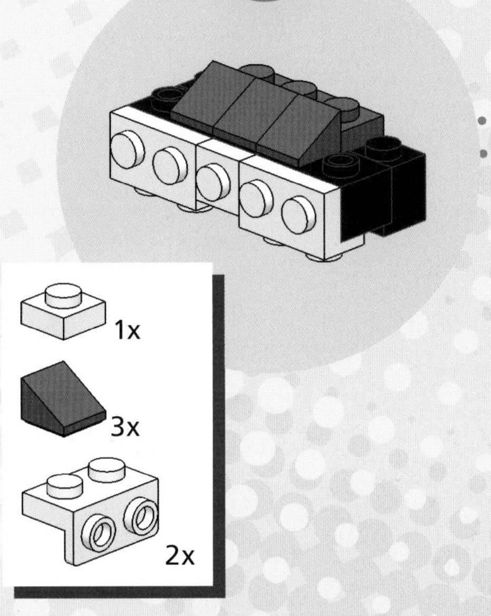

1x

3x

2x

34

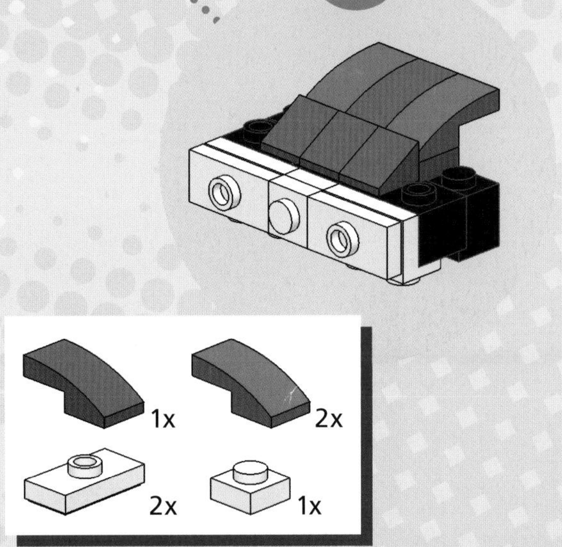

1x

2x

2x

1x

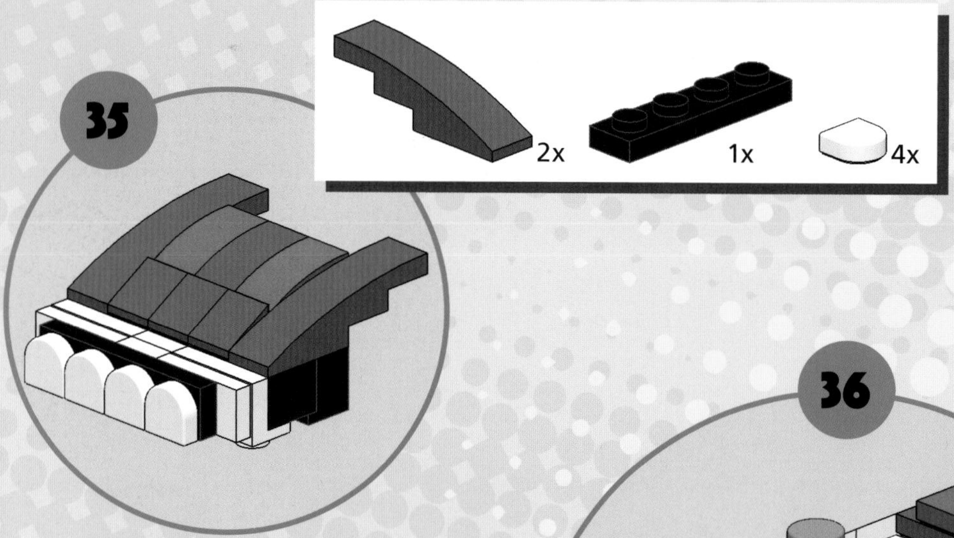

35

2x 1x 4x

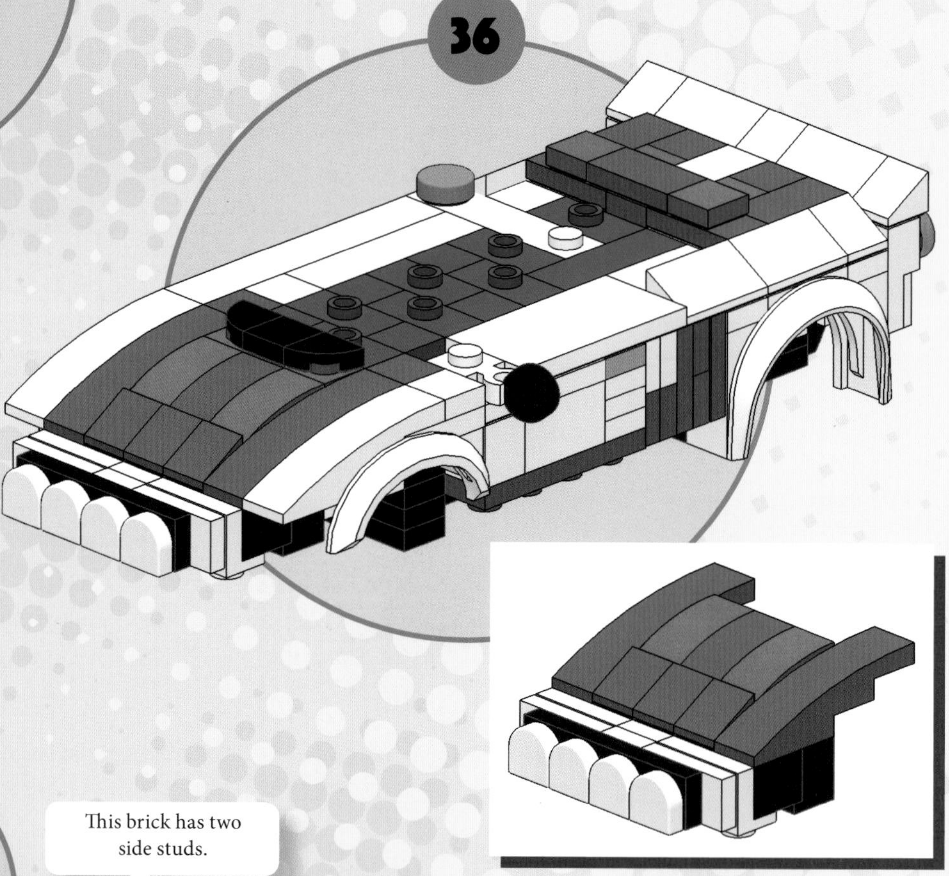

36

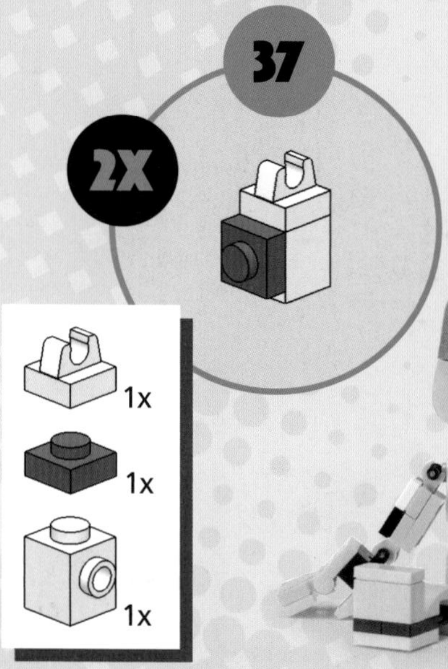

37

2X

1x
1x
1x

This brick has two side studs.

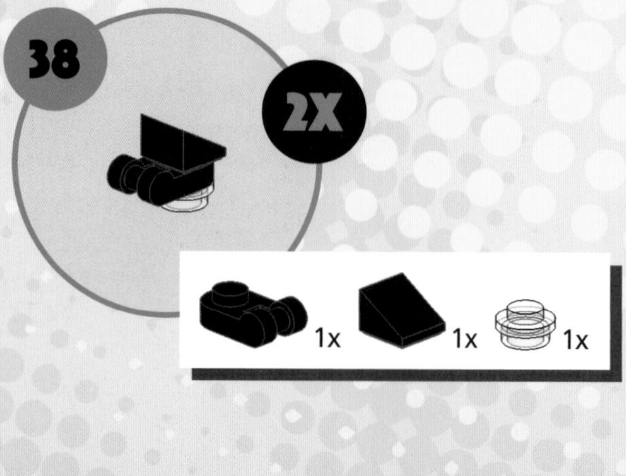

38

2X

1x 1x 1x

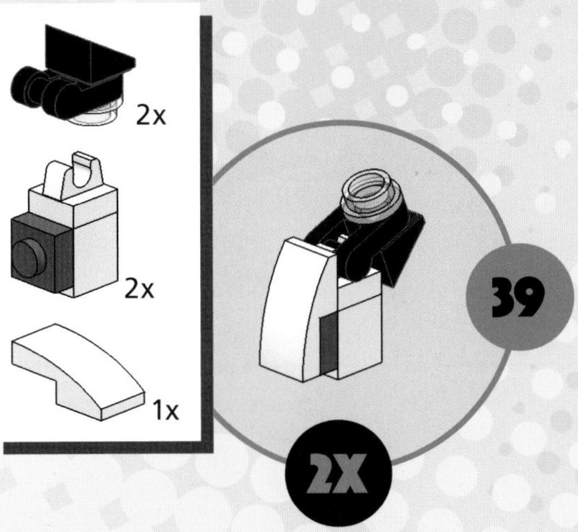

2x

2x

1x

39

2X

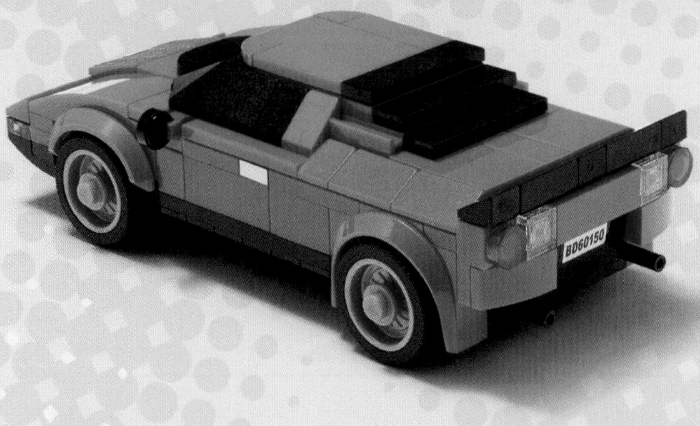

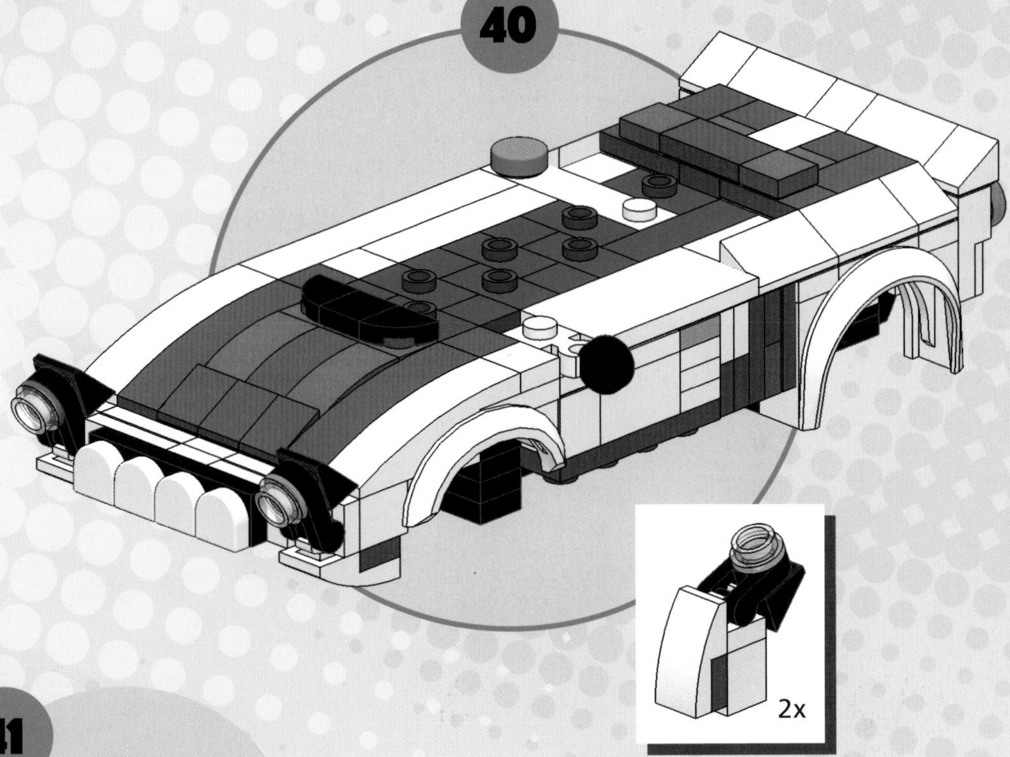

40

2x

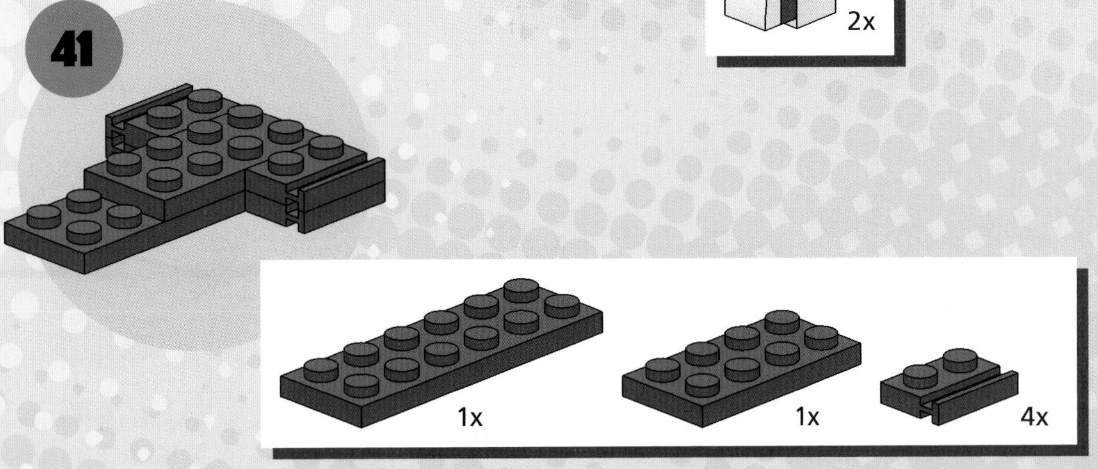

41

1x

1x

4x

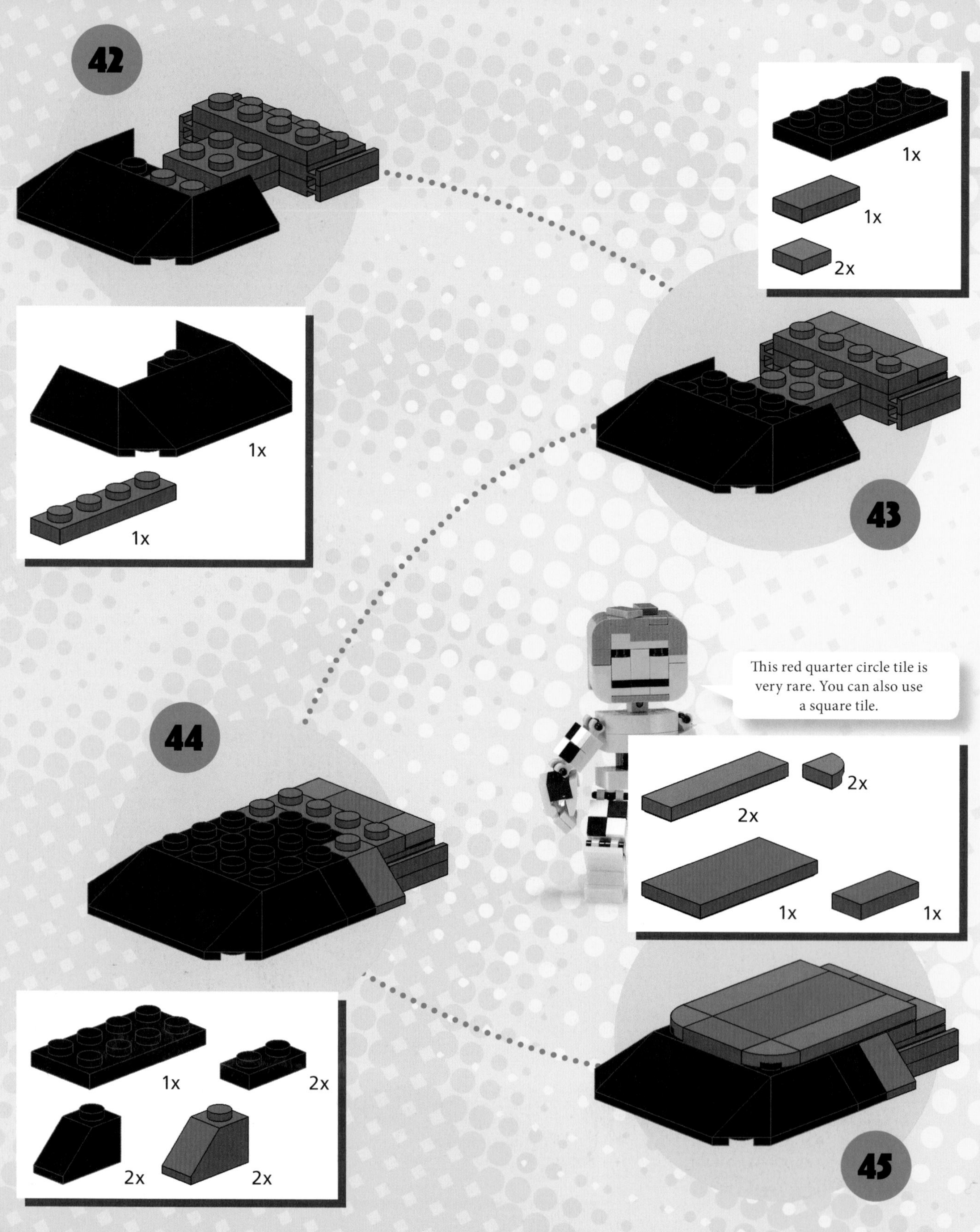
42
1x
1x
1x
1x
2x
43
This red quarter circle tile is very rare. You can also use a square tile.
44
2x
2x
1x
1x
1x
2x
2x
2x
45

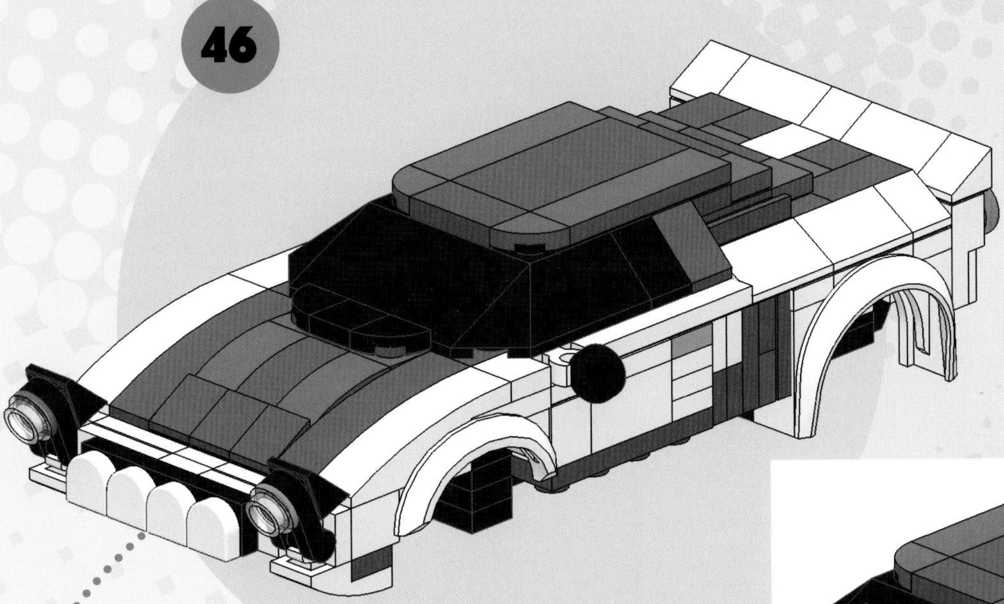

46

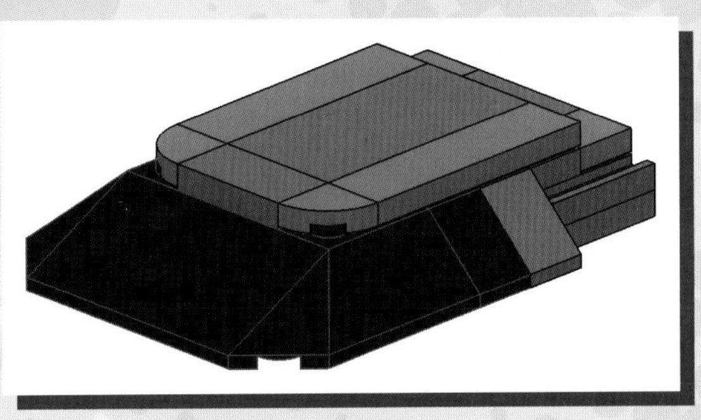

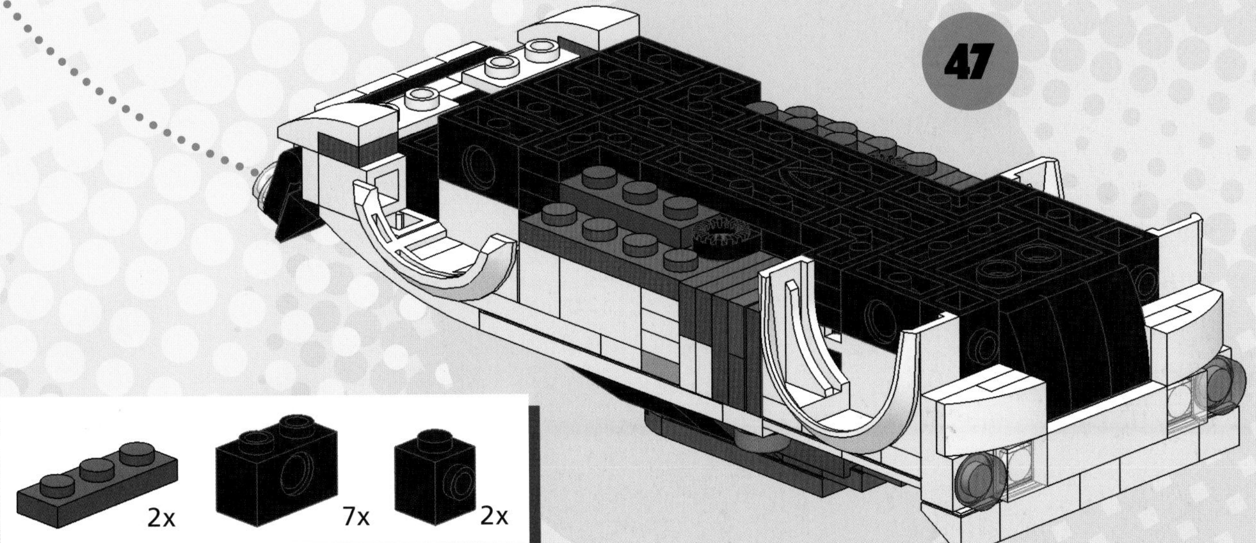

47

2x

7x

2x

48

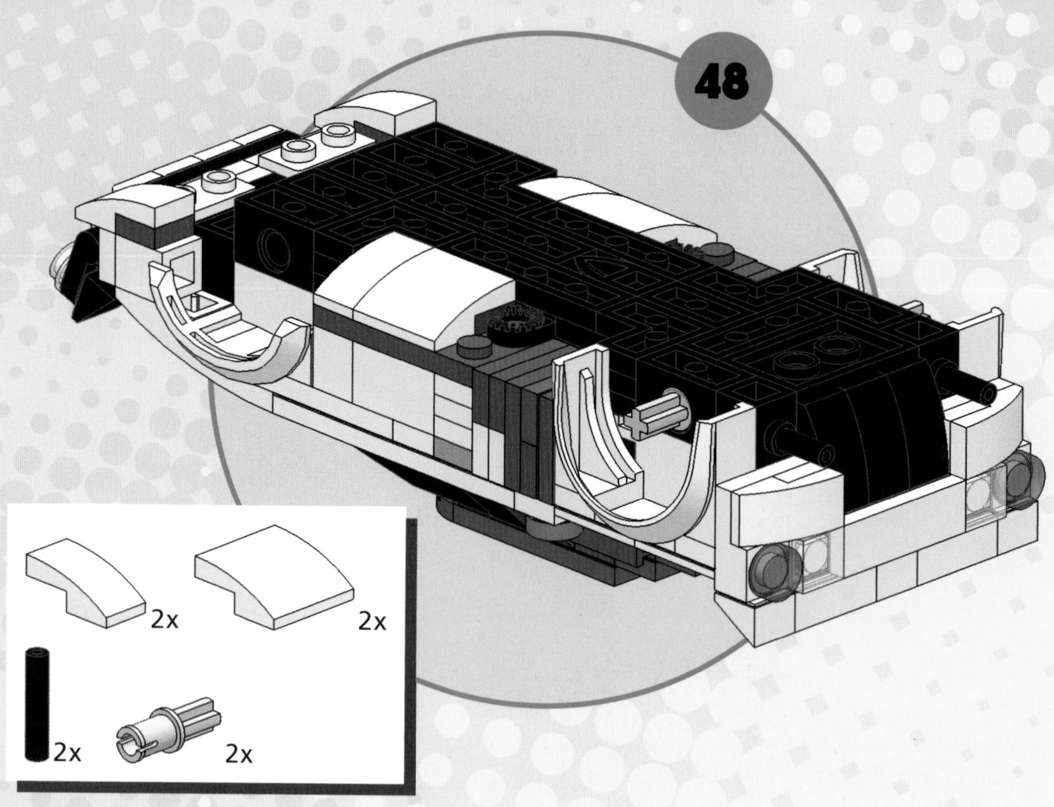

49

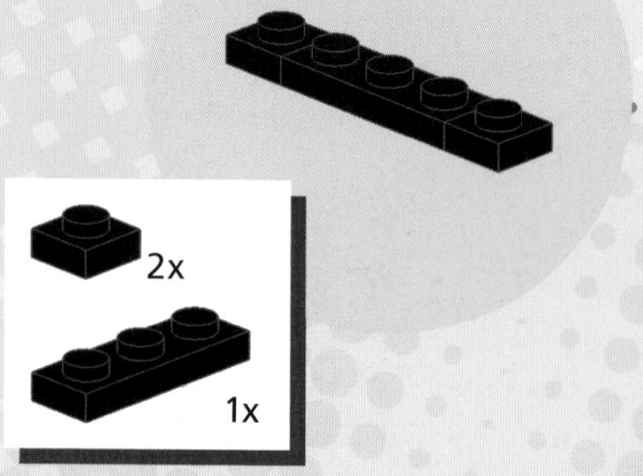

2x

1x

50

1x

2x

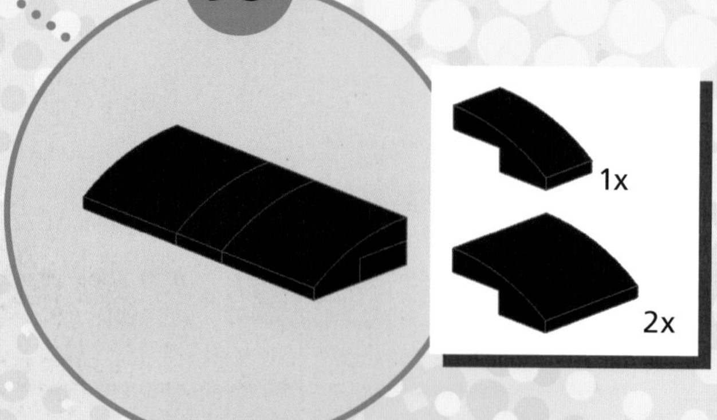

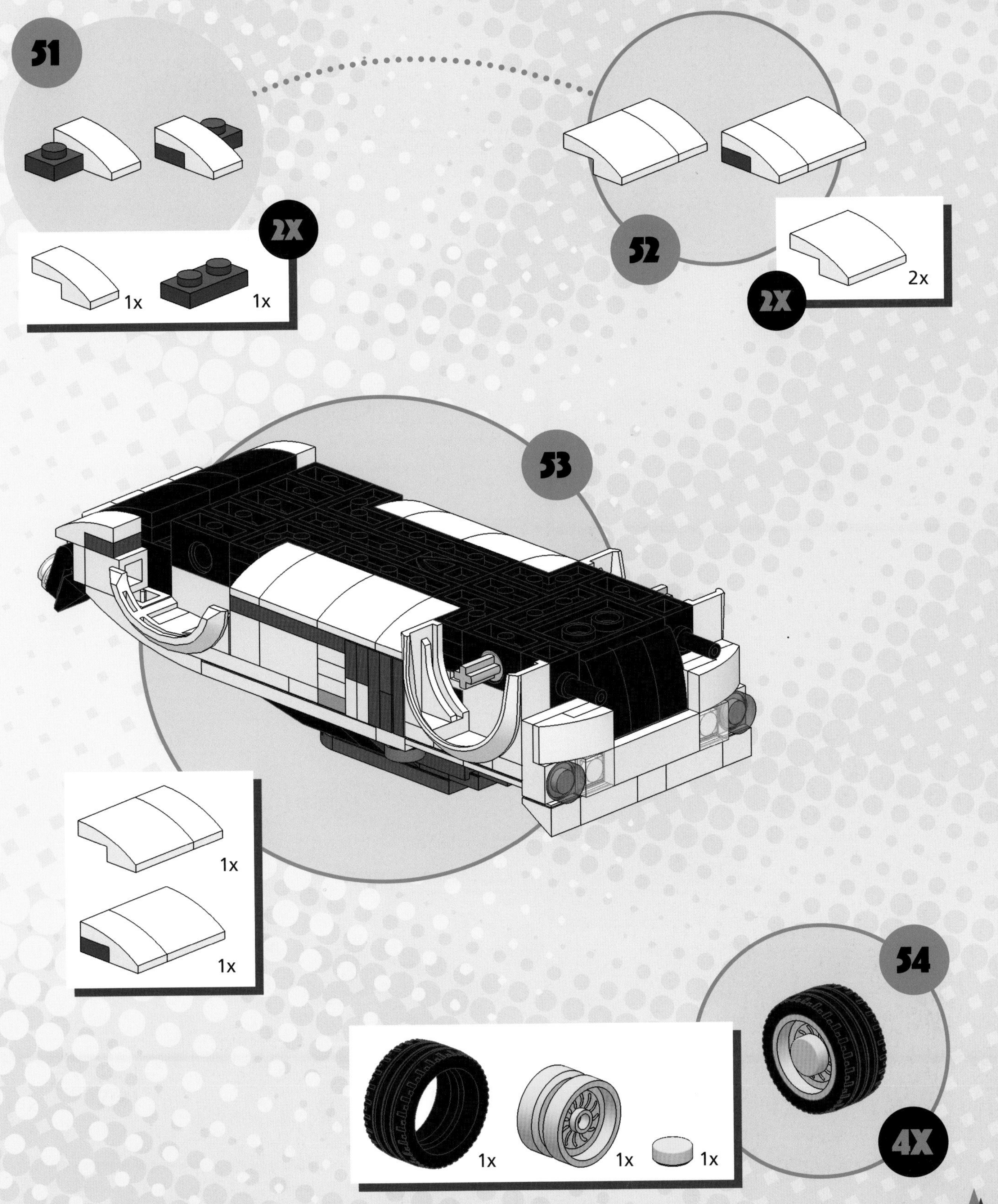
51
2X
1x
1x
52
2X
2x
53
1x
1x
54
1x
1x
1x
4X

55

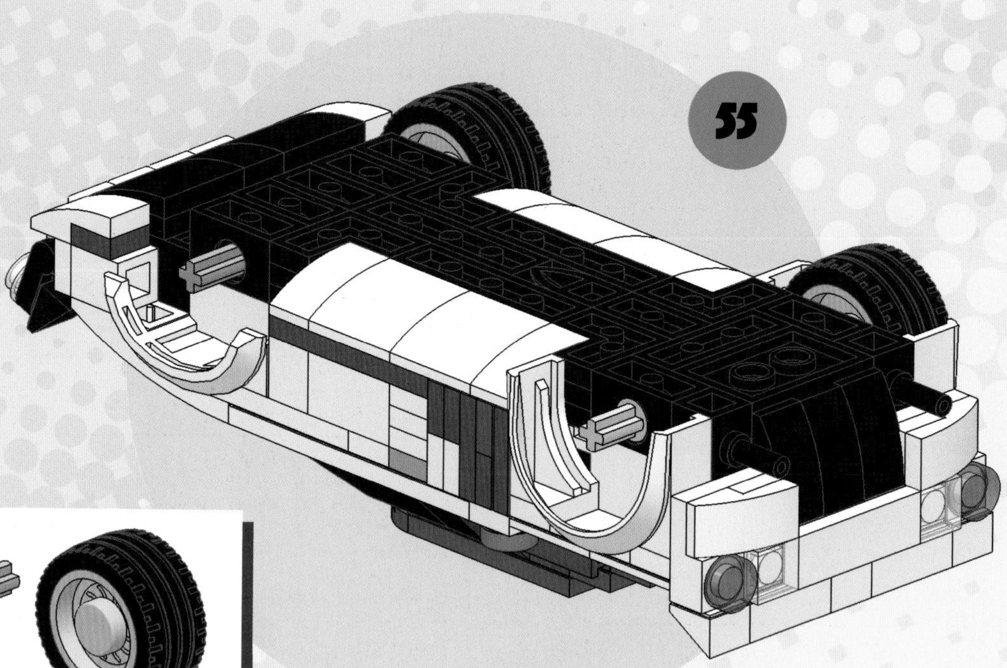

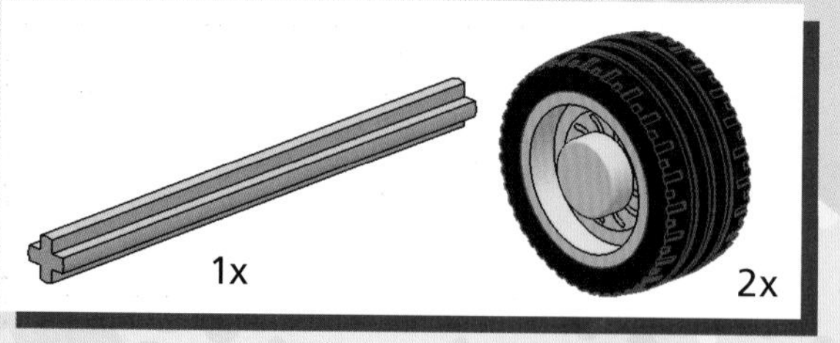

1x

2x

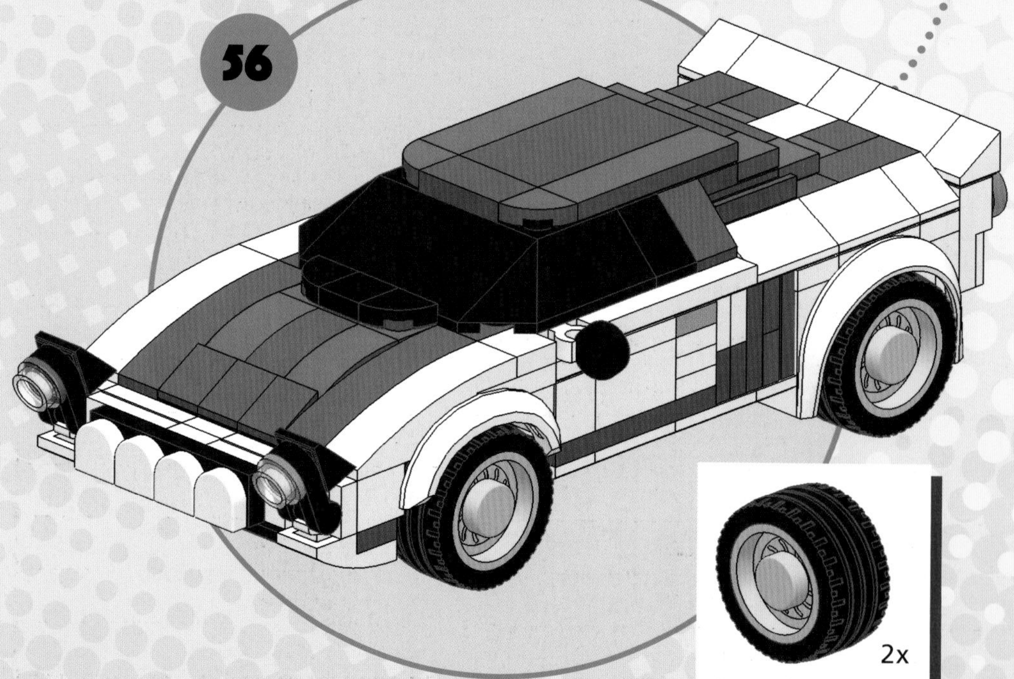

PARTS LIST

Quantity	Color	Element	Element Name	LEGO® Number
2	White	99781	Bracket 1 x 2 - 1 x 2 Down	6018774
5	Black	4070	Brick 1 x 1 with Headlight	407026
3	Black	87087	Brick 1 x 1 with Stud on 1 Side	4558954
5	White	87087	Brick 1 x 1 with Stud on 1 Side	4558952
2	White	47905	Brick 1 x 1 with Studs on Two Opposite Sides	4626882
2	Black	3004	Brick 1 x 2	300426
2	Black	11211	Brick 1 x 2 with Two Studs on One Side	6138173
2	White	11211	Brick 1 x 2 with Two Studs on One Side	6058177
1	Blue	3622	Brick 1 x 3	362223
1	Blue	3010	Brick 1 x 4	301023
2	Blue	3002	Brick 2 x 3	300223
1	White	3002	Brick 2 x 3	300201
1	Blue	3001	Brick 2 x 4	300123
1	White	3001	Brick 2 x 4	300101
2	White	98282	Car Mudguard 4 x 2.5 x 1	4646576, 6170504
2	White	18974	Car Mudguard 4 x 2.5 x 2.333	6102583
6	Black	3024	Plate 1 x 1	302426
3	Green	3024	Plate 1 x 1	302428
2	Metallic Silver	3024	Plate 1 x 1	4528732
11	White	3024	Plate 1 x 1	302401
2	Trans Clear	4073	Plate 1 x 1 Round	3005740
2	Black	26047	Plate 1 x 1 Round with Horizontal Handle on Side	6157554
1	White	60897	Plate 1 x 1 with Clip Vertical (Thick C-Clip)	
1	Black	49668	Plate 1 x 1 with Tooth In-line	4273590
7	Black	3023	Plate 1 x 2	302326
2	Blue	3023	Plate 1 x 2	302323
6	Green	3023	Plate 1 x 2	302328
2	Red	3023	Plate 1 x 2	302321
8	White	3023	Plate 1 x 2	302301

Quantity	Color	Element	Element Name	LEGO® Number
4	Green	32028	Plate 1 x 2 with Door Rail	4107760, 4272665
7	Blue	15573	Plate 1 x 2 with Groove with 1 Centre Stud, without Understud	6092582
2	Green	15573	Plate 1 x 2 with Groove with 1 Centre Stud, without Understud	6092586
3	White	15573	Plate 1 x 2 with Groove with 1 Centre Stud, without Understud	6051511
5	Black	3623	Plate 1 x 3	362326
3	Blue	3623	Plate 1 x 3	362323
1	Green	3623	Plate 1 x 3	4107758
1	Red	3623	Plate 1 x 3	362321
1	White	3623	Plate 1 x 3	362301
4	Black	3710	Plate 1 x 4	371026
1	Green	3710	Plate 1 x 4	371028
1	White	3710	Plate 1 x 4	371001
1	White	92593	Plate 1 x 4 with Two Studs	4597131
7	Black	3666	Plate 1 x 6	366626
4	Blue	3666	Plate 1 x 6	366623
1	Blue	3460	Plate 1 x 8	346023
2	Green	3022	Plate 2 x 2	302228
3	White	3022	Plate 2 x 2	302201, 4613976
6	Black	2420	Plate 2 x 2 Corner	242026
3	White	99206	Plate 2 x 2 x 0.667 with Two Studs On Side and Two Raised	6046979
4	Black	3021	Plate 2 x 3	302126
1	White	3021	Plate 2 x 3	302101
2	Black	3020	Plate 2 x 4	302026
3	Green	3020	Plate 2 x 4	302028
1	White	3020	Plate 2 x 4	302001
1	Green	3795	Plate 2 x 6	379528
2	Black	54200	Slope Brick 31 1 x 1 x 0.667	4287159, 4504382

Quantity	Color	Element	Element Name	LEGO® Number
3	Green	54200	Slope Brick 31 1 x 1 x 0.667	4546705
6	White	54200	Slope Brick 31 1 x 1 x 0.667	4244370, 4504369
6	White	85984	Slope Brick 31 1 x 2 x 0.667	4547489
1	Black	13269	Slope Brick 33/45 6 x 4 with 2 x 2 Cutout	6031790
2	Black	3040	Slope Brick 45 2 x 1	304026, 4121966
2	Green	3040	Slope Brick 45 2 x 1	4109668, 4121969
4	Black	11477	Slope Brick Curved 2 x 1	6047276
1	Green	11477	Slope Brick Curved 2 x 1	6047426
2	Red	11477	Slope Brick Curved 2 x 1	6029946
8	White	11477	Slope Brick Curved 2 x 1	6034044
2	Black	15068	Slope Brick Curved 2 x 2 x 0.667	6053077
4	White	15068	Slope Brick Curved 2 x 2 x 0.667	6047220
2	Green	61678	Slope Brick Curved 4 x 1	4541100, 4541188, 6042951
2	White	61678	Slope Brick Curved 4 x 1	4518992, 6045936
1	Light Bluish Gray	44294	Technic Axle 7	4211805, 44294194
2	Tan	3749	Technic Axle Pin	4186017, 4666579, 65625
7	Black	3700	Technic Brick 1 x 2 with Hole	370026
2	Black	76263	Technic Flex-System Hose 2L	
1	Black	2711	Technic Rotor 2 Blade with 2 Studs	
2	Black	25269	Tile 1 x 1 Corner Round	6172383
2	Red	25269	Tile 1 x 1 Corner Round	6170390
1	Black	98138	Tile 1 x 1 Round with Groove	6139403
1	Flat Silver	98138	Tile 1 x 1 Round with Groove	4655241
2	Trans Red	98138	Tile 1 x 1 Round with Groove	4646864
4	Yellow	98138	Tile 1 x 1 Round with Groove	6070714
2	White	12825	Tile 1 x 1 with Clip with Rounded Tips	
1	Black	3070b	Tile 1 x 1 with Groove	307026
5	Blue	3070b	Tile 1 x 1 with Groove	4206330
4	Green	3070b	Tile 1 x 1 with Groove	4238528, 4558593

Quantity		Color	Element	Element Name	LEGO® Number
6		Red	3070b	Tile 1 x 1 with Groove	307021
2		Trans Clear	3070b	Tile 1 x 1 with Groove	4162145, 6047501
3		White	3070b	Tile 1 x 1 with Groove	307001
4		White	24246	Tile 1 x 1 with Rounded End	6131655
5		Green	3069b	Tile 1 x 2 with Groove	306928
2		White	3069b	Tile 1 x 2 with Groove	306901
1		Blue	63864	Tile 1 x 3 with Groove	4587840
1		White	63864	Tile 1 x 3 with Groove	4558168
2		Red	2431	Tile 1 x 4 with Groove	243121
1		White	2431	Tile 1 x 4 with Groove	243101
1		White	6636	Tile 1 x 6	663601
2		Green	3068b	Tile 2 x 2 with Groove	4107762
1		Green	87079	Tile 2 x 4 with Groove	4566179
1		White	87079	Tile 2 x 4 with Groove	4560178
4		Black	18977	Tyre 11.2/ 28 x 17.6 Intermediate	6102596
4		Yellow	18976	Wheel Rim 11 x 18 with Vented Disc Brake	6176266

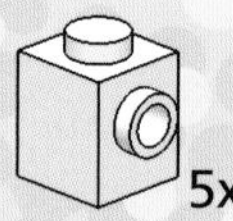

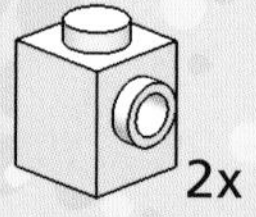

2x

2x

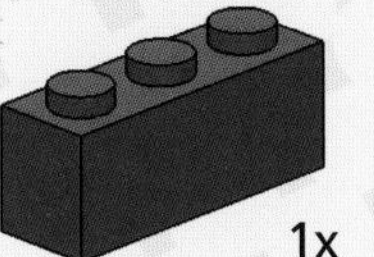
1x

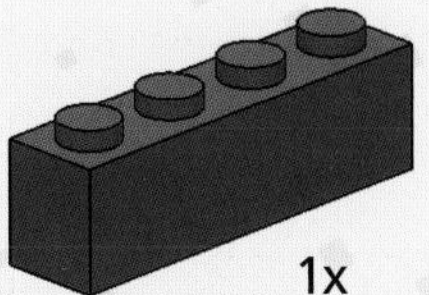
1x

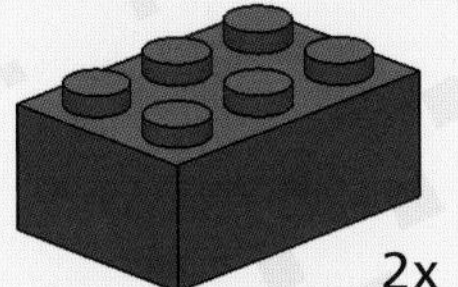
2x

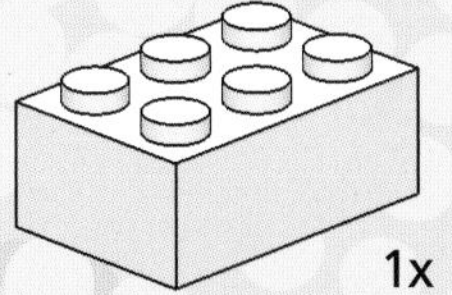
1x

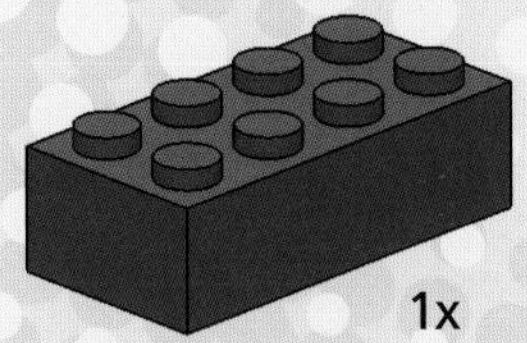
1x

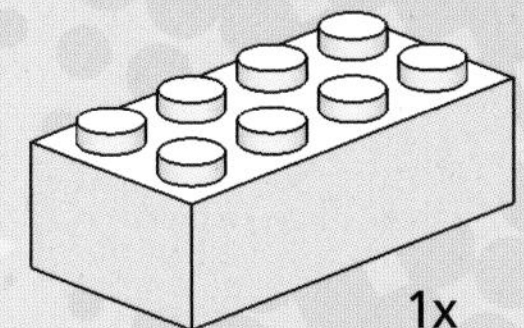
1x

2x

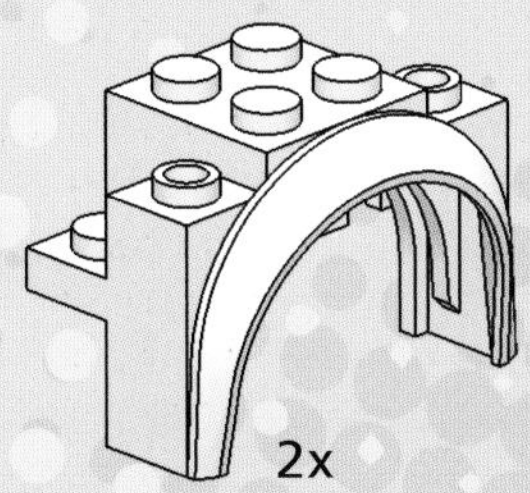
2x

6x

3x

2x

11x

2x

2x

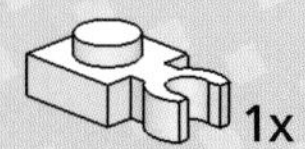
1x

1x

7x

2x

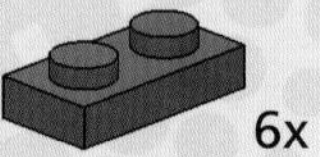
6x

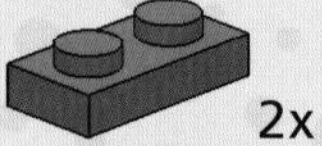
2x

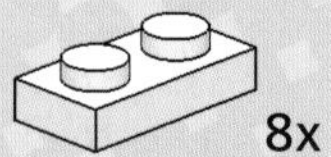
8x

4x

7x

2x

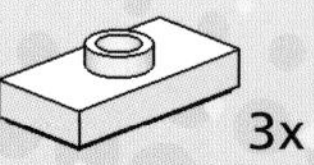
3x

5x

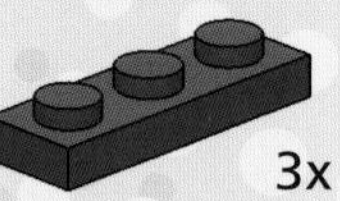
3x

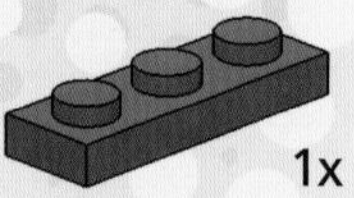
1x

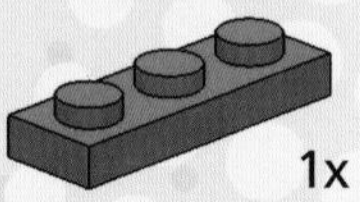
1x

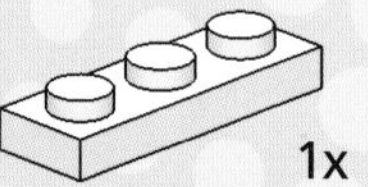
1x

4x

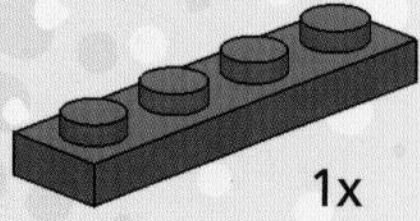
1x

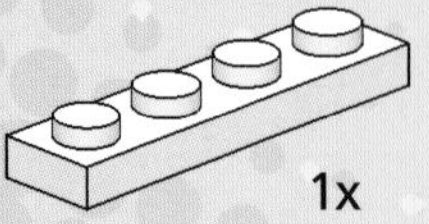
1x

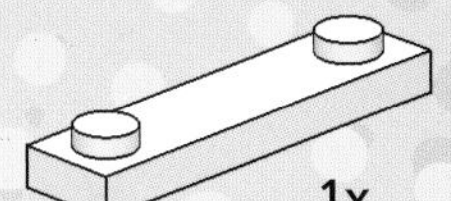
1x

4x

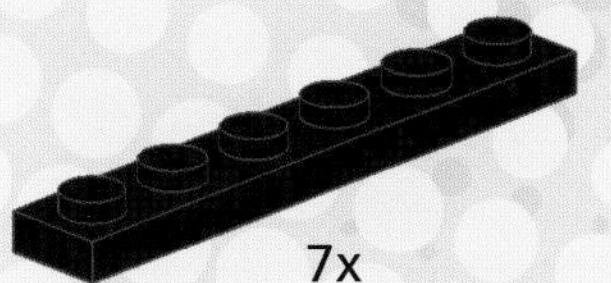
7x

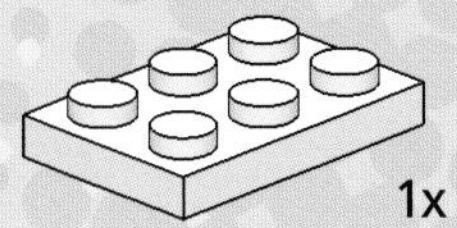
1x

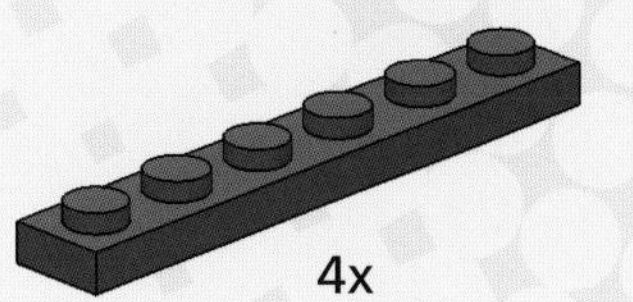
4x

2x

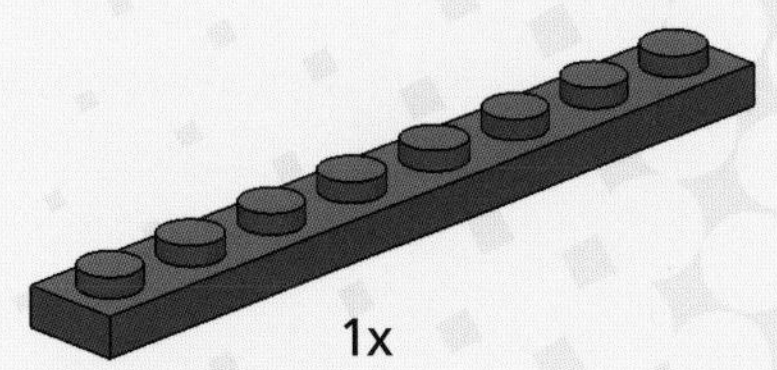
1x

3x

2x

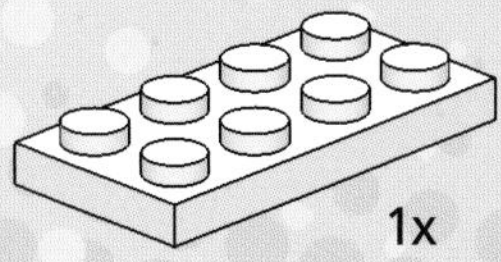
1x

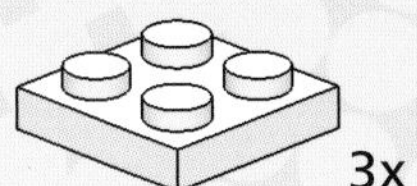
3x

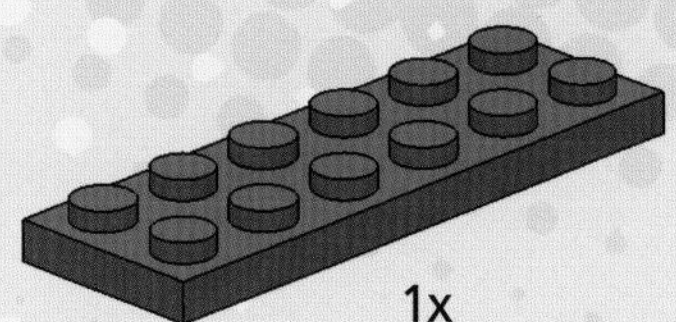
1x

6x

2x

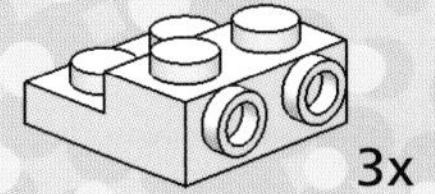
3x

3x

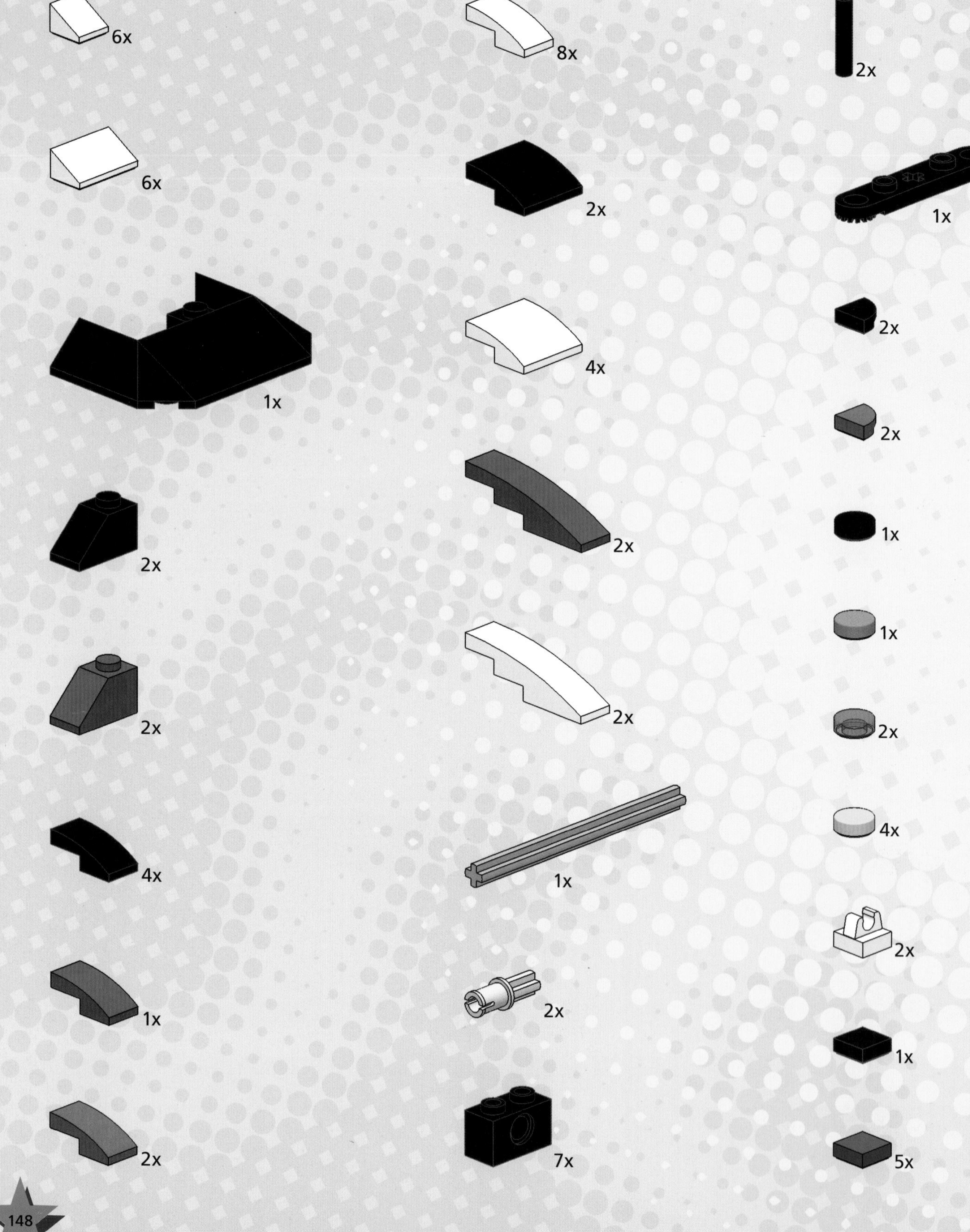
6x
8x
2x
6x
2x
1x
1x
4x
2x
2x
2x
2x
1x
2x
1x
2x
2x
1x
4x
4x
1x
1x
2x
2x
2x
1x
2x
7x
5x

4x

6x

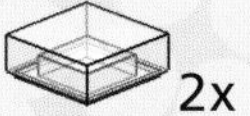
2x

3x

4x

5x

2x

1x

1x

2x

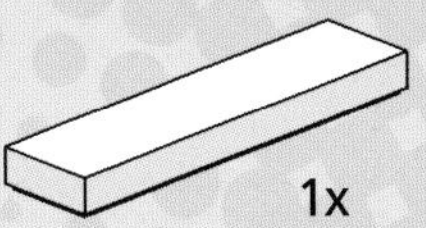
1x

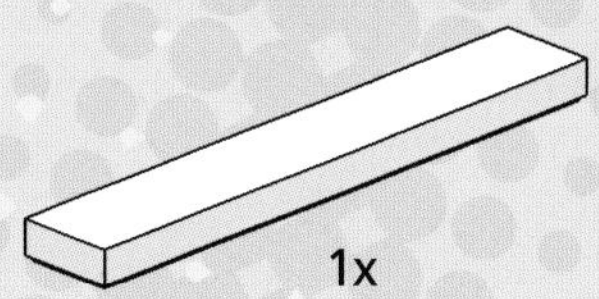
1x

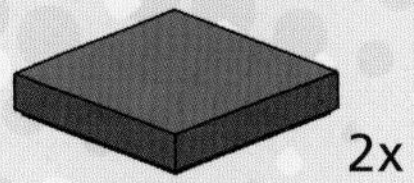
2x

1x

1x

4x

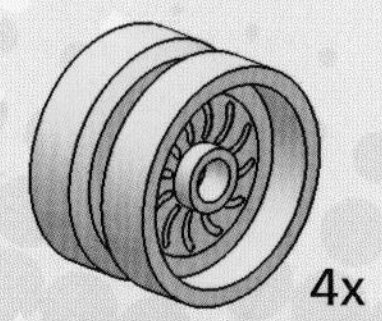
4x

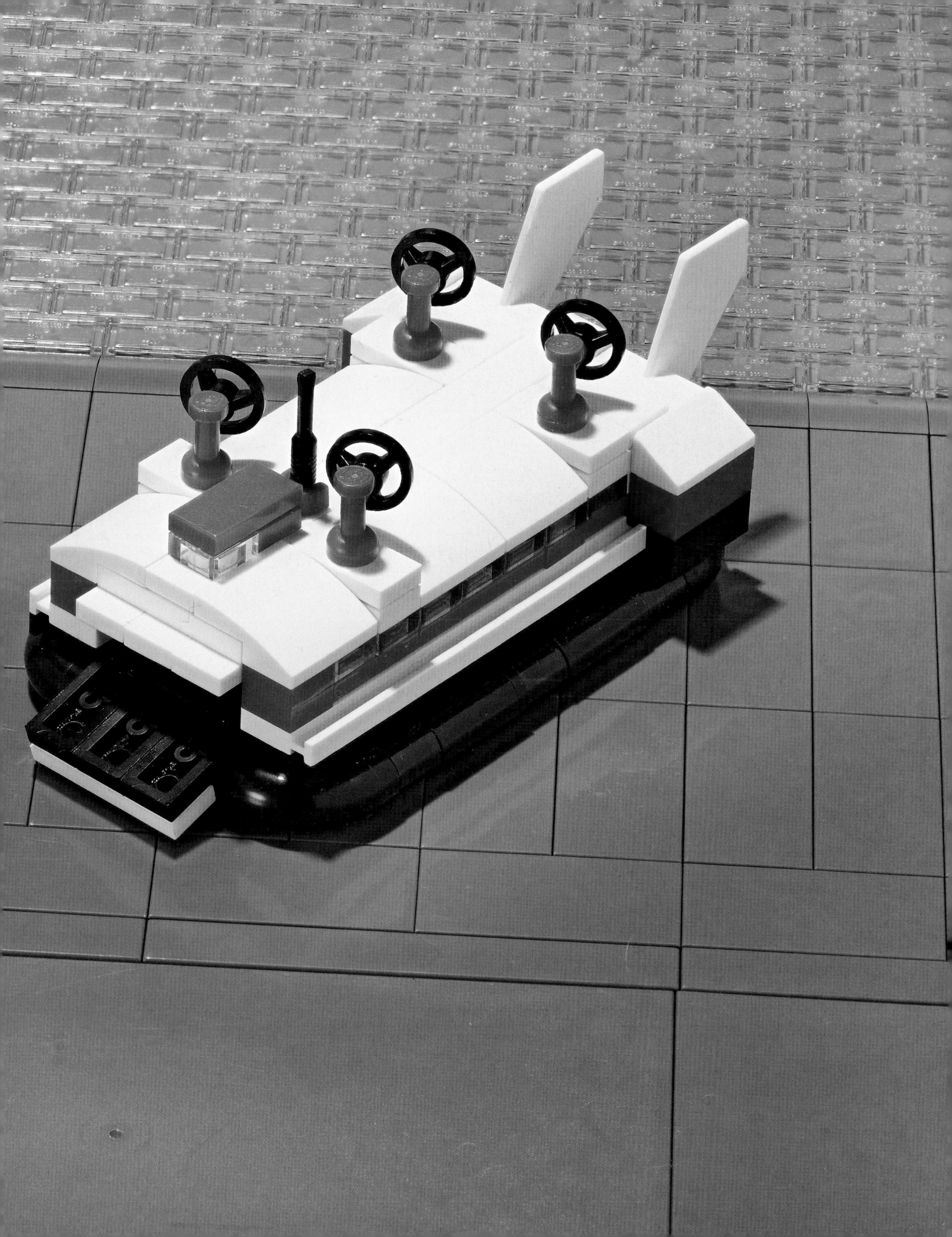

HOVERCRAFT NAUTICAL 4

Who would have thought it? Is it a coincidence that we had a second record vehicle from the company Saunders-Roe here? It's the Nautical 4 Hovercraft. In September 1995 it set a new world record that it is still unbroken today: It crossed the English Channel, travelling from Calais to Dover in just 22 minutes.

OPERATIONAL RANGE:	*450 km (280 miles)*
WEIGHT:	*165,000 kg (182 t)*
TOP SPEED:	*154 km/h (96 mph)*
HP:	*136,000*
TANK CAPACITY:	*10,599 liters (2,800 gal.)*

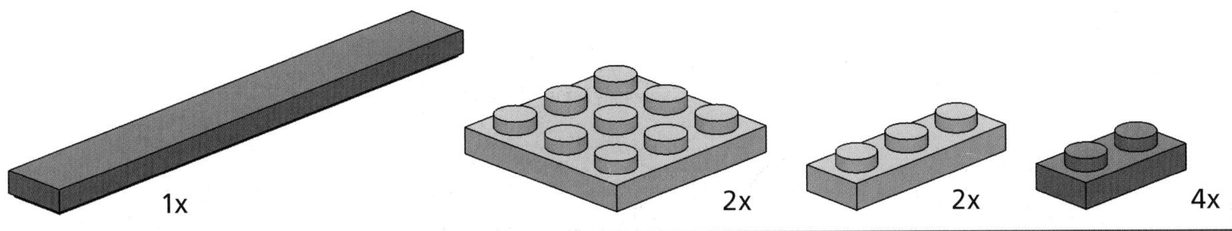

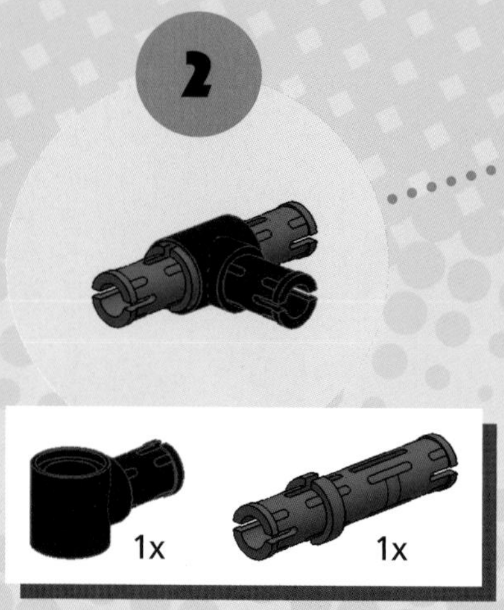

2

1x 1x

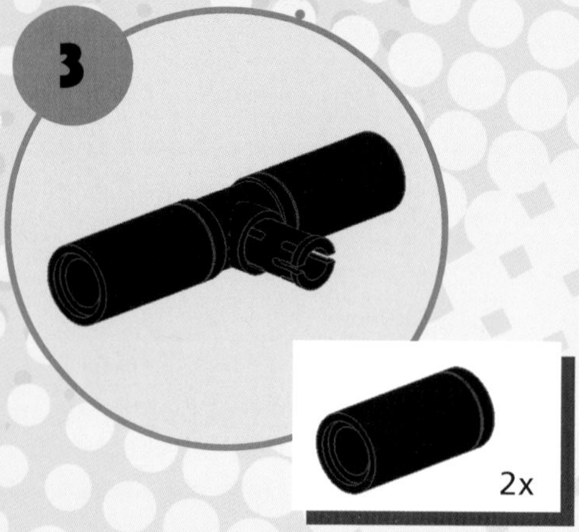

3

2x

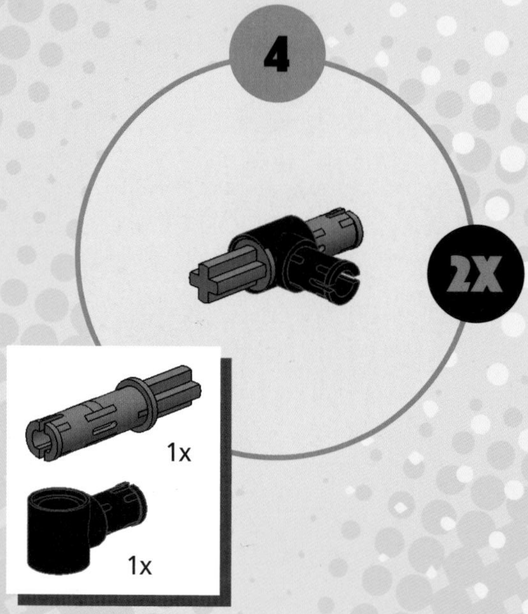

4

2X

1x

1x

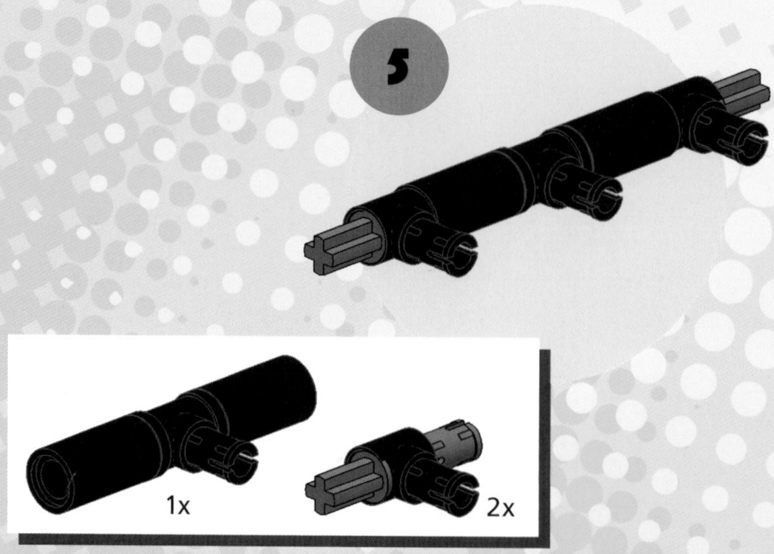

5

1x 2x

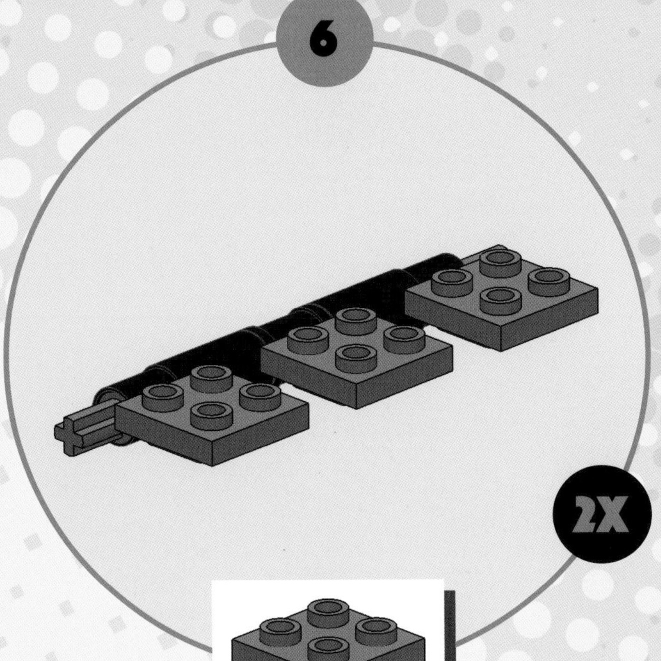

6

2X

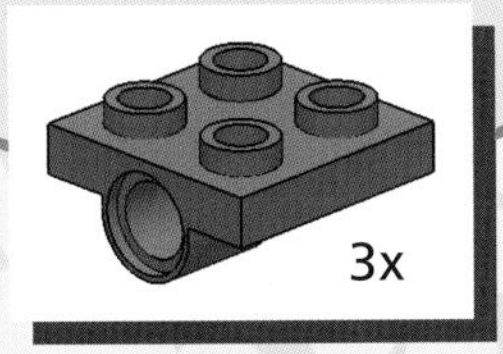

3x

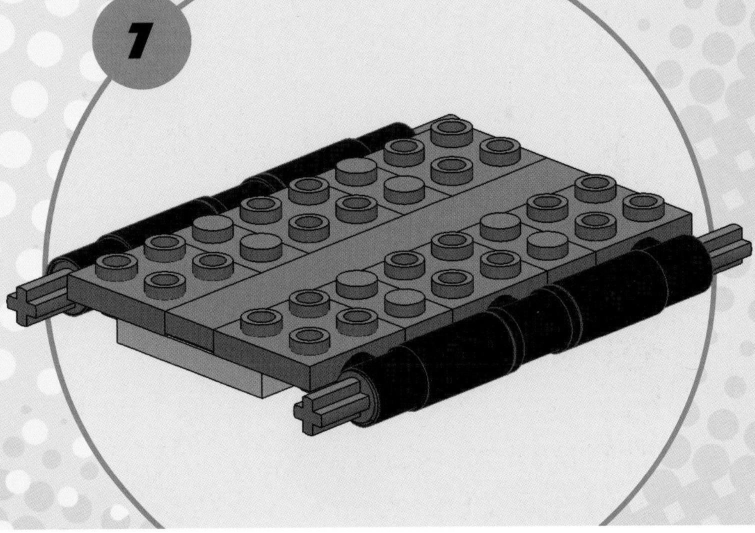

7

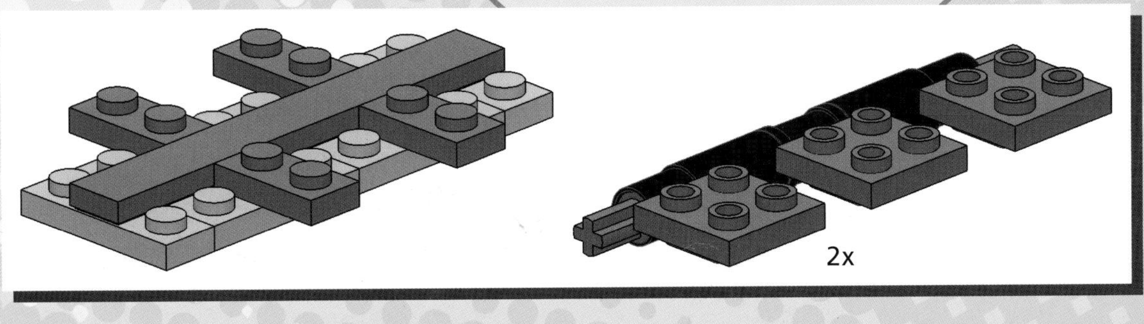

2x

8

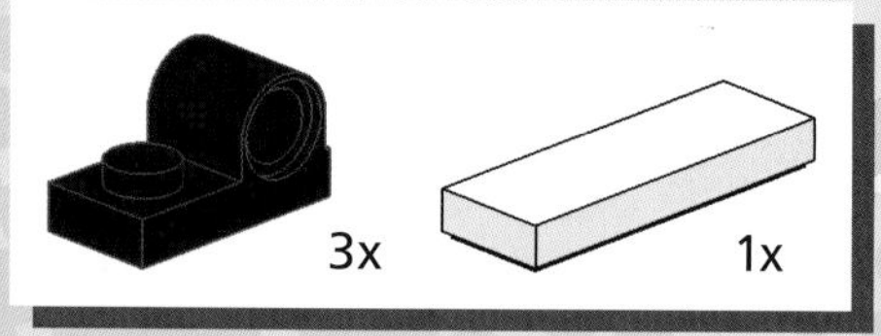

3x 1x

9

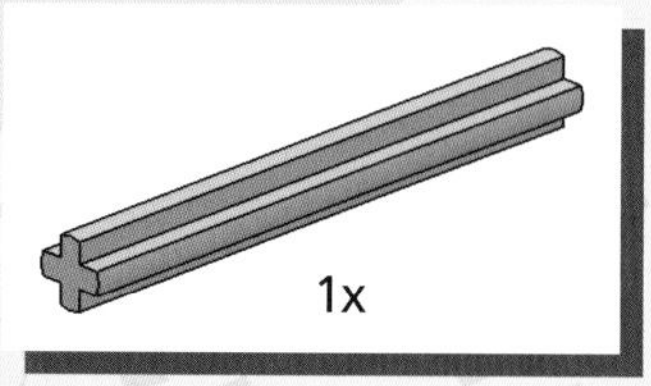

1x

10

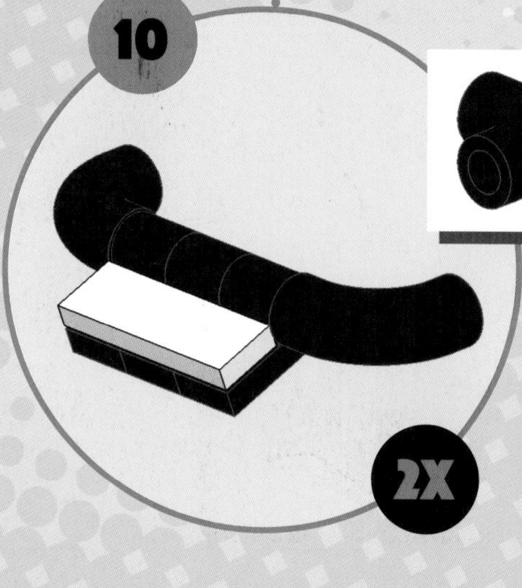

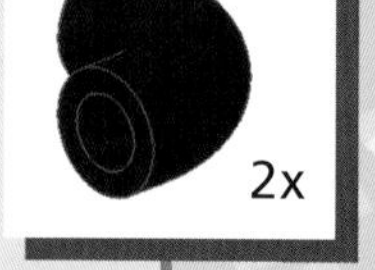

2x

2X

The only set with the curved brick is 21307 (Caterham Seven 620R Sports Car). However, it makes no sense not to use the brick here, in black. You can also get it from LEGO® service or at BrickLink.com.

11

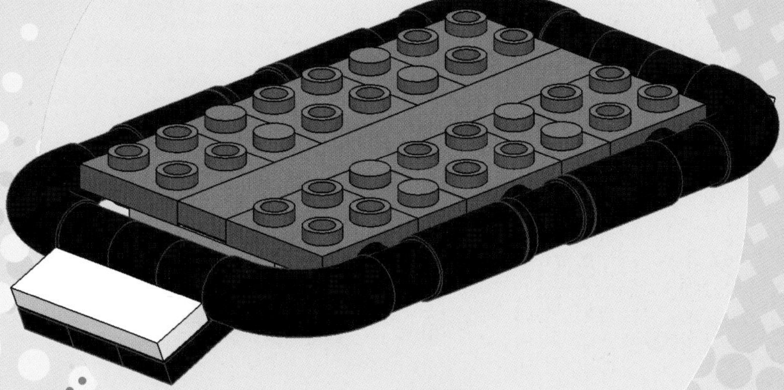

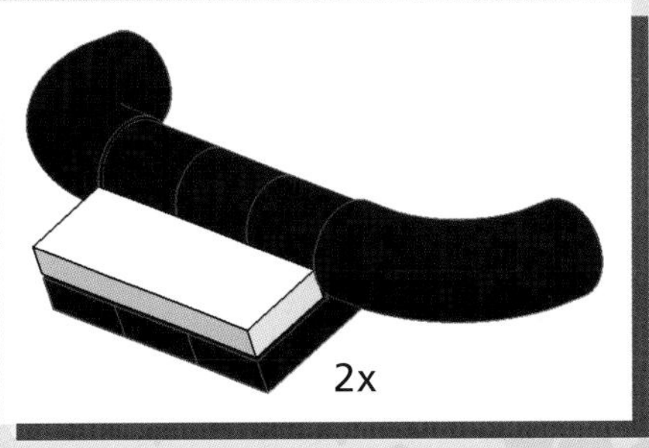

2x

12

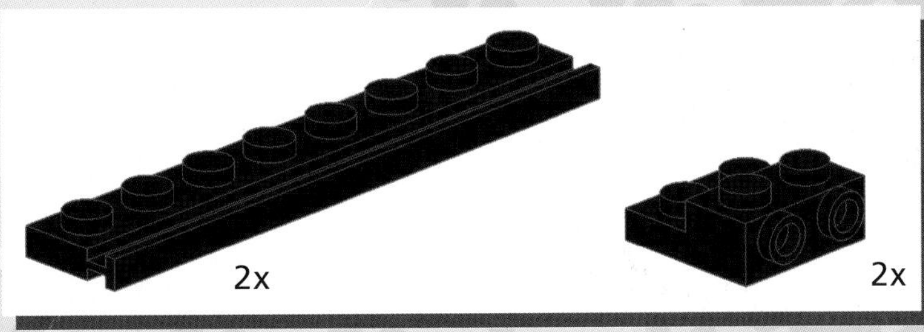

2x

2x

13

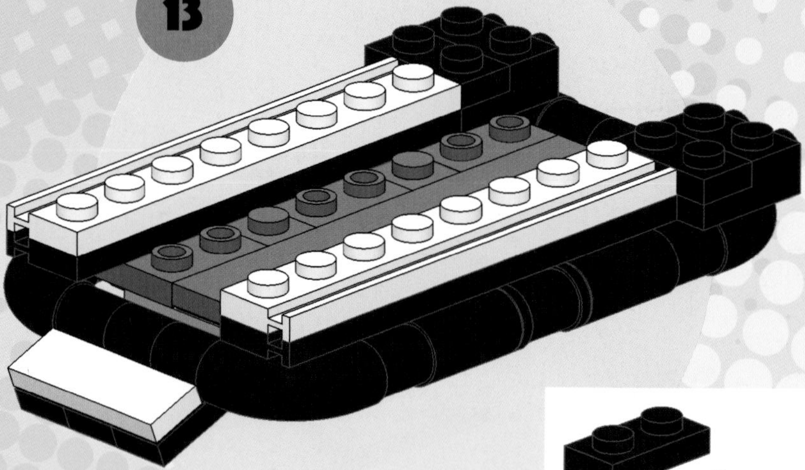

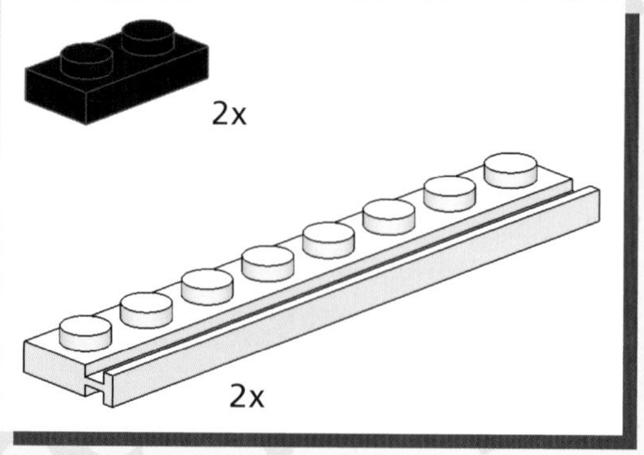

2x

2x

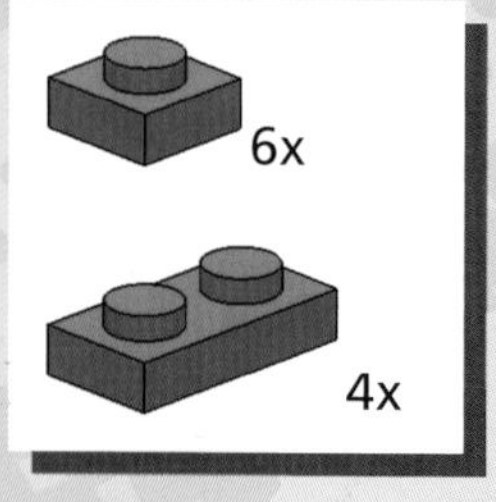

6x

4x

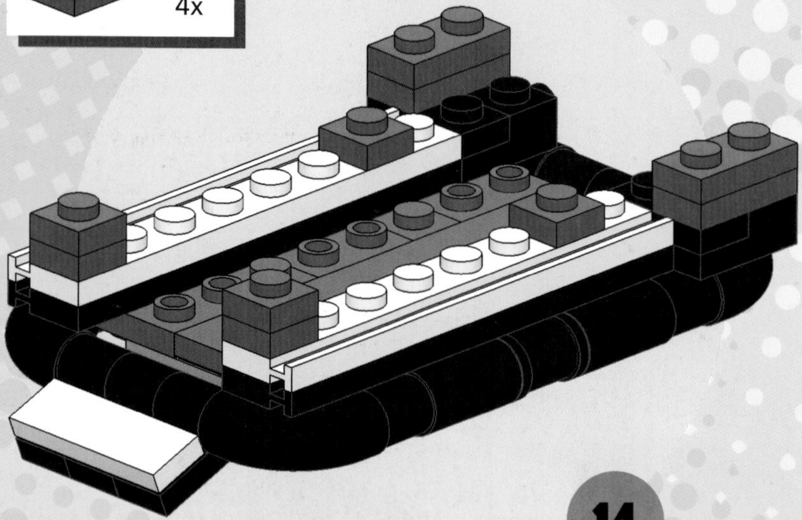

14

15

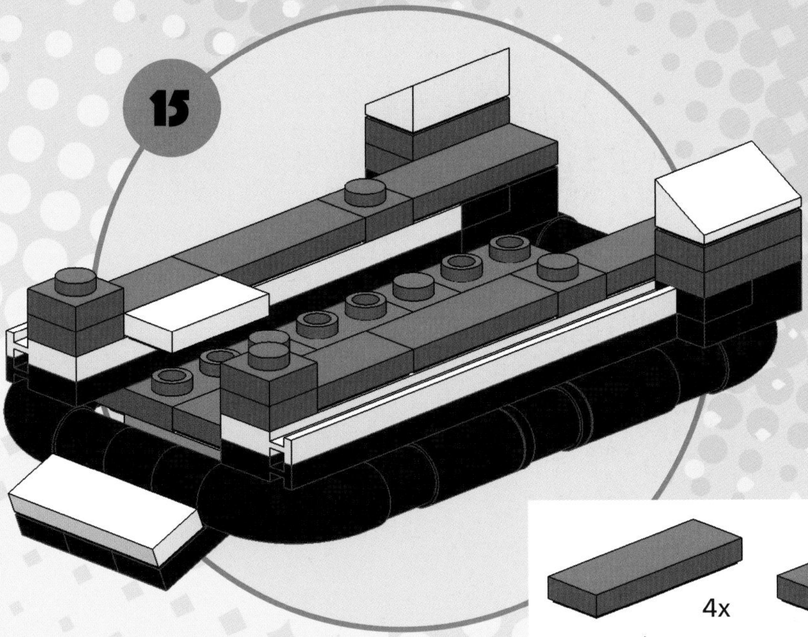

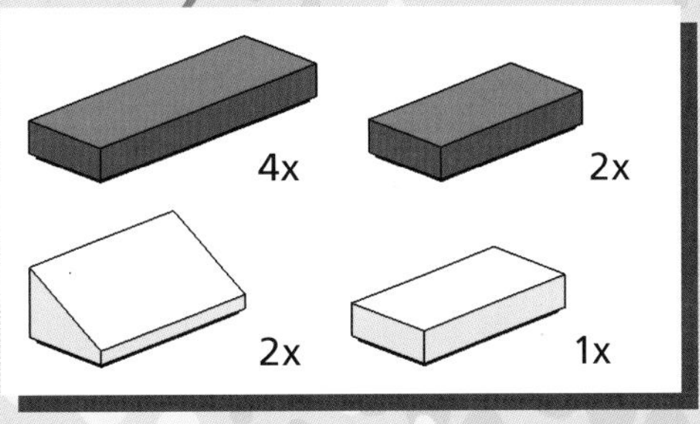

4x

2x

2x

1x

16

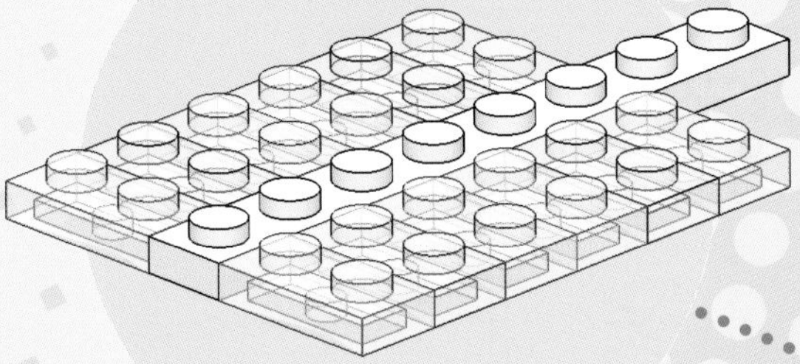

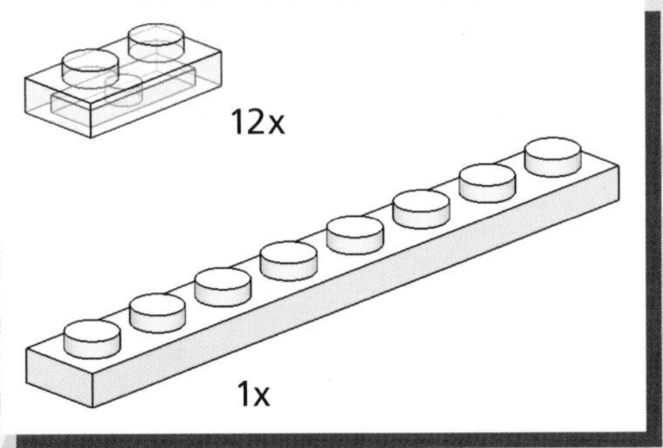

12x

1x

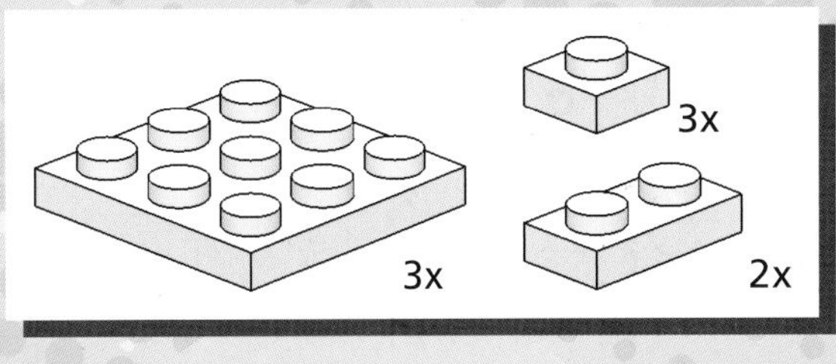

3x

3x

2x

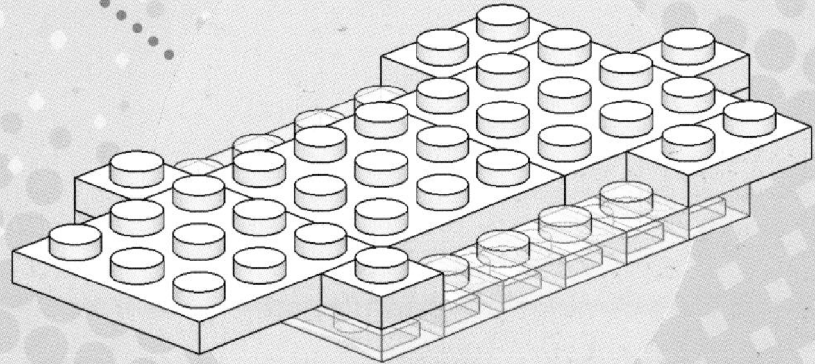

17

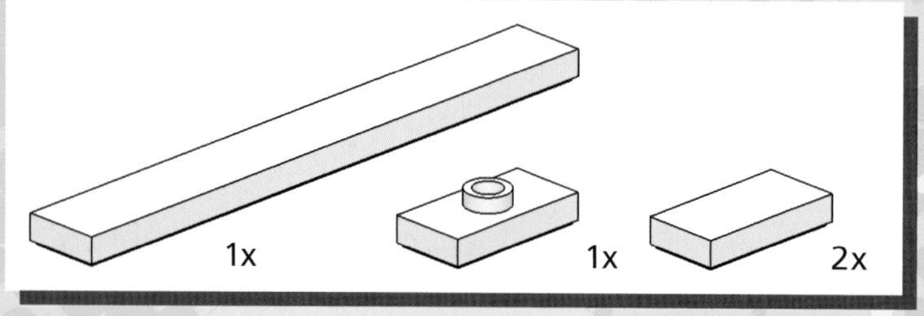

1x

1x

2x

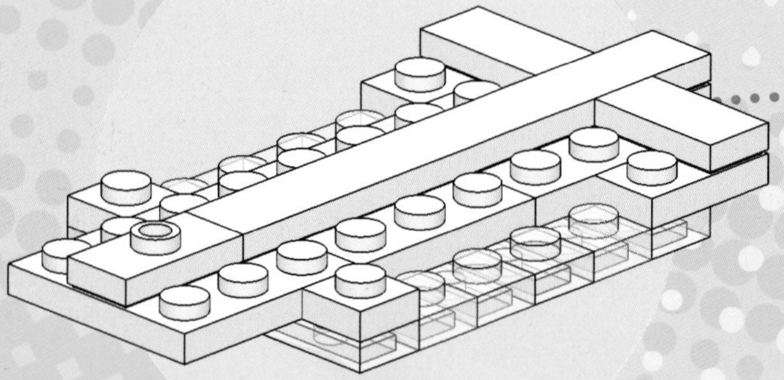

18

19

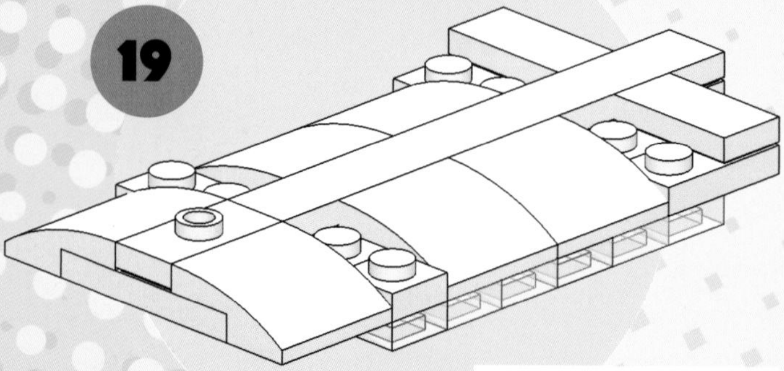

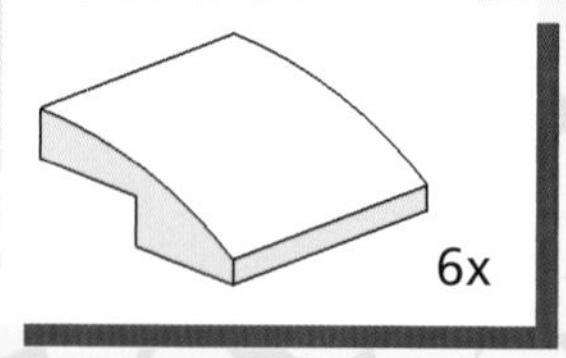

6x

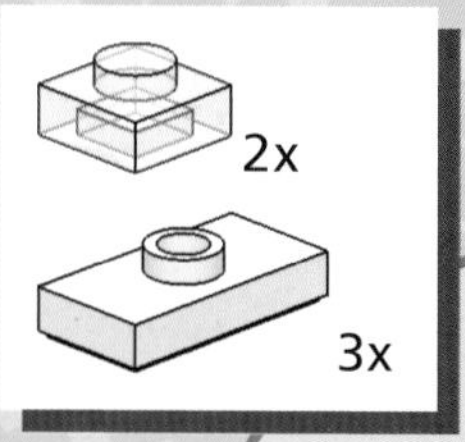

2x

3x

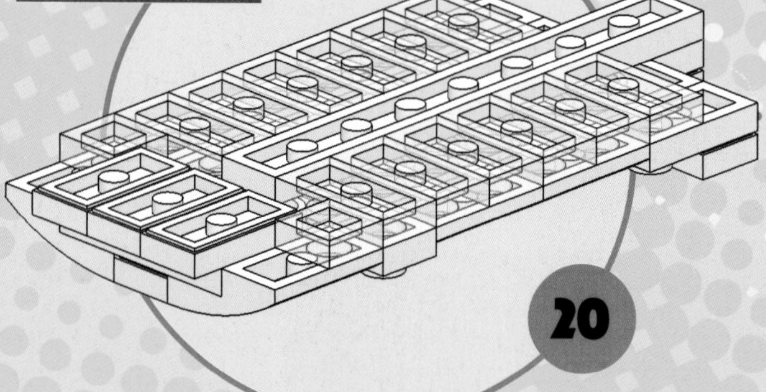

20

21

1x

1x

22

2X

1x

23

1x

1x

1x

1x

24

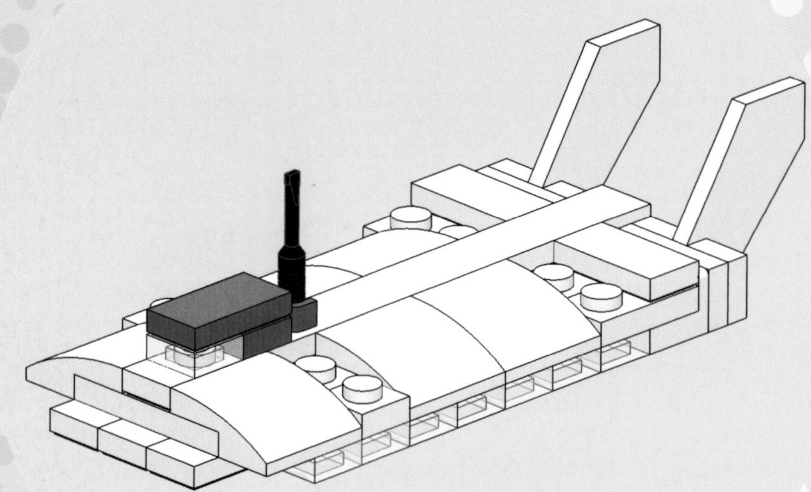

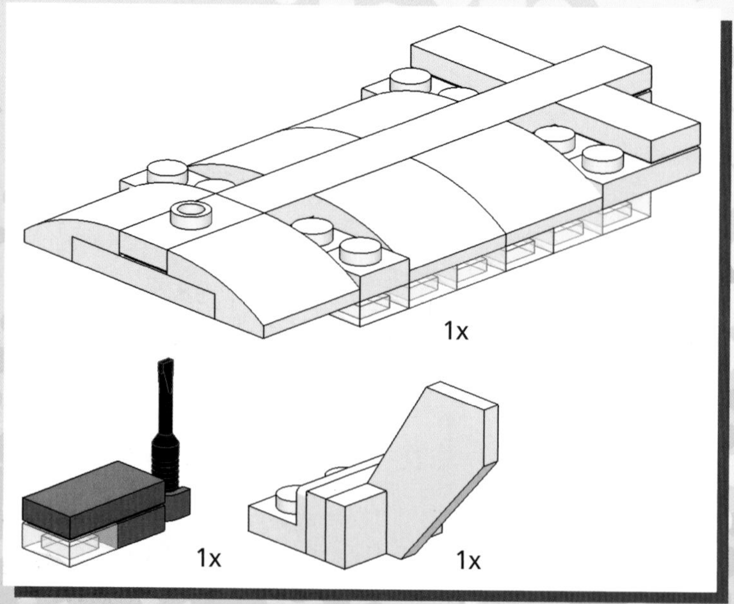

We have included a simple construction for the propellers in the building instructions. In the photo, you can see how to create a delicate solution. To remount the steering wheels, however, you need some strength. They fix on to the water hydrants well and also turn beautifully.

25

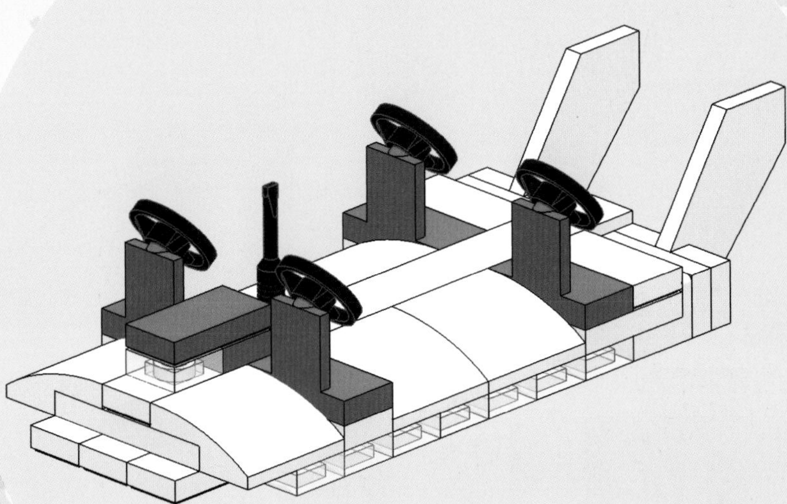

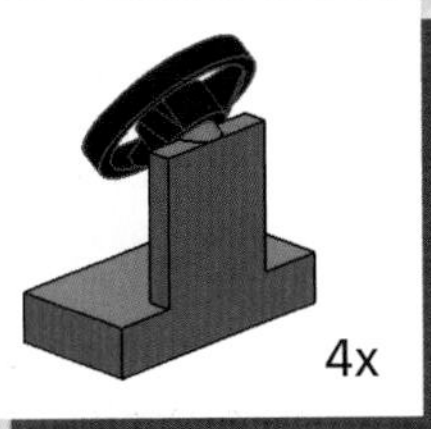

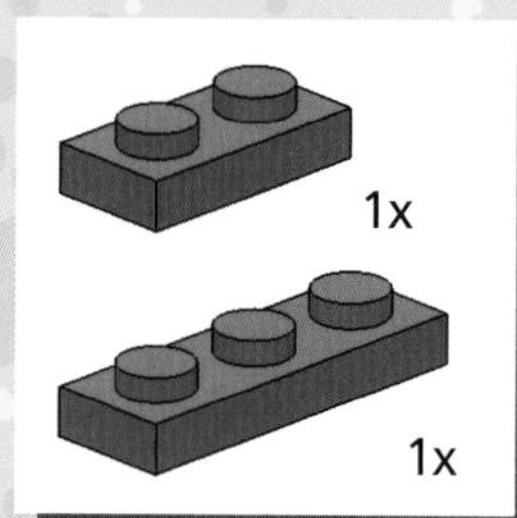

26

27

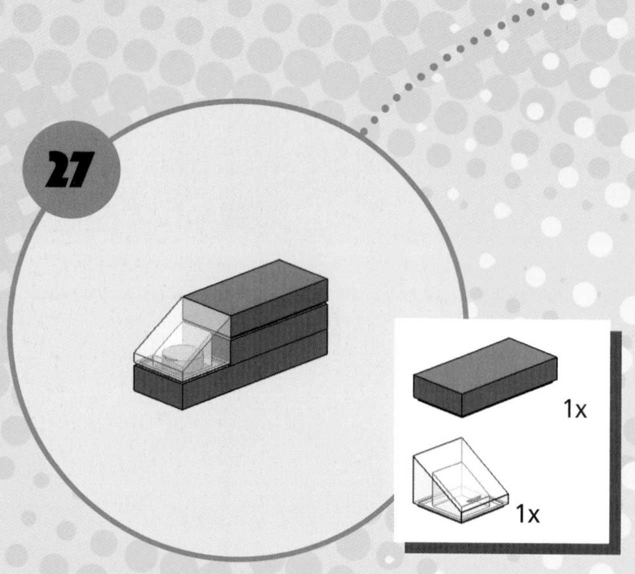

28

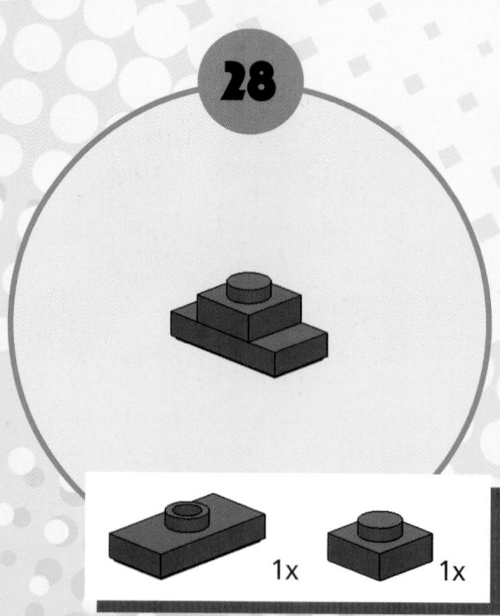

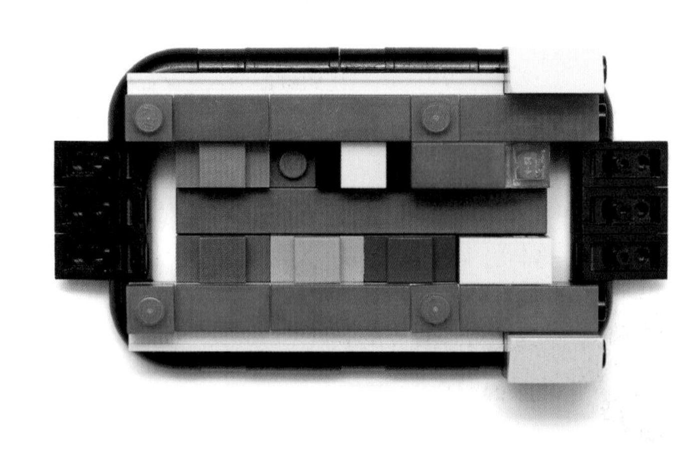

29

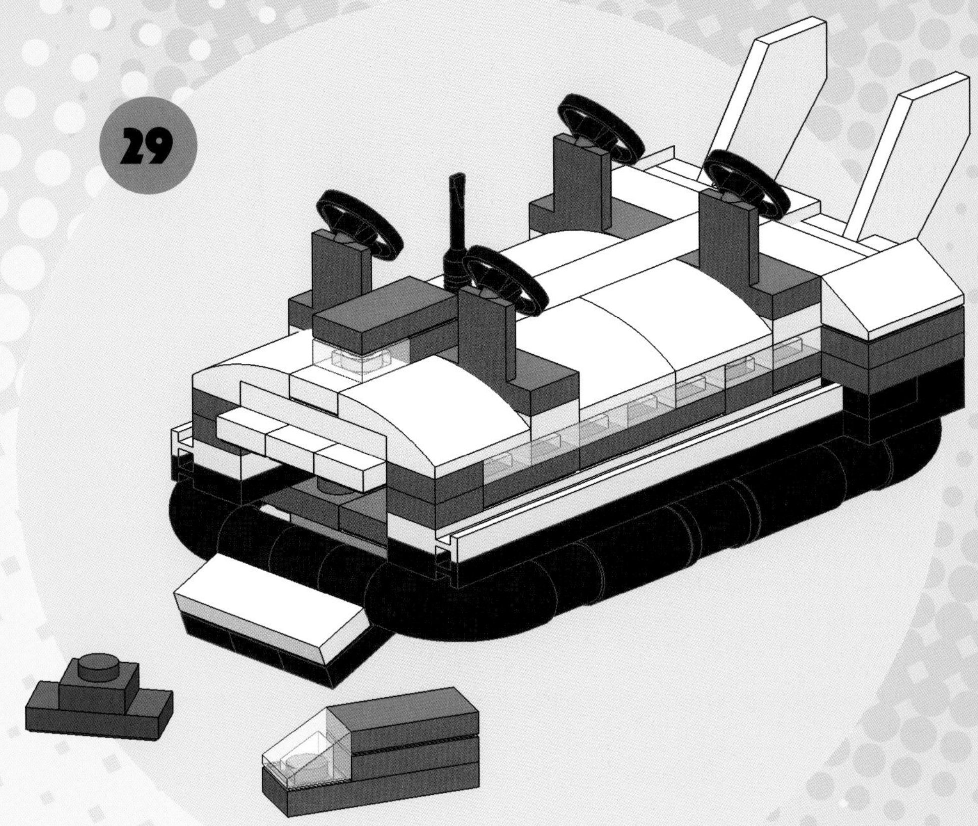

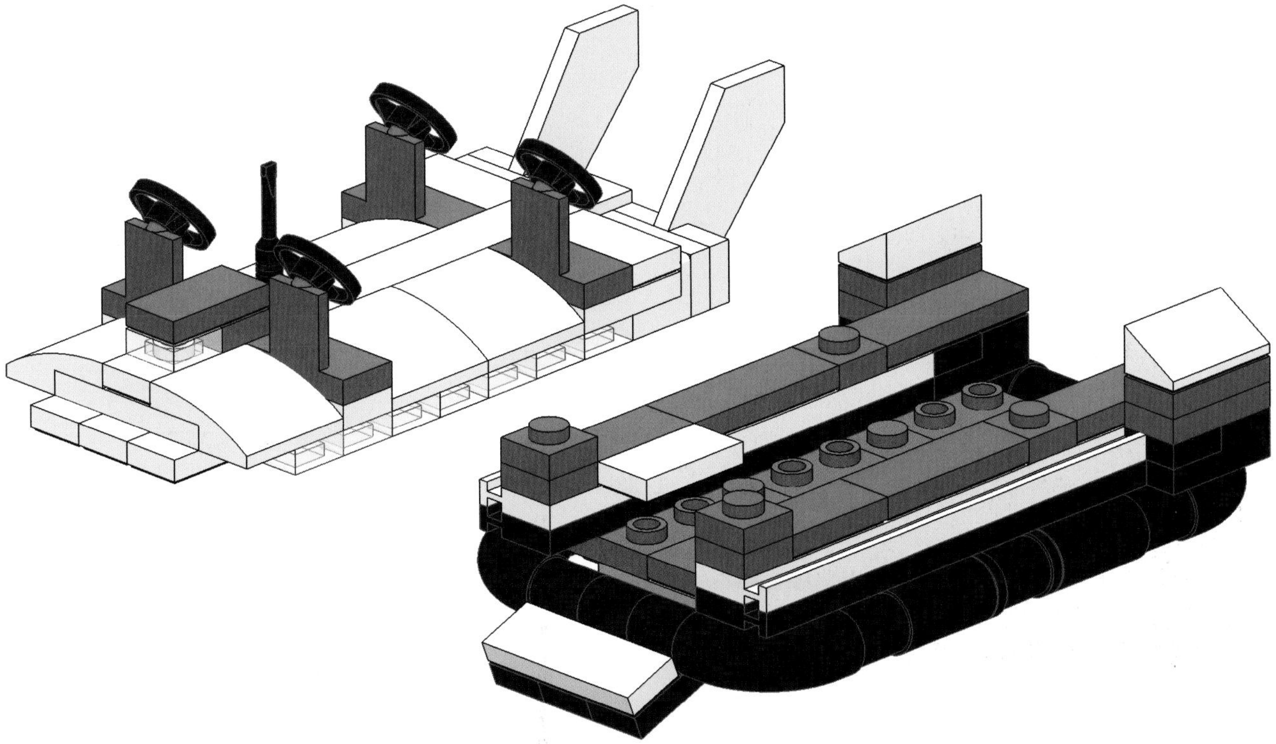

PARTS LIST

Quantity	Color		Element	Element Name	LEGO® Number
2		White	99780	Bracket 1 x 2 - 1 x 2 Up	6070698
4		Red	3829c01	Car Steering Stand and Wheel (Complete)	9552
1		Black	55298	Minifig Tool Screwdriver	
4		Black	25214	Brick, Round 1 x 1 d. 90 Degree Elbow - No Stud - Type 2 - Axle Hole	6179182
1		Dark Blue	3024	Plate 1 x 1	4184108
6		Red	3024	Plate 1 x 1	302421
4		Trans Clear	3024	Plate 1 x 1	3000840
3		White	3024	Plate 1 x 1	302401
1		Red	4085b	Plate 1 x 1 with Clip Vertical (Thin U-Clip)	4542315
2		Black	3023	Plate 1 x 2	302326
4		Dark Bluish Gray	3023	Plate 1 x 2	4211063
5		Red	3023	Plate 1 x 2	302321
12		Trans Clear	3023	Plate 1 x 2	4167842, 622540
4		White	3023	Plate 1 x 2	302301
4		White	3794	Plate 1 x 2 with Groove with 1 Centre Stud	379401
1		Light Bluish Gray	15573	Plate 1 x 2 with Groove with 1 Centre Stud, without Understud	6066097
6		Black	11458	Plate 1 x 2 with Offset Peghole	6114987
2		Light Bluish Gray	3623	Plate 1 x 3	3623194, 4211429
1		Red	3623	Plate 1 x 3	362321
1		White	3460	Plate 1 x 8	346001
2		Black	4510	Plate 1 x 8 with Door Rail	4286009
2		White	4510	Plate 1 x 8 with Door Rail	4250463, 4501853
6		Dark Bluish Gray	10247	Plate 2 x 2 with Hole and Complete Under-side Rib	6047417
2		Black	99206	Plate 2 x 2 x 0.667 with Two Studs On Side and Two Raised	6052126
2		Light Bluish Gray	11212	Plate 3 x 3	6015347

Quantity		Color	Element	Element Name	LEGO® Number
3		White	11212	Plate 3 x 3	6104805
1		Trans Clear	54200	Slope Brick 31 1 x 1 x 0.667	4244362
2		White	85984	Slope Brick 31 1 x 2 x 0.667	4547489
6		White	15068	Slope Brick Curved 2 x 2 x 0.667	6047220
2		White	44661	Tail 2 x 3 x 2 Fin	4288960
2		Light Bluish Gray	32073	Technic Axle 5	32073194, 4211639
4		Dark Bluish Gray	11214	Technic Axle Pin Long with Friction with 2L Pin	6015356
4		Black	75535	Technic Pin Joiner Round	75619
2		Blue	6558	Technic Pin Long with Friction and Slot	4514553
6		Black	15100	Technic Pin with Friction with Perpendicular Pin Hole	6073231
4		Red	3069b	Tile 1 x 2 with Groove	306921
3		White	3069b	Tile 1 x 2 with Groove	306901
4		Red	63864	Tile 1 x 3 with Groove	4533742
2		White	63864	Tile 1 x 3 with Groove	4558168
1		Dark Bluish Gray	4162	Tile 1 x 8	4211008, 5210651
1		White	4162	Tile 1 x 8	416201

2x

4x

1x

4x

1x

6x

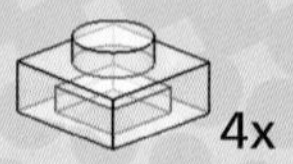
4x

3x

1x

2x

4x

5x

12x

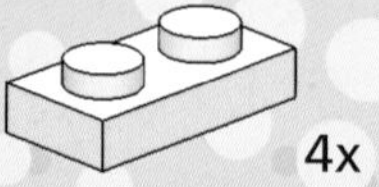
4x

4x

1x

6x

2x

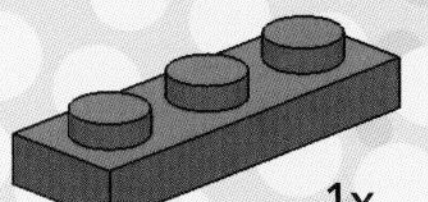
1x

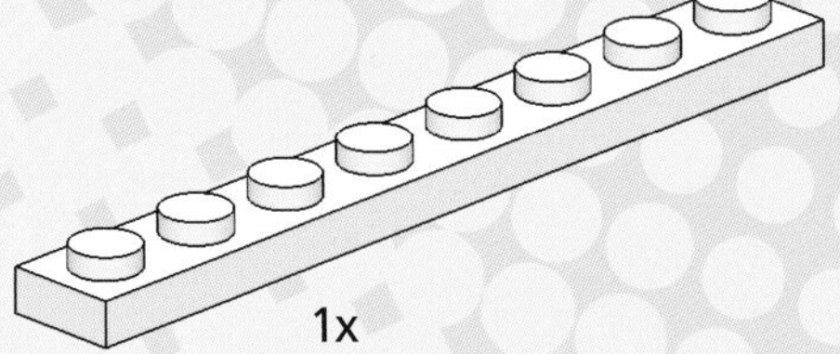
1x

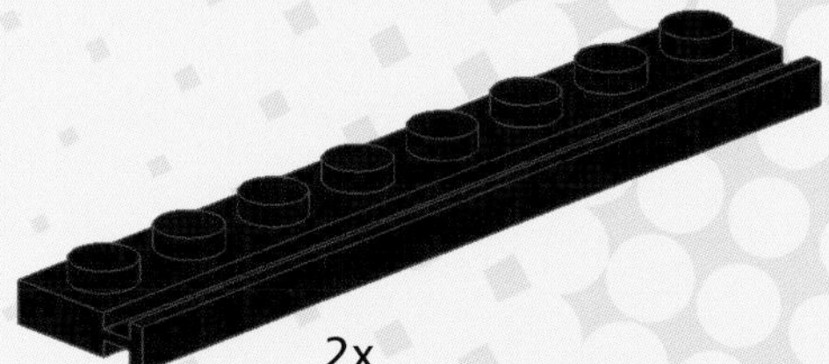
2x

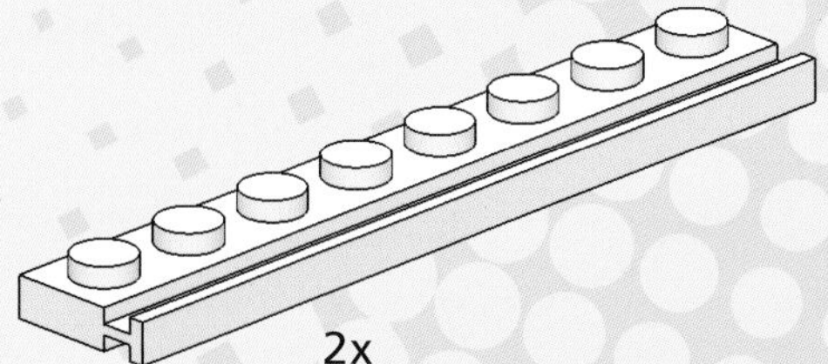
2x

6x

2x

2x

3x

1x

2x

6x

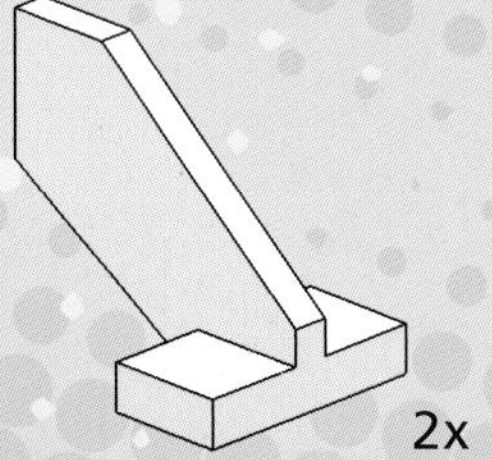
2x

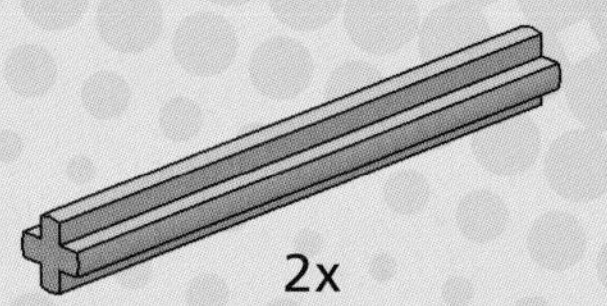
2x

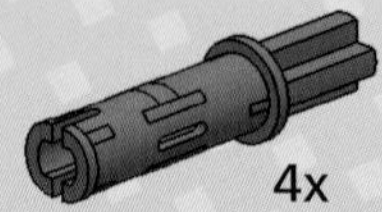

4x

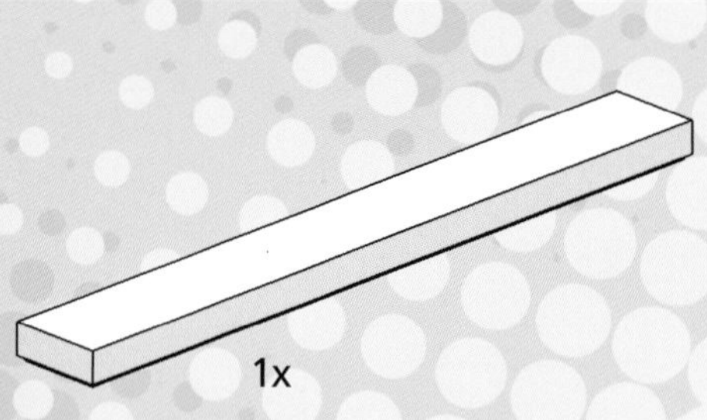

1x

1x

4x

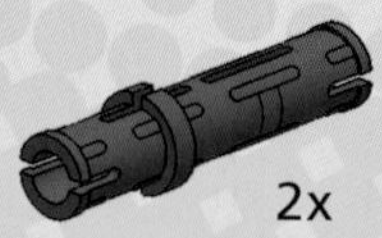

2x

6x

4x

3x

4x

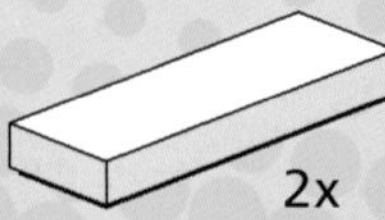

2x

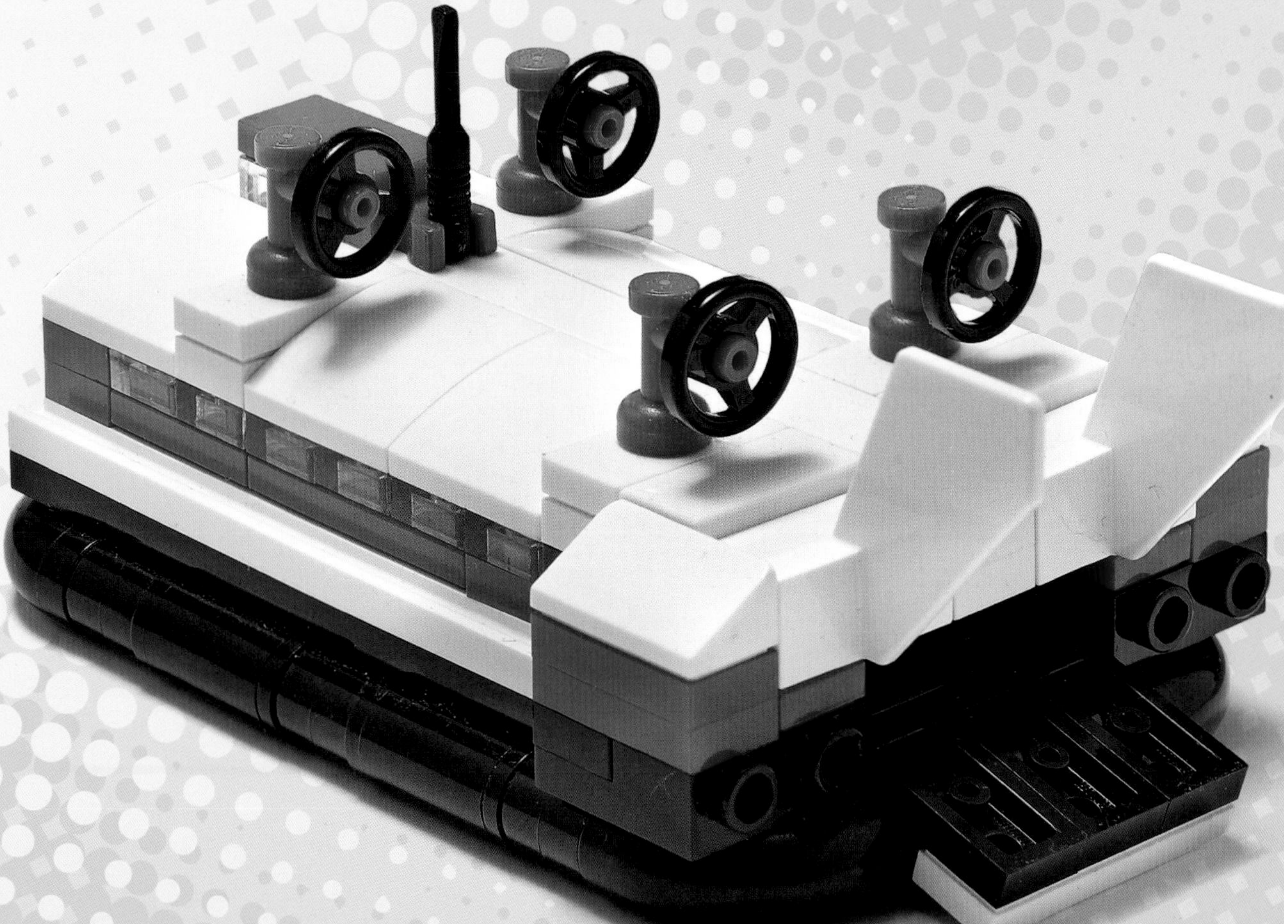

RIVA AQUARAMA

This speedboat is a highlight for many people! The Lamborghini version is the fastest Riva Aquarama motorboat in the world and achieves record selling prices of over 2 million euros. I rebuilt the model after the photo shoot and, true to form, I completely changed the stern around the engine area at the last minute. Your finished version following the building instructions will therefore differ a little from the photos.

WEIGHT:	*2,850 kg*
TOP SPEED:	*89 km/h (55 mph)*
HP:	*700*
TANK CAPACITY:	*96 liters (25 gal.)*

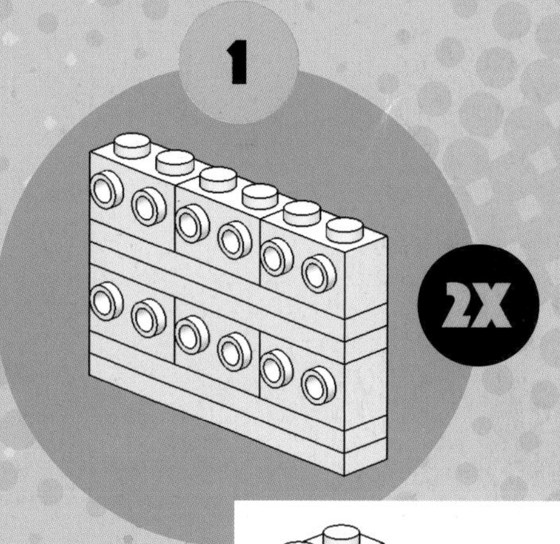

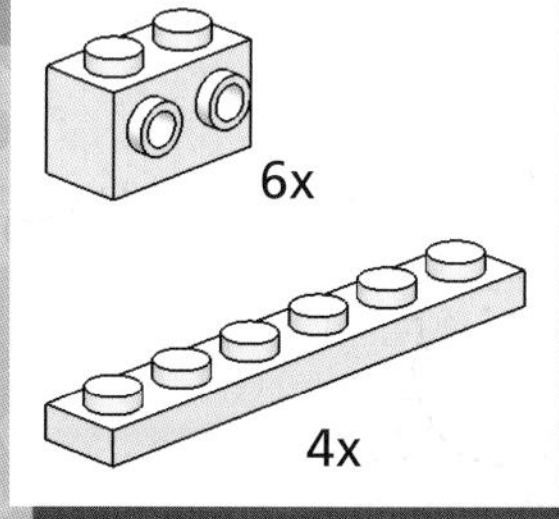

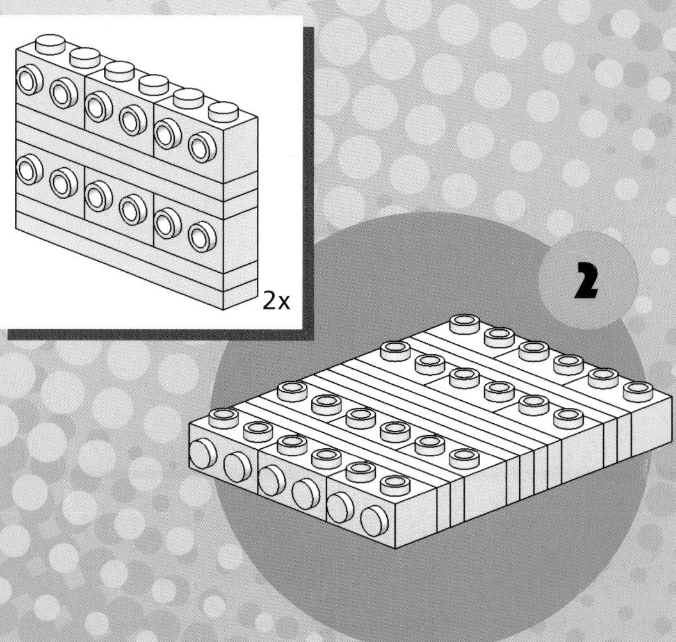

3

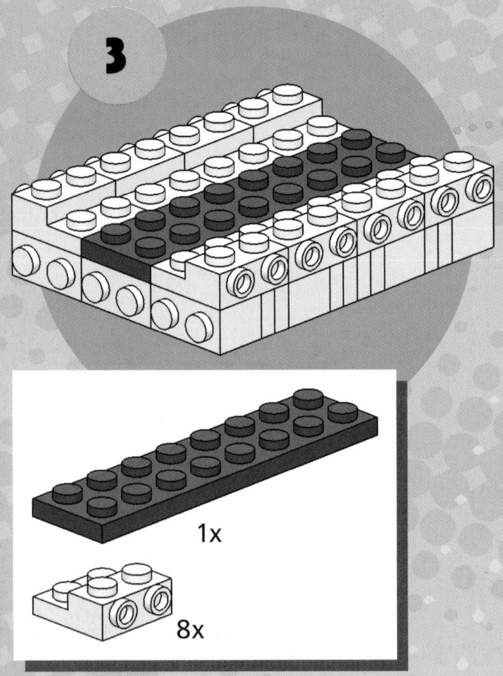

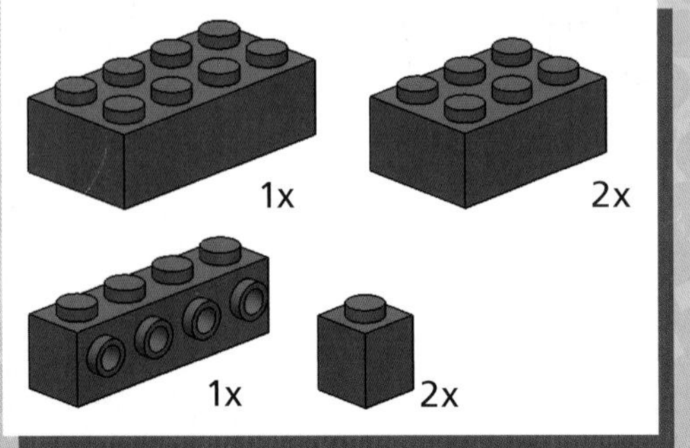

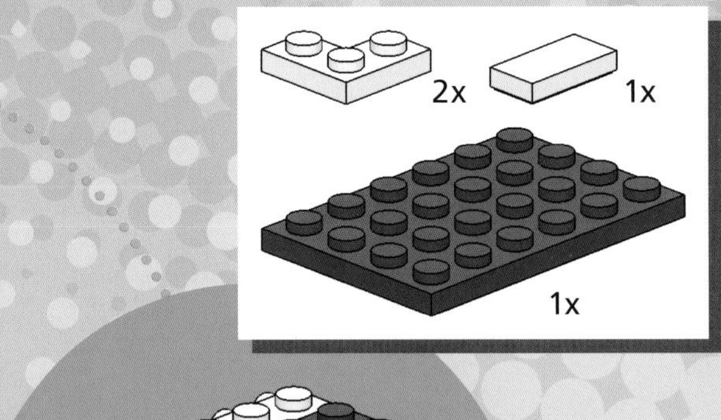

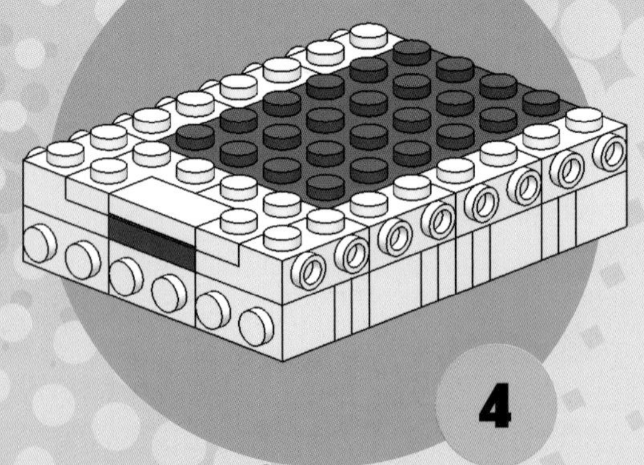

4

5

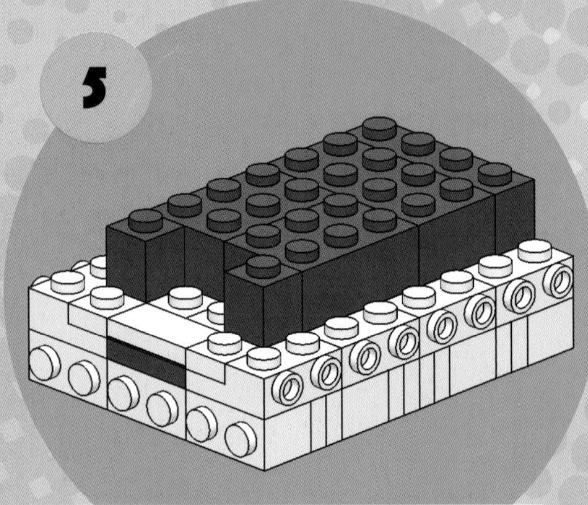

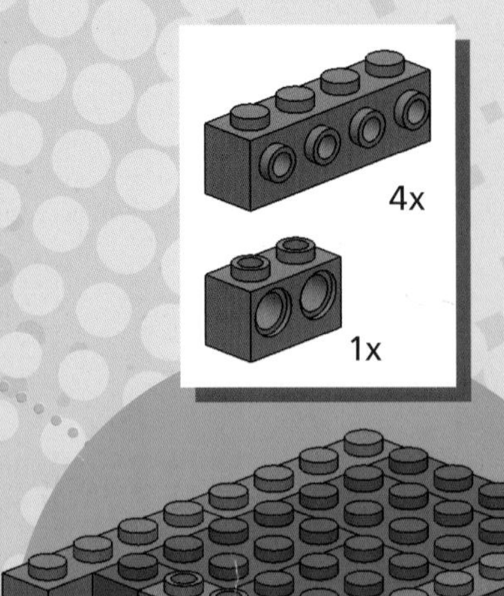

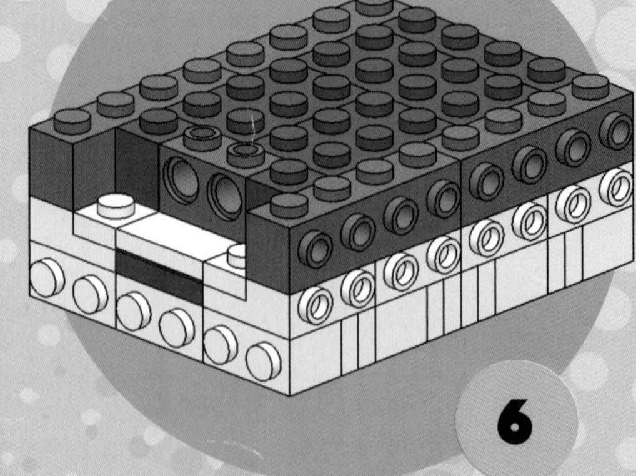

6

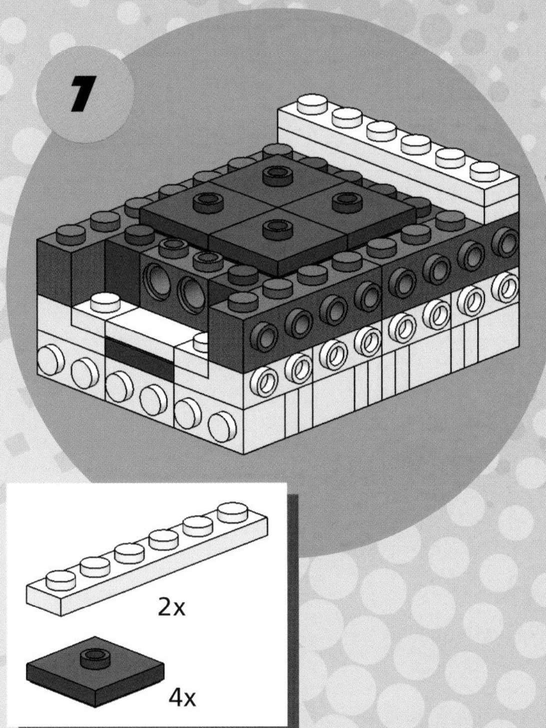

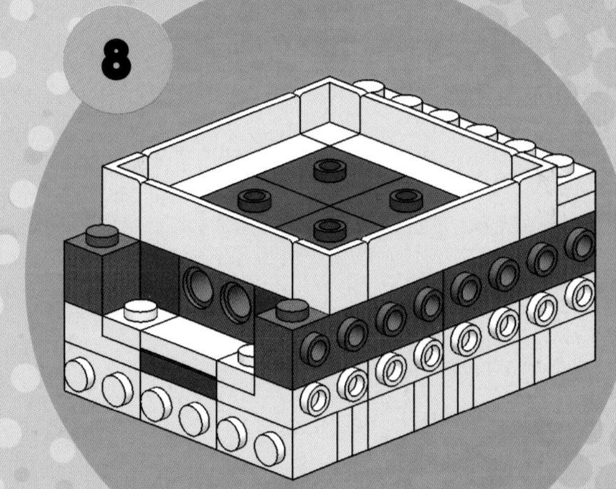

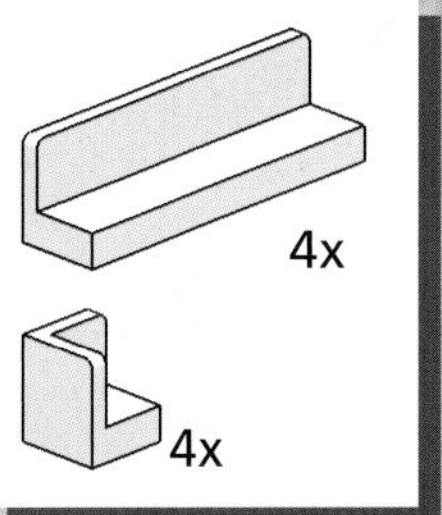

2x 1x
1x 2x 2x

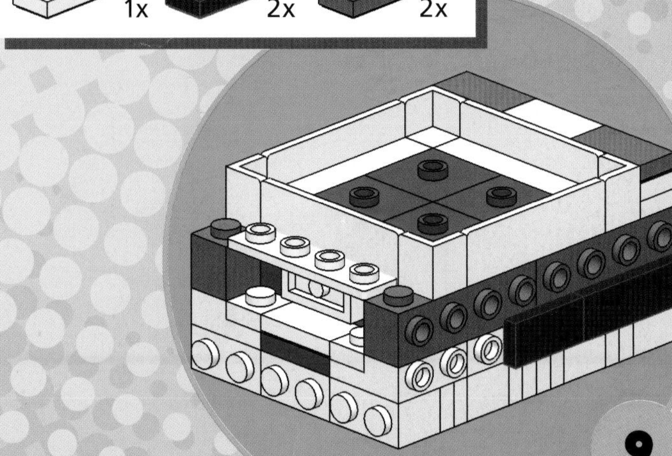

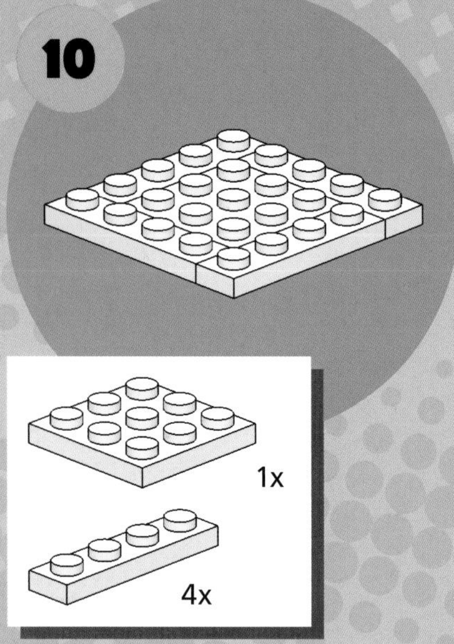
10
1x
4x

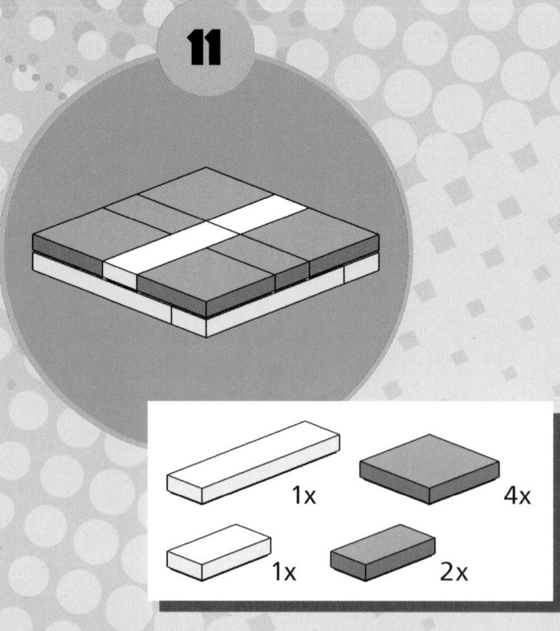
11
1x
4x
1x
2x

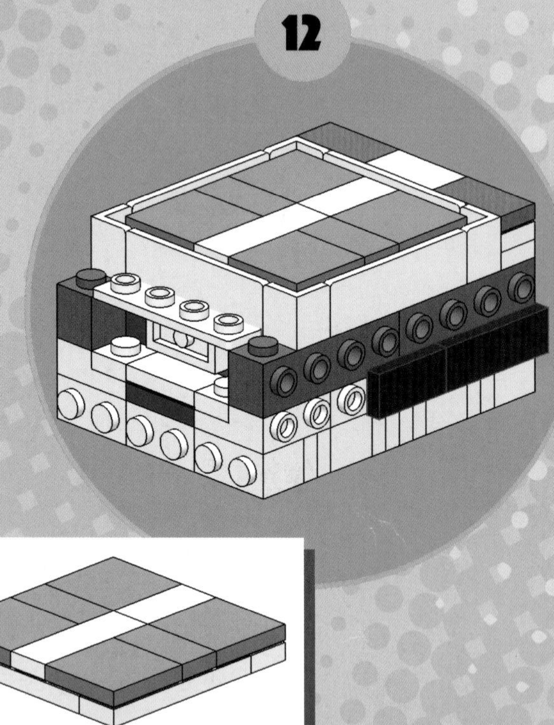
12

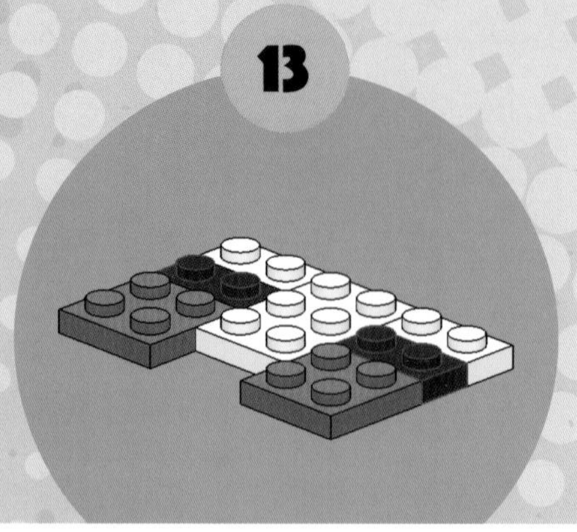
13

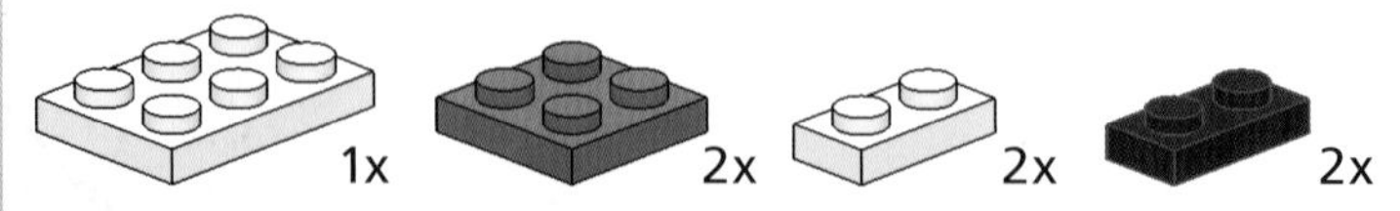
1x
2x
2x
2x

14

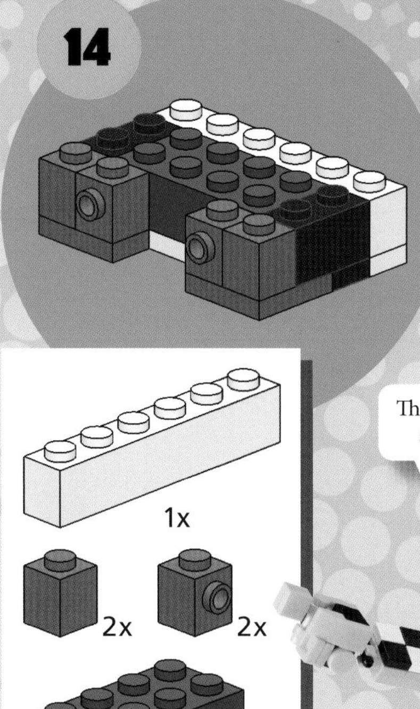
1x
2x
2x
1x
2x

These bricks only have a single side stud.

15

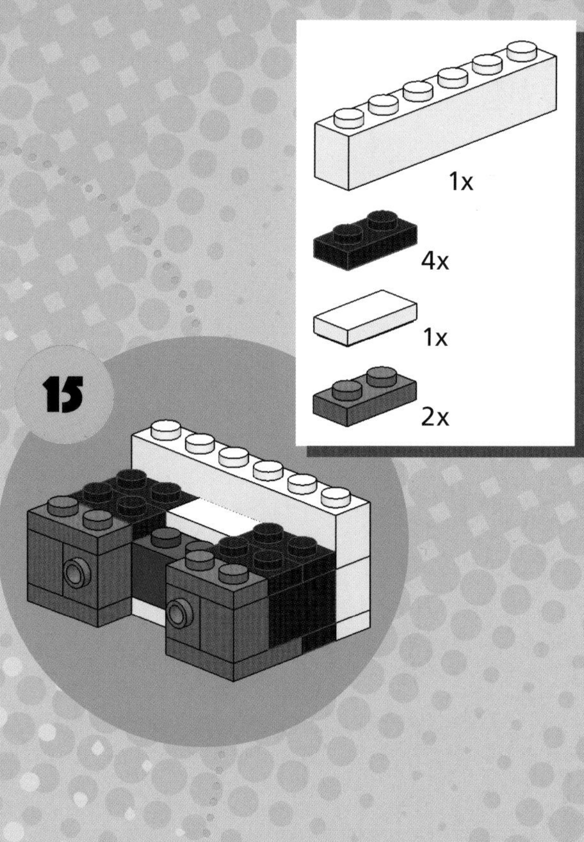
1x
4x
1x
2x

16

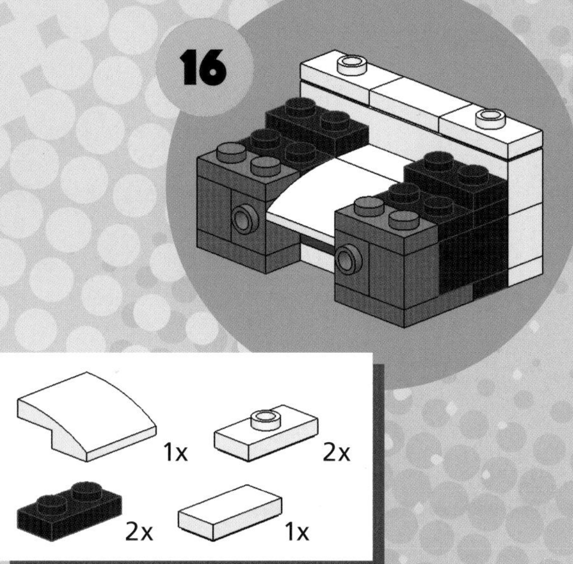
1x
2x
2x
1x

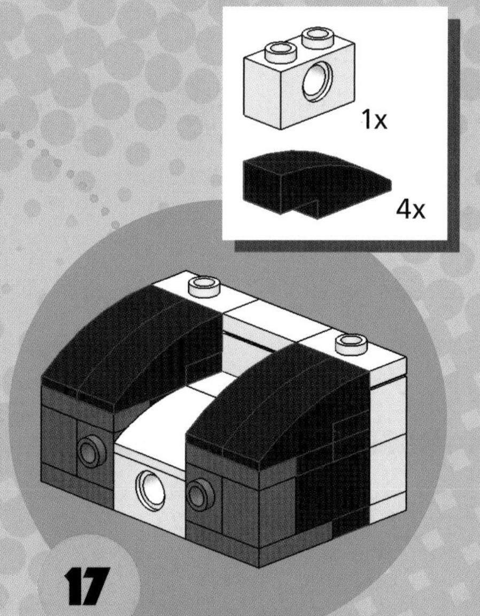
1x
4x

17

1x 2x 2x

18

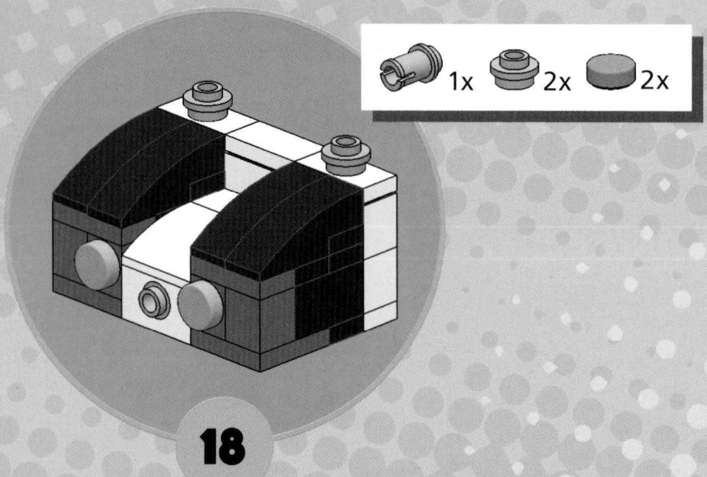

19

1x 1x 1x

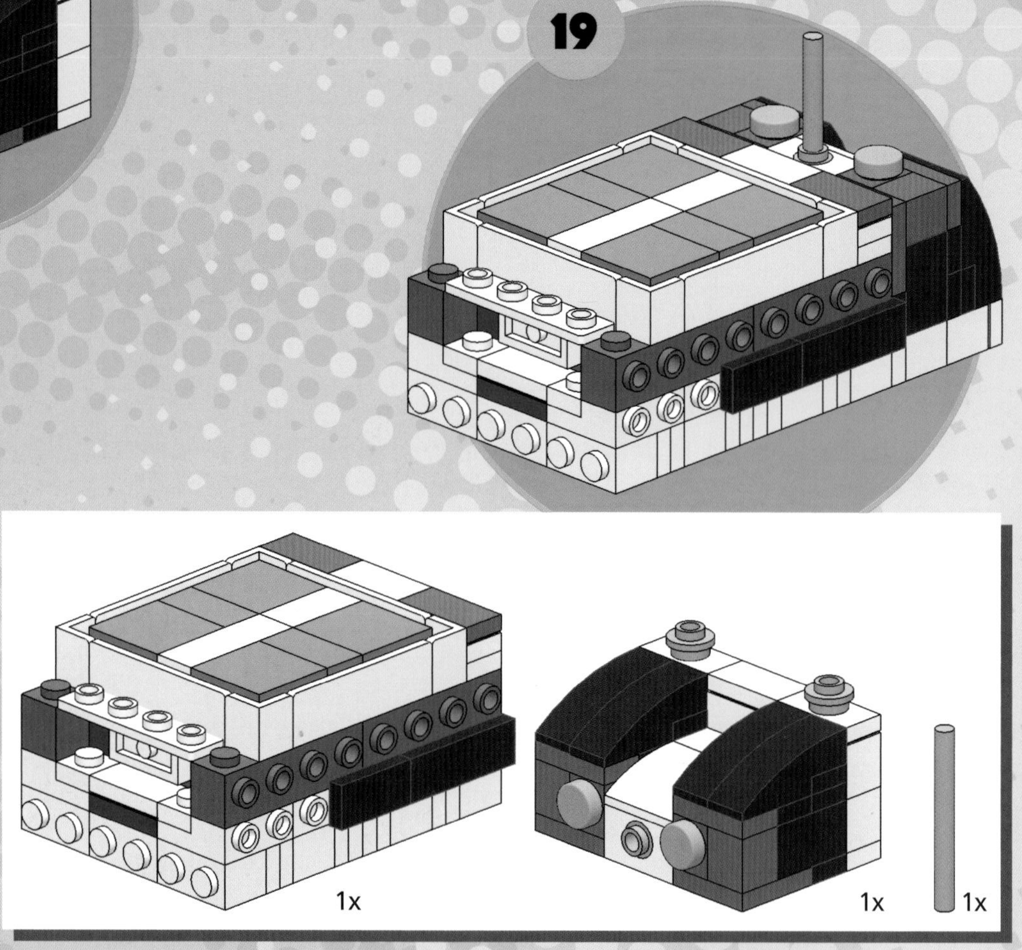

20

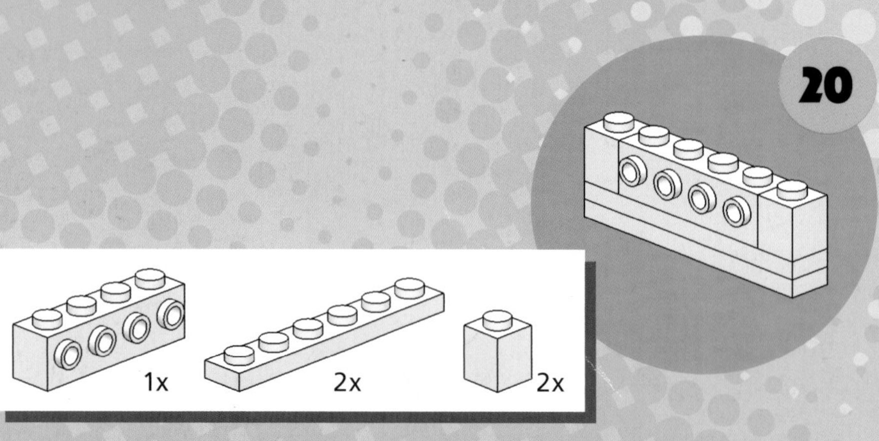

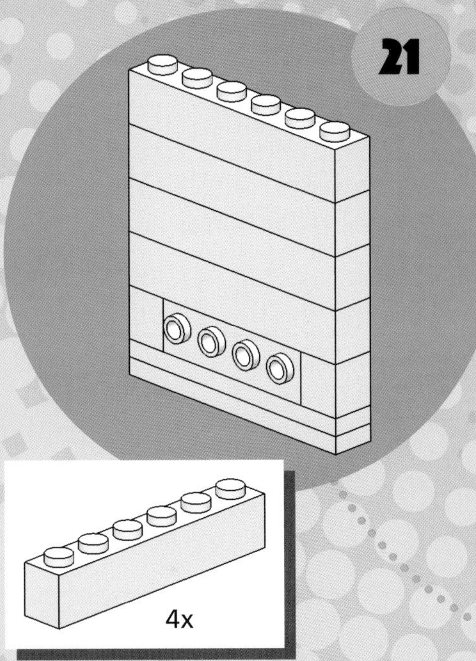
21
4x

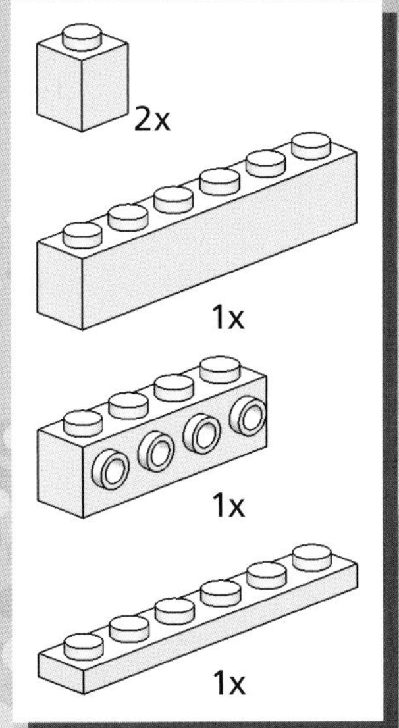
2x
1x
1x
1x

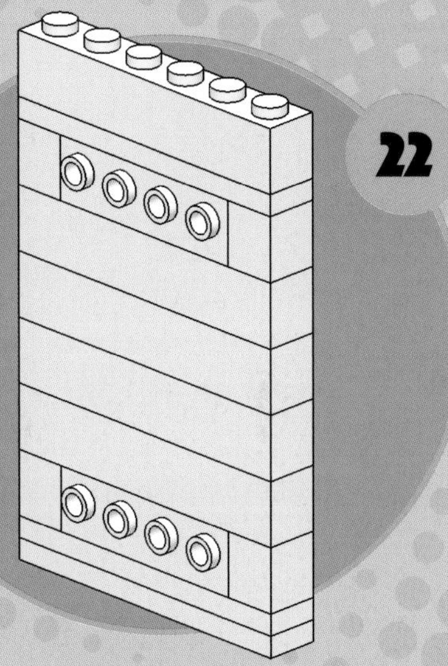
22

23

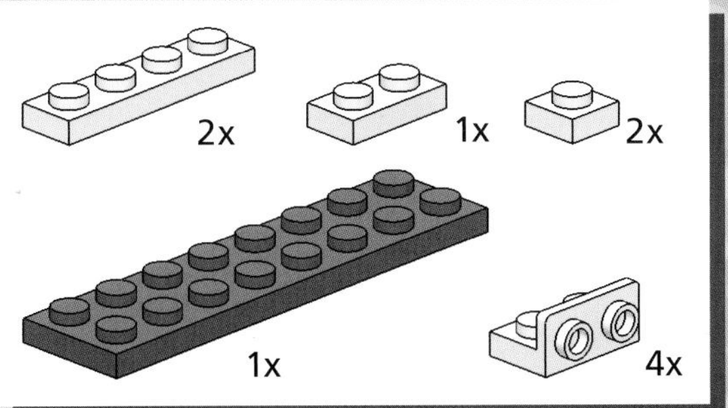
2x
1x
2x
1x
4x

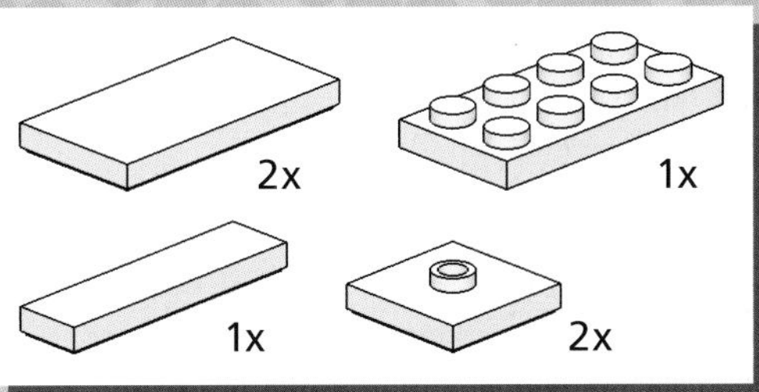
2x
1x
1x
2x

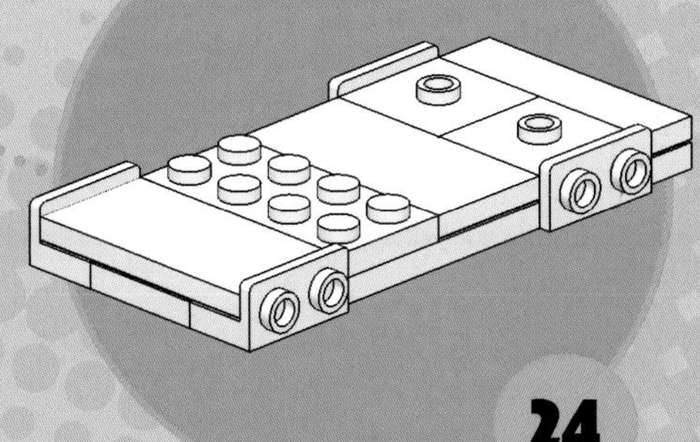
24

25

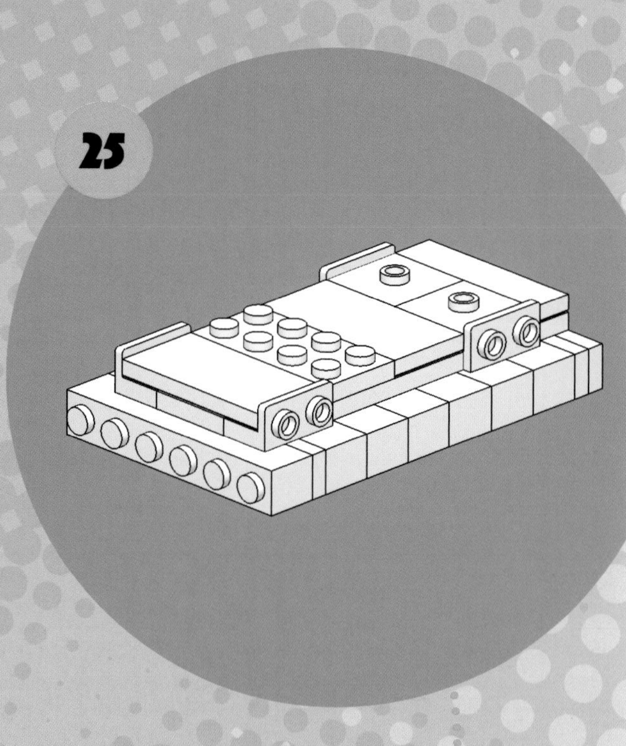

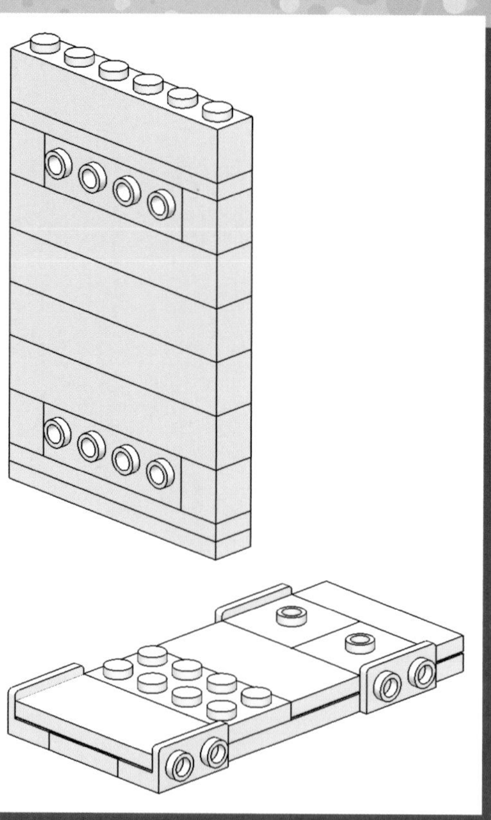

26

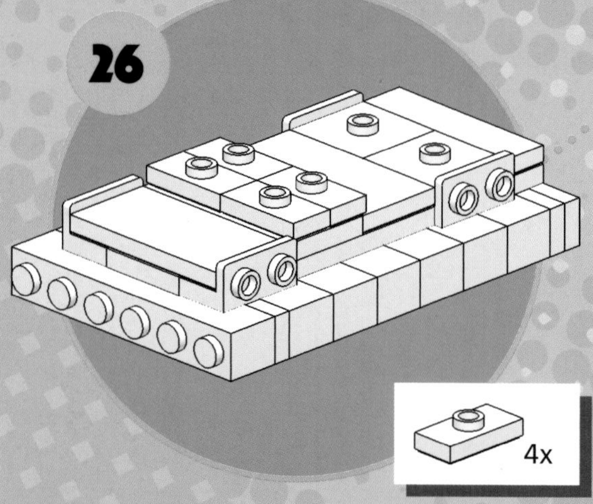

4x

27

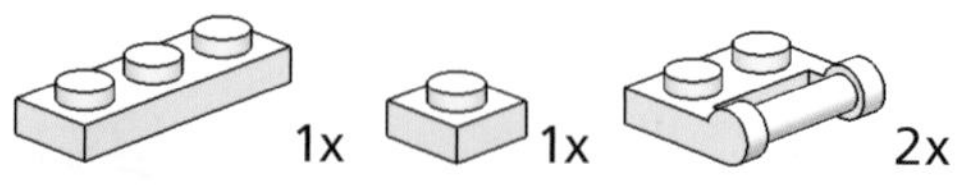

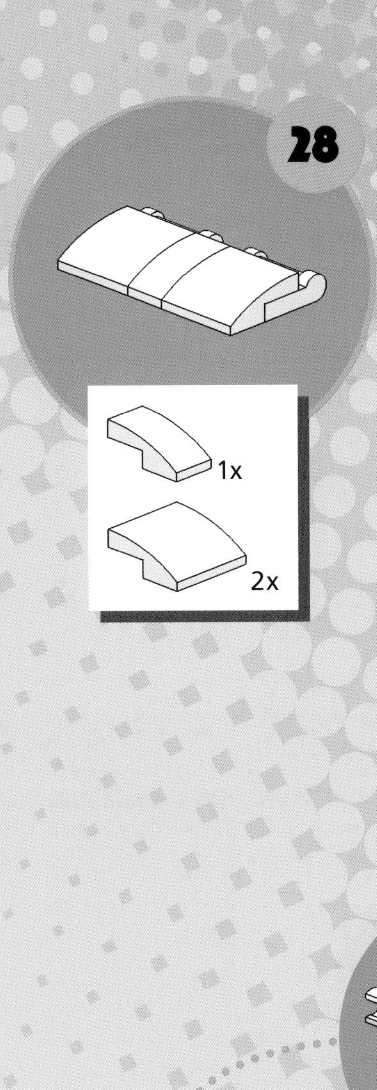

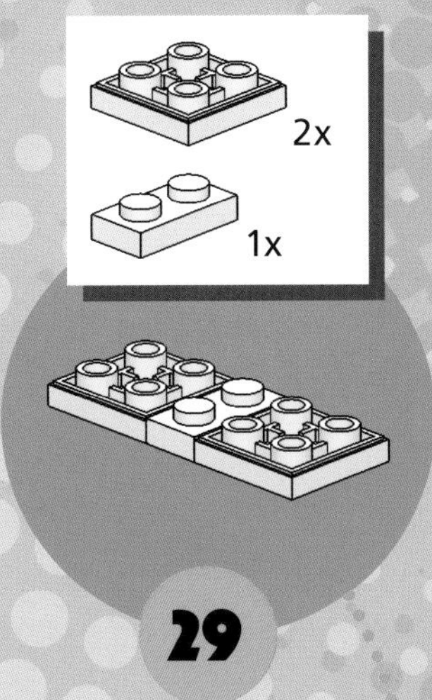

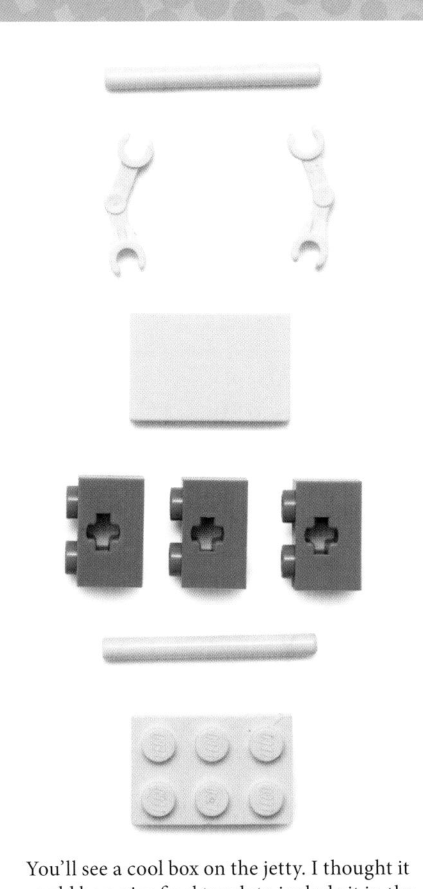

You'll see a cool box on the jetty. I thought it would be a nice final touch to include it in the building instructions.

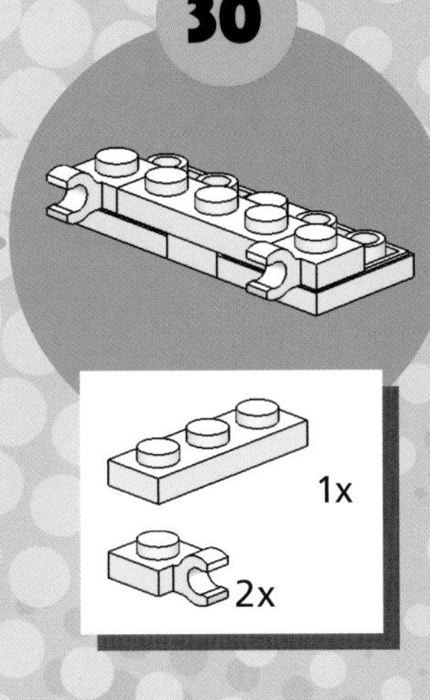

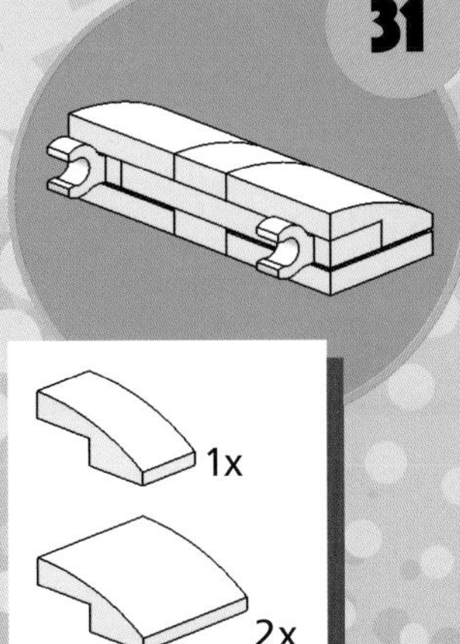

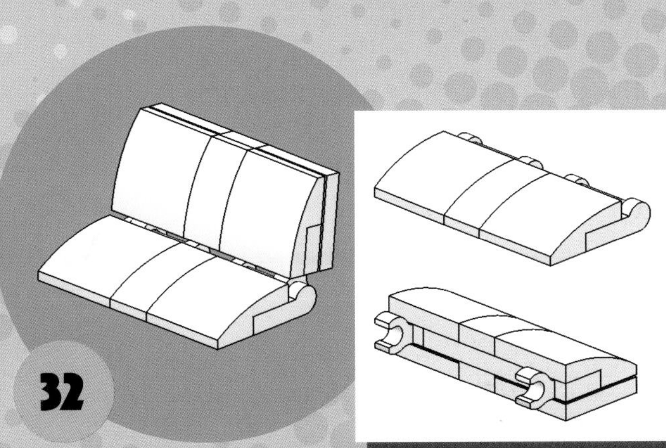

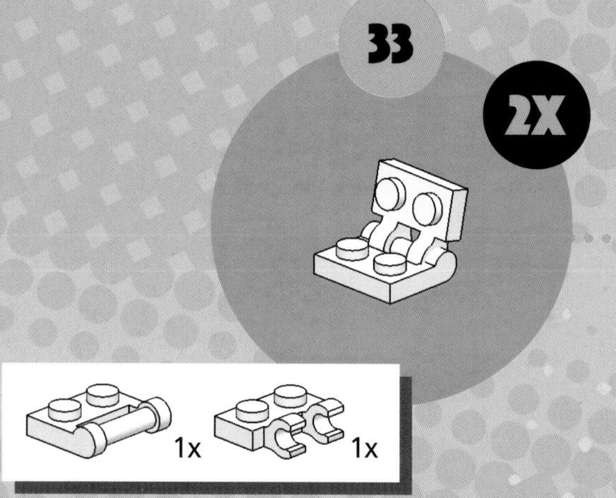
33
2X
1x
1x

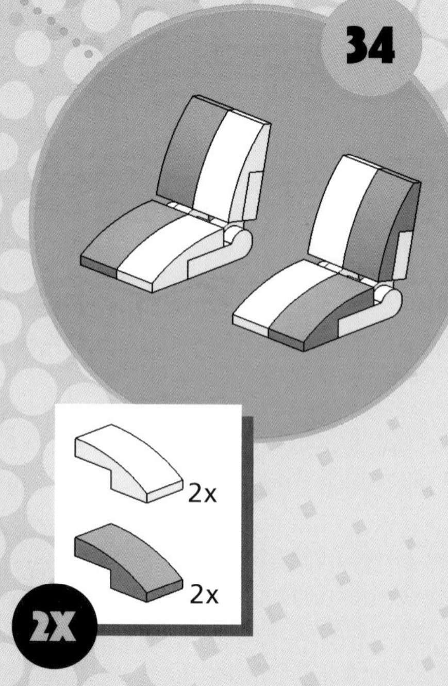
34
2x
2x
2X

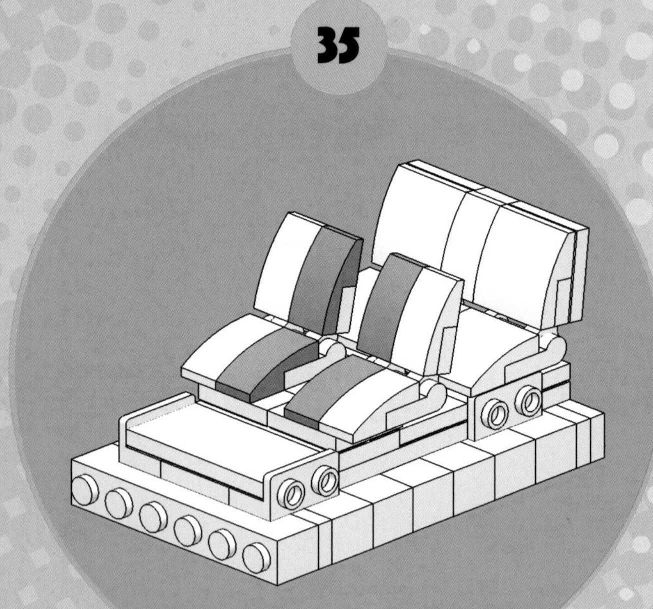
35

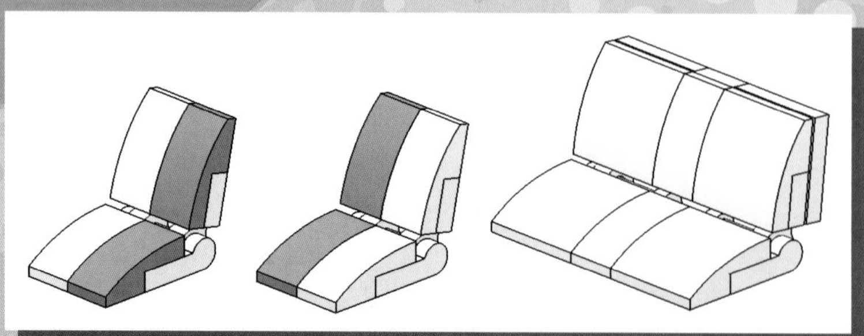

36

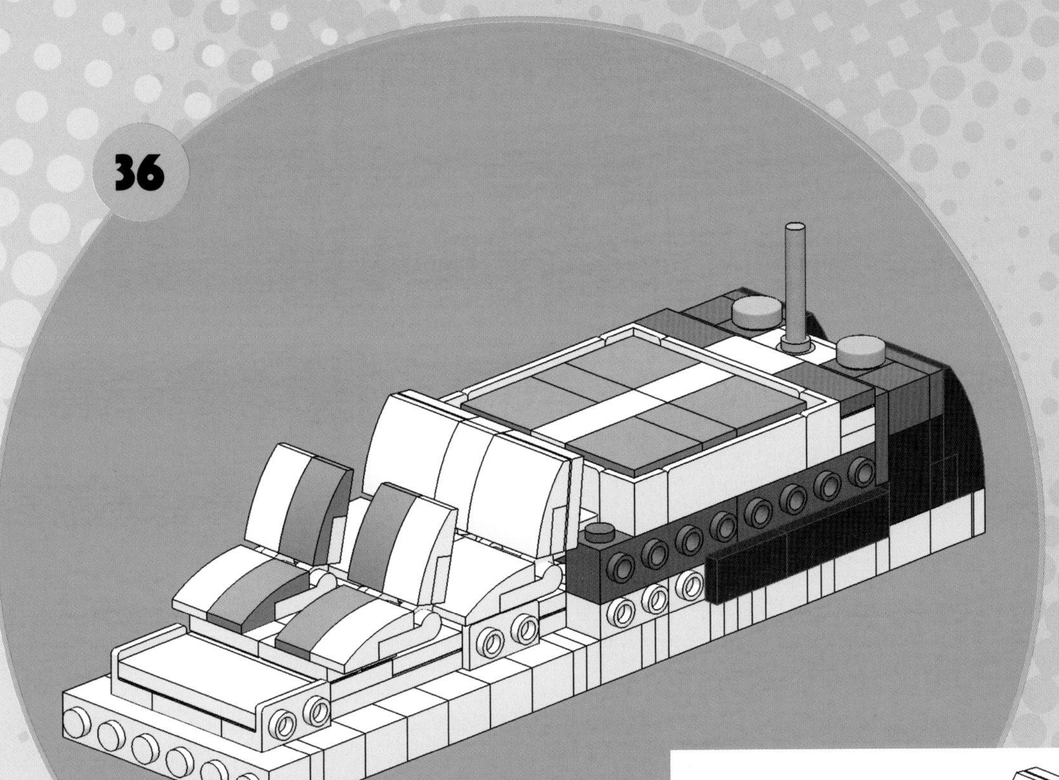

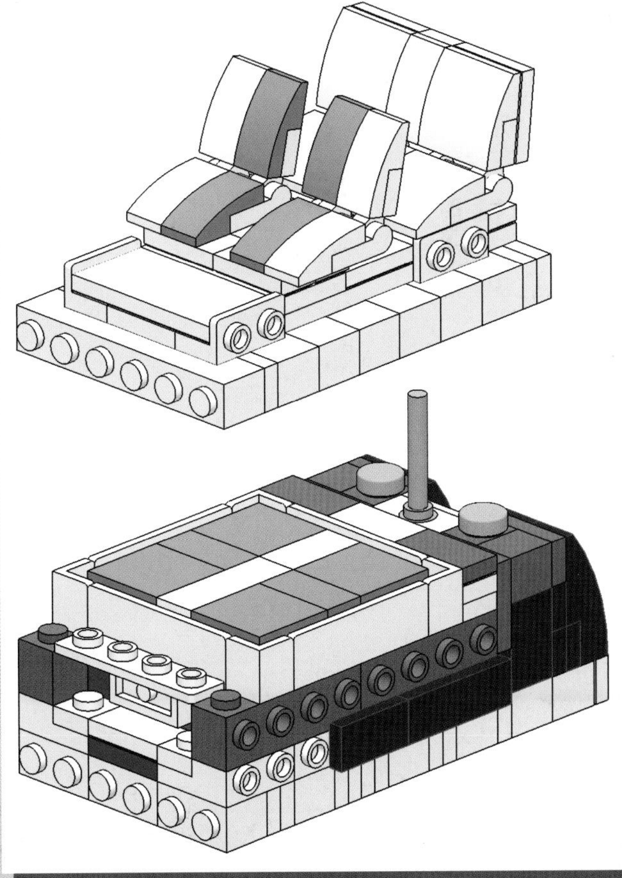

37

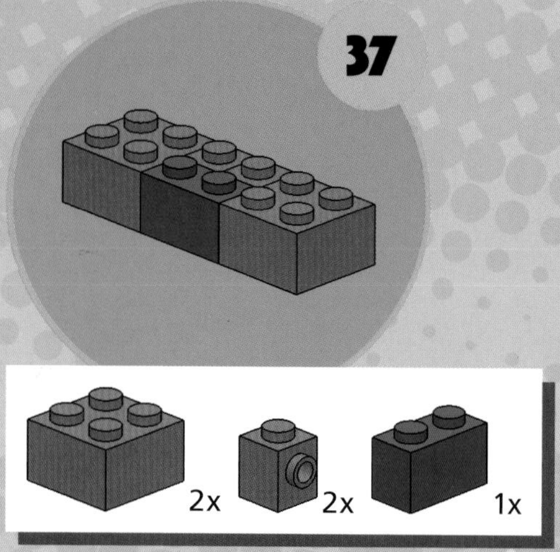

2x 2x 1x

38

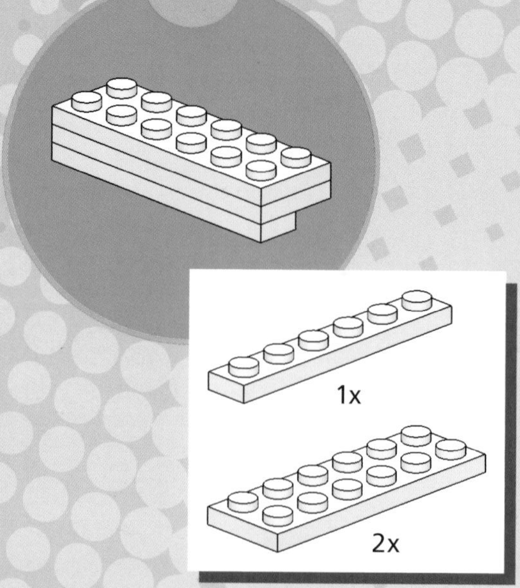

1x

2x

39

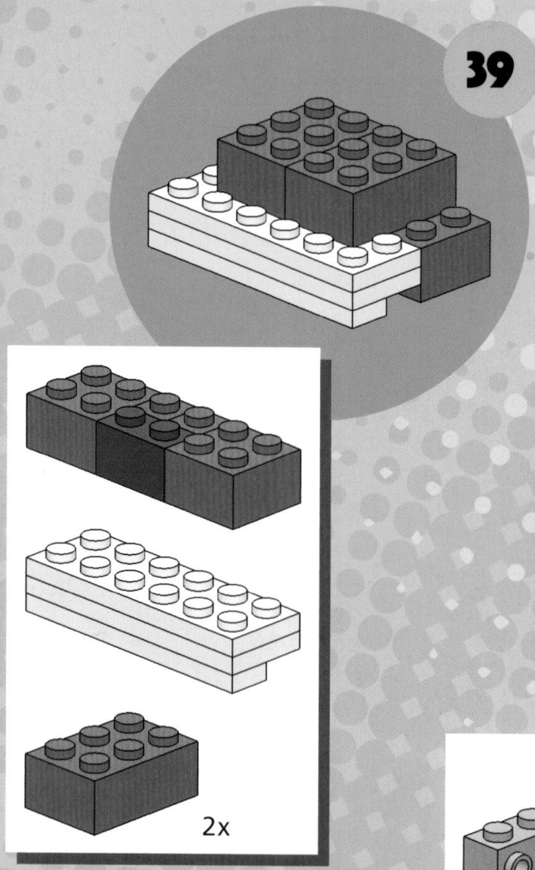

2x

40

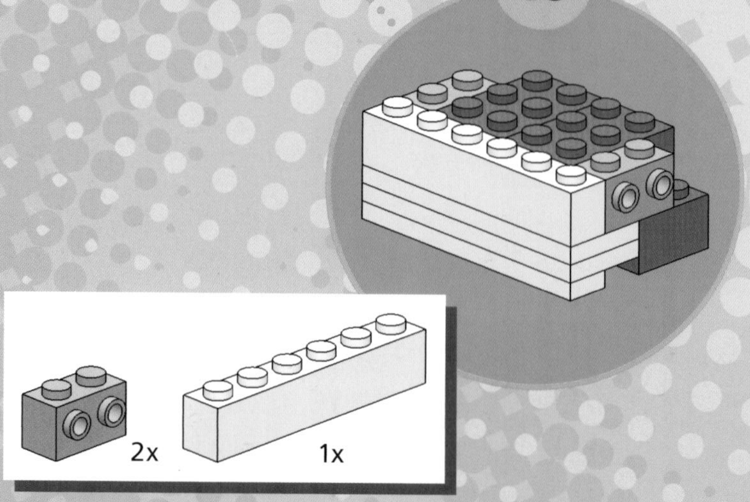

2x 1x

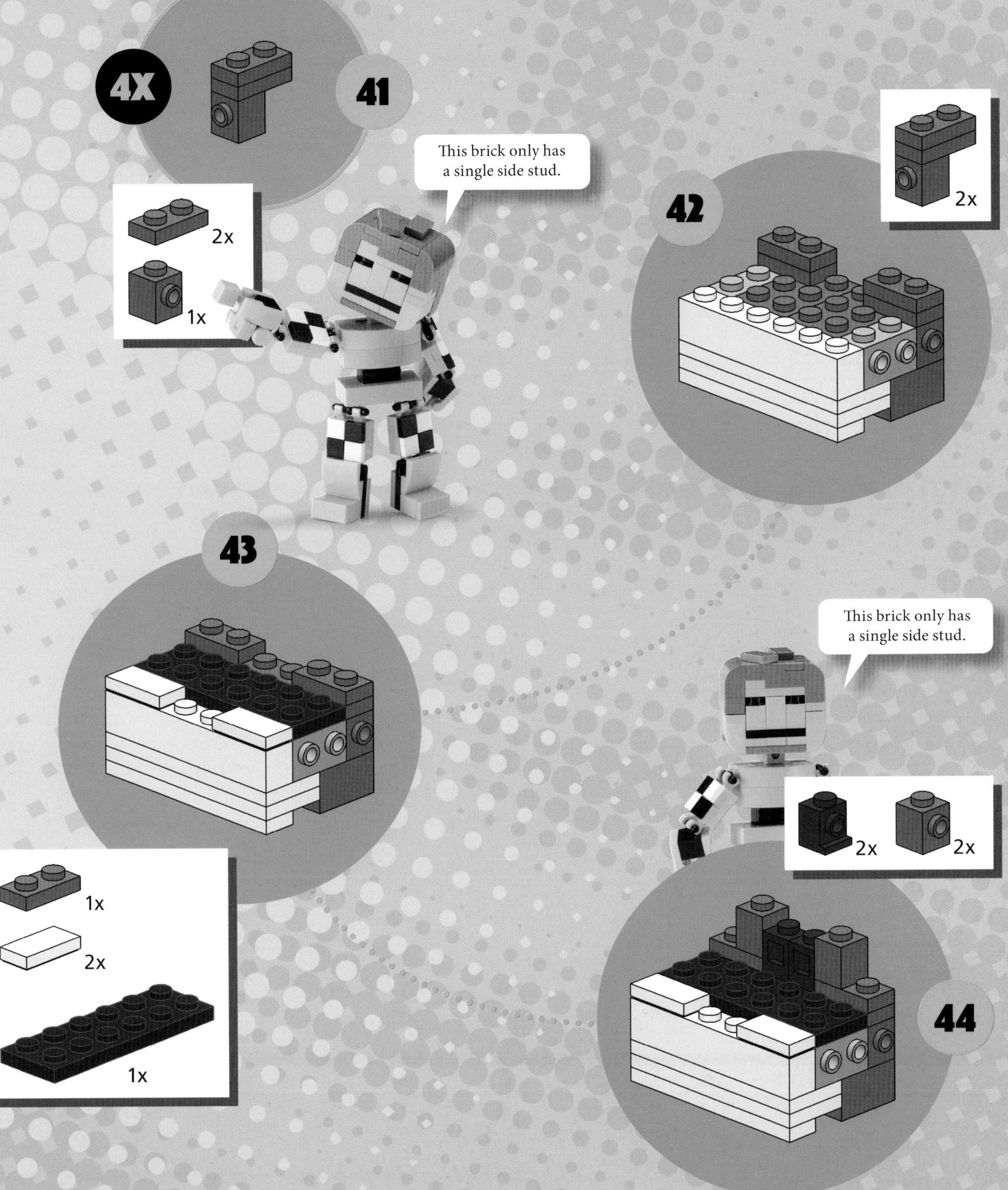
4X
41
This brick only has
a single side stud.
2x
1x
42
2x
43
1x
2x
1x
This brick only has
a single side stud.
2x
2x
44

1x
1x
4x
45

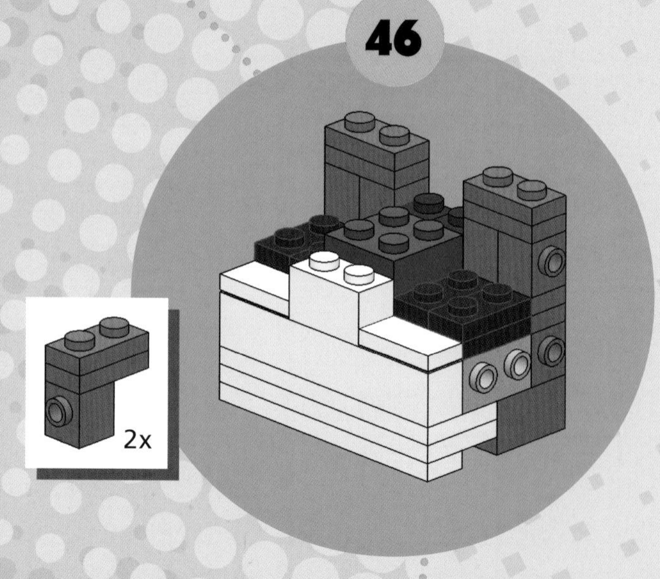
46
2x

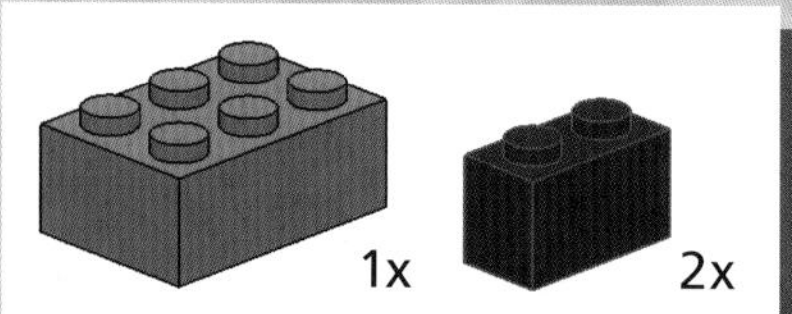
1x
2x

47

48

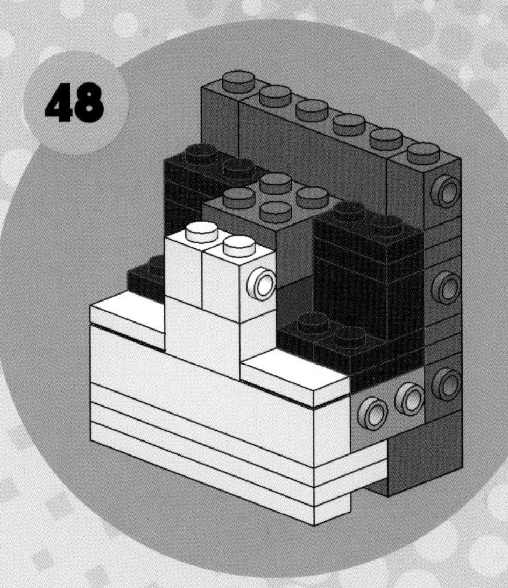

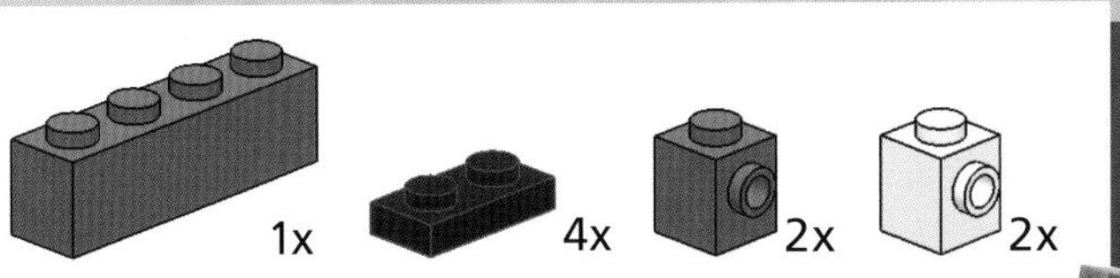

These bricks only have a single side stud.

49

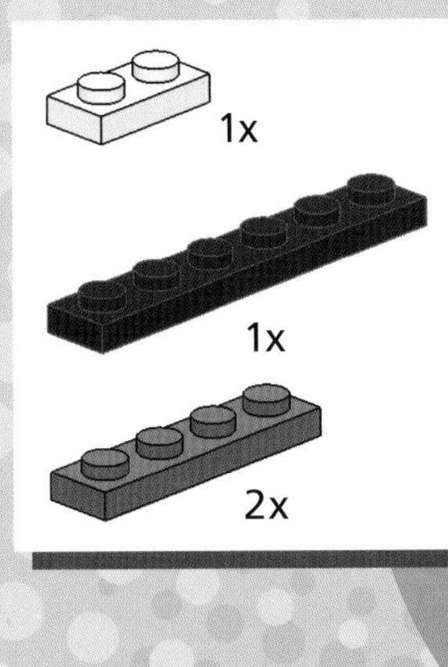

50

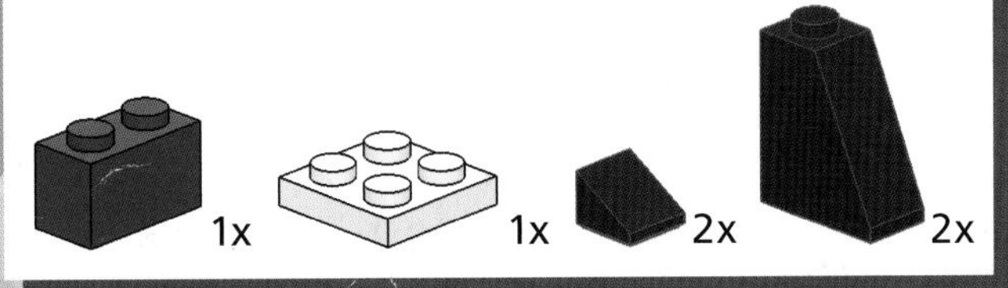

51

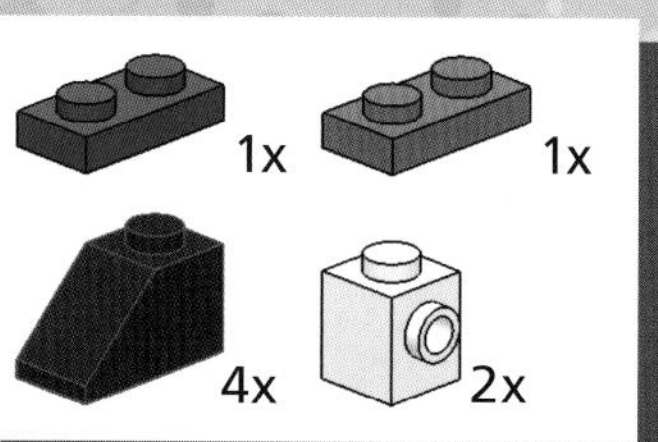
1x
1x
4x
2x

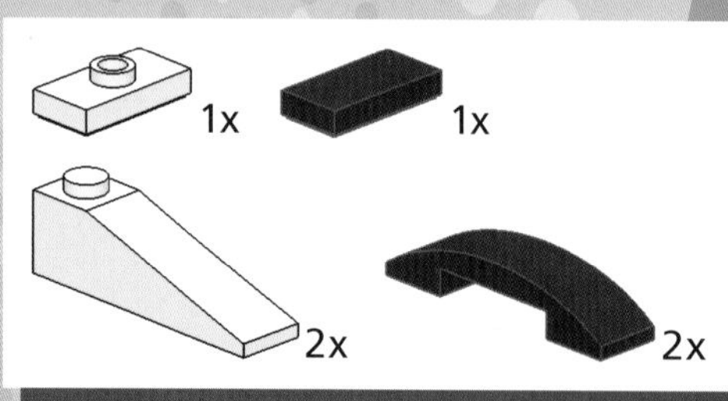
1x
1x
2x
2x

52

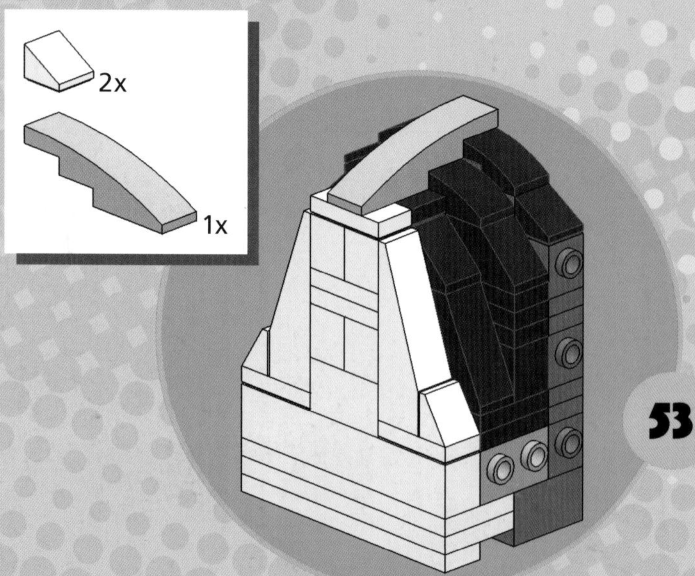
2x
1x
53

54
2X
1x
1x

55
3x
2x
2x
1x

56
2x

57
2x
1x

58
1x
2x
1x

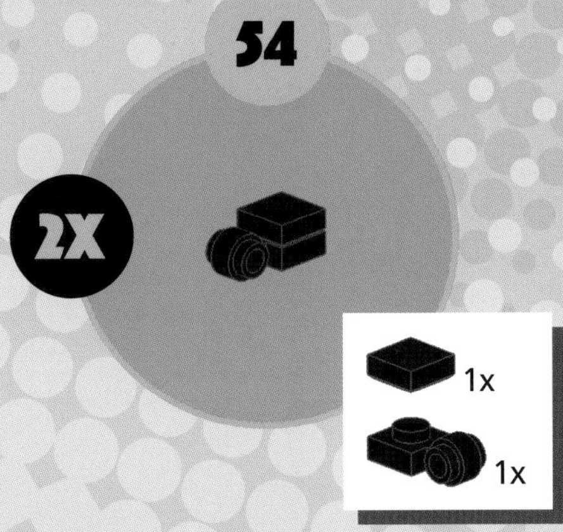

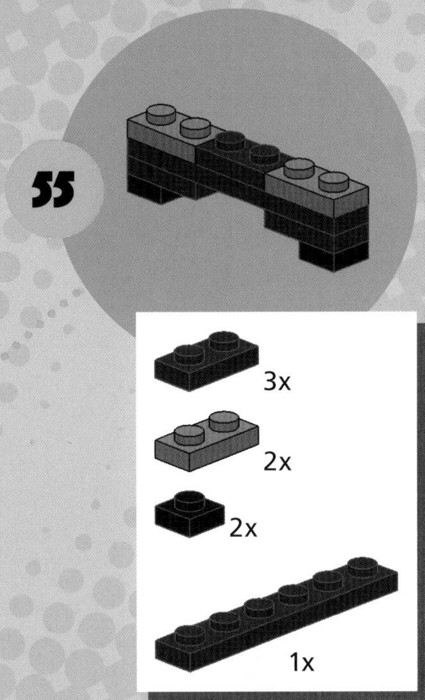

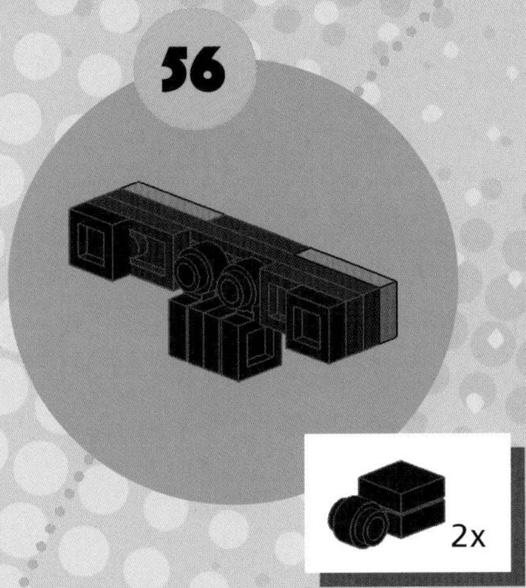

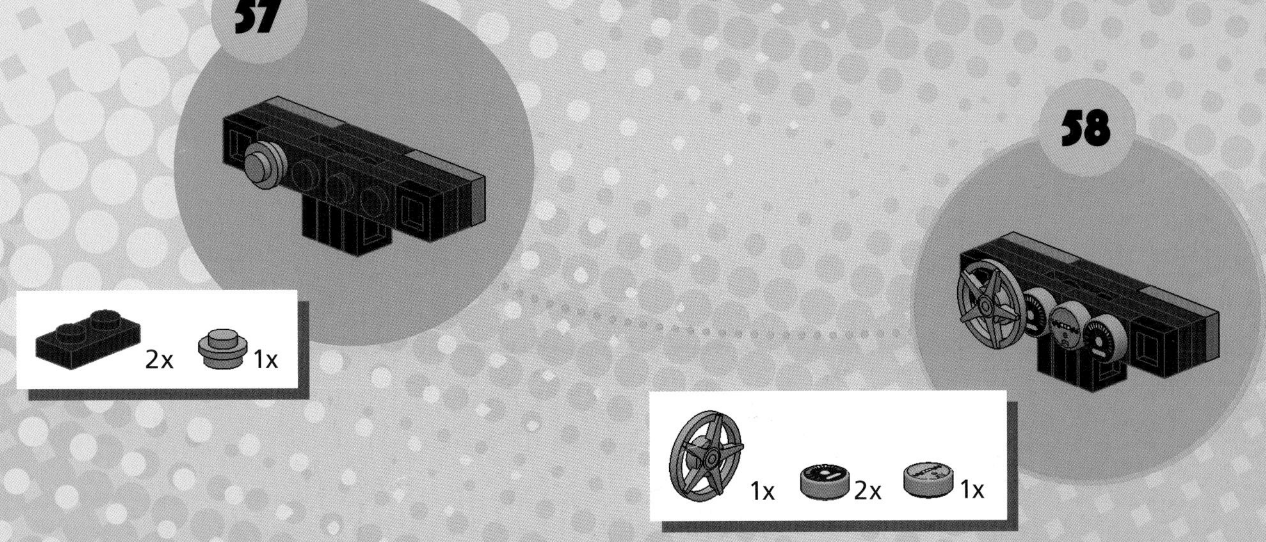

59

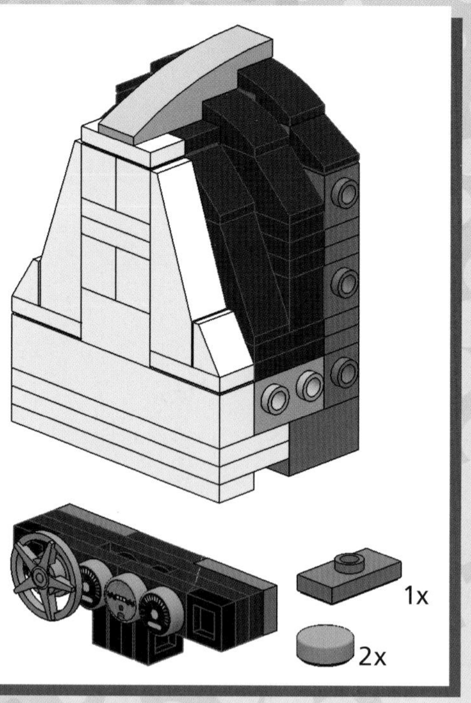

60

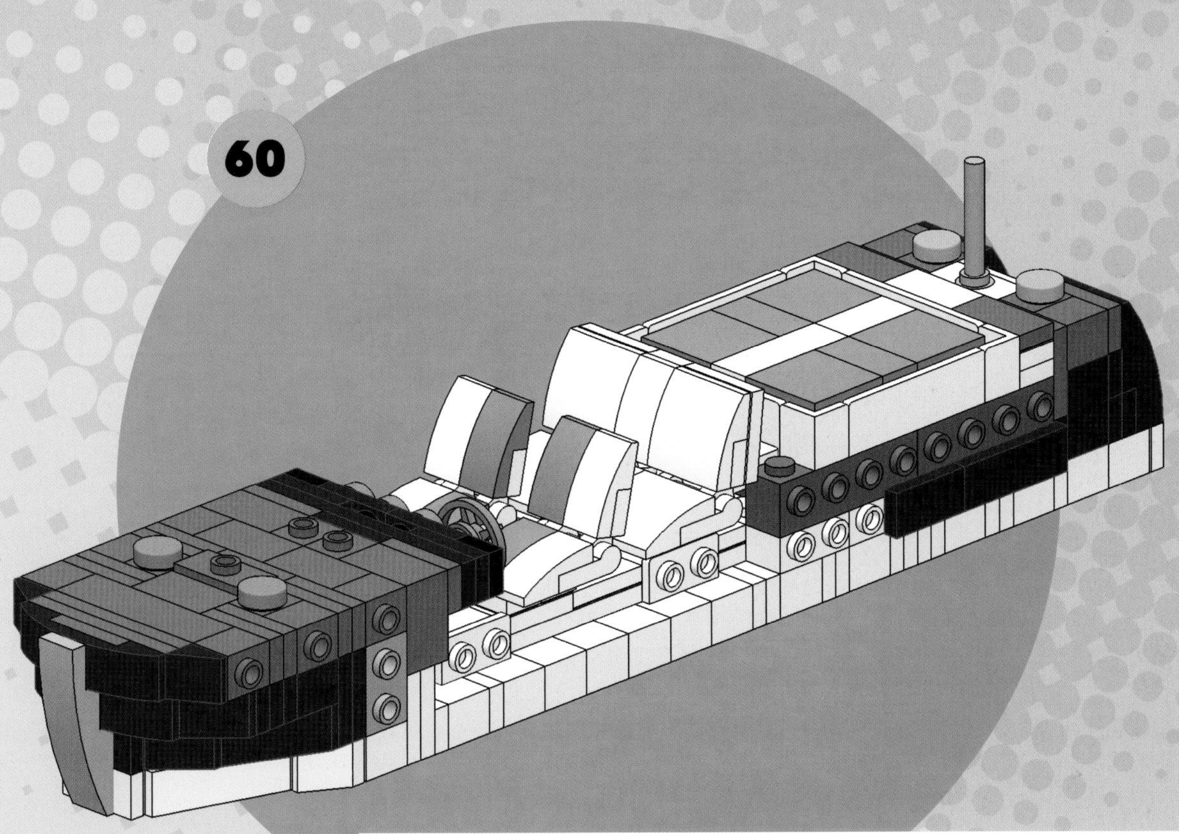

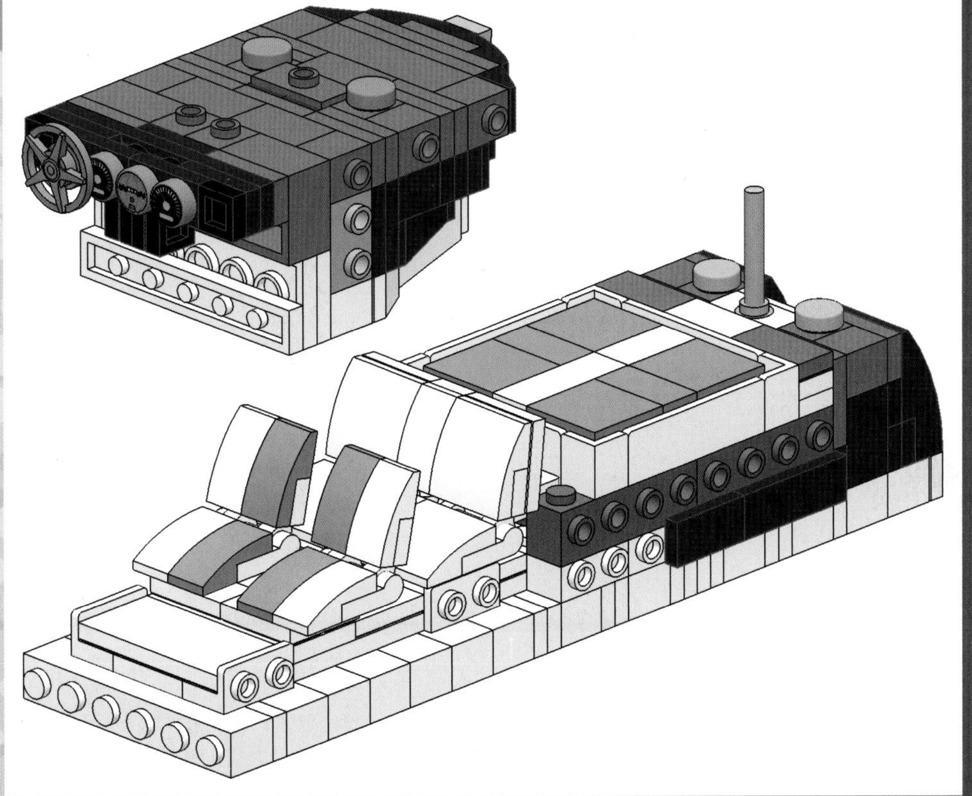

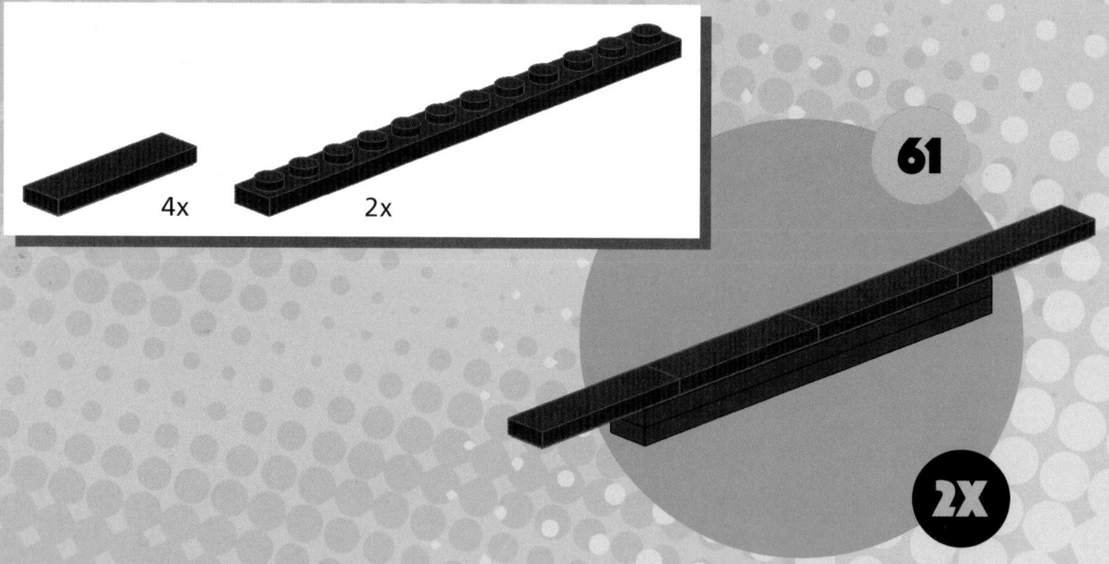

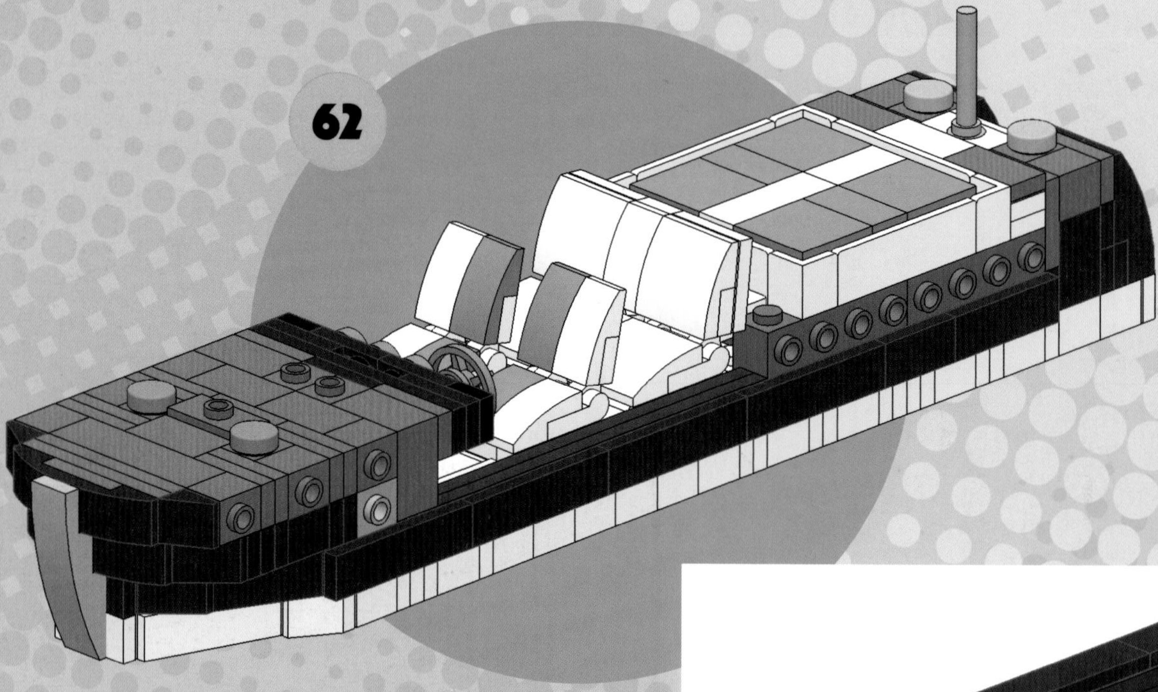

62

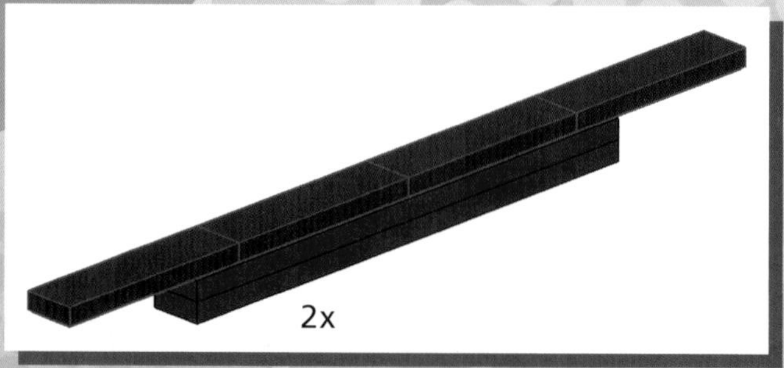

2x

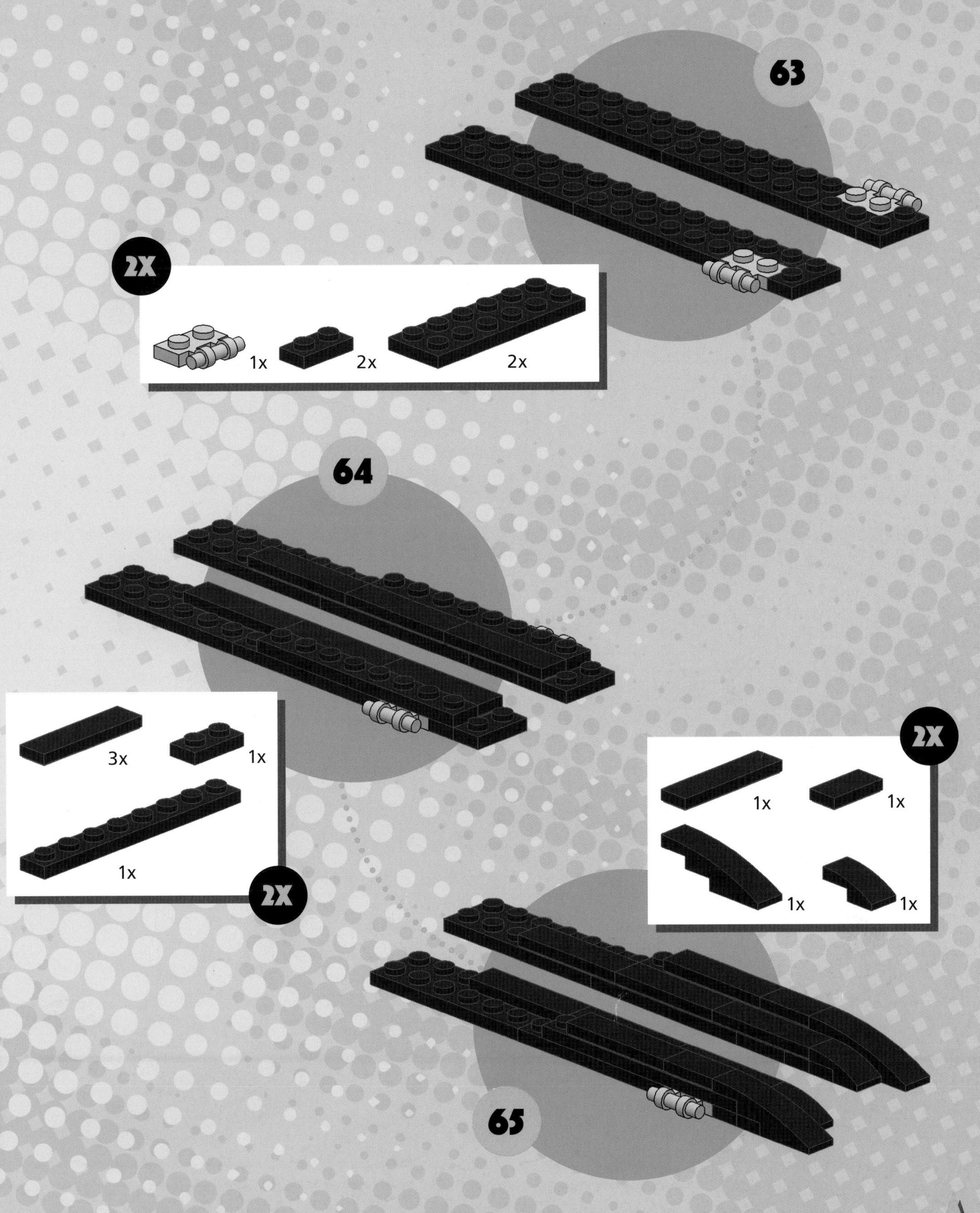
63
2X
1x
2x
2x
64
3x
1x
1x
2X
2X
1x
1x
1x
1x
65

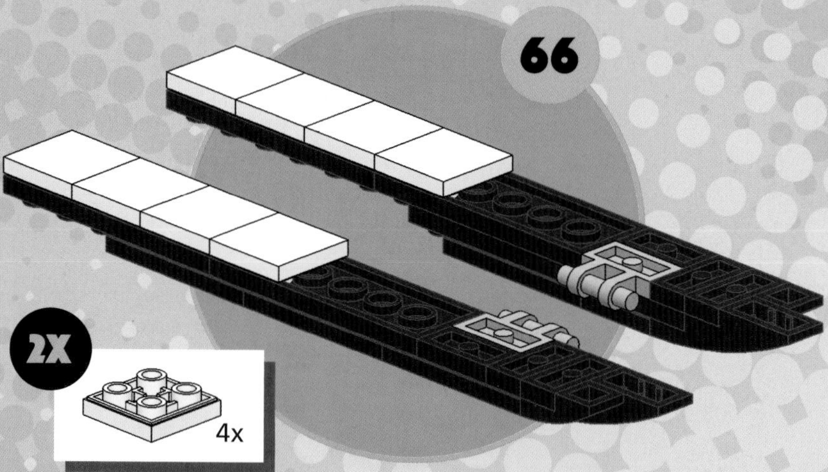

66

2X

4x

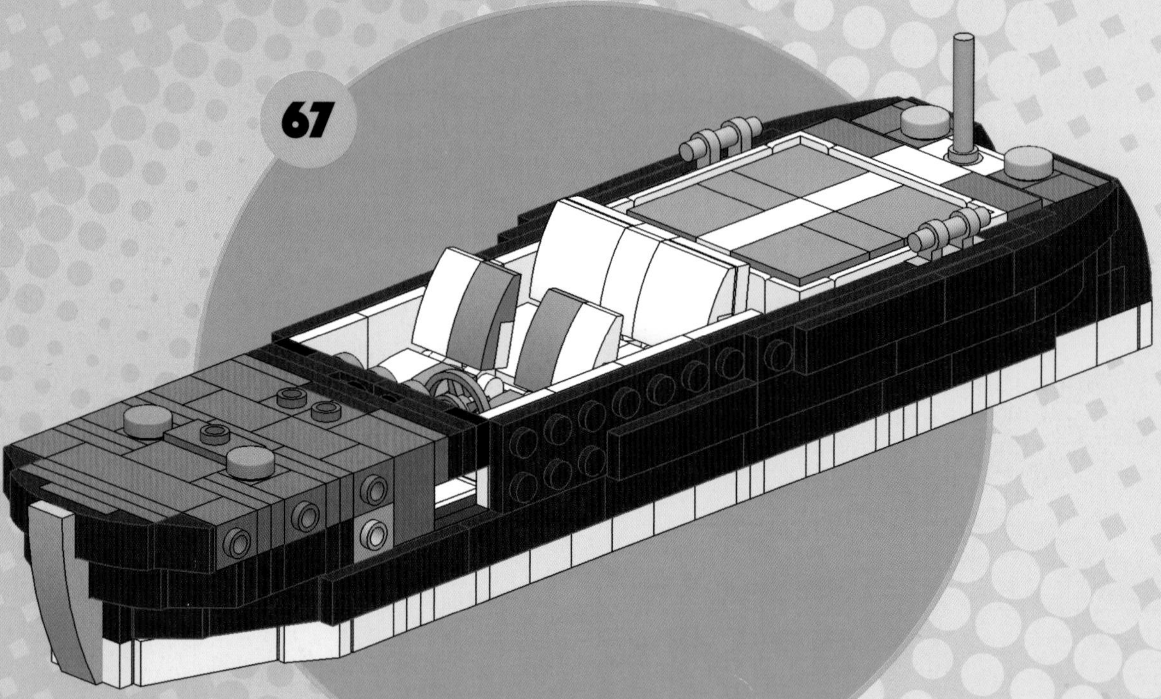

67

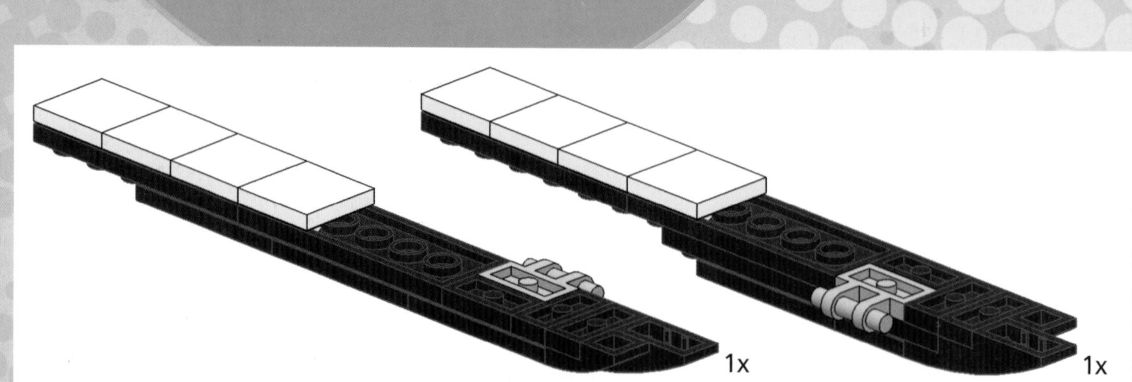

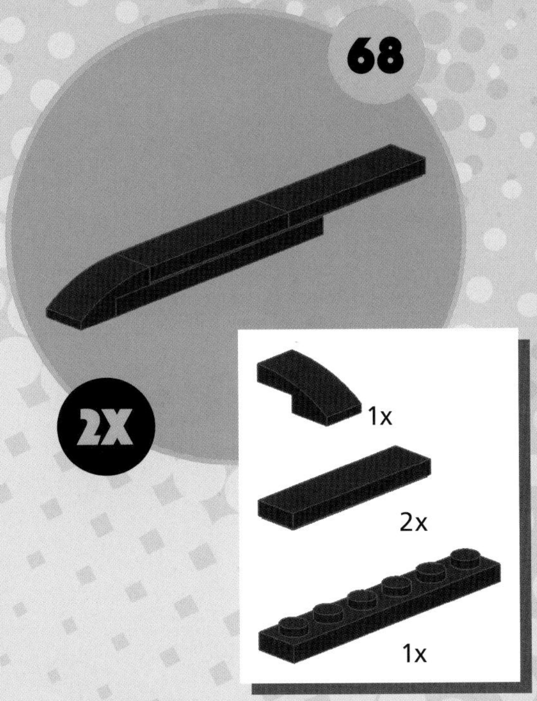

68

2X

1x

2x

1x

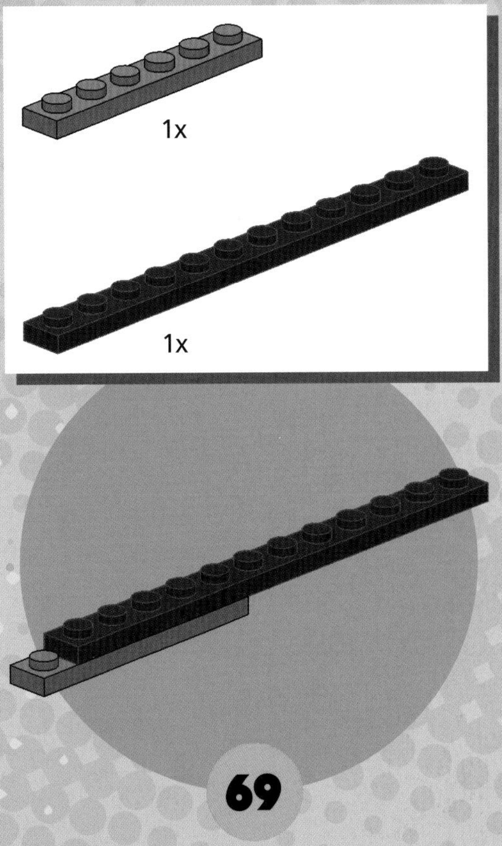

1x

1x

69

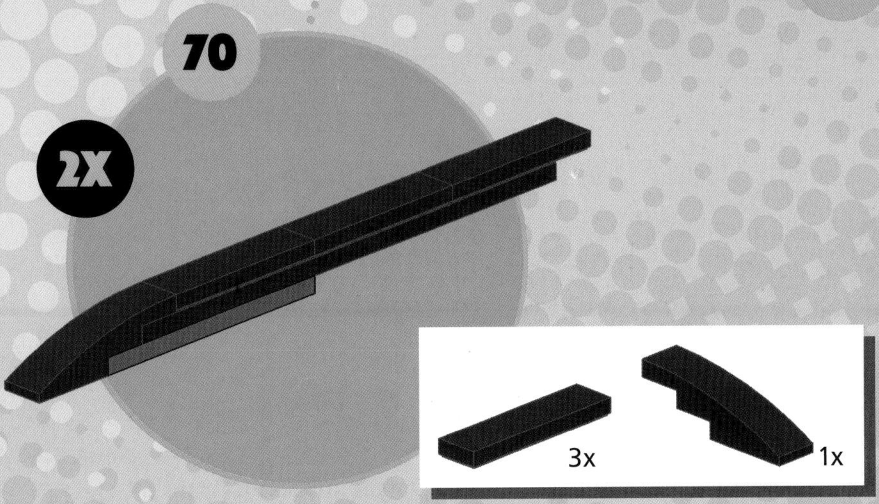

70

2X

3x

1x

71

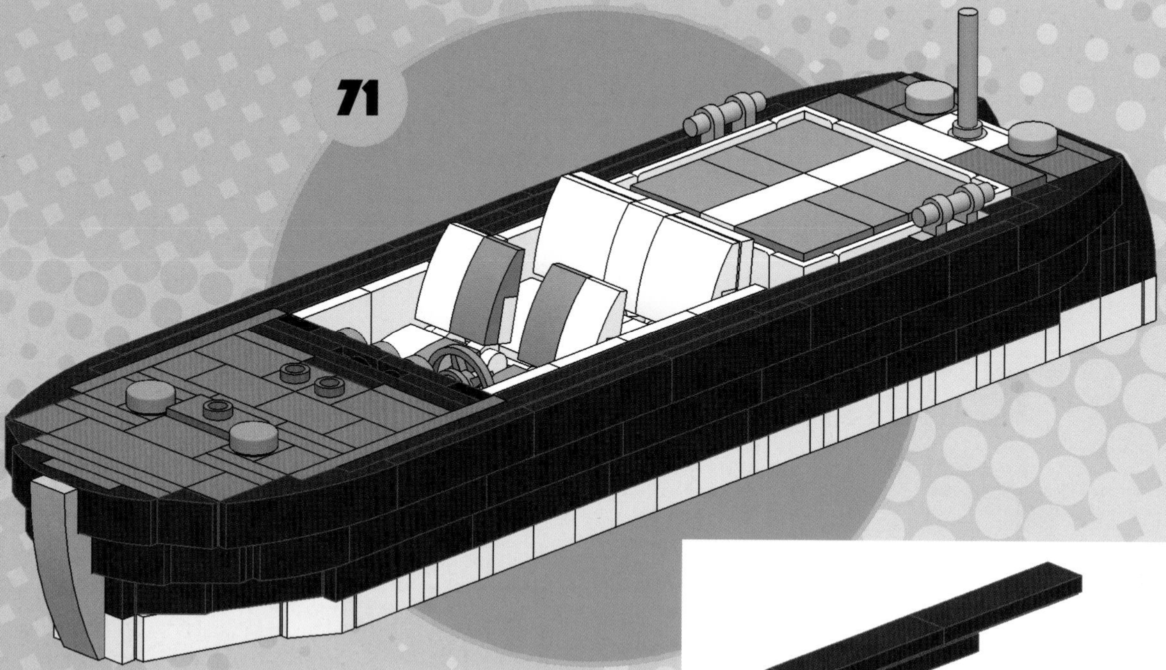

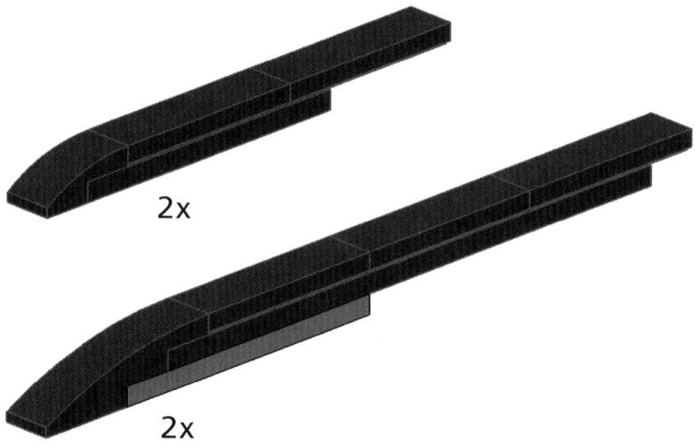

2x

2x

72

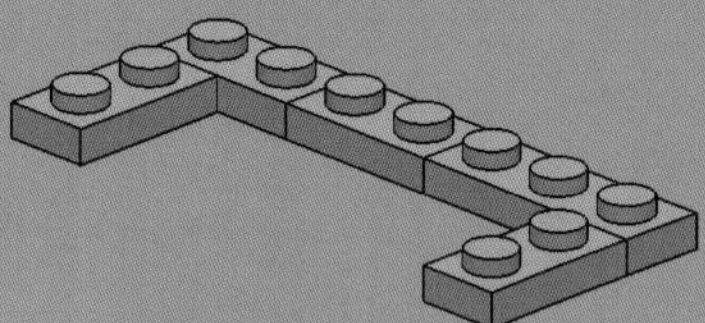

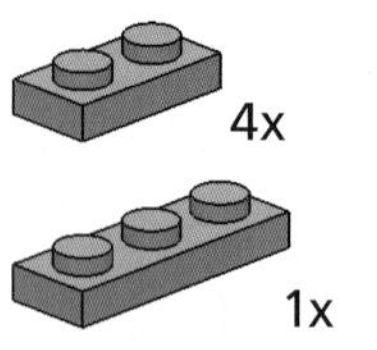

4x

1x

73

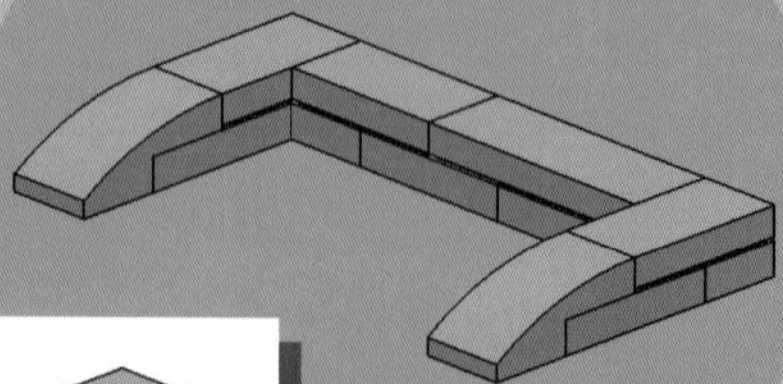

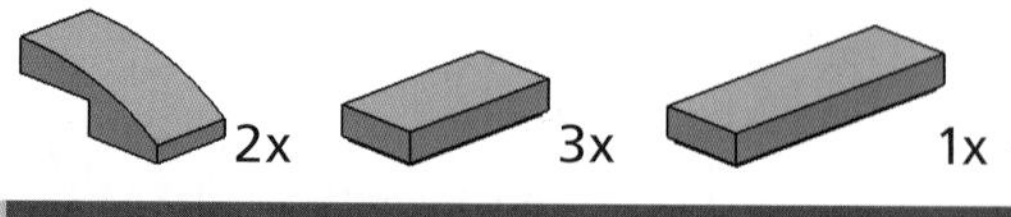

2x 3x 1x

74

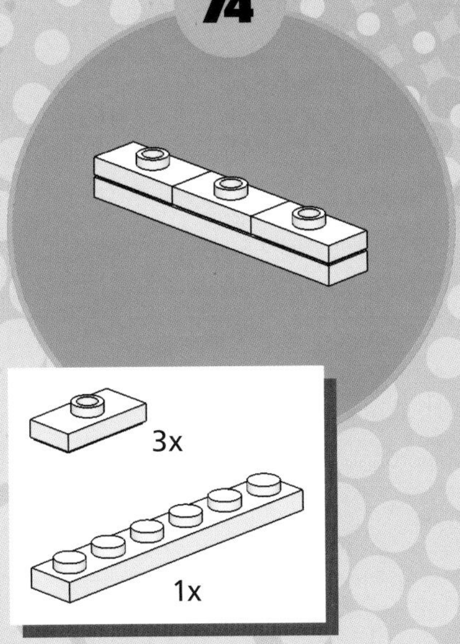

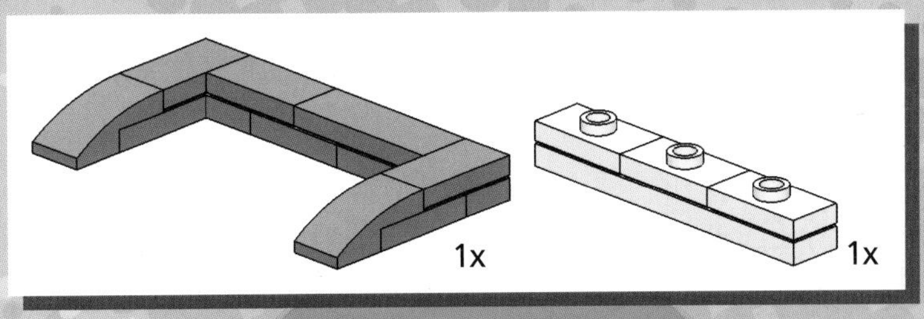

1x

1x

3x

1x

75

1x

1x

1x

1x

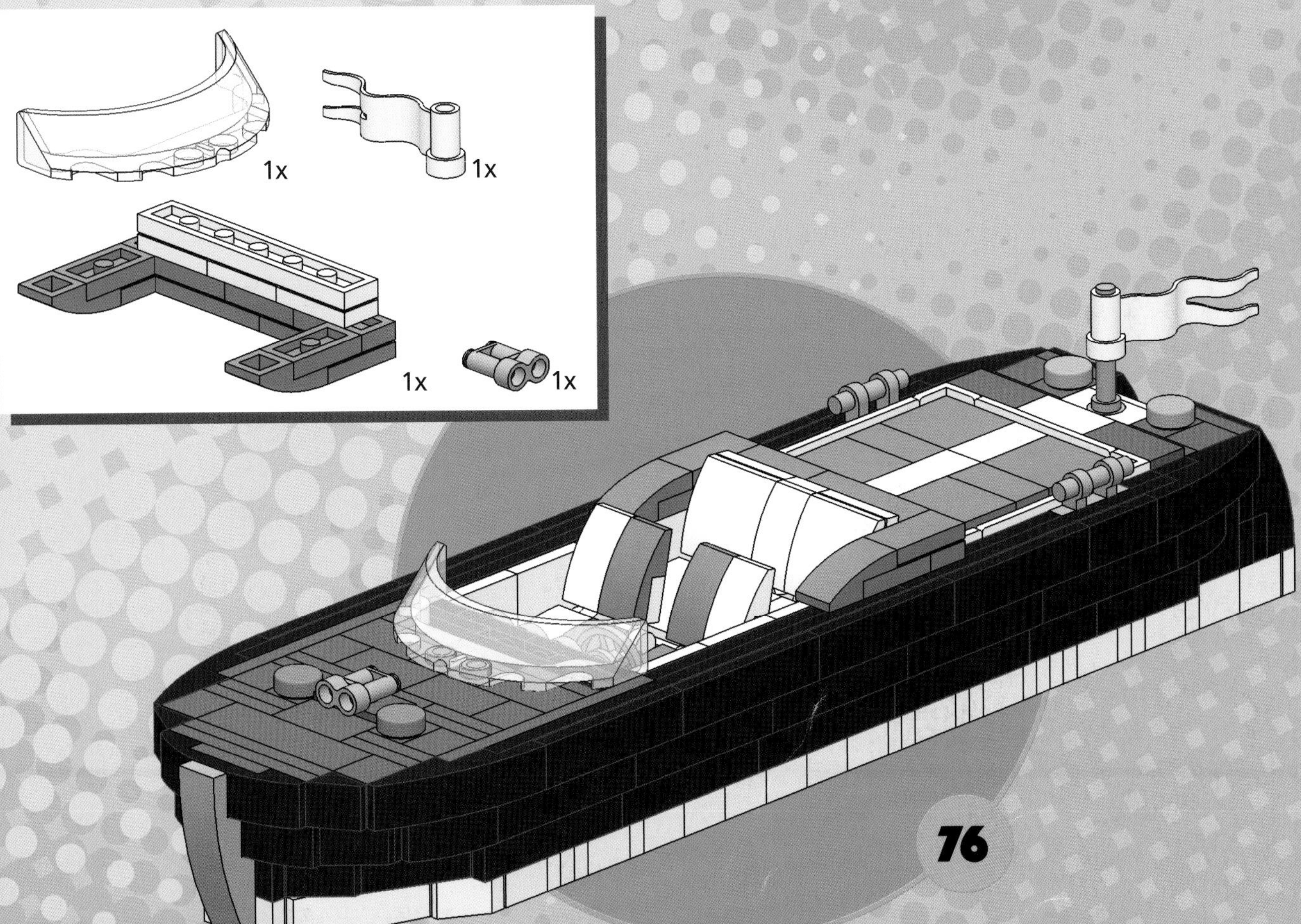

76

PARTS LIST

Quantity	Color	Element	Element Name	LEGO® Number
1	Light Bluish Gray	30374	Bar 4L Light Sabre Blade	4211628, 6116608
4	White	99780	Bracket 1 x 2 - 1 x 2 Up	6070698
1	White	2436b	Bracket 1 x 2 - 1 x 4 with Rounded Corners	6089574
2	Blue	3005	Brick 1 x 1	300523
2	Dark Orange	3005	Brick 1 x 1	4179814, 6000643
4	White	3005	Brick 1 x 1	300501
2	Reddish Brown	4070	Brick 1 x 1 with Headlight	4225469
12	Dark Orange	87087	Brick 1 x 1 with Stud on 1 Side	4666322
4	White	87087	Brick 1 x 1 with Stud on 1 Side	4558952
2	Blue	3004	Brick 1 x 2	300423, 4613959
4	Dark Brown	3004	Brick 1 x 2	4623774, 6058257
1	White	3004	Brick 1 x 2	300401, 4613964
2	Light Bluish Gray	11211	Brick 1 x 2 with Two Studs on One Side	6015344
12	White	11211	Brick 1 x 2 with Two Studs on One Side	6058177
1	Dark Orange	3010	Brick 1 x 4	4164439
1	Blue	30414	Brick 1 x 4 with Studs on Side	4212411
4	Dark Bluish Gray	30414	Brick 1 x 4 with Studs on Side	4210725
2	White	30414	Brick 1 x 4 with Studs on Side	4143254
8	White	3009	Brick 1 x 6	300901
1	Blue	3003	Brick 2 x 2	300323
2	Dark Orange	3003	Brick 2 x 2	4164440
2	Blue	3002	Brick 2 x 3	300223
3	Dark Orange	3002	Brick 2 x 3	4165998
2	Blue	3001	Brick 2 x 4	300123
1	White	4495	Flag 4 x 1 with First Wave Right	
1	Light Bluish Gray	30162	Minifig Binoculars with Round Eyepiece	4212313, 4550170
4	White	6231	Panel 1 x 1 x 1 Corner with Rounded Corners	623101
4	White	30413	Panel 1 x 4 x 1 with Rounded Corners	4173477, 6061047
2	Black	3024	Plate 1 x 1	302426
3	White	3024	Plate 1 x 1	302401

Quantity	Color	Element	Element Name	LEGO® Number
1	Flat Silver	4073	Plate 1 x 1 Round	4633691
2	Light Bluish Gray	85861	Plate 1 x 1 Round with Open Stud	6124825, 6168647
2	White	61252	Plate 1 x 1 with Clip Horizontal (Thick C-Clip)	4538353
2	Black	4081b	Plate 1 x 1 with Clip Light Type 2	408126, 4632571
1	Blue	3023	Plate 1 x 2	302323
4	Medium Azure	3023	Plate 1 x 2	4619511, 6097419
27	Dark Brown	3023	Plate 1 x 2	6058221
14	Dark Orange	3023	Plate 1 x 2	4162217, 4570877
5	White	3023	Plate 1 x 2	302301
2	White	60470b	Plate 1 x 2 with 2 Clips Horizontal (Thick C-Clips)	4556152
1	Dark Orange	15573	Plate 1 x 2 with Groove with 1 Centre Stud, without Understud	6092602
12	White	15573	Plate 1 x 2 with Groove with 1 Centre Stud, without Understud	6051511
2	Light Bluish Gray	2540	Plate 1 x 2 with Handle	4211632
4	White	48336	Plate 1 x 2 with Handle Type 2	4222017
1	Medium Azure	3623	Plate 1 x 3	6119107
2	White	3623	Plate 1 x 3	362301
2	Dark Orange	3710	Plate 1 x 4	4164448, 6074892
6	White	3710	Plate 1 x 4	371001
4	Dark Brown	3666	Plate 1 x 6	4566704
2	Dark Orange	3666	Plate 1 x 6	4244385
15	White	3666	Plate 1 x 6	366601
2	Dark Brown	3460	Plate 1 x 8	4519946
4	Reddish Brown	4477	Plate 1 x 10	4223683
2	Dark Brown	60479	Plate 1 x 12	4519825
2	Dark Orange	3022	Plate 2 x 2	4165522, 4615606

Quantity		Color	Element	Element Name	LEGO® Number
1		White	3022	Plate 2 x 2	302201, 4613976
2		White	2420	Plate 2 x 2 Corner	242001
4		Blue	87580	Plate 2 x 2 with Groove with 1 Center Stud	4565319, 6126049
2		White	87580	Plate 2 x 2 with Groove with 1 Center Stud	4565324, 6126046
8		White	99206	Plate 2 x 2 x 0.667 with Two Studs On Side and Two Raised	6046979
1		White	3021	Plate 2 x 3	302101
1		White	3020	Plate 2 x 4	302001
5		Dark Brown	3795	Plate 2 x 6	4518687
2		White	3795	Plate 2 x 6	379501
1		Blue	3034	Plate 2 x 8	303423
1		Dark Bluish Gray	3034	Plate 2 x 8	4210997
1		White	11212	Plate 3 x 3	6104805
1		Blue	3032	Plate 4 x 6	303223
2		White	60477	Slope Brick 18 4 x 1	4515359
2		Dark Brown	54200	Slope Brick 31 1 x 1 x 0.667	6033014
2		White	54200	Slope Brick 31 1 x 1 x 0.667	4244370, 4504369
4		Dark Brown	3040	Slope Brick 45 2 x 1	4518557
2		Dark Brown	60481	Slope Brick 65 2 x 1 x 2	4624089
6		Medium Azure	11477	Slope Brick Curved 2 x 1	6137300
4		Dark Brown	11477	Slope Brick Curved 2 x 1	6046943
6		White	11477	Slope Brick Curved 2 x 1	6034044
5		White	15068	Slope Brick Curved 2 x 2 x 0.667	6047220
4		Dark Brown	50950	Slope Brick Curved 3 x 1	6022199
4		Dark Brown	61678	Slope Brick Curved 4 x 1	4563023, 6045939
1		Metallic Silver	61678	Slope Brick Curved 4 x 1	4532630
2		Dark Brown	93273	Slope Brick Curved 4 x 1 Double	6135005
1		White	3700	Technic Brick 1 x 2 with Hole	370001

Quantity	Color	Element	Element Name	LEGO® Number
1	Dark Bluish Gray	32000	Technic Brick 1 x 2 with Holes	4210762
1	Light Bluish Gray	4274	Technic Pin 1/2	4211483, 4274194
2	Flat Silver	98138pb010f	Tile 1 x 1 Round with Gauge with red pointer Pattern	6030333
2	Flat Silver	98138	Tile 1 x 1 Round with Groove	4655241
2	Light Bluish Gray	98138	Tile 1 x 1 Round with Groove	4650260
1	Flat Silver	98138ps1	Tile 1 x 1 Round with Thermal Detonator Pattern	6006541
2	Black	3070b	Tile 1 x 1 with Groove	307026
5	Medium Azure	3069b	Tile 1 x 2 with Groove	4649741
5	Dark Brown	3069b	Tile 1 x 2 with Groove	4566688
2	Dark Orange	3069b	Tile 1 x 2 with Groove	4614158
7	White	3069b	Tile 1 x 2 with Groove	306901
1	Medium Azure	63864	Tile 1 x 3 with Groove	6097492
2	Dark Brown	63864	Tile 1 x 3 with Groove	6167928
1	White	63864	Tile 1 x 3 with Groove	4558168
26	Dark Brown	2431	Tile 1 x 4 with Groove	4536989
1	White	2431	Tile 1 x 4 with Groove	243101
10	White	11203	Tile 2 x 2 Inverted with Groove	6013866
4	Medium Azure	3068b	Tile 2 x 2 with Groove	6060857
2	White	87079	Tile 2 x 4 with Groove	4560178
1	Flat Silver	18978a	Wheel Rim 11 x 18 Front with 5 Spokes	6107391
1	Trans Clear	62360	Windscreen 3 x 6 x 1 Curved	4523573

1x

4x

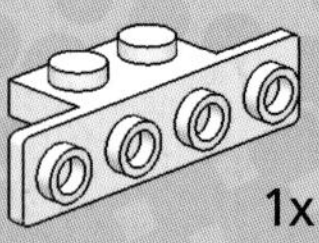
1x

2x

2x

4x

2x

12x

4x

2x

4x

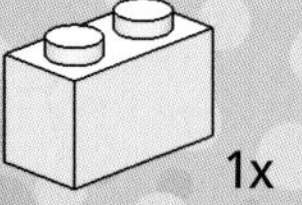
1x

2x

12x

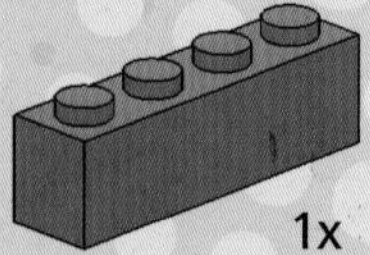
1x

1x

4x

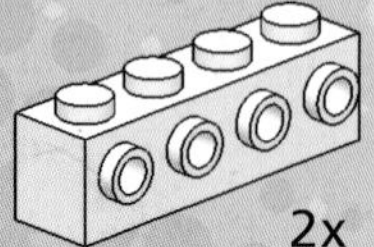
2x

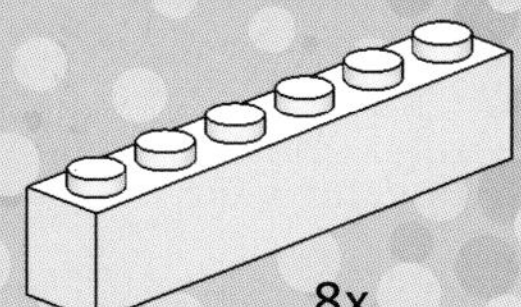
8x

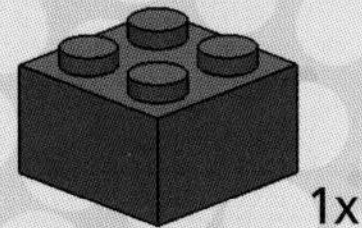
1x

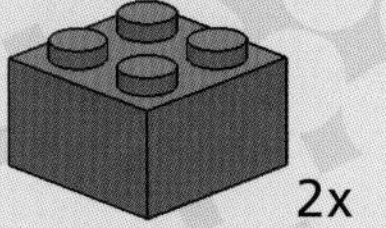
2x

2x

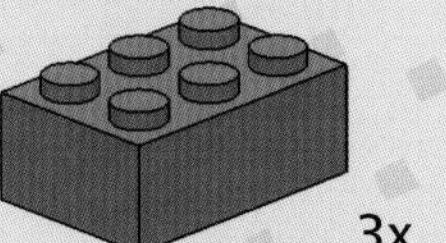
3x

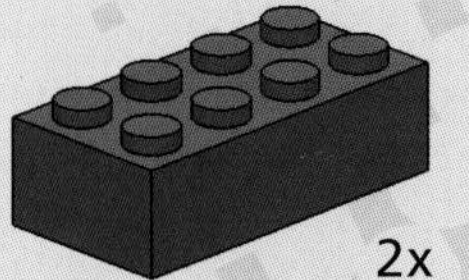
2x

1x

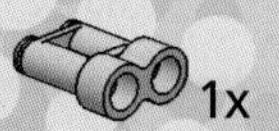
1x

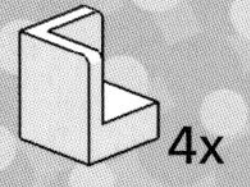
4x

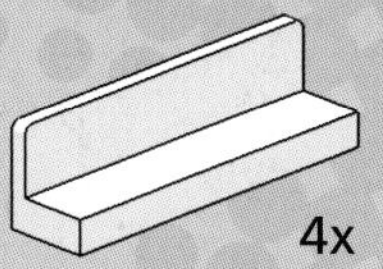
4x

2x

3x

1x

2x

2x

2x

1x

4x

27x

14x

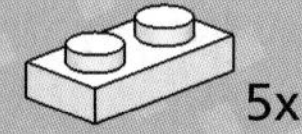
5x

2x

1x

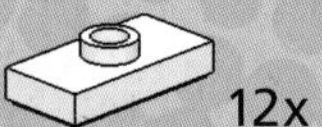
12x

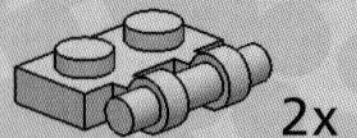
2x

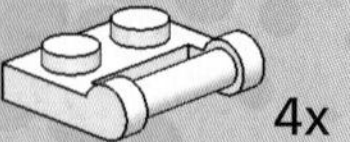
4x

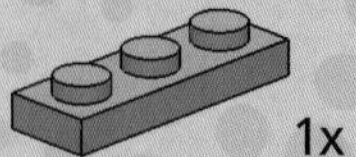
1x

2x

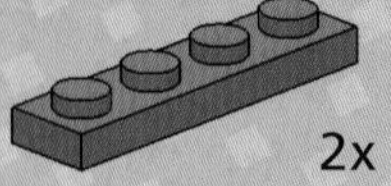
2x

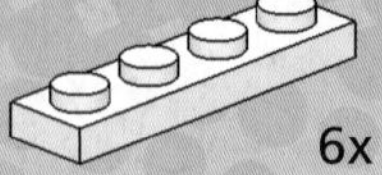
6x

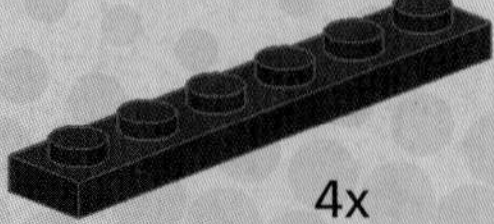
4x

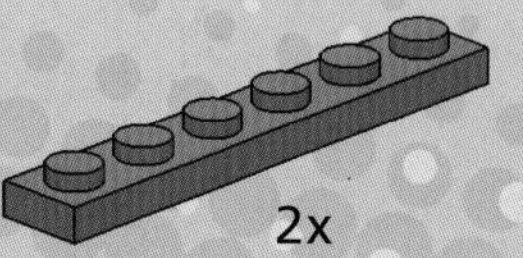
2x

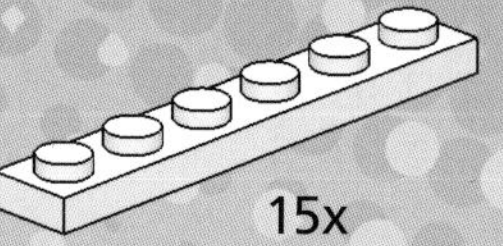
15x

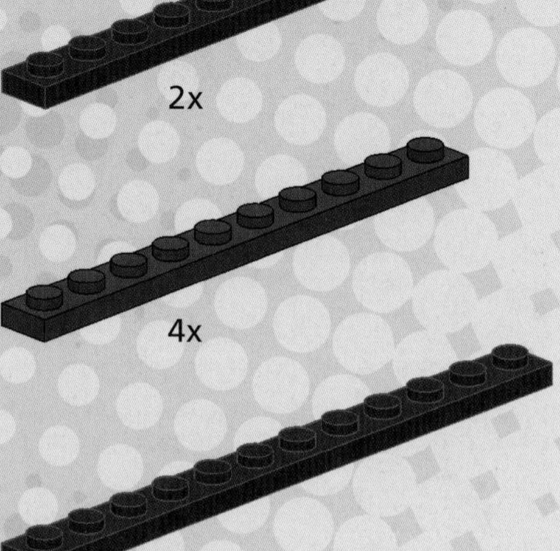
2x

4x

2x

2x

1x

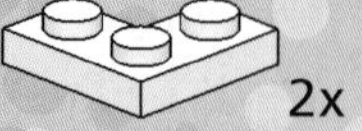
2x

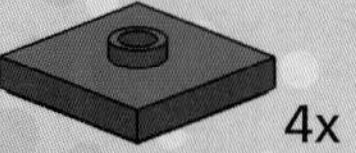
4x

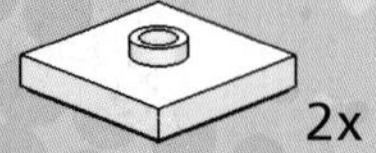
2x

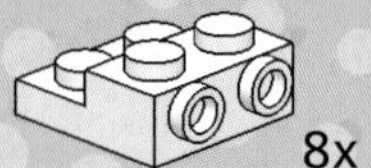
8x

1x

1x

5x

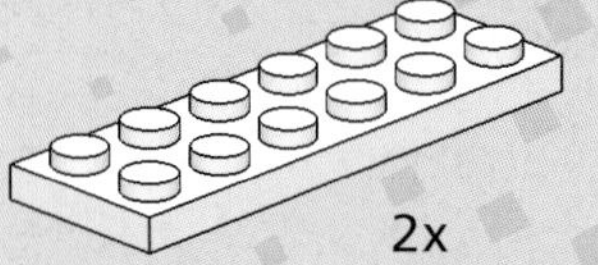
2x

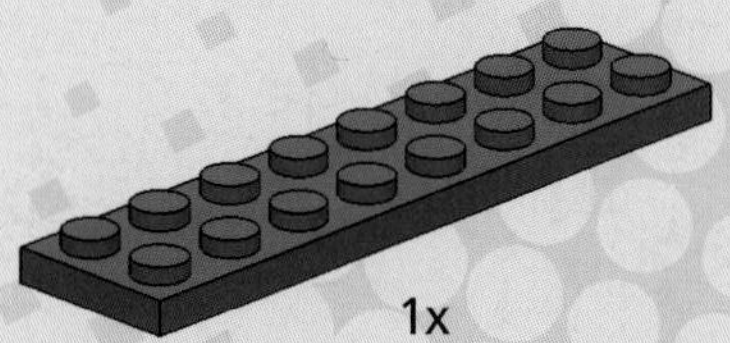
1x

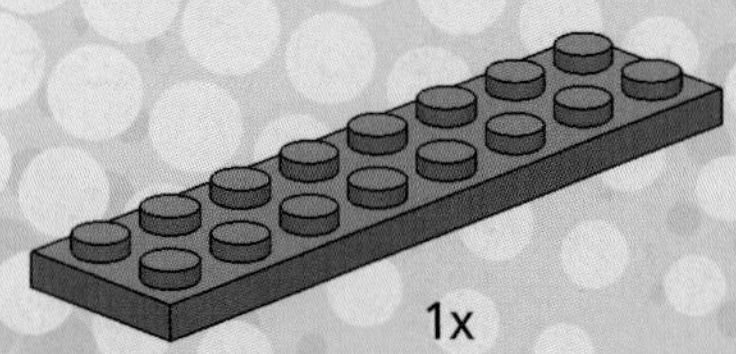
1x

1x

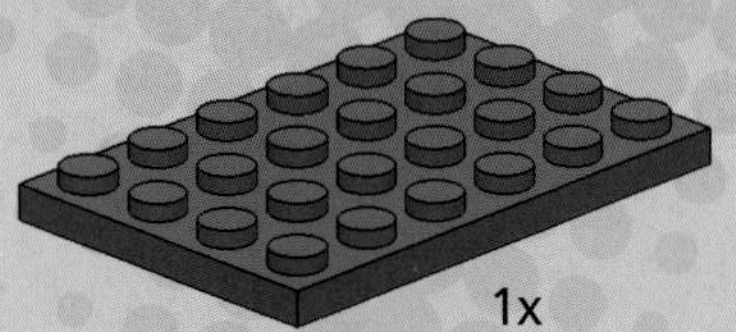
1x

2x

2x

2x

4x

2x

6x

4x

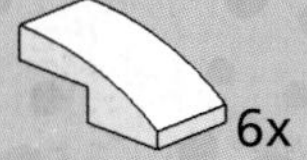
6x

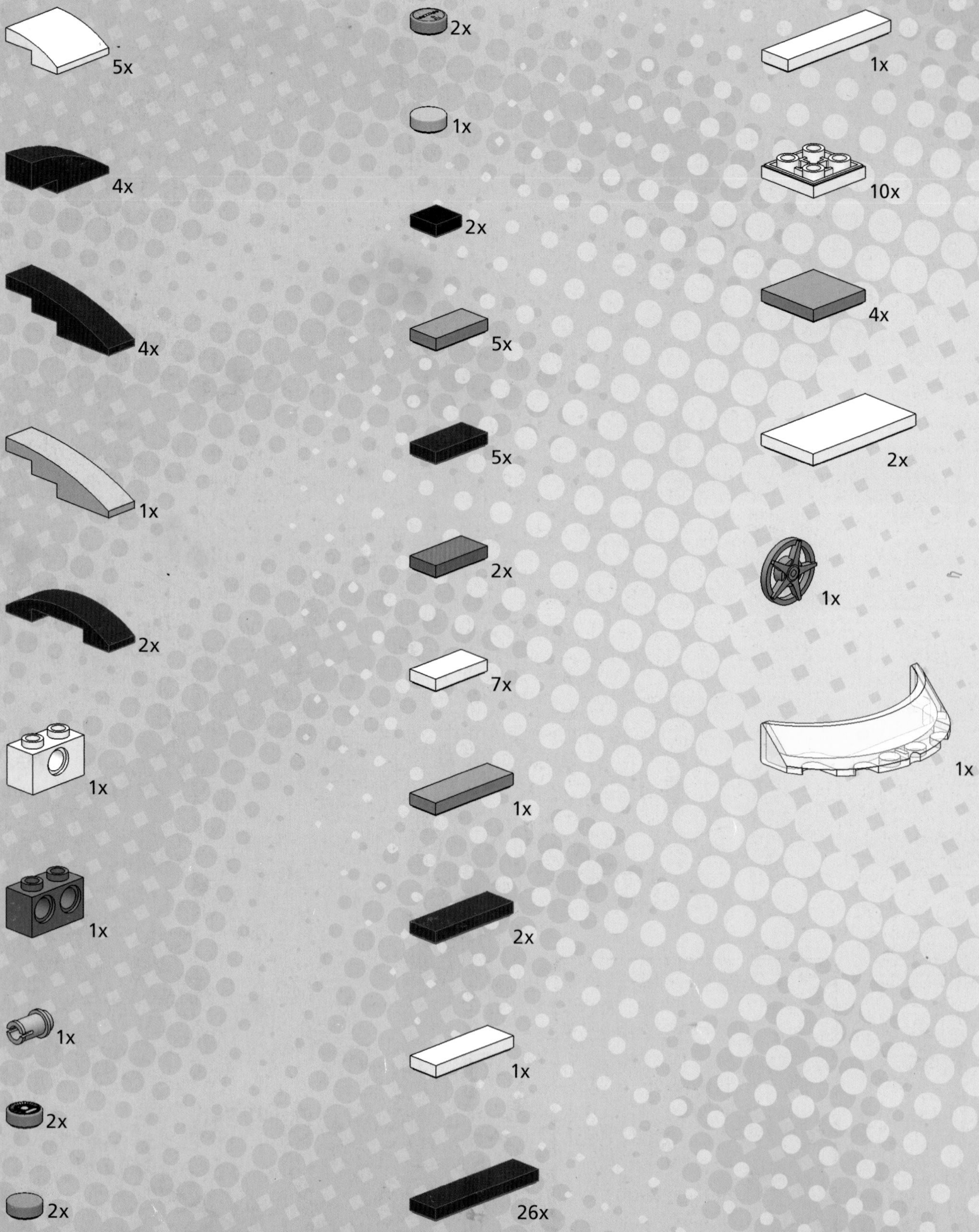

5x

4x

4x

1x

2x

1x

1x

1x

2x

2x

2x

1x

2x

5x

5x

2x

7x

1x

2x

1x

26x

1x

10x

4x

2x

1x

1x